The Flexible Writer

Second Edition

The Flexible Writer

A BASIC GUIDE

Susanna Rich

Kean College of New Jersey

ALLYN AND BACON

Boston   London   Toronto   Sydney   Tokyo   Singapore

Editor in Chief, Humanities: Joseph Opiela
Editorial Assistant: Brenda Conaway
Editorial-Production Administrator: Rowena Dores
Editorial-Production Service: Lauren Green Shafer
Text Designer: Pat Torelli
Cover Administrator: Linda Dickinson
Composition Buyer: Linda Cox
Manufacturing Buyer: Louise Richardson

Library of Congress Cataloging-in-Publication Data

Rich, Susanna.
    The flexible writer : a basic guide / Susanna Rich. — 2nd ed.
      p.   cm.
    Includes bibliographical references and index.
    ISBN 0-205-15934-6 (alk. paper)
      1. English language—Rhetoric.   2. English language—Grammar.
    I. Title.
PE1408.R558   1995
808'.042—dc20   94-28568
                                                                                CIP

This book is printed on
recycled, acid-free paper.

Credits
*Credits are listed in the Endnotes on pages 497–498, which constitute an exten-
sion of the copyright page.*

Printed in the United States of America

10 9 8 7 6 5 4 3 2   98 97 96 95

Contents

To Instructors   xiii
To Students   xx

Part I / THE WRITER   1

Chapter 1 Becoming a Writer   1

Why Write? 1
Free Yourself to Write 2
   Myths About Writing 2
   Fears About Writing 8
   Commitment 11
Freewriting 13
   When to Freewrite 15
The Practice of Writing 16
   Writing Time 16
   Writing Tools 18
   Writing Space 19
   Writing Habits 20
WRITERS WRITING 21

Part II / T H E   W R I T I N G
P R O C E S S

27

Chapter 2   **The Writing Process**   27

Writing for Meaning 28
Phases of the Writing Process 28
Formal and Informal Writing 35
  The Essay 36
Styles of Composing 36
  The Planner's Style 36
  The Explorer's Style 37
New versus Practicing Writers 38
  New Writers 38
  Practicing Writers 38
  Becoming a Flexible Writer 39

Chapter 3   **Purpose and Audience**   42

Purposes for Writing 42
  Kinds of Purpose 43
  Identifying Your Purpose 50
  Purposes in Education 53
Audiences for Writing 55
  Kinds of Audiences 55
  Identifying Your Audiences 56
Audience Appeal 59
  Denotations and Connotations 63
Purpose and Audience in the Writing Process 66
  Focusing 66
  Collecting 66
  Organizing 67
  Consulting 67
  Revising 67

Chapter 4   **Collecting**   69

The Dynamics of Collecting 69
Collecting and the Writing Process 71
  Purpose and Audience 71
  Collecting and Focusing 72
  Collecting and Organizing 72
  Collecting, Consulting, and Revising 72

Journals   73
  Personal Journals   73
  Process Journals   74
  Writer's Journals   74
  Learning Journals   74
  Training Journals   75
  Other Focused Journals   75
  Keeping a Journal   78
Listing and Brainstorming   80
  Listing   80
  Brainstorming   80
Clustering   82
Interviewing   84

Chapter 5   Focusing I: Strategies   87

The Dynamics of Focusing   88
Focusing and the Writing Process   89
Focusing and Purpose   89
  Relevance   90
  Repetition and Redundance   91
  Focusing and Collecting   92
  Focusing and Organizing   93
  Focusing, Consulting, and Revising   93
  Choosing   96
  Specifying   100
  Quoting   105
  Illustrating   111
  Questioning   116
Thesis Statements   121
  Strong and Weak Statements   122
  Writing Thesis Statements   125

Chapter 6   Focusing II: Sense Appeal   131

The Dynamics of Sense Appeal   132
Collecting: Your Six Senses   133
Showing and Telling   140
Subjective and Objective Modes   144
Finding Meaning and Purpose   147
Organizing Sensations   154
Comparisons and Clichés   158
A STUDENT MODEL FOR DISCUSSION   162

Chapter 7 **Organizing** 166

The Dynamics of Organizing   166
Organizing and the Writing Process   167
  Organizing, Focusing, and Coherence   167
  Organizing and Collecting   168
  Organizing, Consulting, and Revising   168
  When to Organize   168
Leads   168
  Fourteen Strategies for Leads   169
  Writing Leads   173
Titles   177
  Writing Titles   177
  Ten Strategies for Titles   177
Endings   179
  Eight Strategies for Endings   179
  Writing Endings   181
The Body   182
  Ten Strategies of Development   182
  Shaping   189
    Deduction and Induction   189
    Diagrams   189
  Writing the Body   196

Chapter 8 **Consulting** 202

A Community of Writers   202
Writing Workshop   204
Responding to Writing   206
  Twelve Responses to Writing: A Model Workshop   207
  Workshop Personalities   216
  Problems and Opportunities in Writing Workshop   217
  Five Variations   220
  Acknowledgments   223
Making the Grade   223
  Holistic Scoring   224
  Learning to Score Holistically   224

Chapter 9 **Revising** 231

Why Revise?   232
Revising Strategies   232
  Revision To-Do List   233

Writer's Journal 234
Copy-editing Strategies 237
Levels of Changes 246
    Recopying 246
    Readjusting 247
Revising in the Writing Process 247
Reflecting on the Revising Process 249

Part III / P U R P O S E S   F O R   W R I T I N G   255

Chapter 10   Writing to Remember   255

The Dynamics of Memory 255
Meaning and Purpose 256
Focusing Memories with Statements 261
Collecting Memories 265
Focusing Memories with Sense Appeal 271
Organizing Memories 274
    Personal History 275
    Family History 279
STUDENTS WRITING TO REMEMBER 282

Chapter 11   Writing to Bridge Cultures   289

What Are Cultures? 290
Why Bridge Cultures? 292
Language and Culture 293
Points of View 297
    Being an Outsider 298
    Ethnicity 302
    Gender 304
    Age 306
STUDENTS WRITING TO BRIDGE CULTURES 309

Chapter 12   Writing to Learn I: Becoming a Responsible Thinker   317

The Need to Learn 317
Writing to Become a Responsible Thinker 318
Purpose and Audience Across the Curriculum 320
    Points of View 320

Focusing: Taking Effective Notes   322
   Key Words   322
   Questions   324
   Key Statements: The Thesis   331
Learning Through the Senses   332
Summarizing   335

Chapter 13   Writing to Learn II: Making Connections   341

Reason and Evidence   342
Drafting: Writing, Itself, Helps You Learn   342
   Learning Journal   343
     Double Entries   343
     Process Entries   345
     Letters   346
Writing Essays: Thesis and Evidence   348
Synthesizing: Forming Theories   351
Comparing and Contrasting   354
   Writing Comparisons and Contrasts   355
   Organizing   357
Special Structures Across the Curriculum   362
STUDENTS WRITING TO LEARN   364

Chapter 14   Writing for Power   370

The Power of Language   370
Appealing to Your Audience   373
   Appeals to Emotion   374
   Appeals to Status   374
   Appeals to Reason   376
   Combinations of Appeals   377
Power and the Writing Process   382
   Establishing Needs   383
   Naming Your Purpose   383
   Focusing   386
   Collecting for Power   389
   Organizing for Power   391
   Consulting for Power   394
   Revising Faulty Reasoning   395
   Results   400
STUDENTS WRITING FOR POWER   401

Part IV / H A N D B O O K 409

Chapter 15 **Grammar** 409

How to Use This Chapter 410
Grammar, Purpose, and Audience 410
PARTS OF SPEECH 415
SENTENCES 417
Phrases 417
   Prepositional Phrases 417
   Verb Phrases 418
Clauses 422
   Independent Clauses 422
   Dependent Clauses 424
   Sentence Variety 428
Parallel Construction 431
PROBLEM SENTENCES 434
Fragments 434
   Identifying Fragments 435
   Revising Fragments 437
Run-ons 441
   Comma Splices 442
   Identifying Run-ons and Comma Splices 443
   Revising Run-ons and Comma Splices 445
Misplaced Modifiers 448
AGREEMENT 450
Subject-Verb Agreement 450
Verb Tense Consistency 455
Pronoun Agreement 457
   Pronouns and Reference 458
   Pronouns, Number, and Case 458
   Pronouns and Consistency 459
   Pronouns and Sexism 460
GRAMMAR REVIEW 463

Chapter 16 **Punctuation** 464

How to Use This Chapter 464
Punctuation, Purpose, and Audience 465
   Myths About Punctuation 467
The Elements of Punctuation 469

Capitalization 469
The Comma   470
The Hyphen   476
The Apostrophe   478
Quotation Marks   481
The Ellipsis   484
Parentheses   485
The Colon   486
The Semicolon   487
The Dash   488
End Marks   489
   The Period   489
   The Question Mark   490
   The Exclamation Point   490
Underlining (Italics)   491
Paragraphing   493
PUNCTUATION REVIEW   495

Endnotes   497
Index   499

To Instructors

The point is that students must be at the
center of their own learning.
—*John Mayher, Nancy Lester, Gordon Pradl*

When I first started to teach developmental writing, I found myself ordering three texts for my classes: a rhetoric, a reader, and a handbook. I soon found it hard to justify three texts for a course focused on writing. Serving as coordinator of a developmental writing program with a constantly changing population of instructors, I found it even more difficult to pre-order texts for other sections of my program that would suit a broad range of teaching styles in a multicultural community with students of varying ages. We needed a more flexible textbook that incorporated the benefits of rhetorics, readers, and handbooks and focused directly on meaning and purpose, person and process. We needed a textbook that would help students of different ages and cultural backgrounds write for different purposes: personal, interpersonal, academic, and professional. I wrote *The Flexible Writer* to address these needs. Here are its features:

Flexibility

The Flexible Writer can be used as a rhetoric, a reader, and a handbook. The book is organized to serve students and instructors with different styles and approaches to basic writing. The chapters can be followed in sequence or, as most writing classes require, used as needed. Also, the text has ample materials for programs that offer a sequence of developmental writing courses that would lead from personal to interpersonal and academic writing.

A Dynamic Model of the Writing Process

There are no shortcuts or mechanical formulas for real writing. *The Flexible Writer* offers a dynamic recursive model of the writing process that reflects the practical experiences of writers. This model focuses on purpose and audience and includes the processes of consulting and revising. Separate chapters offer detailed discussions and Explorations of each of seven identified phases of the writing process.

Emphasis on Writing

Learning to write, like any worthwhile activity, takes time, patience, commitment, and practice, practice, practice. Writing leads to more writing. Therefore, *The Flexible Writer* offers numerous opportunities for students to write.

Focus on Purpose and Audience

Writing is a process of finding and making meaning in particular contexts—for different purposes and audiences. Part III of *The Flexible Writer* helps students appreciate these dynamics and offers opportunities to write for different purposes, from the most personal ("Writing to Remember") to the most public ("Writing for Power"). "Focusing II: Sense Appeal" provides students with opportunities to develop their ability to observe themselves and the world for different purposes. "Writing to Bridge Cultures" invites students to explore experiences of ethnicity, gender, age, race, and religion. Two chapters on "Writing to Learn" are devoted specifically to strategies of academic writing. Part III further serves as a reader of student models.

Numerous Student Models

New writers are much encouraged and inspired by learning about each other's processes and experiences in writing. Therefore, *The Flexible Writer* offers numerous models of student writing both in process and as polished products.

Student-Centered Explorations

Students write more and better when they write about what concerns or interests them. Therefore, *The Flexible Writer* approaches different aspects of writing by offering students a range of Explorations from which to choose and to find their own interests and directions. By understanding and developing their own points of view, students can appreciate and develop strategies to negotiate other points of view.

Emphasis on Community and Collaboration

Writing, like other language activities, is more easily learned in the company of others. *The Flexible Writer* offers a balanced range of Explorations (marked *Together* and *Solo*) to help you and your students create a writing community. Students become conscious of and confident about the linguistic insights they already have and therefore better appreciate and incorporate the insights of others.

Connections Between Reading and Writing

Practiced writers know how to read their own and others' writing. Therefore, *The Flexible Writer* helps students to read writing with an emphasis on how the writing process is reflected in the product.

Multicultural Perspective

Writing is a process of learning how to communicate with different audiences. College communities are becoming increasingly multicultural. Therefore, *The Flexible Writer* provides insights and opportunities to explore the dynamics of how language works in different cultural contexts.

Preparation for Academic Writing

The Flexible Writer provides students with the basic conceptual skills they need for writing to learn. Two chapters focus specifically on reading and responding to academic texts across the curriculum.

Critical Thinking Strategies

As student Bruce Inge stated it, "Writing is a learning process." Thinking shapes writing; writing shapes thinking. Critical thinking strategies and Explorations are provided throughout *The Flexible Writer*.

Flexible Handbook Focused on Meaning

Part IV of *The Flexible Writer* is a handbook that shows students how grammar and punctuation function to create meaning in different contexts. Stylistic issues are approached from a multicultural perspective. The Explorations in this section are designed to help students learn and directly apply basic skills to their own writing.

A Solid Base in Theory and Research

The Flexible Writer is based on my fifteen years of experience as a writer in a wide range of genres, including essays, articles, a novel (and a dissertation about writing it), humor, business memos, translations, and reams of poetry. It is based, as well, on fifteen years of guiding a broad spectrum of students and instructors in composition, creative writing, critical thinking, and research on the teaching of college writing. The approach and methods that are formulated in *The Flexible Writer* reflect the most carefully developed current research on the writing process.

How to Use This Book

The purpose of *The Flexible Writer* is to support you and your students in creating a community of writers that suits your styles and needs. The Explorations are a special feature of this book. Sometimes an Exploration suggests a series of steps to be taken together or solo, or alternating between the two. The purpose of the Explorations is to help students write and talk about writing. Students don't have to take every step or answer every question. Many of the best breakthroughs occur when student writers follow ideas that occur to them independently during the process. The purpose of the suggested class discussions is to practice talking about writing, not to settle on "correct" answers. Finally, even as you are working together as a class on one portion of this book, you can refer students to other portions you feel they need. In some classes, you and your students can decide together which chapters to turn to next and which Explorations to do. For additional support, the *Instructor's Manual* that accompanies *The Flexible Writer* offers suggestions for how to sequence and combine chapters for different purposes, styles, and needs.

The enthusiasm, successes, and breakthroughs of students and instructors who have worked with *The Flexible Writer* are recorded and reflected throughout the book. I hope you will write to me about your experiences with *The Flexible Writer*, as well.

A Word on the Second Edition

Readers of the first edition will notice that I have reorganized the second edition to give greater priority to academic writing. Chapter 2 includes a new section on formal and informal writing and the essay. Elements of the original Chapter 12, "Writing to Learn," have been transferred into sections in Chapter 3, "Purpose and Audience," and Chapter 5, "Focusing I: Strategies." Chapter 5 has been further expanded to include strategies for quoting and illustrating. Because imagery is so fundamental to effective writing, the original Chapter 9, "Writing to Develop Your Senses," has metamorphosed into Chapter 6, "Focusing II: Sense Appeal."

Throughout, the second edition features numerous drafts illustrating various phases and strategies of the writing process. These papers are actual student examples; they include the necessary errors that Professor Mike Rose marks as the places "where education begins." The second edition also offers many new polished essays by developmental writing students.

"Explorations" have been further streamlined to reflect the interests and needs of instructors and students who have been using *The Flexible Writer* nationwide. Sections that were most effective for students, such as "Myths About Writing," have been expanded. Other sections, more appropriate for advanced writing courses, have been either deleted or simplified.

Chapter 15, "Grammar," has been revised for further clarity and user-friendliness. Additional Explorations, student examples, and strategies help students to adjust their own grammar. Confusing technical terms such as *adverbial conjunctions* and *conjunctive adverbs* have been replaced by more descriptive and therefore more useful terms such as *connecting adverbs* and *afterthoughts*. The Index refers readers who are accustomed to traditional terms to these more helpful usages.

Finally, the second edition features sidebars, shaded gray for easy reference, that summarize and highlight important writing strategies.

Acknowledgments

Writing *The Flexible Writer* taught me much about the dynamics of the writing process in general and my own in particular. The single most important lesson I learned was just how central understanding *purpose and audience* is to the making of meaning, even if the only purpose is to express and the only audience, oneself. I learned just how inextricable *consulting* is to the writing process, whether it's as simple as consulting a dictionary for spelling or as complex as consulting teachers about different thinking styles.

I could not have written a textbook flexible enough to fulfill the purposes and serve the broad audience I set out to reach if it weren't for the many people I consulted during the process—some as distant as the memory of my sixth-grade English teacher, some as immediate as the remarks of a current student. The guidance I offer in this book is my current best synthesis of the guidance and support I received from consulting with others in three decades of becoming a writer myself. A comprehensive list of them would fill a city phone book. I mention here only those who have been most obviously focal to the creation of this book.

First, I would like to thank my students at Kean College of New Jersey, Montclair State University, the University of North Carolina at Chapel Hill, New York University, and Sussex County Community College, who inspired me to create the materials that comprise this book. They were models for me in their willingness to write, write, and revise, and to work with and for each other. Their insights, creativity, energy, and successes dispelled any of the fears I had when I first started to teach developmental writing. In particular, I wish to thank students Liz Wells, Karen Wreden, Alan T. Russell, Donna Mekita Kuhl, Lydia Gordon, Jennifer Carter, Annie E. Lee, Marsha Fructer, Nochus Berry, Maurice Lozzi, and Leonie Infantry for their interest and enthusiasm.

I am grateful to my past and current teachers who continue to be a source of inspiration for me. They include Paul Ziff, Carl Schmidt, Mitchell A. Leaska, John Mayher, Gordon Pradl, Lil Brannon, Dixie Goswami, Nancy Sommers, Mimi Schwartz, Neil Postman, Joan Aleshire, John Skoyles, Sharon Olds, and Robert Wrigley. In addition, there are those teachers who have mentored me only from their writings: Mina P. Shaughnessy, Peter Elbow, Mike Rose, Janet Emig, Ann E. Berthoff, James Moffett, Kenneth Bruffee, and Grace M. Fernald. I thank these teachers for inspiring what is worthy in this book.

Many of my colleagues at Kean College worked with these materials in process and provided invaluable insights, ideas, student feedback, and encouragement. They have taught me much by their example about effective teaching and collaboration. I am especially grateful to Ira Berkowitz, Bob Cirasa, Dorothy Goldberg, John Gruesser, Ruth Hamann, Sid Krueger, Jay Mahoney, Joanne McAneny, Joan Migton, Mary Newman, Maria Perez, Jessie Reppy, Betsy Rodriguez-Bachiller, Gregory Ryan, Mary Scotto, Kevin Toth, Bernie Weinstein, and Sue Woulfin. My special thanks to Carole Shaffer-Koros, Chair of the English Department at Kean; to Dean Mary Lewis, Dean Ed Weil, and Mark Lender; and to Kean College of

New Jersey for providing the context, time, resources, and encouragement I needed to write this book.

In addition, the generous, detailed comments of many other writing instructors helped transform *The Flexible Writer* into its present form. My thanks to E. Jennifer Monaghan, Brooklyn College; Arthur B. Powell, Rutgers University; Peter Adams, Essex Community College; Peter Carino, Indiana State University; Duncan Carter, Portland State University; Theresa Enos, University of Arizona; Pamela Gay, SUNY–Binghamton; C. Jeriel Howard, Northeastern Illinois University; Frances Kurilich, Santa Monica College; Cecilia Macheski, La Guardia Community College; Martin McCoski, University of Akron; Randall Popken, Tarleton State University; Judith Stanford, Rivier College; and Fran Zaniello, Northern Kentucky University. For comments offered during the preparation of the second edition, I am grateful to Timothy J. Evans, Richard Bland College; Eric Hibbison, J. Sargeant Reynolds Community College; Eileen Master, Rowan College of New Jersey; Sylvia Robb, Tomball College; Mary Sauer, Indiana University Purdue University at Indianapolis; Rick Shannon, Community College of Allegheny County; and Kathryn Waltz-Freel, Indiana Vocational Technical College.

I wish to thank Rowena Dores, Brenda Conaway, and Ellen Mann at Allyn & Bacon for the energy and creativity they devoted to helping *The Flexible Writer* reach its audience and fulfill its purpose. My thanks also to Lauren Green Shafer, Kathryn Graehl, and Marilyn Graber for their patience, thoroughness, and perseverance in bringing *The Flexible Writer* through production.

There are three persons without whom this book could not have been written, and to whom I am most grateful. Joe Opiela is a writer's ideal editor. His devotion to producing quality English textbooks, his patience, flexibility, expertise, accessibility, and diplomacy allowed me to develop what is best in *The Flexible Writer*. Priscilla Donenfeld is a textbook writer's ideal assistant. Her devotion, patience, flexibility, teaching and writing expertise, and, incidentally, strong typing hands were crucial to the realization of this text. Most of all I would like to thank Morton D. Rich for being a writer's ideal husband and friend. He was my first methods teacher twenty-three years ago and still dazzles me with the depth and creativity of his teaching. His devotion and patience, ideas and expertise, flexibility and support allowed me, through this process, to discover what is best in me as a teacher, writer, and person.

Susanna Lippoczy Rich
Kean College of New Jersey

To Students

Part of becoming a writer is the desire to have
everything mean something.
—*Louise Erdrich*

If you are like most student writers, you may be worried about writing. Perhaps you have been discouraged by previous experiences. You may feel as other students have felt at the beginning of a developmental writing course: deprived, scared about what others will say, out of place, and panicky.

Know that you are not alone. Most writers, even professionals, have these feelings. The difference between them and you is that they have learned strategies for making the writing process satisfying, no matter how they feel at first. These writers know that writing is not a matter of following rigid rules, that writing is a process that takes time, practice, patience, and commitment. *The Flexible Writer*—based on my years of writing and working with writers like you—offers you the strategies of practicing writers so that you too can enjoy the following benefits:

- The confidence that comes from recognizing that you already know more about writing than you thought you did
- The productive habits of practicing writers
- The chance to practice writing without fear of mistakes
- The freedom to choose topics that concern and interest you
- The opportunity to write for different purposes and audiences
- The ability to use a variety of writing strategies
- The skills of reading like a writer
- The skills of a responsible thinker
- The opportunity to learn through writing

- The means to bridge cultural, intellectual, and other gaps between you and others
- The opportunity to work collaboratively with your peers

Features of This Book

In order to help you gain the benefits of writing, this book has these features:

- Numerous opportunities to practice writing
- A strong focus on the writing process
- Student models and reflections on writing
- Opportunities to write alone (solo) and together
- Opportunities to revise your writing
- Sidebars and quotes you can use as reminders
- Ideas for how to manage your grammar and punctuation

How This Book Is Organized

The Flexible Writer is divided into four parts:

Part I offers you practical suggestions for arranging your time, space, and habits for writing. This part introduces you to the experiences of other writers and offers you strategies for success.

Part II offers you a dynamic model of the phases of the writing process, which starts with needs and ends with results. The phases in between are: identifying purpose and audience, collecting, focusing, organizing, drafting, consulting, and revising. A separate chapter is devoted to each of these phases. With your instructor, you can decide whether to work through these chapters one after another or to refer to them as needed while you work with chapters in Part III.

Part III offers you chapters focused on writing for different purposes: writing to remember, writing to bridge cultures, writing to learn, and writing for power.

Part IV is a handbook. This section helps you understand how grammar and punctuation affect the meaning of what you write. Here too, you can decide whether to work through all the chapters or to refer to portions as you need them. The Table of Contents and the Index will help you to find what you need.

How to Use This Book

The purpose of *The Flexible Writer* is to provide you with the support you need to become a writer and to develop your own style. Even as you are working together with your instructor and fellow students, turn to other portions of this book that interest you. Have the courage and independence to take what this book has to offer, whether or not you are assigned to work with a particular section. Review portions that you need to review, even after the class has stopped working on those portions.

The Explorations are a special feature of this book. They are marked *Together, Solo,* or a combination of *Together* and *Solo. Together* Explorations are designed for class and small group work. *Solo* Explorations are designed for individual work. Sometimes an Exploration suggests a series of steps to be taken together or solo or alternating between the two. In doing Explorations, remember that the most important purpose of them is to help you to start and keep writing. If an Exploration inspires an idea that is not explicitly suggested in the Exploration, follow your inspiration. As long as you are writing, don't feel as if you have to take every step or answer every question. Remember, as well, that the point of class discussions is to practice talking about writing, not to settle on "correct" answers.

I enjoyed writing *The Flexible Writer* and hope you will enjoy reading it and writing with it. Write me a letter to tell me about your experiences with the book. Send me some of your writing as well.

Susanna Lippoczy Rich
Kean College of New Jersey

Chapter **1**

Becoming a Writer

This chapter offers opportunities to
- —Explore **myths and fears** about writing
- —**Freewrite**
- —Make a **commitment** to writing
- —Create the **time, space,** and **habits** for becoming a writer
- —Discover the dynamics of **language and beliefs**

> Everybody is talented and original and
> has something important to say.
> —*Brenda Ueland,*
> *Writer, Teacher*

> But better by far to write twaddle or
> anything, anything, than nothing at all.
> —*Katherine Mansfield,*
> *Fiction writer*

Why Write?

A father needs to reassure his son, so he tacks a note onto the refrigerator saying, "Back by noon." A student rewrites her notes to prepare for an exam. Two heads of state want to end a war, so they write and sign an agreement. People write for many reasons: to express feelings, to remember, to develop their senses, to learn, to solve problems, to ask for help or to offer it, to have fun, to complain, to argue, to mourn. In short, people write to live. One student writer says, "I write because I like that 'Wow' feeling I get when I find out I know more than I thought I knew." Another student writer, who is very career oriented, says she writes in order to create high expectations in a prospective employer. "Then I have something to live up to," she says. I'm writing this book because I love to write and want more people to enjoy the benefits of writing, too.

Free Yourself to Write

Writing can be very flexible and useful. So it's a wonder that more of us don't write more often. Some people suffer from "writer's block," an inability to write because of fears, false beliefs, and unproductive habits. This section offers some insights and explorations to help you free yourself from writer's block and become a flexible writer.

Myths About Writing

The word *myths* applies to stories of heroes and heroines, fantastic dragons and unicorns, quests for magical powers, and perfect solutions to human problems. Such myths can tell the history of a people, reflect their emotional and spiritual needs, and offer hope and moral guidance. For example, the movie *Star Wars* is a cinematic myth for the twentieth century. In it, Luke Skywalker uses technology to call on "the Force," a creative, spiritual energy that enables him to encounter and survive a destructive force represented by Darth Vader. Princess Leia is no "damsel in distress" who must wait for someone to save her. She is active and powerful, and she collaborates *with* the hero. One of the lessons of this myth is that technology must be used for positive purposes. It reminds us of the values of courage and friendship, and it discourages mere hunger for power. It is a myth that embodies the newfound power women have embraced in this past century.

But the word *myth* also applies to superstitions and false beliefs that can rob people of their powers to grow and create. A long-distance swimmer, Melanie, once told this story of how a myth limited her ability to swim:

> For twenty years I couldn't swim the crawl because I believed you *had* to blow the air out into the water before you come up for air. But

the bubbles flew back into my face, disorienting me. I kept swallowing water and gasping for air. I gave up swimming.

One day while I was wistfully watching people doing laps, I asked the lifeguard if there was any other way to manage my breathing. "Sure," she said, "Just blow out the air when you come up. You can take your next breath right after." I tried it and a whole new world opened up for me. Before long I was swimming a half mile regularly with strong, even strokes. I'm training now for a long-distance race. Recently, I experimented with blowing the air out with my face in the water. Because I have greater confidence as a swimmer now, I'm not disturbed by the bubbles anymore. I can even swim faster: the bubbles just trail behind me.

Unquestioned beliefs and rigid rules can stop you from writing just as Melanie's rigid belief about breathing stopped her from swimming. Here are some myths about writing that may be stopping you from getting into the swim of it.

Myth 1: Writers are born, not made.

If you believe writers are born, not made, you may feel like giving up even before you start. But the ability to write is learned, not given to you. If you can speak a language, you are already 80 percent there. After all, you have been learning, helping, arguing, and so on since you first started to talk. Just like ballet dancers, concert pianists, football players, and master carpenters, writers train for years, decades, and lifetimes to perfect their writing. Perhaps you may be only a weekend jogger and not a winner of marathon races, but to be a runner you have to run. You may not want to be a professional writer, but if you are to enjoy the benefits of writing, you have to work and play like a writer.

Myth 2: There is one right way to write.

If you believe there is one right way to write, you may feel so tense and discouraged by your early exploratory attempts that you give up too soon. But minds are not mass-produced pages to be shaped and filled in the same way. You have to develop your own mind so that it will be uniquely your own and not just a copy of those around you. Writing is one of the most effective tools you have for knowing and developing your mind. To seek a *right way* is just to follow someone else's way. Find your own. The *A* paper usually takes risks and sounds unique. It would be comforting if there were *one* right way, but ultimately that would be stifling.

Myth 3: You have to get it right the first time.

The most destructive belief that beginning writers may have about writing is that if you don't get it right the first time, you can never get it right. But in reality, what you read on a published page is rarely, if ever, a first draft. Novelist Ernest Hemingway revised his book *The Old Man and the Sea* more than two hundred times. Marcy Syms, chief operating officer of Syms Stores, says that in her office people are constantly checking with each other on how to phrase and rephrase thoughts in letters and in memos. A teacher's first draft may need more work than a student's. The difference between a piece of writing that works and one that doesn't may be the number of times it's been rewritten.

Myth 4: You have to get it right all the time.

You wouldn't devote the same amount of attention to choosing every outfit you wear—every minute of every day—or you would never get out of your closet and on with your life. Yet, some new writers waste so much energy perfecting one response to an exam question that they fail because they don't move on to the others. They worry so much about their first sentence in a first draft of a paper that they lose ideas that would have emerged had they kept writing.

If you believe that everything you write has to be perfect, you will miss the pleasure of the new ideas and subjects that develop with a more flexible approach to writing. Especially for a new writer, it's important to explore many new directions. Informal writing such as freewrites (defined on pages 13–16), diary entries, informal letters to your instructor, and early drafts of your papers can include tangents, changes of subject, and errors. Polished writing such as job résumés and term papers deserve more attention, more drafts, and more time.

Myth 5: Only better is good enough.

This myth is a variation on Myth 4. Some new writers feel that unless later drafts are better than earlier ones, they will never succeed. Discouraged, they may give up, saying, "I just don't have what it takes." But this is not true. Writing does not develop in a straight, upward-sloping line, any more than health regimens or achievements in sports do. Often people find that they get worse before they get better: fevers, rashes, and other "detox" symptoms are sometimes necessary for regaining health. Successful workouts are often followed by aches, setbacks, and frustration.

The more you commit yourself to excellence, the more likely it is that your work will get worse before it gets better. Your standards will rise, and sometimes you'll stumble. Frustration is a badge of commitment, not an invitation to failure.

Myth 6: Product is more important than process.

In a finished piece of writing, what you see is not how the writer got there but what he or she got to. When you buy a worthwhile garment, you rarely, if ever, will see the patterns, loose threads, chalk marks, pins, scissors, and leftover scraps of material needed to make it. It takes many, many people to get that garment to your store.

When you read a book, you don't see the twenty attempts to start, the crumpled drafts, the worn-out dictionary and library card. The really effective beginning is often written last—after the writer has thought things through in the process of writing. If there is a thesis sentence (a sentence that states the main point the author wants to get across), it is often discovered and reshaped as the writer writes. The arrangement of paragraphs, the purpose, and the author's sense of the audience will often change in the process of writing. The Foreword of this book was written and rewritten as ideas unfolded and developed in the process. It was finished last.

Being too worried about grades is partly a result of focusing too much on the end product and not on the activities of the writing process. Being impatient with yourself and what you write is also an indication that you are putting too much emphasis on the product. Engage fully in the *process* of writing. The more you do, the better your final product will be.

Myth 7: Writing is just recorded speech.

If you believe writing is just recorded speech, then you may be confused by the demands teachers make on you in writing classes. Here are some ways in which writing and speaking differ:

- Writing is *permanent*, whereas speech (unless it is recorded) is gone as soon as it is spoken.

- Writing is *solitary*. When you speak, your face, body, and voice help express what you mean. But when you write, the words you choose and the way you arrange them have to communicate some of what your face, body, and voice would if you were speaking instead of writing.

- Writing can be *riskier* than speaking. When you write, you are never sure who will pick up your writing. You can't be there to reinterpret or soften what you say. That's why you have to make even more careful decisions about what you decide to leave in finished papers. Others can hold you to something in writing much more than they can hold you to your spoken word.

- Writing can be *safer*. When you speak, words can tumble out before you realize what you are saying and what effect it can have. Once you have said something, it's hard to take it back. One of the benefits of writing is that you can adjust what you write before it reaches your intended audience. So, for example, it's helpful to write some letters you never send: you express your feelings without having to cope with the consequences of having done so. Having formulated your ideas, the next time you speak with the person you will be able to express yourself more clearly and with more control.

- Writing is *solid*. When you put your thoughts on paper, they become as real as clay. While you are writing, you can change and learn from your words because you can see and manipulate them. You can't hold silent thoughts or spoken words in the same way.

- Writing is *independent* of speech. Writing doesn't just record speech, although early drafts may approximate it. How you punctuate does not always follow the rhythms of speech. How you hear a word in English is not always how you spell it. How you communicate on the page may be very different from how you communicate in person.

Myth 8: No pain, no gain.

In the past you may have become convinced that writing is painful, and so now, naturally, you avoid it. But although writing is work, so is playing football, creating a special meal, building an engine, or breeding cats. Meaningful work—a labor of love—is what people seek. It is human nature to do so.

A closed fist can only punch and pound. A relaxed hand is flexible enough to create a world. Writing doesn't have to hurt. Writing is a process of experimenting with ideas and words until you find the ones that work. Researchers have noticed that the students who do best in writing are the ones who know how to design their schedules, choose their topics, work with others, and challenge themselves in ways that enable them to *enjoy* writing. As you develop as a writer, notice your strengths and use them. If you are bored, challenge yourself. If you are frustrated, relax. Try another strategy or topic for a while.

On the other hand, don't fall into the pleasure trap: just because something is easy or *you* like it doesn't mean that it's as good as it can be. Writing is satisfying work, but it is *work*. And sometimes work is hard. The better you are as a writer, the more aware you are of problems, and the higher your standards will be. Listen to what others suggest about your writing, and grow. Listen to your own best instincts. Writing develops over time.

Myth 9: You have to go it alone.

Many of the benefits of writing stem from its being a solitary activity: you have time to think things through, opportunities to change your mind, space to be your own person on your own terms. But although part of writing is done alone, more often than not, writing happens as a result of anticipating an audience and consulting with others. Just read the Acknowledgments at the beginning of this book and you will see that hundreds of people were involved in its creation. You, as an anticipated reader, are crucial to the process. Biographies of great authors are filled with stories of how poets, novelists, playwrights, humorists, and essayists worked with and for each other. Business, legal, medical, and scientific professionals are constantly collaborating with each other in the preparation of documents.

Myth 10: Only the teacher knows.

Some students and teachers believe that it is the writing teacher's job to tell the student exactly what to write and how to write it, and then to correct the student's grammar and punctuation. These students become discouraged because they don't feel in charge of their own minds and development. They don't write what they really want or need to say because they don't want to be criticized for it. They don't take risks. Teachers become frustrated, as well, if they feel they are doing the work students need to learn to do for themselves.

The teaching of writing has gone through many changes in the past decades. Teachers realize more fully that writing is an expression of a whole human being. Students have many insights into language that the teacher may not have. In addition, students know things that their writing teachers may not but would like to learn. The teacher's role is seen to be more like that of a coach. Teachers can't write it for you, but they can help you find your way. Teachers and students find the new ways of learning to write more meaningful and exciting. The purpose of this book is to help you discover your strengths.

*E*xplorations

1. *Together or Solo.* Discuss which of the ten myths about writing you have believed. How have these myths affected you as a writer? Offer a specific incident as an example of a myth in action.

2. *Together.* Discuss how the following myths formulated by student writer Sandra Spillman would affect you as a writer:

   a. Each sentence when writing a paper must be perfect. If it is not, I may not go on to the next.

   b. When finished with writing the paper, I must not need corrections and, therefore, do not need to make changes.

    c. My vocabulary must sound intelligent—the more complex, the better.

    d. Each piece of work must be finished at the end of each session. I may never hand in an incomplete work.

    e. I must keep to my regular format and not try anything different in case it may be wrong.

    f. I must not write about anything that may not interest every single reader of my work.

    g. My work must sound as though an English major wrote it.

3. *Together or Solo.* List some rules about writing that you learned or adopted during your years in elementary and high school. How have each of these rules benefited or hindered your development as a writer?

4. *Solo.* Choose one of the following topics, and write about how your beliefs about writing were affected by your experience:

- Your earliest experience with writing

- Your worst experience with writing

- Your best experience with writing

5. a. *Solo.* Write a letter introducing yourself to your classmates. Decide how you want them to see you, whether it be entertaining, serious, outgoing, shy, or assertive. Tell them what is most important about you. Relate how you feel about writing, what you hope to gain from the class, and how you can contribute to the class.

    b. *Together.* In small groups, read these letters to each other. Ask questions that arise. Note similarities and differences between group members.

    c. *Solo.* Rewrite your letter, including aspects of yourself that occurred to you during the small group conversation.

    d. *Together.* Form small groups with other students to read and discuss your rewritten letters.

Fears About Writing

If you fear writing, you may become so paralyzed that you won't write. Naming fears is a first step to facing them. Here are some insights that other students have had into why they fear or avoid writing:

Fear of Success.   Sometimes success can be even worse than failure. It can put pressure on you, as it did on Jane. She wrote this:

> I avoid doing well in school because whenever I do well my parents and teachers expect too much out of me. I can't take the pressure. So I go sour on school and do as little as I can. I tell myself I can't do it, so I don't.

The problem was that Jane exchanged one set of pressures for another. Instead of having to cope with pressures to succeed, she had to cope with the pressures of not having the skills she needed to land a satisfying job.

Fear of Failure. If you have had difficulty with grammar in the past, you might write sentences that are too simple to express your ideas. If you have difficulty with spelling, you might avoid writing interesting words that you don't know how to spell. If an instructor gave you a low grade because you disagreed with a popular political statement, you might avoid taking a stand in your work. But writing to avoid failure—writing "safe"—diminishes you and your skills.

Fear of failure breeds failure. What makes gold medals at the Olympic Games, landings on the moon, flourishing vegetable gardens, and best-selling books is the ability to fall down and get right up again. A professional basketball player will have made more mistakes than an amateur. A successful student or writer is someone who is willing to work through mistakes until a piece of writing fulfills its purpose.

The best way to develop confidence in writing is to write, write, write. Here's what a student, Sharon DiNicola, discovered:

> I couldn't wait to finish revising to tell you how I am improving. You were right. I was very negative about my last paper and felt too discouraged to do anything about it. Well, this time around, I sat down and said I was going to have a positive attitude toward this revision. I told myself, "I know what I'm doing. I *can* do this."
>
> I expanded a few paragraphs and used more effective words to make my point clearer. I am learning to write and go back and fix certain areas. Every time I revise, I feel more and more proud of myself.

Fear of Losing Friends. Sam's friends made fun of him when he showed interest in classes. They called him a "nerd," so Sam hid his books, stopped asking questions in classes, and refused invitations from teachers to join debates and the school newspaper staff. He was afraid of losing his friends if he did well. They were afraid of the same thing. The trouble was, he became bored and irritable because he was starving his mind. His friendships suffered.

Fear of Exposure.   You may feel embarrassed or shy about revealing who you are to people you don't know. This is what Kerrie Losche wrote:

> My shyness supposedly keeps me safe from any kind of embarrassment and stops me from taking risks. I've been shy all my whole life, stopping myself from doing little things like oral reports, raising my hand in class to give an answer, introducing myself to a class, and especially writing well-developed essays. I always told myself I would sound dumb and I really believed it.

The problem for Kerrie was that the more she retreated, the less she learned and the more she needed to hide her lack of knowing.

Fear of Change.   Another student felt torn about learning to speak and write in English. José Campis was born in Puerto Rico and loved the beautiful landscapes, people, and way of life he knew as a youngster. He wanted to do well when his family moved to New Jersey, but somehow, adopting standard academic English felt as if he were betraying his Puerto Rican heritage. Many of us closely identify with the language of our family and community. Adopting a different language or way of communicating may threaten our sense of belonging. José felt more and more torn and lost.

Misery Likes Company.   Sometimes you can adopt another person's fears. Ed realized that succeeding in a world of words threatened his relationship with his father, who had not had the same educational opportunities as he had had. In writing the following, Ed was able to appreciate why he held back from greater involvement in his school work:

> I really get interested in some things about science and nature. This sometimes hurts me when I talk to my father. If he is doing something and I tell him an easier way to do it, he sort of shuns me. He mainly does this if there are other people around. I think he does it because he resents his son being able to tell him something that he doesn't know. This makes him look dumb in front of people. He still loves me, but I don't think he can accept my knowledge about certain things he doesn't know. I usually don't let this bother me, but sometimes if I know something more about what my dad is doing, I just keep quiet. I also don't put much effort into school anymore.

Ed decided that his failing school would just make his father feel worse. Ed hoped that by doing well in school he would eventually make his father proud of him.

Commitment

Commitment is the cure for myths and fears. Commitment is taking charge of your life. You stop waiting for others to push you or "do it for you." You decide to make things happen in your life, for yourself. If you don't, you will probably settle for superficial novelty and pleasure that soon wear off. Falling in love is novelty and pleasure; marriage is a commitment to work through hard times so as to enjoy a lasting and meaningful relationship.

Writing is a commitment. If you write only when it's easy or safe, you will enjoy such superficial pleasures as "getting it over with." But success comes from working through as many rough drafts as is necessary to realize the potential of your writing projects. Resisting writing tasks because they might be inconvenient is self-defeating. A successful writer is willing to write something more challenging and meaningful than a merely error-free, easy essay. A successful writer takes on challenging topics, recognizes problems, and then revises a piece of writing until it fulfills a satisfying purpose.

When fears arise about writing, when you find yourself resisting a writing task, take a deep breath and *do it anyway*. The more you write, the more you assert that you *are* a writer. Get organized; make a commitment to yourself as a writer. Here are two lists that contrast the actions of a committed and an uncommitted writer:

Committed writer	**Uncommitted writer**
Buys both the more complete hardcover dictionary for home and a portable paperback for commuting.	Reluctantly buys the cheapest dictionary and loses it—buys a new CD with the money saved.
Attends all writing classes and makes special arrangements to be on time.	Gets to classes only when the weather is suitable and no work is due.
Asks the instructor for appointments. Arranges for a tutor when necessary. Asks questions often in class.	Complains to others that the instructor doesn't explain things, but doesn't talk to the instructor directly.
Types and proofreads all papers.	Writes papers on the bus on the way to class. Drops them into a puddle.
Makes contact with several other students in class to study together and review class notes and assignments.	Makes excuses for not knowing assignments.

Committed writer	Uncommitted writer
Uses school work as a way to cope with personal and family difficulties and to develop a firmer hold on life by adopting teachers as friends, studying family and social relationships, researching diseases, and so on.	Frequently uses personal and family difficulties as excuses for not attending class and doing assignments.
Treats "mistakes" as necessary for growth. Welcomes adjustments and critiques offered by teachers and others.	Uses "mistakes" as excuses for giving up too soon.
Organizes time and space to support writing.	Procrastinates.

*E*xplorations

1. *Solo.* Write about a time when you overcame a fear to succeed at something important to you. Choose one or more of these questions to inspire you:

   - What did you fear?

   - What myths did you believe?

   - How did you avoid confronting your fear?

   - What finally caused you to confront your fear?

   - What did you do?

   - What happened?

   - What did you learn?

2. *Solo.* Write about a particular time when you failed at something, such as writing, a sport, a relationship, or a project. Respond to one or more of these questions to inspire you:

   - What happened?

   - Who was involved?

   - What changed?

   - What did you fear?

   - What myths did you believe?

   - If you had to do it over again, what would you do?

3. *Solo.* Write about someone you know or have heard of (this could be you, as well) who overcame a fear or handicap in order to succeed.

Discuss in detail the person's problems and how he or she overcame them. What did you learn from writing about this person that you can apply to your own life?

4. *Solo.* Poet Diane Wakoski said, "We become the words we speak." Language can shape your life through self-fulfilling prophecies and social prejudices. For example, if a teacher expects a student to be intelligent, then she or he will treat the student with more respect. That respect can help the student develop the confidence needed to work and thereby succeed. On the other hand, making snap judgments about a person because of how she or he seems can lead to misunderstandings, at the very least. Write about some experience you have had with social prejudice, whether because of your age, sex, race, religion, physical traits, past record, or cultural background. The prejudice may be positive or negative. What were the beliefs that shaped this experience? What were some of the words others applied to you? What did you learn about how language changes the way we perceive and behave?

5. **a.** *Solo and Together.* Add to the lists of actions of committed and uncommitted writers. Draw on your experience. Be honest.

   b. *Solo.* Write a letter to your instructor, making a commitment to actively participate in your writing class. Record any problems that you anticipate and how you plan to solve them. Ask for specific kinds of support. From time to time during the semester, revise and add to this letter.

Freewriting

The best way to learn *how* to write is to write: learn by doing. *Freewriting* is a special strategy that will help you write past myths and fears. When you freewrite, you get words onto the page or computer screen as fast as possible. You are like a runner leaping over the hurdles of worries and indecision, speeding past the blocks of confusion and resistance. Freewriting helps you relax so your ideas can flow. As one student writer, Satonya Gardner, put it, "Freewriting helps you break down walls." Frank Kisselman, another student, said, "Sometimes when I freewrite, my mind wanders. Sometimes what emerges is more worth writing than what I started out with."*

The elements of freewriting are focus, time, speed, and freedom. Read the basic procedure detailed in the sidebar.

---

*The concept of freewriting was formalized by Peter Elbow in *Writing Without Teachers* (New York: Oxford, 1973).

How to Freewrite

1. *Focus.* Choose a topic (for example, a word, idea, image, or quote) and record it at the top of a sheet of paper or a clear computer screen.

2. *Time.* Commit yourself to writing for a specific number of minutes. (Start with sessions of five or ten minutes.) If you need to write longer, go ahead.

3. *Speed.* Write as quickly as you can without physically hurting yourself. Speed helps you run through blocks and distractions.

4. *Flow.* Keep your pen or keyboard active. If you feel stalled, repeat the same word or expression until you find something else to write.

5. *Freedom.* Don't reread or correct while you are freewriting. If you can't think of a word, draw a line to fill in later. Spell words any way that lets you move on. Follow novelist John Steinbeck's advice:

    > Write freely and rapidly as possible and throw the whole thing on paper. Never correct or rewrite until the whole thing is down. Rewriting in process is usually found to be an excuse for not going on. It also interferes with flow and rhythm which can only come from a kind of unconscious association with the material.[1]

To keep going as you freewrite, you may want to record your reflections on the writing process as you proceed. Be honest! You may have to start by writing, "I don't know where to start." Remember that focus is the first element of freewriting, even if it means to focus on your not being able to focus. You'll be surprised how this can loosen you up. When you freewrite another time, you may want to choose a favorite sentence, image, or word from a previous freewrite.

Strange, silly, or forbidden thoughts and words may come to your mind as you freewrite. *Write them down.* No one has to see a freewrite that you don't want to show. At times, a mind is like a clogged faucet—jammed with words held back for fear of someone's disapproval, especially your own. Once you get the "sludge" out—the old rusts and "musts"—you get a clear flow. The idea you needed may be just behind one you don't want. And you never know—on second thought, one of those silly or forbidden thoughts may turn out to be exactly the one you were looking for.

Virginia Woolf is one of the most admired writers in English literature. Notice how flexibly she uses freewriting to focus herself in "A Sketch of the Past":

> Two days ago—Sunday 16th April 1939 to be precise—Nessa said that if I did not start writing my memoirs I should soon be too old. I

should be eighty-five, and should have forgotten—witness the unhappy case of Lady Strachey. As it happens that I am sick of writing Roger's life, perhaps I will spend two or three mornings making a sketch. There are several difficulties. In the first place, the enormous number of things I can remember; in the second, the number of different ways in which memoirs can be written. As a great memoir reader, I know many different ways. But if I begin to go through them and to analyse them and their merits and faults, the mornings—I cannot take more than two or three at most—will be gone. So without stopping to choose my way, in the sure and certain knowledge that it will find itself—or if not it will not matter—I begin: the first memory.

  This was of red and purple flowers on a black ground—my mother's dress; and she was sitting either in a train or in an omnibus, and I was on her lap.[2]

*R*eflections _____

1. Which parts of Virginia Woolf's freewriting sound as if she's talking to herself? Point to particular words, phrases, and sentences.

2. Which parts may need further explanation?

3. Which parts are most interesting to you? Why?

4. How did freewriting help Woolf clear her mind and find ideas on which to write?

When to Freewrite

Freewriting can help you with any writing task. Here are some purposes it can help you satisfy:

- To express a strong feeling
- To generate ideas
- To discover and choose details
- To get warmed up for an essay exam—freewrite your answer on a separate sheet of paper before writing on the exam paper
- To start writing when you are tired
- To rehearse a conversation
- To test different beginnings for a writing project
- To entertain different solutions to a problem
- To pass time

Exploration _____

Together and Solo.

1. Choose a thing (such as snow, roses, milk, or beer) or a person (such as a talk show host) that the whole class knows. Individually, do a timed ten-minute freewrite about the subject you chose together.

2. Read aloud to each other what you wrote, and compare the different directions people took from the same starting point.

3. Name any fears or concerns about writing that occurred as you wrote.

4. Choose your favorite sentences, phrases, or ideas from your freewrites. You might want to record them on a board. Discuss what you like and why. Do another freewrite starting with a sentence, phrase, or idea from your own or someone else's freewrite. Read portions of these freewrites to each other and discuss what you learned.

The Practice of Writing

The following practical ideas will help you manage your time, tools, space, and habits so that you can put into practice your commitment to being a writer.

Writing Time

To manage your time, you need goals, regularity, flexibility, and planning. With your instructor, set a *goal* for the number of papers and pages you are to submit on schedule. Then strive to be *regular* in your writing habits, the way most practicing writers are. So, for example, just like a runner deciding to run a mile every day at 6:30 P.M., you may decide to practice writing every day for fifteen minutes at 6:30 P.M. Then do it wherever you are. Let your friends think you are strange when you go off to another room during a party. They will admire you, too. And it might be fun to go off and gossip with yourself about them in writing. Use made-up names in case others find what you wrote.

Be *flexible* in how you plan, so your schedule will work *for* you. For example, because campus parking is difficult, several students decided to drive to school by 7:45 A.M. so that they could park where they wanted to, without wasting time. During the hours before class, they found places in the library or in an empty auditorium, studio, classroom, or lounge to study or work. Three other students, with small children, arranged for

	SUN	MON	TUES	WED	THU	FRI	SAT
MARCH 1995				1	2	3	4
	5	6	7	8 PAPER ASSIGNED LIST TOPICS	9	10 CONSULT MR. JAUGS ON FOCUS	11
	12	13 LIBRARY- COLLECT INFO.	14	15 ORGANIZE- DRAFT LEAD	16	17	18 DRAFT PAPER- JOURNAL
	19 CONSULT BRUCE ON PAPER	20 COLLECT MISSING INFO.	21	22 REVISE TYPE	23 PROOF WITH MARY	24 PAPER DUE	25
	26	27	28	29	30	31	

FIGURE 1.1   A Writing Time Plan

one babysitter to care for all of their children one afternoon a week. The students used those afternoons to meet at the library to work on their papers together.

Plan your writing time. Start early and make and beat your *own* deadlines. Break down your writing projects into manageable parts. The next chapter maps out the different phases of the writing process. Once you become familiar with it, you will be able to decide which phase of the writing process you want to do next *before* you stop a particular writing session. Then you will feel more confident because you will know where to start. Figure 1.1 is an example of how one student planned his time to write a long paper. He wrote his writing time plan in pencil and made frequent adjustments as he went along.

Procrastination.   *Procrastination* means "to put off until tomorrow." There are two kinds of procrastination: creative and self-deceiving. *Creative procrastination* is taking time off from a particular phase of a task *already started* to reorganize, re-energize, and give ideas and events time to evolve. It can also be staying at your workplace and doing either nothing or your work. The first seven minutes of a task are usually the hardest, and 50 percent of the task is getting yourself settled. One student, working on a long paper, would sit for an hour at her desk without producing more than a paragraph. But sitting there reaffirmed her commitment. After a while, she had few dry spells. It was more interesting to work on her writing than to sit there doing nothing.

The point of *self-deceiving procrastination*, the second type, is to avoid giving enough time to a task. Self-deceiving procrastination shows up in two ways: putting off the task constantly, or trying to "get it over with" too soon. Either way, the person puts off real development for another day. The self-deceiving procrastinator tends to claim, "I work best under pressure." If you put work off, this is what can happen:

1. You tend to make more errors because you're working too fast.

2. You may run out of time, because it's hard to judge exactly how long a project will take.

3. You are cheating yourself because you don't give yourself the opportunity to develop your skills.

4. If you realize that you could have done the task if you had started earlier, you will probably lose confidence and self-esteem. Loss of confidence is an invitation to give up too soon.

Writing Tools

Instruments.   Mechanics have their wrenches; writers have their pens. Your tools are there to serve you the way a scalpel serves a surgeon. As a student writer in the 1990s, your challenge is to experiment with different writing instruments. You will need a typewriter or computer for college and work-related writing so that you can produce presentable materials. In addition, studies have shown that, for many writers, a typewriter or computer enhances not only the speed with which they compose but also the process of developing ideas. (This works even if you are only a two-finger typist as fiction writer John Cheever was.)

Tape Recorder.   If you are a talker but freeze when facing a page, make the most of your gifts by talking your early drafts into a tape recorder. Then you can play back and write down your ideas. In addition, if you are a commuter, you may find that ideas come to you while you are riding. Tape them for later.

Supplies.   If you were a lawyer, you wouldn't tell the judge you couldn't complete your case because you ran out of typewriter ribbon the night before. *Being a student is your profession.* Part of a profession is to keep plenty of supplies (such as paper, typewriter ribbons, pens, and notecards) so that you can complete your work properly. Next time you run out of ribbon, be ready to go to class and tell your instructor, "I ran out of typewriter ribbon." Watch the person's face change, ready for the excuse. Then say, "But I had a backup, and here's the freshly typed copy." Then you can both laugh.

Writing Space

Incense, flowers, high ceilings, organ music, and a pulpit invite a congregation to worship. Loud, rhythmic music and strobe lights inspire people to dance. To write, you need to find or create the right conditions. When you establish that a place is a writing place, just going there will help you to get started or at least to practice creative procrastination.

William Oatman, a student, wrote about how he created his writing space:

> First of all, when I write, I have to bring myself into my own world. I'll put Marvin Gaye's "What's Going On" on the tape recorder to block out noise that will bring my mind back into reality. When I write, I have to be physically alone: anyone around me seems to be a threat. It's like they're looking over my shoulder trying to correct or give me advice. Even if the person doesn't know me, I feel uncomfortable.

Robin Livelli, another student, reported some of the discomfort she had while writing:

> My body becomes very tense because most of the time when I write I am not using a table; I use my lap. Therefore, I have to make a hard enough surface to write on. My head is always swaying from side to side. Don't ask me why. I think that maybe by moving my head around, I feel it will shake the information out. My hand always cramps because I hold my pen or pencil too tight. In grammar school, I was taught that if the teacher could not pull the pen or pencil out of your hand easily then you were holding it incorrectly. But I still hang on too tight.

Her classmate Raul Sanchez gave her some ideas about how to cope:

> When I write I sit in a chair in an upright position with both my feet on the floor so that there's a consistent blood flow. This helps me to relax my body. Once I relax the writing gets better. Once in a while I get up to stretch, walk around, or even do some sit-ups. I also have to have a good lamp and a desk with a big surface.

Writing Habits

To establish the habits of a writer, take the following advice adapted from William James's essay "Habit: Its Importance for Psychology":[3]

1. Launch yourself into writing with energy.
2. Make no exceptions to your routine until the new habit is established in your life.
3. Start today.
4. Write every day (even if only for ten minutes).

Writing is its own reward. But *do* reward yourself for your new habits with a treat: a new something, a game of basketball, a hot bath, or a walk in the park. Keep a record of how much you write on any given day, what research you did, and what you learned so you can monitor and be proud of your progress.

Explorations

1. **a.** *Solo.* One writer writes on an ironing board; another prefers writing in bed. Describe what happens in your mind, body, and emotions when you write. How do you create your environment to enhance your work? What changes could you make in your environment or in your habits to help you better harness your writing energies?

    b. *Together.* Read your essays to each other and swap and develop strategies.

2. **a.** *Solo.* List problems that you anticipate in creating or acquiring the time, tools, space, and habits that are conductive to becoming a writer.

    b. *Together.* In small groups, share these concerns and then devise strategies that will help you turn problems into opportunities. If possible, find ways in which you can work to support each other, such as forming study groups or car pools, sharing supplies and tools, or swapping services (for example, typing a paper for an oil change).

3. *Solo.* Keep a record of your writing activities. Each time you perform some writing task, mark it down in a particular place such as the inside cover of your notebook. This will help you to monitor your work. If you haven't worked, it can remind you to do so. If you have progressed, it can enhance your self-esteem and inspire you to do more.

4. *Together.* Using insights you developed through reading and working with this chapter, write a group letter of advice to student writers.

WRITERS WRITING

Read and discuss the essays that follow, using these reflection questions and suggestions to guide you.

*R*eflections _____

1. *Together or Solo.* Choose your favorite essay. Discuss the following:
   - Why you like it more than the others
   - What similar experiences you have had in your life
   - Which words, phrases, or sentences you especially like
   - What purpose you think it served the writer
   - What questions you would ask the writer

2. *Solo.* Write a letter to the writer in response to his or her essay.

3. *Solo.* Write about an experience you remember as a result of reading the essay you like best.

Owning My Words

Student Annie E. Lee

It felt like someone was constantly whispering in my ears, "You don't know how to articulate your words. Your grammar is horrible. How can people understand you?" These fears were always there, causing me to fear speaking before a group.

I guess it began when I came to New Jersey from the south. Southern people have a deep accent and some have a tendency to talk fast—I was one of them.

Some people criticized me for my southern accent. I had this one friend in particular, Karen Jones, who thought she was more intelligent than others. Whenever I talked, she listened very closely to see how I pronounced words. She told me that I added endings to words such as "mucha" instead of "much" and "hurted" instead of "hurt." Or, I might leave endings off words such as "start" when it was appropriate, instead of saying "started." Sometimes we could be talking and she would say to me, "I don't know what you are trying to say: spell it out for me." She even told me once that I don't put my words in the right places. She always was trying to correct me and always in the presence of other people. This made me feel stupid and insecure and caused me not to want

21

to talk to people. Or, I would choose certain words that I thought people would understand. I started to lose confidence in myself and it hindered me for a long time. I came to the point where I didn't want to talk with her because I was so afraid that I would say the wrong thing. She was the only person I had this problem with.

Just this past Sunday, I had dinner at my house with some friends and invited Karen over. I was sharing my experience of baking my first cake with my friends. The first cake I baked fell because I put too much baking powder in it. I was baking this cake for a birthday, so I had to call my mother and get the right ingredients. Where I put three teaspoons of baking powder, I should have put ¼ teaspoon. I told my friends that my mother said to use confectioners' sugar instead of granulated sugar. Well, not only did Karen have a better solution, but she also tried to correct me again. With her head up high and a tone in her voice that said, "You don't know what you are talking about," she said, "If you don't have confection*ary* sugar, you can always sift granulated sugar and it will be just as good." Her statement made me feel stupid and embarrassed because she emphasized "confection*ary*" as a way to not-so-subtly correct my saying "confection*ers'.*" My attention was not directed to my guests any more. I was sitting there thinking that I misused "confectioners'." My fears started to work on me saying "You can't, you didn't, you shouldn't . . ." So, to put my mind to rest, I looked at the name on the box of sugar I used and also consulted *The American Heritage Dictionary,* and I saw that the correct expression *was* "confection*ers'* sugar." It made me feel much more in control, and Karen doesn't seem so intimidating to me anymore.

Coming Back to Writing

*Sue Woulfin**

As I sit here facing my English class, I sometimes wonder how I got to be a college writing instructor. Certainly, I have not always enjoyed English. In fact, there was a time in high school when I dreaded every English class and was totally frustrated by every essay assigned. As I look back now, this fear was probably due to an English teacher I had early in my high school career.

Mr. X was a brand new teacher, and I was a brand new high school student. He loved analyzing literature but never spent time on writing

---

*Instructor of Developmental Writing at Kean College of New Jersey. An essay by Ed Metz, one of her students, is on page 24.

and grammar. Up to that point in my life I had always been a fairly good writer. I made that judgment based on the generally good critiques I'd received from previous English teachers. However, I had only written creative pieces. I had no idea how to develop an analytical essay, compare and contrast ideas, or delve into a nonfiction work. Mr. X noticed this deficit.

At the end of the semester, Mr. X called me into his office to discuss my future. He noted that I was in an accelerated math class and suggested I seriously consider devoting myself to a career in math. This was his way of telling me that I was being placed in a lower track in English. Mr. X then stated that I shouldn't be concerned about this change because math people were always pretty poor in English.

From that point on, his prophecy came true. I could never write an essay without hearing his words. Naturally, those words became self-fulfilling. I never did well in a high school English class again.

It wasn't until I got to college and met an English professor who seemed genuinely interested in me that my attitude toward English changed. She asked me why I wasn't majoring in the field. It was her interest that finally got me to question Mr. X's evaluation of my abilities. As I sit here writing this, I realize I'm glad I did. But why did it take so long?

I Need To Improve

Student Tamara Tolbert

I used to be a pretty good writer, but as I got older, I got more careless and impatient and I worried more about the quantity than the quality. So from that point on I went downhill. Yet I still thought I didn't need to improve. Even when I wrote my essay on the placement test. It didn't hit me until now when I see I was placed in a more basic writing class than I thought I needed.

Another flaw I have is my spelling. I always think I spelled a word right and so I never bothered checking it. You see, I used to be an excellent speller a long time ago and so for some reason that image stuck on me and I began to get overconfident. Needless to say my vocabulary has changed over the years and the words have gotten harder and it's about time I came to grips with the fact that I can't spell every word correctly.

The last problem I have is this misconception that the teacher is always right and only they know the secret in writing a "perfect" paper. That also slackened my confidence a little.

A Great Experience with Writing

Student Ed Metz

Throughout my four years of high school, I was never really fond of writing. I mean every time I handed in an essay, poem, sonnet, or even a term paper, it would always come back to me with red correction marks. Some of the teacher's comments would be, "too wordy," "lacks parallelism," or "run-on sentences." Errors in my punctuation were another area the teacher seemed to make sure not to miss marking up my papers with. The teachers were like the knights of King Arthur's court, and their pens like lances dripping with the blood of their enemies. Whenever the teacher would strike with her lance, she would leave trails of blood along my papers.

All of these bad experiences with writing always drove me further away from trying to write any better.

During my last year of high school, our English teacher gave us a choice of topics. We had to write a clear and concise essay, sonnet, poem, or paper and hand it in. This would account for one-half of our quarter grade. I said to myself, "I'm getting tired of being stabbed with the lance of a teacher." I wasn't about to die.

I'm pretty good with making words rhyme and matching syllables, so I chose to write a sonnet. I wrote a fourteen-line sonnet in iambic pentameter. I considered this my love sonnet. Every word rhymed, every other line was in rhythm with each other.

We handed the papers in all together. The teacher exclaimed, "I'll have them back to you tomorrow." All day long, I couldn't think during my other classes. I was sweating profusely. My heart was beating like the old man's evil eye in "The Tell-Tale Heart." The next day finally arrived. I was in English class. I sat in the back as though I didn't care about that sonnet, but I did: this was the biggest grade of my life.

The teacher handed back our papers. When I looked at mine from a distance, I could see the "blood marks" from the teacher's lance on my paper as if to say, "Ha! You've lost again." But to my surprise these marks were those of victory. The teacher made comments such as "good diction, well-worded, one of the best sonnets I've ever read." I earned an *A* on my paper.

Chapter Review _____

1. *Solo.* Define yourself as a writer, using the ideas, readings, discussions, and strategies you explored in this chapter. You may want to ask these questions of yourself for inspiration:

- Where have I been as a writer? Why?
- Where am I as a writer now? Why?
- What are my specific challenges as a writer?
- Where do I want to be as a writer? How am I going to get there?

2. *Together.*

   a. In a small group of three or four, write a letter to your instructor saying what you hope to gain from your writing class. Mention your fears. Ask your instructor to clarify her or his expectations of you as a writer. Make a commitment as a class to helping everyone develop as a writer. Suggest any ideas that you believe will help make this a satisfying venture for all of you.

   b. Read your small group letters to the whole class. Notice what they had in common and how they were different. How does your instructor react? What did you learn from this group exploration?

Chapter **2**

The Writing Process

This chapter offers opportunities to

—Identify *seven phases of the writing process*

—Distinguish *formal* from *informal* writing

—Discover your *style of composing*

—Learn what an *essay* is

You write by sitting down and writing.

—*Bernard Malamud, Novelist*

You are like a mechanic trying to design something, sitting at a table with . . . little bits and pieces scattered about, sorting them out with a forefinger, pushing one to the side, ousting another altogether, bringing the first one back, finding it doesn't match with something that you've meanwhile chosen; deciding, perhaps, that it's so good that you must consider abandoning all the rest and starting over again with this as the main component.

—*Christianna Brand, Mystery writer*

You have to try something harder to do better.

—*Laura Silwones, Athlete, Massage therapist*

Writing for Meaning

Writing is a process that leads from a need to a product and, ideally, a result that is meant to satisfy the need. What a piece of writing *means* to you is determined by the combined effect of your need, purpose, audience, and results. If you write only to have an instructor read and grade what you write, the writing itself may not mean much to you. If you write because you are horrified at drug dealers in your neighborhood (you have a need to protect yourself) and want to convince the government (your audience) to provide more police protection (your purpose is to persuade), the writing itself will be very meaningful. If, as a result of writing, the situation actually changes as you want it to, you will be experiencing the full power of written language.

The more important the need, purpose, and results of writing are to you, the more meaningful your writing will be. The less important the need, purpose, and results of writing, the less it will mean.

Needs + Purpose + Audience + Results = Meaning

Often, you can't control needs or the results of writing. These are relatively *passive* phases of the writing process. But you *can* decide whether and how to react to needs and results. Your options are the seven *active* phases of the writing process: identifying purpose and audience, drafting, collecting, focusing, organizing, consulting, and revising. By working with these active phases your needs and results will further transform and inspire your writing.

This chapter offers an overview of the seven phases of the writing process. This model emphasizes the importance of writing for meaning and for an audience that includes, at the very least, not only your instructor but your peers. You may decide to work through the chapters that are devoted to different phases of the writing process first. Or you may decide to explore writing for different purposes in Part III of *The Flexible Writer*—to remember, to bridge cultures, to learn, to gain power—and return as the need arises to explore the phases of the writing process in Part II.

Phases of the Writing Process

How you write (the process you go through) is not *what* you finally produce (the product or result). The rehearsal (the process) is not the play (the product or result)—the production line is not the car. Much work goes into the process of producing a Madonna for her audience: long daily workouts with a personal trainer; hours of nail, hair, and skin work by beauty experts; lessons with dance, voice, and acting coaches; experiments with wardrobe consultants, composers, musicians, technicians, and many more. Her music videos are a product of much trial and error, outtakes, and surprises in the process. You see only the results, not the many hours of preparation and mistakes. So too with writing—what is published is the result of consulting with peers and experts, trial and error, outtakes, and surprises in the process.

The writing process can be divided into nine phases, as shown in Figure 2.1. You enter the process because of some need. The center of the writing process is identifying your purpose (what you hope to accomplish for yourself and others through writing) and identifying your audience (who you want to reach with your writing). The writing process culminates in some result, which in turn may create another need to write.

As you can see, this model of the writing process is not a straight line leading from a need to a result. According to this model, there is no set order in which to move through the phases of the writing process. Also, the way you move between phases will change for different writing tasks. Notice that the arrows pointing to the phases go both ways. This is to illustrate that any phase can be repeated as needed. As you move into one phase of the writing process, ideas for other phases of the writing process will probably arise. Look at the summary of these phases in Figure 2.1.

Needs. The writing process begins with a need. This need may be as simple as a need to design a schedule or as complex as a need to express anger over a political issue. Educator Claire Weinstein distinguishes two kinds of needs for learning: *performance* and *mastery*. If you do your assignments just to get a grade and pass a course, then you are only creating a performance. You will expend your energy figuring out what the instructor wants and will fulfill only the requirements you perceive. You make your instructor a dictator and thus give over your power. If you do your assignments to master a body of information or a set of skills, then your interest is mastery. You will perceive the instructor as a guide, not a dictator. Assignments will be a stimulus for exploration and discovery. You will take initiative and assume responsibility for your own development.

What Weinstein says about learning applies to writing in most situations. For example, you might write a memo in order to perform for your boss, just so he will notice you for the next promotion. Or you might write the same memo to develop your ideas about marketing a new product. The irony is that the person who works for mastery is the person who is most

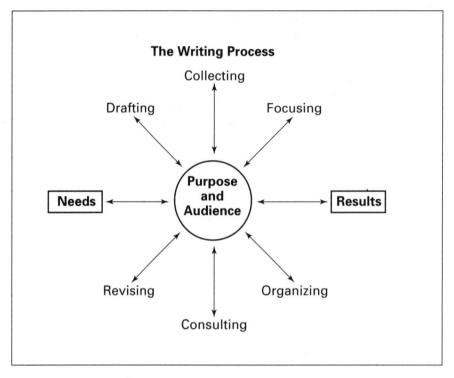

FIGURE 2.1 The Writing Process

likely to perform well. The person who works only to perform may become stuck in a mere power struggle.

The least inspiring motivation for writing may be to merely fulfill a course requirement. But you can turn almost any assignment into something satisfying if you can discover some way to address more basic needs such as curiosity, a need for adventure, a need to assert your individuality, a need for precision, a need to be included in a community, or a need to express yourself. A given piece of writing may fulfill a single need or a complex of needs. To understand this phase of the writing process, ask yourself such questions as these:

- How do I feel about this topic?
- Which aspect of this topic is important to me?
- What human interest do I find in this?
- What basic need could writing this satisfy for me?
- What does writing this *mean* to me?
- Am I writing for performance or mastery?

Identifying Purpose and Audience.   When you enter the active phases of the writing process, you make a commitment to fulfill your need. This commitment to action transforms your need into a purpose. Since writing is communicating, as soon as you enter the writing process you are also anticipating who your audience (or receiver) will be, even if it's just yourself as reader.

Your purpose and audience will determine what and how you write. For example, if you write a letter to your senator (your audience) to win a vote against a nuclear plant in your city (your purpose), you would not want to attack her personal campaign strategies. This could alienate her and undermine your purpose. However, you could write an additional letter to the editor of your local newspaper stressing your concerns and thus make the senator more willing to please her constituents.

The purposes and audiences for writing are as varied and numerous as there are life situations. Any given piece of writing may have more than one purpose and audience, although some may be more important to you. To engage in this phase of the writing process, ask yourself these questions:

- Why am I writing this?
- Is my reason personal, intellectual, economic, physical, or social?
- Who is my audience?
- What does my audience know?
- What does my audience want?
- How can I capture and keep my audience's attention?
- How can I best fulfill my purpose?

Drafting.   To experiment with and learn from writing, you put words on the page. Drafting is this process of actually creating the written document. You may use many different methods of drafting: audiotaping, writing longhand, typing, cutting and pasting, or word processing. To manage your documents so that you can monitor and ensure your progress, you create a filing system. To engage in this phase of the writing process, ask yourself this question:

- How can I create an environment that includes the tools I need to support my writing process?

Collecting.   To discover, develop, and create ideas that will serve your purpose and reach your audience, you need to collect memories, sensations, experiences, and ideas. You will read, talk, watch films, and listen to the radio. You may visit a museum, try hang gliding, or cook seaweed so that you can better understand your subject. Chapter 1 invited you to experiment with *freewriting,* a basic tool for collecting and creating ideas. Additional collecting strategies are introduced in Chapter 4: *listing, brainstorming, clustering, interviewing,* and *writing journals.* To engage in this phase of the writing process, ask yourself these questions:

- What information, experiences, and ideas do I need in order to accomplish my purpose?
- How can I most effectively collect what I need?

Focusing.   To divide your writing task into manageable bits, and to hold your own attention as well as that of your audience, you focus your writing. By focusing, you create *unity* in your work—including all and only those ideas that are relevant and necessary to fulfill your purpose.

1.   *Strategies.* Six focusing strategies are explored in Chapter 5: choosing, specifying, quoting, illustrating, questioning, and stating. To engage in this phase of the writing process, ask yourself these questions:

- What's relevant to my purpose?
- What choices do I need to make?
- How can I be more specific?
- Which examples could enliven my writing?
- What exactly am I writing about?
- What questions do I need to answer to be clearer?
- How can I state my purpose and point of view?

2.   *Sense appeal.* To enliven your writing and engage your audience, you focus on sensory images of sight, hearing, smell, taste, and touch as well as bodily sensations of motion, pleasure, and pain. Chapter 6 offers you strategies for giving your work sense appeal. You will learn how to describe, how to distinguish showing from telling, how to balance objective and subjective approaches to writing, and how to use comparisons to enliven your work. To engage in this phase of the writing process, ask yourself these questions:

- Have I used sensory images?
- Have I ignored any senses that might be relevant?
- How can I prime my senses with objects, photographs, or audio- and videotapes?
- What firsthand experience could prime my senses?
- Do I illustrate important claims?
- What do the images mean to me?

Organizing.   To guide yourself and your reader, you organize your work so it holds together. A well-organized piece of writing will thereby have *coherence.* You pay special attention to titles, leads (beginnings), the body of your work, transitions, and endings. Chapter 7 offers you strategies for managing these elements of your writing and also for developing, shaping, and outlining your work. To engage in this phase of the writing process, ask yourself these questions:

- How can I shape this writing so that it will engage me in the process of developing ideas?
- How can I organize this writing so that it holds my audience's attention, from an effective beginning through a body of ideas to a memorable last impression?

Consulting.   To grow as a writer, a thinker, and a person, you consult with others who can help you develop. These people may include peers, teachers, librarians, family, friends, and others. To develop your own writing intuitions, you, in turn, respond to the writings of others. Helping them, you help yourself. We learn best what we teach. To engage in this phase of the writing process, ask yourself these questions:

- Who can respond to my work?
- What do I want others to help me do in my writing?
- How can I best help other writers?

Revising.   To develop your early drafts, you look for opportunities to improve and build on them: this is the process of revising. In revising, you reconsider your purpose and audience and decide which phases of the writing process you need to perform. The best way to learn how to adjust your writing for your purpose and audience is to consult with others. To engage yourself in this phase of the writing process, ask yourself these questions:

- How can I revise this writing to most effectively do what I want it to do?
- What am I learning from revising?

Results.   A stopping point in a particular writing process is publication. This may be as limited as reading a paper aloud in class or sending in a résumé to a prospective employer. It may be as broad as having a book published. Other results may occur, including return mail, a grade, a job offer or rejection, money, a new love, or ideas for more writing. A most disappointing result may be no reaction or result at all. You may follow up this result by choosing to address a different need, a different purpose, a different audience, or a different way of presenting your ideas.

Publication of some sort—either in print or in a public speech or reading—is often the desired result of writing. In school, publication may be as limited as handing in a paper to your instructor or as wide as having your work published in a newspaper, magazine, or book. The results may be as limited as a grade or as far-reaching as finding an instructor who becomes actively engaged in helping you with your academic career.

Because publication is so motivating in the real world of writing, you may want to set a goal of producing a class newsletter or magazine. You may want to arrange for an evening of reading your work for family, friends, and members of the campus and community. Sometimes you can pair up with another section of a course and present your work to each other. Working toward such goals offers opportunities for community and accomplishment. To respond to this phase of the writing process, ask yourself these questions:

- Am I satisfied with this result?
- With whom can I further share my writing?
- How can we, as a community, publish together?
- Do I need to write more or differently?

*E*xplorations

1. *Solo.* The purpose of this exploration is to help you further understand process. Identify some specific activity—serious or humorous—at which you consider yourself to be an expert. Here are some examples:

    Throwing a fastball   Messing up relationships

    Eating pizza   Making peanut butter sand-
    Arranging a bouquet of flowers   wiches

    Losing things   Mowing a lawn

    Rebuilding a carburetor   Growing snap peas

    Creating parties

    Describe how you go from need to result in your chosen activity. You may want to use different phases of the writing process as a guide. So, for example, you *need*/crave an apple pie; the *purpose* for it may be to celebrate a raise; the *audience* can be your friends; the *collecting* activities may include picking apples; and so on. For each phase of your activity, offer special instructions. *How* do you select apples? *How* do you make the crust flaky?

2. *Together.* Read what you wrote in Exploration 1. Discuss your different processes. If two people wrote about a similar activity, compare their processes. Discuss what lessons you can draw for your writing process from what you know about process in other activities.

3. *Solo.* Describe how you wrote your last piece of writing. Identify which phases of the writing process you used and which you didn't. Would you have written the paper differently if you had used the model of the writing process described in this chapter? If so, how? If not, why not?

4. *Together.* Set a goal for publishing your work this semester either by creating a class book or by giving a public reading to family, friends, and members of the campus and the community.

Formal and Informal Writing

Different writing tasks emphasize different phases of the writing process. If you are writing a diary entry, you are less likely to move into the consulting and revising phases of the writing process than if you were writing a business proposal. Similarly, if you are writing a first draft of a paper, you may be less concerned about organizing your thoughts than you are in just collecting and drafting what comes to mind.

In considering how to approach the phases of the writing process, it is helpful to distinguish *informal* and *formal* writing tasks. One definition of the word *formal* is "shaped." Informal writing does not have to be shaped as carefully as formal writing does. Informal writing focuses more on the drafting and collecting phases of the writing process. The more formal a piece of writing is, and the more important its audience, the more fully you must enter every phase of the writing process. Notice how some formal and informal writings compare:

Formal	Informal
Clean printout	Illegible handwritten draft
Focused	Exploratory
Concise	Searching
Researched	Incomplete
Organized	Digressive (with tangents)
Passed consultation	Unreviewed
Revised	Uncorrected

Here are some parallel examples of formal and informal writing:

Formal	Informal
Polished paper	Freewrite
Business proposal	Short memo
Letter to a senator	Letter to a good friend
Exam essay	Class notes
Produced play	Party charade

The Essay

An essay is a composition focused on a single topic, supported by examples and illustrations. One purpose of writing an essay is to explore ideas. In fact, the verb form of the word *essay* means "to try" or "to make an attempt." Another purpose of writing an essay is to present your personal point of view on a topic. Often, the essay is an attempt to convince your audience to see the world as you do. The essay is a fundamental form of writing that helps you develop as a student and a professional.

The model of the writing process in *The Flexible Writer* is tailored to help you write essays. Focusing helps you to commit yourself to a single topic. It helps you to illustrate your topic so you can, in turn, focus your audience's attention on what you have to say. Collecting invites you to explore and test different ideas and sensations. Organizing allows you to develop a structure that will support your focus. Consulting and revising offer you opportunities to test and learn more about your purpose, your audience, and your topic.

Styles of Composing

You may discover that you have special abilities in particular phases of the writing process or that you prefer some phases of the writing process over others. You may discover that you are a natural researcher and prefer collecting information to revising. You may be an editor and enjoy revising more than drafting. You may be a doer who likes to dive right into drafting. You may be social and enjoy the consulting phase over organizing. This section offers you some insights into tastes in and styles of composing.

The Planner's Style

As you practice writing, you may discover that you have a current favorite way of moving from one phase of the writing process to another. For example, you may prefer a particular straight-line style because you tend to be a *planner:* collect information, choose a topic, organize an outline, write a focused statement, draft your paper, proofread, submit. A planner tends to know ahead of time how a writing project will look when it is finished. The benefit of the planner's style is the security of knowing what to do next. This style works well for papers in which you report simple information.

The drawback of the planner's straight-line style is that it may restrict the writer. One of the benefits of writing is that you learn and create new ideas during the process. Often in the writing process new insights arise in one phase that will require you to refocus, reorganize, or redraft if you are to include them. If you adhere too strictly to your original plans and ideas, you lose the benefit of writing your way to better ideas. Also, different writing tasks call for different approaches. What may work for you in writing academic papers may not necessarily serve you in writing business letters or project proposals. Longer, more creative writing projects take more time, readjustment, and flexibility than short writing pieces that are meant only to transfer simple information.

The Explorer's Style

The person who takes an *explorer's* approach to the writing process moves back and forth between different phases as needed and is comfortable with revising as many times as is necessary. For example, an explorer may draft several attempts first, find a focus, collect information, draft again, consult with others, organize, revise, refocus, collect more information, redraft, publish. The benefit of the explorer's style is freedom and the discovery of new ideas.

The drawback of the explorer's style is that it may initially confuse or frustrate you. Writing can help you steady your mind when you focus and organize your thoughts. Having a clear plan can offer you the structure you need to develop confidence in yourself as a thinker and social being. If you entertain too many ideas at once, you may confuse yourself and become bored. Shorter tasks such as essay exam questions do not require the same kind of exploration as longer, more creative papers, proposals, and projects do.

Experiment with both the planner's and the explorer's styles. Ask yourself which writing tasks call for which approach, and when. Although you may favor one style over the other (and some writing tasks require more of one and less of the other), you will find yourself both planning and exploring in most tasks. Here, as in any aspect of the writing process, be flexible.

New versus Practicing Writers

New Writers

Being a new writer can be very exciting. It is a time for discovering abilities you already have but didn't recognize in yourself. It is a time for exploration, adventure, and discovery—it is a time for developing friendships with other writers. Each time you start a kind of writing with which you are unfamiliar, you have an opportunity to recapture this excitement. If you are fully engaged with the process, you can take on the attitude of a new writer each time you write.

But some new writers—afraid of criticism—get stuck in a familiar phase of the writing process. Often this is the revising or consulting phase. Even before they start putting words on the page, these new writers *revise* in their heads. They tell themselves things like "That won't work," "I can't write that," "They won't understand." It's almost as if they were trying to avoid the disapproval of a harsh authority figure. So they give up before they have to and depend almost entirely—without discussion or negotiation—on teachers or tutors to perform the other phases of writing *for* them, including assigning topics (identifying purpose and audience, and focusing), offering ideas to include (collecting), telling them how to organize their work, and correcting their grammar and punctuation (a part of revising). These writers may rush through their assignments and thus lower their satisfaction in writing. The purpose of this textbook is to help you to gradually make these choices for yourself.

Then there are new writers who go to the other extreme and won't take any advice at all. They tend to believe statements such as "My writing is just fine. What's good is just a matter of my taste against yours." They are suffering from denial. Shutting themselves off from others' reactions, these blocked writers can slow their growth or even stunt it.

The problem for both the underconfident and the overconfident new writer is fear of not getting it *right* the first time. If you fear not being able to write *right,* you let others perform phases of the writing process for you or you make believe you don't need any help.

Ignore your fears. Focus on experimenting with the different phases of the writing process for yourself. If you get stuck in one phase, skip to another. You may find your answer there. Keep moving. Become a *practicing* writer.

Practicing Writers

Flexibility is the hallmark of practicing writers. They move more easily from one writing phase to another and back, as needed. For example, when practicing writers get too involved collecting information (to the point of being jammed with more research than will ever be needed to write a certain paper), they may return to the center of the writing process and ask, "What is my purpose in writing this paper?" They may move to revising an introduction (noticing that it is more likely to engage an audience) and then move right to drafting. Practicing writers acknowledge that they may need more practice in a particular phase of writing and then get it. Acknowledging that different writing tasks may call for different approaches to the writing process, practicing writers don't get stuck with any particular sequence in which to perform the phases.

Practicing writers are *aware* of their audience, so they consult with others to read drafts. Practicing writers are willing to *revise* as many times as needed to reach readers and fulfill their purposes. Because they consult with others and experiment with different versions of what they write, practicing writers know how to talk about writing and become more and more *aware* of their own writing processes.

Becoming a Flexible Writer

The difference between a new and a practicing writer is that the practicing writer has probably made more mistakes in writing than the new writer has—just as a tennis pro has hit more balls out of bounds in a career than an amateur has. There are days and days of frustrating rehearsal, miles of rejected film, and sometimes millions of dollars worth of false starts, bloopers, and outtakes behind the smooth surface of a finished movie. There can be years of work and piles of rejected words behind a well-written book. Have the courage to be imperfect. The more you practice one kind of writing, the more perspective and flexibility you'll have for other kinds of writing. A practicing writer gets through possible blocks by being willing to experiment, explore, and try as many ways as needed to create the desired results. The practicing writer makes enough time for writing, so that new ideas can emerge and the process can be enjoyed. The more you practice as a writer, the more automatically you can move from one phase of the writing process to another.

One student, Edem Ikurekong, summarizes the benefits of learning to be flexible during the writing process: "Not trying to be too perfect while I'm in the writing process enables me to be a man of my own and be able to say what I want to say and not what I'm expected to say. If I was trying to be too perfect, I'd be searching for somebody else's *right way* to write." The good news is that you can become a practicing writer very quickly, just by committing time, energy, and attention to the process. Each time you write notes, experiment with an idea on paper, consult with someone, turn to a book (such as this one) to guide you, collect information, or even just shop for the proper supplies, you are acting as a practicing writer, a flexible writer.

Chapter Review _____

1. *Solo and Together.* Answer "yes" or "no" on the lines of the following questionnaire to determine whether you currently prefer a planner's or an explorer's style of composing. Check the Answer Key below, and then discuss your results.

    a. _____ Do you write an outline before starting to write?

    b. _____ Do you need to know exactly how to write something?

    c. _____ Once you start, do you need to finish writing quickly and be done with it?

    d. _____ Do you revise when you get new ideas as you write?

    e. _____ Do you look forward to learning as you write?

    f. _____ Do you prefer thinking things through before writing?

    g. _____ Do you write down your ideas first and revise later?

    h. _____ Do you like to revise?

    i. _____ Do you prefer reading to writing?

    j. _____ Do you believe that there is a right sequence of steps to take in the writing process?

2. *Solo.* Determine which phase of the writing process has given you the most difficulty in the past. Read the chapter that is devoted to that phase. Freewrite a letter to your instructor, quoting your three favorite statements from that chapter. In your letter, make a commitment to becoming an expert on that phase. Adopt that chapter; refer to it often; help others with that phase of the writing process.

_____

Answer Key:

The planner tends to answer "yes" to a, b, c, f, i, j. The explorer tends to answer "yes" to d, e, g, h.

3. *Solo.* For your next essay—and whenever possible—write a self-review by responding to these questions:

   a. Why did I write this?

   b. Who is my audience?

   c. How did I maintain focus?

   d. How did I organize?

   e. How did I collect information?

   f. What did I learn from consulting others?

   g. What efforts did I make to revise?

   h. What problems did I have in the process?

   i. What did I learn about my writing process and skills?

   j. What more could I do to enliven this work for myself and for my readers?

Chapter *3*

Purpose and Audience

This chapter offers opportunities to

—Identify **purpose** and **audience** in the writing process

—Find **meaning** and **purpose** in writing

—Learn how to **engage readers**

—Distinguish four purposes of education: **information, skills, interpretation,** and **experimentation**

—Explore the dynamics of **denotation** and **connotation**

Why write? To live, of course.

—*Gunter Kunert,*
Author of over sixty books

Ancient Egyptians believed that the mere action of writing could provide protection against calamity.

—*Joseph Campbell, Mythologist*

Purposes for Writing

The writing process is usually motivated by some combination of real-life needs: personal, emotional, intellectual, physical, social, or economic.

If you choose to satisfy your need through the act of writing, you transform your need into a purpose. Some purposes are more inspiring than others.

If you write merely to avoid disapproval—to get an assignment "over with"—the reward of writing may be as removed from your real-life needs as a grade on a dusty transcript. It is far more meaningful to write in order to explore feelings, questions, ideas, topics, and interactions that concern you fully and directly. How engaged you are shows in the writing. If you're bored with your writing, your reader will be too. Even if you are writing only for someone else's approval, paying attention to the phases of the writing process will help you discover some way to transform each writing task into something that satisfies you more fully and directly—something that meets *your* approval. Your work itself will thereby improve, and so will your grades. But then the grade won't have to be the point any more.

Kinds of Purpose

Writing can serve three kinds of needs or purposes: (1) *self-expressive*—the need to be heard; (2) *interpersonal*—the need to get something done with others; and (3) *aesthetic*—the need for order, beauty, pleasure, and creativity.[4] A given piece of writing may serve some of or all these purposes, depending on the writer's purpose and audience. Practicing writers know how to gauge the kind of writing (or combination of kinds of writing) that is appropriate in a given situation. These writers don't try to write a mostly self-expressive piece when an interpersonal one is in order, nor do they treat something aesthetically when they mean only to be self-expressive.

Self-expressive Writing.   Self-expressive writing helps you to formulate your experiences in words so that you can "get them out of your system." The main purpose of self-expressive writing is to fulfill the need

When to Explore Purpose and Audience

1. You are beginning a writing project.
2. You are worried about readers' reactions.
3. Readers don't respond as you had hoped they would.
4. You are bored or frustrated.
5. You don't know what to do next.

to be heard. Self-expressive writing allows you to vent your anger as well as to express love, to remember your childhood as well as to dream of your future. Sometimes the purpose of this kind of writing is fulfilled just in the act of writing. Self-expressive writing often takes the form of first-draft diary entries, letters, autobiographies, poems, and songs. Here is a self-expressive paragraph written by student Samantha Renner:

> I am terrified of the idea of war. All I can think of are those films of houses gutted by bombs, children lying half-naked and dead in the streets, and blood everywhere. Sometimes at night, I wake up to the sirens from the fire station down the block, and I panic: What if they are not signaling for a fire? What if, somehow, there are planes coming to bomb our town? This must be just a little of what people must feel who are actually in a war zone. It's terrible.

In this example, Samantha is expressing her feelings about war. The self-expressive purpose of the piece is fulfilled by writing, itself.

Interpersonal Writing.   Interpersonal writing is social. The main purpose of interpersonal writing is to help you connect, break, or negotiate lines of communication between different aspects of yourself and others. These others are called your *audience,* a word that literally means "those who listen." Your anticipated audience may be as far away as a reader in another country whom you may never meet, or your audience may be as close as yourself. Your anticipated audience may be as specific as your instructor or as general as all college students. More than one audience may exist for a given piece of writing. Your task is to decide which audiences you mainly want to reach.

In interpersonal writing, you try to get someone else to recognize you, to do something for or with you, to agree with you, or to change in some way. The *essay,* a written interpretation of experiences and information, is a very important form of interpersonal writing in the academic world, in journalism, and in business and the professions. In the essay, you show what you know and contribute your perspectives to the community. Interpersonal writing may take other forms such as letters, proposals, reports, business and legal memos, recipes, instructions, exams, essays, legal documents, and editorials. The following paragraph is an example of interpersonal writing that contrasts with the self-expressive writing in Samantha's paragraph about war. In this second paragraph, Samantha is trying to persuade the audience of her position:

> Before a country declares war on another country I believe that several things should take place:

1. There should be an open debate on television between those who are for the war and those who are against it. The debators should include the parents of draftable people, military personnel, lawmakers, and conscientious objectors.

2. There should be films of wars played on television showing people who have been hurt or killed.

3. There should be a vote taken by the general population.

4. There should be an active campaign to ensure that at least 50 percent of the population votes.

5. The people of the country on whom we are planning to declare war should be allowed to speak to the people of this country. In short, we should spend at least as much time, money, and thought in deciding on whether to declare war as we do on a presidential campaign.

Aesthetic Writing. The main purpose of aesthetic writing is the challenge and pleasure of learning how to use language in interesting ways. When you focus on your writing style for its own sake, you are writing for an aesthetic purpose: to create beautiful language. Even a harsh situation can be aesthetically described if the language is precise and effective. Writing about your feelings about war may start out to be a self-expressive act, but if you then revise it into a polished poem, play, story, or creative essay, you are writing for an aesthetic purpose. Samantha transformed her paragraph into a poem. She shaped her work using techniques that display the beauty and power of language: clear images, meaningful line breaks, musical sounds, appropriate rhythms, and comparisons. Using these strategies, she engages her readers' attention so that she can more effectively relate her message on a difficult subject:

When Will We Awaken?

The sirens shriek,
3:30 in the morning, again.
Somewhere nearby there is a fire.
This one will be cooled by water.
The children will be carried
by people in wet rubber coats.
What of the shrieking in another place
Where no one can carry the children
Away from bombs bursting in air
Giving proof through the night
That a flag may wave?

Combinations.   Good writing often satisfies different needs or purposes at the same time. For example, it is hard to separate the aesthetic from the self-expressive and from the interpersonal in some writing. A poem that is written to satisfy an aesthetic need may also satisfy a self-expressive purpose, as Samantha's poem does. This same poem may serve to convince others to avoid war. Paying attention to how words are put together—writing something in an aesthetic way—often helps you to better satisfy your self-expressive and interpersonal needs. Furthermore, self-expressive writing can form the basis for interpersonal writing, and, in turn, interpersonal writing can lead to more self-expression, as it did for Samantha.

To see for yourself how combinations of purpose work in process, read the first draft of student Cassandra "K.K." Reid's essay on joining the army:

First draft

When I was in the eleventh grade, I decided I wanted to enter the armed forces when I graduated. I went to the recruiter office and signed up. I then was given a date to take the entrance test. The instructor was in the Army. He handed out the test and you were told to put the test on the desk when you finished. When the recruiter contacted me, he notified me that I passed.

So the next week after graduation. I was to report to Newark Airport where a sergeant would be waiting for me. It was like waking up being in another time and place. You boarded a plane with other people and when you landed you were in another life. This place was Columbia, South Carolina. A sergeant met the group at the airport and led us to a bus. I thought this bus ride was the longest ride I ever took.

K.K. brought her first draft to class to consult with her peers. Here are some questions they asked her in response to her draft:

- Why did you join the army?
- How did the sergeant talk you into it?
- Weren't you afraid of doing it?
- Why did it feel like you were landing in another life?
- What made the ride seem so long to you?
- Who was with you?

K.K.'s peers needed to know what her experiences *meant* to her, what purpose they served for her. She had limited her essay to just listing events, as if her purpose were to write a job report. In her work in Army communications, that was the kind of writing she was used to doing. Notice how more engaging her writing became when she became more self-expressive:

Second draft

The Decision

In the eighth grade, I had an close friend Malcome, who lived across the street from the armory. I used to pass through the armory parking lot to go home. This was a short cut. So I became familiar with the army personnel, one sergeant in particular, Pat. I don't remember Pat's last name, because I don't think I ever used it. Pat was Italian, well built and very friendly. I really don't know how our meeting began, but it became a long, lasting friendship.

The armory became an community center for me. In the basement, there was a pool table and a bar with a television. So this is where you would find me. Playing pool most of the time, I became a young pool shark.

The armory started having roller skating on the weekends. On Friday and Saturday nights, this would be the place to be. In Plainfield, the town was separated into two parts. The east end and the west end. Soon on the weekends everybody from both ends of town would show up. The line would always be long. What made these nights special is that Pat was in charge and I helped him.

We would block off a section of the drill floor hall and put up road cones to mark off a big oval. All the skaters were supposed to skate around that oval. Then when the skaters came, I would help to hand out skates. At the end I would collect them. In between, I was an official skating guard, making sure everyone went in one direction and people didn't get into fights. We used to play vinyl records in those days and Pat let me run the record player. Sometimes I would talk to the skaters over the microphone. But that was Pat's favorite thing to do.

The doors would open up at eight o'clock. People would start to come around seven, to be in front of the line. I wouldn't show up sometimes until ten minutes to eight, opening time. I would feel as though I was the class queen, gliding my way in front of the line. I could hear people commenting, "Hey, where do you think you're going?" Some people would try to do the same thing. As a result, since they weren't official like me, they were barred from getting in.

Once I entered the door and got onto the drill floor, I would be greeted by the other people that also helped. I enjoyed being there. When everybody was let in and the skates were issued, the floor vibrated with the many people skating around in a circle. I heard the wheels singing and chanting, whirl, whirl, whisk. I felt a slight whiff as people rode by.

Most of my time was at the armory, and it become my second home. I decided one day, I might want to be part of the armed forces for good. It was not until years later when I did let my dream come true. In the eleventh grade, I did sign up. Most of my friends went to college; some had jobs. I wanted to get away for adventure. So I had a commitment which meant something to me. I look back and I dream of the times I had at the armory. If there was one main inspiration on my decision, I would have to say it would be Pat. He made me feel important and wanted.

*R*eflections

1. What topics did K.K. try to cover in her first draft?

2. What was the main focus of K.K.'s second draft?

3. Which portions of K.K.'s second draft do you like the best? Why?

4. What was the purpose of K.K.'s first draft? Her second?

5. To which questions by her peers did K.K. decide to respond?

6. Which questions have become irrelevant to her second draft?

7. Which of K.K.'s drafts would be more effective if her purpose were to recruit new personnel for the Army? Why?

8. Would K.K.'s second draft serve self-expressive as well as interpersonal purposes?

9. How could K.K. further revise her essay if her purpose were to reach recruits?

10. What other papers could K.K. write about her experiences in the Army?

In your own writing, balance self-expressive, interpersonal, and aesthetic purposes. The following Explorations help you to identify different purposes for which you write or have written.

Explorations

1. **a.** *Together.* List different kinds of writing you've done, from shopping lists to essay exams, telephone messages to formal proposals.

   b. *Solo.* Choose two pieces of writing you've done: a particularly meaningful piece and one that you found less satisfying. For each piece, consider the following:

   - The purpose for writing
   - Who the audience was or would be
   - The difficulties you may have had in writing
   - How you managed problems with writing
   - Who supported you in the writing
   - The satisfactions you had from the writing
   - The results of the writing

   c. *Together.* As a whole class or in small groups, discuss what you learned from this exploration.

2. *Together.*

   a. There are some down-to-earth reasons people need to write. These include personal, emotional, intellectual, economic, and social purposes such as the following:

   - To release stress
   - To make others like them
   - To be heard when no one seems to listen
   - To earn a good grade

   Add to this list, being as honest and straightforward as you can be.

   b. Group the reasons on your list into the following categories, according to the main need they satisfy for you: self-expressive, interpersonal, aesthetic.

   c. Discuss which reasons for writing are the most satisfying to you. Which reasons cause you the most tension? Which of these are more directly related to writing? Which of these are indirectly related to writing?

3. **a.** *Together.* Add to this list of professions:

Mechanic	Real estate broker
Homemaker	Psychiatrist

   b. *Solo and Together.* Interview a person from a profession or business with which you aren't familiar but that interests you. Ask the person to show you samples of the kinds of writing done in the normal course of her or his duties. Use these questions to guide your discussion of individual pieces of writing:

- Why did you write this?

- Who were your anticipated readers?

- What problems did you have in writing this?

- How did you solve your writing problems?

- Whom did you consult?

- What advice helped you the most?

- What satisfactions did you have from writing this?

- What results did this piece bring?

- Would you do it differently next time? If so, how?

c. *Together.* Bring the materials and ideas you collect to class and discuss what you learned.

Identifying Your Purpose

Purpose and audience are closely connected in the writing process. What you want to accomplish—your purpose—will determine your choice of audience. The audience you're writing to or for determines—to a great extent—what purposes you can fulfill.

The range of things you can do with language is as broad as life itself. For example, expressing, proposing, promising, betting, and naming can be done entirely with words and don't necessarily anticipate reactions from others. Just stating "I promise" is a promise. Just stating "I bet" is a bet.[5] Other actions—such as persuading, negotiating, arguing, and stopping—anticipate reactions from others and may require a more complex statement. You have to learn about your audience's interests, access to information, and expectations. You have to anticipate your audience's responses to shape your own.

By writing, you *connect* with, *separate* from, or *negotiate* with others. For example, to marry, apologize, compliment, or inform is to attempt to connect with others. To argue against, ridicule, intimidate, or blame may serve to create separation. To discuss, plan, or persuade is to negotiate.

The following Explorations will help you to discover some of the purposes that language can serve and to see how it allows you to connect, separate, or negotiate.

*E*xploterations ⎯⎯⎯⎯⎯⎯⎯⎯⎯⎯⎯⎯⎯⎯⎯⎯⎯⎯⎯⎯⎯⎯⎯⎯⎯

This Exploration provides the language you need to discuss the purposes of your own papers.

1. *Together.*

   a. Generate a list of thirty-five verbs that refer to verbal communication. You may wish to use dictionaries and thesauruses. Start with these words:

discuss	scold
argue	flatter
persuade	ask
entertain	insult

   Let the words above lead to other words that lead to other words. Strive for variety and quantity.

   b. Group these language activities according to whether they help you *connect* with, *separate* from, or *negotiate* with others.

Letters often focus on well-defined purposes. The following Explorations offer you focused opportunities to explore how awareness of purpose and audience shapes writing.

2. *Together and Solo.* Referring to the verbs listed in Exploration 1a, name the purposes of different sentences in the following letters. For example, Cornelius Vanderbilt starts by *accusing the reader of cheating him.* What does he do next?

   a.

   Dear Sir:

   You have undertaken to cheat me. I will not sue you because the law takes too long. I will ruin you.

   Sincerely,

   Cornelius Vanderbilt[6]

   b.

   Dear Mrs. Allen,

   Don't you hate to hear the ring of the alarm clock early in the morning? I do. I suspect my reason is that I dislike to be reminded of an obligation.

   I guess that's common with everybody. We all have a feeling of irritation when reminded of something we might overlook or forget. So, I want you to know that I don't like to remind you of the account of $435.40 that was due a few days ago. But, like the alarm clock, I must speak my piece.

If you've already placed your check in the mail, please ignore this note and consider it bookkeeping on our part.

And, thank you!

Sincerely yours,

P.S. I'm sure we'll both continue to dislike—but recognize the necessity of—pesky reminder devices. Right?[7]

c.

Dear Miss,

After three years of schooling at Barbiana I took, in June, my exams for the intermediate diploma as a private-school candidate. The composition topic was: "The Railroad Cars Speak."

At Barbiana I had learned that the rules of good writing are: Have something important to say, something useful to everyone or at least to many. Know for whom you are writing. Gather all useful materials. Find a logical pattern with which to develop the theme. Eliminate useless words. Eliminate every word not used in the spoken language. Never set time limits.

That is the way my schoolmates and I are writing this letter. That is the way my pupils will write, I hope, when I am a teacher.

But, facing that composition topic, what use could I make of the humble and sound rules of the art of writing in all ages? If I wanted to be honest I should have left the page blank, or else criticized the theme and whoever had thought it up.

But I was fourteen years old and I came from the mountains . . . I tried to write the way you want us to. I can easily believe I was not a success.[8]

3. *Together or Solo.*

   a. Suppose you have just accidentally damaged a car you borrowed from a family member or friend. Imagine the accident in as much detail as you can. Write letters to each of the following: the owner of the car, the officer who is going to file the accident report, and someone who would be on your side.

   b. Read these letters aloud to each other. Using words you discovered in Exploration 1a, decide on the following:

   - The purposes of the letter
   - The most important purpose
   - Why the letter is or is not likely to accomplish your purpose
   - Whether the letter attempts to connect, separate, or negotiate
   - How you could change the letter so that it would be more likely to achieve its purpose

4. **a.** *Solo.* Write a letter that you *don't* intend to send. Your audience should be someone with whom you have an important relationship, such as a family member, a friend, a lover, a boss, a co-worker, or an instructor. Your subject should be something that concerns you deeply. Your purpose in this letter is to express your feelings and position.

    b. *Solo.* Write another letter to the same person and on the same subject, this time with the intention of sending it. As you write and modify what you write, decide on your purpose and the result you want.

    c. *Solo or Together.* Compare your sets of letters. What changes have you made in the letters you intend to send? What did you include, exclude, emphasize, or de-emphasize? Which letters are more likely to succeed, and why?

5. **a.** *Together and Solo.* Choose a controversial public figure who is currently in the news and write her or him a letter with a specific purpose in mind. As you write, negotiate your approach and discuss the purpose as it develops in the writing.

    b. *Solo.* Choose a person you admire (either alive or dead) to whom you would like to say something. This person can be either a private or a public figure. Write a letter to this person, noting your purpose.

    c. *Together.* Discuss the letters you wrote to persons you admired, paying special attention to purpose and audience.

Purposes in Education

To focus your studies in a particular academic course, become conscious of the major purpose or emphasis of the course. Four major emphases of courses are (1) information, (2) skills, (3) interpretation, and (4) experimentation.

Information.   When the focus is on *information,* you concentrate on what people in a particular academic discipline consider to be important and relevant facts. When information is emphasized, you tend to concern yourself with others' statements and points of view: You memorize more and question less. You take more short-answer exams. There certainly are benefits and satisfactions in knowing a lot of information. Otherwise, games like Jeopardy and Trivial Pursuit—based on information—wouldn't be as popular as they are. It *is* satisfying to score 100 percent on a multiple-choice test. But more important, knowing what others know in an academic community helps you become a part of that community. Fundamentally, knowledge *is* power.

Remember, however, that just because people believe something is a fact doesn't mean that it is or that it shouldn't be questioned. For example, at one time some scientists erroneously believed that women were intellectually inferior to males. "Facts" sometimes are no more than statements that are commonly believed by a group of people. Maintain the position of a responsible thinker. Have the courage to question "facts." If you disagree with the information you are offered, the more you know about it, the better you can question it and convince others of your point of view: *You* become a maker of knowledge.

Skills.   When the focus in a course is on *skills*, you will engage in a variety of activities that go beyond collecting and memorizing what others consider to be important information. The focus of this book is on skills. Approaching this book as if it were focused on information would be inappropriate. You could memorize this whole book and be able to score 100 percent on a multiple-choice test about it. But, if you didn't write and consult with others about writing, you wouldn't acquire the skills this book can help you develop.

Interpretation.   When the focus in a course is on *interpretation*, you combine a command of information and general skills with the ability to respond as an individual. Morals and art, for example, are considered to be more matters of "point of view" than matters of "fact." Each discipline and subdiscipline provides you with skills for responding to subject matter in an individual way. For example, in an art course, you are taught how to interpret the mood or statement that a painting suggests through the use of colors, shapes, shadows, and organization. In a poetry course, you are taught to interpret the feelings or insights a poem suggests through the use of sound, rhythm, and sensory images. Be careful to notice if, in a particular course, someone claims that a certain interpretation is "the right one." That person may have confused a matter of fact with a matter of interpretation. One interpretation may be clearer or may account for more parts of a painting or a poem than another, but that doesn't mean that that is the *only* good interpretation.

Experimentation.   When *experimentation* is the focus in a course, you concentrate on questioning, experimenting, and exploring. You are encouraged to *discover* information more through trial and error than through collecting and memorizing. Whereas an information-based course offers the security of easy ways of learning and testing, an experimentation-based course offers you the excitement and satisfaction of creating and inventing new ideas and skills.

There is no easy way to assign these emphases by disciplines because much depends on your instructor's style of thinking and teaching and your style of thinking and learning. But courses such as basic chemistry may emphasize information and structured experimentation more than interpretation. Your writing course is more likely to emphasize skills, interpretation, and experimentation over information. Whenever you move from one class or situation to another, and whenever there is a shift in what you are required to do in a class, identify the main emphasis of your work.

Explorations

1. *Together.* Bring college catalogs to class. List a number of interesting courses representing the full range of disciplines. Using catalog descriptions as aids, state in your own words the purpose or emphasis of each course and the academic discipline of which it is a part.

2. *Together.* List the courses that members in the class are currently taking or have recently taken. For each course, arrange the following in terms of their importance to the class: information, skills, interpretation, experimentation.

3. *Together.* List the different kinds of tests, papers, and reports you are required to do in the courses you are currently taking or have recently taken. Which assignments stress information? Skills? Interpretation? Experimentation? Which assignments require you to have a command of more than one of these?

Audiences for Writing

Kinds of Audiences

Writing has three kinds of audiences: (1) general, (2) focused, and (3) specific. If you are writing for a *general audience,* you must consider that it may include people of different sexes, ages, and ethnic origins, with a variety of tastes, interests, and political and religious beliefs. Large newspapers and national magazines are likely to be written for a broad general audience. Writing for general audiences is difficult because so many different factors must be considered, including the following:

- How much information can you assume that everyone knows?
- On what kinds of information would most people agree?
- What are the most popular interests of your audience?

- How many people would stop reading the publication if you included certain topics and information?

As a student writer, develop your skills by writing for *focused audiences,* such as children from eight to ten years old, photographers, stamp collectors, homemakers, or college students. The amounts and kinds of information that would interest such a focused audience are easier to gauge. Magazines, small newspapers, and books on topics of more limited interest are usually written for special audiences.

Finally, a *specific audience* will include only one person or at most a few people. This audience may be just yourself, your instructor, a group of co-workers, your boss, a business associate, or a friend. Journals, letters, and memos are often written for specific audiences.

Identifying Your Audiences

How much information you offer in a piece of writing is determined by the main audience you target for your writing. If, for example, you were trying to decide whether to pursue your college degree now, you could write about it to clarify the pros and cons, decide what to do, and ultimately ease the discomfort of being split by indecision. Because you know yourself and the details of your situation, you would be less likely to include information that would be necessary if you intended your writing to be read by someone else. The following journal entry, written by student Manny Ricardo when he was in high school, may be meaningful to him, but it leaves out information that an audience beyond him and his family would need to know:

> Dad has his reasons for wanting me to wait a year before entering college and when I'm talking to him I agree. But when I walk away I don't feel right. There are so many things I need to learn and I want to get started right away. I wish Mom would talk to him because she agrees with me.

However, if you were writing a letter introducing yourself to a prospective college admissions officer, you would be wise to research the college, its offerings, and its admissions requirements. In writing the letter you would be creating lines of communication between what you believe the college wants and what you know and want. You would have to convince the people in the admissions office to accept you by telling them relevant information about yourself. In a letter he drafted for his application to college, Manny included information that he would not have needed to include in a quick journal entry:

Ever since I was eight years old, scuba diving in a lagoon near my family's cottage, I have been fascinated by the ecological balance between different forms of marine life. I am applying to Ocean State College to make my dream of becoming a marine biologist and educator come true because you have one of the most reputable departments in the field. As my résumé shows, I have spent many summers serving as a Marine Life Counselor training children. I hope that you will consider me as a candidate.

My only concern at this point is financial. My father recently sustained a permanent injury and the funds that were saved for my education are now being used for living and medical expenses. I believe that if I can win a scholarship, including room and board, I can start my education, ease the financial burdens of my family, and more quickly find a job in the field so that I can support them in turn.

Because this letter was written to people who didn't know Manny, he was careful to include information that would support the purpose of his application: to gain admission to Ocean State College with a full scholarship. As he broadened his audience, Manny included more information. His original letter would appeal to the special audience of admissions personnel. With some changes, he wrote a paper that could appeal to an audience of college students:

Ever since I was eight years old, scuba diving in a lagoon near my family's cottage, I have been fascinated by the ecological balance between different forms of marine life. It has been important to me that I be able to devote my time and energy to this interest. Very early on I looked for jobs that were related in some way to the ocean. I spent many summers serving as a Marine Life Counselor training children. During the winter I worked at a scuba diving store that serviced people who vacationed in the Bahamas and Virgin Islands. Every time I had to write a paper in school I asked my teacher if there was some way I could pitch it toward some topic on marine life.

Who your prospective audience is determines—to a great extent—what and how much you write. You might write a friend to express your anger about the job market, but only under extraordinary circumstances would you include this information on your college application. Also, you would not write the same words on an exam as you would write to someone who has demolished your new car—unless your purpose was to shock the professor and fail the exam. In general, don't assume that what you notice is exactly what your reader will notice. Be as clear and thorough as is appropriate to your task.

The following Explorations will help you sharpen your awareness of audience—the person or persons who may read what you write.

Explorations _____

1. *Together or Solo.* Read through the following excerpts and determine the likely audience for each. Is the audience general, focused, or specific? Who is not likely to read a particular excerpt? Why? Consider such factors as these:

age	education	nationality
sex	economic status	family role
occupation	politics	residence
health	religious leanings	
experience	environment	

   a. When you get your new camera, read the instruction booklet that comes with it before you try to use it. The battery and film go in only one way, and you want to do it right so your first roll of film is good.

   b. Among the new films, Kodak's Ektar 25 offers the finest definition, resulting in high acutance at all apertures. Ektar shot at small apertures with a tripod-mounted camera will enable you to make grainless 16 × 20's of a portion of a 35-mm negative.

   c. The camera you are holding is an ideal travel companion. Compact, easy to hold and set, weatherproof, and comfortable for eyeglass wearers, this camera will faithfully record all those places you have dreamed of visiting.

   d. You can now make a fashion statement with the camera you sport. Formerly colors were limited to chrome or black, but several new models are available in a creamy off-white that blends well with any outfit you choose for day or evening.

   e. Here's the camera I promised to send. I've already loaded it with high-speed film because you told me you want to take some indoor pictures of your team without using the flash. You said the flash really annoys the players when they're playing. When you turn the camera on, you'll need to turn the flash off. It has a red button with an arrow on it. Just point and shoot. Make a few baskets for me.

2. a. *Solo.* Write three sets of directions for a specific everyday activity you know well, such as baking chocolate brownies, changing a tire, braiding hair, or cleaning a window. Vary the audience and therefore the directions and information you include. The first audience can be a peer who has never done the activity; the second, a child; and the third, an expert in the activity.

b. *Together.* Read these directions to each other and notice what changes as the audience changes. How does the amount and kind of information vary with the audience?

3. *Together or Solo.* Describe a particular place on campus to these three audiences: a person from the time of the American Revolution, a person from another planet, and a contemporary interior decorator. Notice how the information changes as you adjust to what you believe will interest your audience and what your audience already knows. Notice how much you need to learn to better understand your audience and topic.

4. *Together.* In small groups or as class, read some essays you are writing for a class or your job. Identify the audience or audiences that would be interested in this writing. Does the writer show an awareness of audience? Which words, phrases, or sentences show this awareness? What is the writer's purpose? Will that purpose be satisfied as a result of this paper? Why or why not?

Audience Appeal

To be effective, your writing needs *audience appeal.* Otherwise, readers won't engage with your work long enough for you to fulfill your purpose. To be appealing doesn't necessarily mean to please—it means to engage and interest. In order to appeal to your audience, *take care of your readers.* Even if you disagree with your readers or want to express hostility, consider how you can best help them to get the point.

Whether your audience finds your work appealing depends on the attitude you convey. If you are fearful or dishonest, your audience will not find your work as appealing as if you are confident and honest. Using the suggestions in the Reflections below, compare the difference in attitude, and therefore appeal, that student Ziggy Jamieson brought to two drafts he wrote about writing:

First draft

I will try to do my best in this class. In the past I didn't understand the assignment. Now I will read the book and do the assignment. I will hand it in on time. I will be a good writer. I will pass this course. The teacher knows what is best and I will do that.

Second draft

I never liked to write. I never felt that my teachers listened to what I was writing about. Sometimes I felt that they didn't even read what I wrote. So why should I care? I was good at art though. In that class, I could try different things. Always my teacher seemed to like me and what I did. So I worked even harder. I'm afraid I just can't feel that way about writing. I don't know if I could get a teacher to make me feel good enough so I will want to try.

*R*eflections _____

1. Which draft do you prefer? Why?

2. Who is Ziggy's anticipated audience?

3. What are Ziggy's feelings and attitudes toward the audience in the first draft? In the second draft?

4. Point to specific words, phrases, and sentences that show Ziggy's feelings and attitudes.

5. What is Ziggy's purpose in the first draft? In the second draft?

6. What changed between the first and second drafts?

7. What's the difference in audience appeal between the two drafts?

8. What do you think helped Ziggy to change?

9. How does Ziggy take care of his reader in the first draft? In the second draft?

10. What are the likely responses and results to the first draft? To the second draft?

Whenever you get stuck in a particular phase of the writing process, remind yourself of your purpose and audience. Write an informal "pretend" letter to your audience to help you puzzle out your attitude and whether or not it will appeal to your audience. Another purpose of this letter is to discover how to take care of your reader. Here are some questions to ask yourself and your intended audience while writing your letter:

- What is my purpose?
- What are my feelings and attitudes toward you as my audience?
- As my audience, what are your feelings and attitudes on this subject?
- What do you already know?
- What do you need to know?

- Would this writing appeal to you?
- What more do I need to know or convey about this topic so as to best fulfill my purpose with you as my audience?

Explorations

1. *Together.* Generate a list of words that refer to writers' attitudes toward audiences. You may want to use dictionaries and thesauruses. Here are some words to help you get started:

fearful	self-enhancing
friendly	hostile
unsure	playful
bored	worried

2. *Together.* Using words generated in Exploration 1, compare the following introductory paragraphs of two student papers on abortion. What attitudes does each convey? Which paper has more audience appeal? Why? Do class members disagree on which has more appeal? If so, why? How would you change these essays?

Student A

Abortion: Pro-Choice or Pro-Life?

The topic of abortion has become very controversial. Meaning everyone has their beliefs and views on the situation. Some people are pro-choice, meaning that it should be up to that person on whether or not they want to or is able to keep the baby. Now on the other hand, there are some who are pro-life, now they believe that once a woman is pregnant, they should keep the baby no matter what the circumstances are such as being "too young", poor, and just not fit for whatever reason. Now I must say that I firmly agree with that and I have many reasons why.

Student B

The Dark Side of Abortion

Abortion is a confusing issue that fires the emotions of everyone. I should warn both the conservatives and liberals in advance that I'm about to throw "another log on the fire." To understand my views, you first need to know the current issues in debate. The popular titles for the debating groups are The Right to Life, who take the conservative position, and Pro-Choice, who take the liberal side.

The conservatives believe that every human being has a right to life, the fetus is a human being, and killing a human being is morally wrong. Thus, abortion is morally wrong. They will go to great extremes, armed with a mountain of facts, to convince you that the fetus is a human being. Their stance hinges on this premise.

The liberal view proposes that abortion should be a woman's right to choose but restricted in some way. The phrase "restricted in some way" presents a lot of controversy within the liberal camp. It seems that they cannot agree on when the fetus becomes a human being. The problem here revolves around their inability to define the point at which the embryo or fetus becomes a human being. There are as many ideas of when this happens as there are people in their ranks. When the embryo or fetus becomes human is anyone's unscientific guess. For the sake of argument, I will accept that this happens at conception.

3. **a.** *Solo.* Bring an essay in process to class. Using specific words such as those listed in Exploration 1, write a brief statement of your purpose, your feelings, and your attitudes toward the anticipated audience of the essay.

   b. *Together.* In small groups or as a class, read each of the essays aloud.

   - Determine its intended audience.

   - Name and discuss the feelings and attitudes the writer seems to have toward the anticipated audience.

   - Point to specific words, phrases, and sentences that convey these feelings and attitudes.

   - Decide whether the essay has audience appeal.

   - Anticipate what purpose this essay might serve with its intended audience.

   c. *Together and Solo.* For each essay, compare the writer's statement of feelings and attitudes with those ascribed by the group discussion. If there are differences, develop ways to revise the essay to best fulfill its intended purpose. If a better purpose arose in the discussion, suggest ways to satisfy this new purpose.

4. *Solo.* Write a "pretend" letter to the anticipated audience of a particular letter, memo, or essay you are writing. Using insights you develop in the letter, adjust your attitude toward your audience and revise

your work accordingly. What did you learn about yourself and writing from doing this exploration?

Denotations and Connotations

If you want your writing to reach a broader audience than yourself or those who know and already agree with you, and if you want to satisfy your purposes, you need to anticipate your audience's reactions to your tone and your point of view. In writing, just as in speaking, *tone* is the feelings and attitudes that come through in *how* you use words. Your *point of view* is the opinions and beliefs about persons, places, objects, ideas, and events that your choice of words communicates. The following sections of this chapter invite you to explore how tone and point of view are created in writing.

In writing, your attitude toward your topic is shown by your choice of words. For example, a person named Harriet Sloan can be referred to—among many other ways—with these expressions:

Dr. Sloan	Dearie
Mrs. Sloan	Mommy
Ms. Sloan	Harriet
Reverend	Honey
That witch	Lady
Miss Know-It-All	The doctor

All these expressions can be used to refer to the same person, so they all have the same denotation. A *denotation* is the meaning that most people would agree a word has. A denotation is the meaning that the dictionary will offer. But each of the expressions used for Harriet Sloan also suggests different attitudes and feelings toward her. These terms have different meanings or connotations. A *connotation* is the attitude or feeling that a word or expression conveys.

Unless used humorously or sarcastically, "Dr. Sloan" shows an attitude of respect, for it recognizes Harriet Sloan as a member of an educated culture. The expression is likely to be used in a professional setting. "Mrs. Sloan" focuses on Harriet Sloan's marital status and can suggest a culture in which women are subordinate to their husbands. However, if Harriet Sloan was born closer to the beginning of the century, when marital status was a matter of more prestige, she might consider "Mrs. Sloan" to be respectful. "Ms. Sloan" is meant to be more neutral and signals a culture in which the issue of the equality of the sexes is recognized. Furthermore, the term a person uses says as much about his or her cultural leanings as it does about Harriet Sloan. If a person insists on calling her "Mrs. Sloan" in a professional setting where "Dr. Sloan" would be more appropriate, that person may be expressing disrespect.

What is true of names is true of most words. In a given situation, a word can convey a positive, negative, or neutral tone. Some words are more strongly positive or more strongly negative. To say someone is a "bulldozer" conveys a strong negative tone. To say the person is "aggressive" is a weaker negative comment. To say someone is "assertive" can be a strong compliment. But to refer to someone as an "entrepreneur" conveys a much stronger positive tone.

When you write, decide how strong you want your tone to be. Using the right words will help you emphasize or de-emphasize those points that will enable you to fulfill your purpose with a given audience. To deepen your understanding of denotation and connotation, turn to pages 122–125 in Chapter 5, which will help you distinguish strong from weak statements.

Do one or more of the following Explorations to sharpen your sense of how your choice of words conveys different connotations and attitudes toward your audience.

Explorations _____

1. *Together.* Discuss the terms that can be used to refer to Harriet Sloan, considering the following questions:

   - In which situations are they respectful?
   - In which situations are they disrespectful?
   - What attitudes, feelings, or cultural leanings would a person have in using each of these terms? What circumstances could change the connotations?

2. **a.** *Together.* List some words used to exclude or diminish people who don't belong to your social group.

   b. *Solo.* Write about a time when you were made uncomfortable by others who used diminishing terms about you. Contrast this with examples of how diminishing words can be used playfully or affectionately within a group.

   c. *Solo.* Write about how you use diminishing language to separate yourself from people who are different from you.

3. **a.** *Together.* In small groups, choose one of the following words. Recall or find as many words as you can with the same *denotation*.

(You may want to use dictionaries and thesauruses.) Be sure to include terms that occur to you from your own experience.

mentally ill	persuade
thrifty	humorous
intoxicated	lie
request	play
slim	different

    b. In each group, put the words in order, beginning with the word with the strongest *negative connotation* and ending with the word with the strongest *positive connotation*. Decide which word you think is most neutral and why.

    c. Present the findings of each group to the class. Add further words and insights as a class.

4. *Solo or Together.* The practice essay "A Lot of Got" is filled with forms of the verb *to get. Get* tends to be a weak word. Underline every occurrence of it in the essay. Then replace forms of *get* with stronger verbs. Add to, delete from, and reorganize the essay to make it more engaging and interesting. Write another paragraph or two to finish the story. Avoid forms of *get, do,* and *have.* Use strong verbs instead.

A Lot of Got

    I got up this morning and realized I had gotten a headache. I got myself over to the medicine cabinet and got out the aspirin. I got it down with some water that my sister got for me. I got better.

    I got myself outside to get the newspaper where it had gotten lost under the bushes. I got my breakfast. After getting through that and the newspaper, I got dressed. It was getting late, so I got outside and got the bus to get to work. No sooner had I gotten my seat than I realized I had forgotten my briefcase. I got really mad. How do I get myself into these situations? I had gotten an interview with the CEO of my company and now I was going to get there without all the charts I had gotten ready the night before (which is probably why I got a headache).

5. *Together and Solo.*

    a. Choose some papers that you are currently writing for either your writing class or other purposes. Underline ten strong words in each. Discuss the connotations of these words and how they would affect a reader in a given situation.

b. Underline ten weak words in each paper. Find stronger words that will serve the purpose of each paper more effectively.

Purpose and Audience in the Writing Process

Focusing

Meaningful writing responds to real-life needs. Sometimes you may recognize the need before you start writing. Often you may discover it as you move through different phases of the writing process.

The same is true for identifying your purpose and audience. Sometimes you discover your purpose and audience as you write. For example, you may start writing a letter thanking your aunt for the weekend you spent at her shore house. As you write, you may notice that you keep thinking of how your two cousins were arguing about who would paint the house this summer. You may find you want to readjust your purpose in writing the letter and offer to help paint the house. So your purpose will expand from merely *thanking* your aunt to *offering to help* her.

Your audience may shift as well. Suppose you start writing about some painful incident in your family. At first, you may be writing just for yourself—to assert how you feel. Then you may realize you want to adopt your cousin as your audience. As you write, you may decide to write a paper as an appeal for sympathy to a more neutral audience.

A given piece of writing may serve many purposes and address a variety of audiences. But, at some point in the writing process, you need to choose what your *main* purpose and audience will be. Devote your energies to this. Chapters 5 and 6 offer you specific strategies for focusing so that you will earn the trust and interest of your audience.

Collecting

Even if your audience is very focused or specific, do not assume that your audience knows what you know or is interested in what interests you. Even if your audience knows what you know, refreshing your audience's memory is usually a good idea. It helps you to clarify your position and engage your reader. Collect the kinds of information and examples that will engage your readers and enliven your writing. Chapter 4 offers you basic strategies you can use to collect the kinds of information that will best capture your audience.

Strategies for Managing Purpose and Audience

- *Identify the main need or purpose* a particular piece of writing is meant to satisfy. Ask yourself, "Why am I writing this? Am I writing it mainly for a self-expressive, interpersonal, or aesthetic purpose?"

- *Identify the relevant characteristics of your anticipated audience.* Ask yourself, "Which audience am I trying to reach? What is my anticipated audience like?"

- *Adjust the amount of information* you give to your audience. Ask yourself, "What information does my audience already know? What information do I need to offer or emphasize?"

- *Be aware of connotations.* Ask yourself, "What attitude do these word choices convey to my reader? Are my words appropriately strong?"

- *Write a letter* to your anticipated audience. Ask your audience, "What is your perspective? How can I connect with, separate from, or negotiate with you?"

Organizing

Shape your writing with the purpose of guiding your readers. Offer them a clear sense of the direction you are taking. Help your readers remember what you want remembered. How you begin a letter or essay is crucial for establishing both your relationship with your audience and the purpose for which you are writing. How you develop the body of your writing determines whether or not you will maintain your audience's attention. How you end a piece of writing determines whether or not you leave a lasting impression that serves your purpose. Chapter 7 helps you to develop and strengthen your organizing skills.

Consulting

The ideal way to identify your purpose and audience and accomplish what you want with your writing is to consult with other readers. Voice your concerns to them. Listen to their responses and watch their reactions. Adjust your writing with the insights you gain from them. Chapter 8 offers you strategies for successfully consulting with others.

Revising

Once you have spoken something, it's hard to take it back. One of the benefits of writing is that you can adjust it before it reaches your audience.

In some cases, you can negotiate with the anticipated audience. For example, some instructors will allow you to revise before you hand in work for a final grade, and bosses may support you in revising proposals before they are formally submitted. If that opportunity is not offered, request it. The request itself shows respect and commitment and will help you to accomplish your purposes with your audience. Chapter 9 offers you strategies for effectively revising your work.

Chapter Review

1. *Solo.*

    a. Copy three statements from this chapter that you want to remember for yourself. For each statement, write a sentence saying why or for what purpose you chose it.

    b. If you were your instructor, what three statements would you have chosen for the class? Why would she or he choose those same three?

    c. Do your choices differ from the ones you believe your instructor would have chosen? What considerations of audience and purpose account for the differences?

2. *Together.* Discuss the results of doing Exploration 1. Notice the different statements students chose for themselves and on behalf of the instructor. At the end of the discussion, have your instructor reveal what her or his choices would have been for the class, and why.

Chapter *4*

Collecting

This chapter offers opportunities to
    —***Collect*** interesting subjects for writing
    —Create a ***journal***
    —Practice ***listing, brainstorming,*** and ***clustering***
    —***Interview*** people

> Science is built with facts, as a house is with stones. But a collection of facts is no more a science than a heap of stones is a house.
>
> *—Jules-Henri Poincaré,*
> *Mathematician, Physicist*

The Dynamics of Collecting

Supermarket carts overflowing on a Friday evening, long lines of cars queuing up at gas stations during a fuel crisis, stacks of family photographs, stadiums filled with fans—for survival and for happiness, people collect.

Learning is a process of collecting and a powerful human need. We collect and transmit much learning by way of letters, the telephone, television, movies, computer networks, newspapers, magazines, and books. Writing is our most effective tool for collecting and remembering what we want to pass on to others.

What you collect for your writing will be determined by your purpose and your intended audience. The four main sources from which you can collect information, observations, and ideas—moving from the more direct to the more indirect—are (1) *yourself* (what you remember and experience); (2) *the world* (what you observe directly of the physical world, including people); (3) *other people* (what they say and show you); and (4) *documents* (what you can learn from visual, audio, and written reports of the experiences and interpretations of others).

Here is a list of sources from which to collect what you need for your writing:

Memory	Interviews
Direct observation	Surveys
Conversations	Photographs
Lectures	Video- or audiotapes
Experiences	Written documents

Different writing tasks may require different methods of collecting. For example, notice how you would proceed in college courses. In chemistry, you would probably collect observations by experimenting directly with chemicals in the laboratory; in early childhood education, you would be likely to observe and interact with young children directly; and in art, you would develop skills by handling different materials. In other courses, the favorite method of collecting could be reading. Of course, which methods of collecting information are favored in a course will depend on your instructor's objectives and how you interpret them. When you write papers, reports, and answers to exams, use the collecting method that best suits the purpose of the course.

Collecting Guide

Ask yourself these five questions whenever you begin to collect information and ideas:

1. What do I already know?
2. What do I already have that I can use?
3. What do I need to find?
4. What can I directly observe or do to find what I need?
5. Whom can I ask directly?

Chapter 1 introduced you to freewriting—a basic way of collecting what you already know. The main tools and strategies presented in this chapter are the journal, listing and brainstorming, clustering, and interviewing.

How you collect your information and ideas will be determined not only by your purpose, your audience, and the availability of sources but also by your particular style. If you are a planner, you may prefer writing a *focused* journal and listing. If you are an explorer, you may prefer freewriting and brainstorming. Artists, especially, and people who like physical activity enjoy clustering. If you are a talker, interviewing may be for you. If you are shy, reading may feel more secure.

As you experiment with different methods of collecting, notice which work best for you and in which circumstances. Strive to be flexible.

Exploration

a. *Together.* On the board, list things people tend to collect, such as stamps, newspaper clippings, Star Trek souvenirs, or family photographs. Try to think of unusual collections.

b. *Solo.* Choose something you or someone close to you collects. Write an essay about the collection. What is collected? How is it collected? What does the collection mean? How does the collecting and the collection affect you, the collector, or other people?

Collecting and the Writing Process

Purpose and Audience

Just as you need bricks, wood, metal, and other materials to build a house (or people, telephones, printing presses, and the mail to run a political campaign), so too you need subjects, ideas, experiences, and information to develop your writing. But even if you collect all the information in the world, if you don't have a purpose, you will just end up with clutter. Throughout this book you will be offered specific strategies for collecting what you need in order to write for particular purposes and audiences. This chapter offers you some *basic* ways to streamline your collecting of subjects, information, and ideas so that you can reach the audiences you want to reach and satisfy the purposes for which you are writing. Tailor your collecting activities to best suit your style and achieve your purposes.

To monitor your purpose and audience while collecting, ask yourself these questions:

- Why am I writing this?
- What does my audience need to know?

Collecting and Focusing

Collecting and focusing are complementary phases of the writing process. Just as the heart has to expand and contract to control the flow of blood, in the writing process, you need to both collect—expand—and focus—contract. Sometimes while you collect information, observations, ideas, and memories, your focus will emerge in the process. You may find yourself moving back and forth between scanning for or collecting your thoughts and focusing on or choosing certain ones. Once you focus, choose only relevant details: those that will help you most effectively fulfill your purpose. Remember that a starting focus makes your collecting easier and more productive. Notice that throughout this chapter all the collecting activities focus on a word, phrase, statement, or question.

To keep yourself focused while collecting, ask yourself these questions:

- Which details are most relevant?
- How can I enliven my work with sense appeal?

Collecting and Organizing

Collecting and organizing are also complementary activities. To avoid overwhelming or confusing yourself or your readers, ask yourself these questions:

- Which ideas and what information belong together?
- What is the most effective order in which to arrange them?

Develop a working plan for how to organize what you choose to include. Be careful, however, not to slow down the collecting by organizing your material into a rigid plan too soon. During the writing process you will move in and out of the collecting and organizing phases.

Collecting, Consulting, and Revising

The collecting phase does not stop with your first draft. You will find, as you reread your work and consult with others, that you may be missing

> ### *Signals to Collect*
>
> - You have a focus.
> - You feel as if you have nothing to say.
> - You are not interested in an assigned topic or in what you already have to say.
> - Your readers need more examples or details.
> - A new focus emerges.

some important materials that would help you better fulfill your purpose with a larger audience. Return to the collecting phase as needed. Ask others for support in finding the sources you may need.

Journals

> Anyone who doesn't write doesn't know how wonderful it is. . . . I am grateful . . . for this gift, this possibility of developing myself and of writing, of expressing all that is in me.
>
> —*Anne Frank*

In this book, the word *journal* is used instead of *diary*. Both words come from words that mean "day" in Latin. But the word *diary* most often applies to personal daybooks, whereas *journal* can apply to many more kinds of daybooks, including not only the personal daybook but daybooks with special purposes. A journal is a home base for collecting what interests you and concerns you, what happens *to* you and *because* of you. The more focused your journal is, the easier it will be for you to continue to write one. Here are some focused journals you can keep.

Personal Journals

During World War II, Anne Frank and her family had to hide in an attic from the Nazis. Keeping a diary helped Anne to understand and find meaning and dignity during a time of terrible oppression and hardships. Her diary was, in many ways, her best friend, and she started her entries with "Dear Kitty." Of course, the person she was writing to was a part of herself—her perfect listener. In writing a diary she created and re-created herself. Her diary satisfied a need to express herself, but it also created a record of her experiences for others.

Many students have found writing personal journals for the purpose of self-expression very satisfying. Sean keeps a personal journal to release pent-up tensions and concerns. Victor is able to steady himself during family conflicts by keeping a journal to show his counselor. Jane writes Bible quotations in her journal and writes about how they apply to her life.

A personal journal—unless it is focused—can become merely a listing of events or a jumble of complaints. From time to time, choose a focus for your personal journal such as one of the following:

Wedding	Leaving home
Children	Religious concerns
Managing the budget	Grandpa
Surviving school	Health

Process Journals

A lawyer keeps a record of the proceedings of a murder trial; a scientist records observations and theories about a series of drug experiments for AIDS; a pastry chef records changes and variations in a new chocolate mousse recipe—all these people are keeping *process* journals. A process journal is a notebook in which you follow your progress, experiments, and failed attempts in a particular endeavor.

Writer's Journals

Practicing writers often keep their journals nearby so they can talk to themselves about what they are writing, what they would like to accomplish with it, how they feel, what they need or plan to do, and which phase of the writing process needs more attention. At times, practicing writers begin and end writing sessions by writing in their journals. You might find it very helpful, as you write, to reflect on your processes in a writer's journal.

Learning Journals

In any intensive learning situation, such as school, travel, or projects, a journal is a tool to help you focus, plan, and direct your energies and to collect and test ideas. Writing helps you learn. One of the most basic ways to use a learning journal is to record a particular question, statement, or event that interests or puzzles you. Then freewrite about it to discover what you already know, name what you need to learn, make connections between different courses and learning situations, and engage more fully in the learning process. You can devote a separate journal to each course or keep a larger journal for them all. Starting a learning journal is simple if you remember to start your freewrites with a focus. Student James Anglin learned a great deal about himself and the world by keeping a focused journal while reading Alice Walker's *The Color Purple.* Student José A. Lopez keeps a journal to help him monitor his learning process in his mathematics courses. Here are some other possible focuses for your learning journal:

Readings	Medical facts
A current event	A journal of your first year in college
Legal issues	
Chemistry problems	

Training Journals

Athletes, especially, find a journal very helpful to their training and development. For example, runners will record how far and fast they run each day, what physical changes they felt, how the route affected their workout, and what other exercises they performed. They will plan their training in the journal and entertain different solutions to physical obstacles and limitations. Runners also write about their psychological blocks and breakthroughs during the running process. A journal is also a place for a runner to record experiences of races won and awards earned. If you are training for sports, dance, singing, acting, pottery, painting—or any other activity—start and maintain a training journal. Here are some possible focuses:

Dieting	Drawing
Weight lifting	Playing an instrument
Singing	Landscaping

Other Focused Journals

Throughout history politicians, explorers, scientists, adventurers, parents, and artists (among others) have kept journals for particular purposes. Some people like to keep focused journals dedicated to one interest. In *The Golden Notebook,* novelist Doris Lessing writes about a character who keeps five different journals responding to five different aspects of her life. Here are some more ideas for focused journals:

Travel journal	Solving-a-problem journal
Journal of a campaign	Business transactions
Journal of an illness	Current events

*R*eflections

1. *Together.* Read the journal entries below. Choose your favorite one. Write about it, discussing the following:

   - Why you like the entry more than the others
   - What similar experiences you have had in your life
   - Which words, phrases, or sentences you especially like
   - What purpose you think the entry served for the writer
   - What audience or audiences are anticipated by the writer, if any

2. *Together or Solo.* Write a letter to the writer in response to a journal entry.

3. *Solo.* Write entries in your journal that are inspired by the ones you read here.

Journal Entries

a. Here's my journal entry on finishing one of the drafts of Chapter 2, "The Writing Process." If you like, you might want, as a class, to compare a paragraph from that chapter with how I write in my journal. Discuss, too, how my journal might have been different if I had written it only for myself. What might I have excluded or included?

6/5/90 12:30 P.M.

   I have just finished redrafting the chapter "The Writing Process"—two hours of intense work. Time to break. I think I'll go back to Chapter 1 and make sure I haven't repeated myself. I do talk about confidence and fears in both chapters and don't want to belabor the point. I'm feeling the usual excitement and fear when I finish one phase of this project and go on to the next. (I notice that, since I decided to include this entry in the book, I'm more conscious of what I believe would be helpful to my readers. It's amazing how writing changes when you expect someone will read it.)

   In any case, I need to recheck my working outline to see what I want/need to do next or else I'll be too agitated to enjoy lunch. Originally, the plan was to include "focusing" in this chapter but I still believe it needs its own. Since the original plan, I combined the chapters "Why Write" and "Audience and Purpose" to form Chapter

1 and decided to use "The Writing Process" as a chapter title because most writing teachers could relate to it. I hope Joe will like the outline I've developed, since we revised the earlier one together.

Of course here I am still writing away after I decided it was time for a break. See you later.

12:51

b. These are the first two paragraphs of Anne Frank's second entry in her diary:

Saturday, 20 June, 1942

Dear Kitty,

I haven't written for a few days, because I wanted first of all to think about my diary. It's an odd idea for someone like me to keep a diary; not only because I have never done so before, but because it seems to me that neither I—nor for that matter anyone else—will be interested in the unbosomings of a thirteen-year-old schoolgirl. Still, what does that matter? I want to write, but more than that, I want to bring out all kinds of things that lie buried deep in my heart.

There is a saying that "paper is more patient than man"; it came back to me on one of my slightly melancholy days, while I sat chin in hand, feeling too bored and limp even to make up my mind whether to go out or stay at home. Yes, there is no doubt that paper is patient and as I don't intend to show this cardboard-covered notebook, bearing the proud name of "diary," to anyone, unless I find a real friend, boy or girl, probably nobody cares. And now I come to the root of the matter, the reason for starting a diary: it is that I have no such real friend.[9]

c. This is what student Altovise Smith wrote:

Well as I was reading my *Learning to Learn* textbook, a question came to mind. The question was how could I generate questions about my interest in criminal justice. So I thought of things such as how should a lawyer prepare for a case, how should a lawyer make a person seem like he or she is innocent when really guilty, and how in the world of law and justice I could come to conclusions about those issues.

I figured studying might help me for the knowledge part but I won't actually know how to do it unless I set my mind on actual court cases so I would be prepared for my first court appearance. But it would never stop there. You still have so much to learn. You have to know about kinds of people you are defending. The personalities you studied about might not be the personalities you are working with. So being a lawyer you have to try very hard to enforce your honesty and good judgment. I know it's hard because you always get people who are guilty and they know that you have to prove that they are innocent because you were hired to protect them.

d. Student John Gaines reflected on his literature class in his learning journal:

> This is my first English Literature class today and it seems it is going to be very interesting. We discussed the poem "The Chimney Sweep" by William Blake. There was an enormous amount of input by us students. We discussed the different meanings that the poem created for us. I interpreted the poem as someone standing from afar watching what became of this boy as these things happened to him. I did not relate it as others did. Some related it to Martin Luther King and Cinderella. I did not relate it to anyone else because I don't make an attempt to relate poems to something outside of them. I make an attempt to take what was written for itself. I occasionally have a problem understanding things. I don't make a connection to try to relate it to something so I can understand it. My teacher has taught me to take what I have in front of me, whether familiar or not, and try to apply it to something that I do know and do understand.

e. This is what runner Beth Avery wrote in her training journal:

> Another tough day. Cold, wet, sinuses kicked in halfway through the run. Decided to walk the rest of the five miles. Coach says it's the distance not the speed, for now. Dad says why do it? Thought a lot about the meet as I walked. I've trained too hard and long not to give this my best shot. Will experiment with not eating any dairy, meat, or sugar. Seems that some people say that will help my sinuses. Will use the steamer before the run, too. Take my time to prepare: steam, stretch, walk, run, cool down.

Keeping a Journal

Choose a journal book that pleases you. You can keep your journal in a spiral-bound notebook, in a blank artist's pad, or in an accountant's ledger. You can handwrite or type your journal, or you can keep the pages in a ring binder. You can use a word processor and keep your entries on file. Be creative. Your journal is *your* record. If you like to draw, you might want to draw in yours.

Plan a regular time for writing in your journal and, in the beginning, especially, stick to the schedule to develop the habit of it. Record the date, day of the week, and time you are writing. Bring this journal book to class to do your in-class writing Explorations. This journal can be a resource of ideas and topics from which you can choose to develop longer papers. (If at any time you feel inspired to write something off the topic, do so. It's *your* journal.)

Explorations _____

1. *Solo.* Choose one of the following kinds of journals. Commit yourself to writing it for a week. Find or create a journal book or use a new computer disk. Write in this journal at a particular time each day.

   a. *A personal journal* in which you record the highlight and low point of each day. Or, you might want to focus on a particular concern for the week, such as a relationship. A journal of just your dreams might be interesting as well.

   b. *A process journal* in which you record experiences with a particular project you are doing. Record what you did, what you learned, and what you want to do next.

   c. *A writing journal* in which you record your concerns with writing. Before or after each writing session (and class), freewrite for ten minutes on what you did, what you learned, and what you want to do next.

   d. *A learning journal* in which you record experiences with a course of learning. For each assignment (and class), choose a particular statement or question and freewrite for ten minutes on what it means to you and what more you need to learn.

   e. *A training journal* in which you record your experiences with training in some performance activity such as a sport, dancing, singing, an art, or a craft.

   f. *A current events* journal in which you record your reactions to news items. For example, clip an article, attach it to your journal, and freewrite. If possible, follow that issue for a week.

2. *Solo.*

   a. Write a journal with another focus for a week. At the end of the week, write about the benefits and challenges of having written this kind of journal.

   b. Commit yourself to keeping a journal for another month or for the whole semester.

   c. Once a month, reread your journal, noticing what changes and what stays the same. Recommit yourself to writing for another month.

3. *Together.* Read portions of your journals to each other in small groups. Discuss the benefits of having written focused journals. Write letters to each other in response to certain entries.

Listing and Brainstorming

Listing

Whenever you are presented with a writing or thinking task, one of the most basic ways you can respond is by listing words, phrases, or sentences. Write and underline a short descriptive title. Write your list underneath it. For example, when student Maurice Lozzi was presented with the assignment to write about some aspect of conditions in the United States today, he listed the following possible topics:

<u>United States Today</u>
Land of opportunity
Helping foreign nations with money
Controlling other governments
Homeless in the street
Vietnam
Terrorists in other countries
Media coverage of politics

As you will see on page 96, Maurice used this list to start a paper.

Brainstorming

When you brainstorm, you say or write whatever comes to mind without stopping to wonder whether you're right or whether the ideas are relevant or make sense. Listing remains focused on a chosen topic. Brainstorming is more like freewriting in that it can take any direction you want. It allows you to clear your mind, create a flow of ideas, and discover new connections. This strategy is best done without much reflection. *Allow your brainstorming to be as long as you like. Cover an entire board space or page. Or decide to brainstorm for a certain time.* Your brainstorming may take the form of a list, or you can write over a page (or board) at random. Notice the different directions some students took while brainstorming on the topic of <u>Education</u>:

Jail	Urban schools
Imprisonment	Drugs
Nelson Mandela	Teen pregnancy
South Africa	Sex education

This brainstorming showed the kinds of things that concerned the people involved. The first item, "Jail," came out spontaneously. If anyone had stopped to question the connection, the other ideas might not have emerged. By not stopping and by allowing themselves freedom to let one idea lead to another, the students were able to collect enough ideas so they could identify topics they wanted to write about. Brainstorming works just as effectively if you do it by yourself.

Once you have listed or brainstormed, you will be able to see some of your options in writing. Choose the item or idea that is most interesting or relevant to your purpose. Start developing your written response: write your chosen item at the top of your page or screen and freewrite for a particular length of time. From there you will find yourself either listing, brainstorming, or freewriting some more, or maybe you will be ready to move on to another phase of the writing process. Perhaps you will return to collecting more information by interviewing someone or reading. Maurice used his list to start a paper that eventually developed into a piece on Vietnam. Student Maria DaFonseca eventually wrote a paper incorporating the ideas of imprisonment and drugs generated during the brainstorming she did with others in class. The story of Maurice's process and paper is featured on pages 96–99 in Chapter 5. Maria's paper appears on pages 251–253.

To practice listing and brainstorming, do one or both of the following Explorations.

*E**xplorations*

1. *Together and/or Solo.* Create a list under one of the following headings, or brainstorm on it:

   Things at which I'm an expert

   Things that happen once in a lifetime

   Animals

   Outsiders

   Things to do to get through college

   Medicine

   Things to do to survive your job

   Problems that need to be solved in the United States

   Challenges for the elderly

2. *Solo and Together.* Choose an interesting item or group of items from the list you created, and do a timed ten-minute freewrite on it. Read

the freewrite to your classmates and note the different directions people took using the same list.

Clustering

Although writing occurs in straight lines on the page, the thinking that goes into it is much more complex than a straight line. As you may have noticed from brainstorming, a word or phrase can point you in many different directions. *Clustering* is a method of collecting your thoughts that reflects this complex shape of thinking.* Artists and people who enjoy physical activities such as sports and dancing especially enjoy clustering because it treats ideas as if they were moving around in space.

Clustering is different from brainstorming in that it shows how one idea is linked to another. Clustering is like brainstorming in that it is freer than focused listing: you can take any direction you want when you cluster.

In Figure 4.1, notice how student Michelle Willabus clustered her thoughts around a word that is important to her: *perfection.* She circled the word and let it lead to other words that she also circled. She drew lines to show which ideas were connected to others. When she found a word or cluster of ideas that interested her, she created new clusters from it.

Michelle found this clustering useful because it helped her identify some topics about which she wanted to write. Eventually, she created papers about her relationship with her boyfriend (see Chapter 5, pages 107–108) and her fear of falling (see Chapter 10, pages 258–260). These papers fulfilled many purposes, including Michelle's need to define perfection for herself, to express her fears, to come to terms with a lost relationship, and to overcome the limitations that perfectionism can impose.

Follow clustering just as you would listing and brainstorming. Choose a particular segment of connected thoughts that most interests you. Start developing an essay by freewriting. This freewrite may lead you to another phase of the writing process, or it may inspire some more collecting activities.

---

*Clustering was formulated by Gabrielle Lusser Rico in *Writing the Natural Way: Using Right-Brain Techniques to Release Your Expressive Powers* (Los Angeles: J. P. Tarcher, 1983).

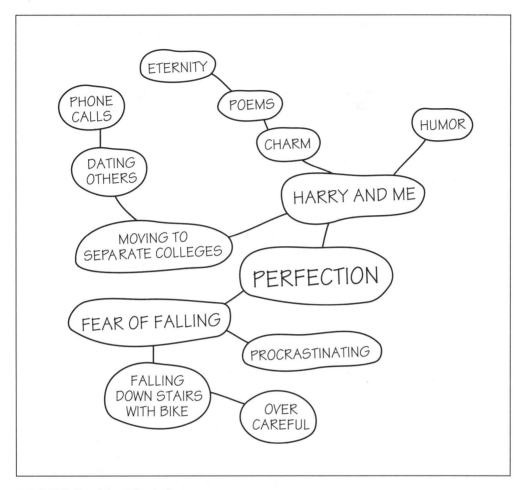

FIGURE 4.1 Clustering

Exploration

Together.

a. Brainstorm a list of words that are important to you for some reason. This list may include words that refer to people, events, emotions, objects, or places. Or you might want to consider the courses you are taking and list important terms from them, such as impressionist painting (art), depression (psychology), energy sources (ecology), or carcinogens (biochemistry).

b. Choose a word that interests you. Write your topic down and circle it. Now create clusters around the word. Write, circle, and link ideas as they come to you, anywhere on your page or on the board.

    c. Notice if any particular string of words becomes long and/or very interesting. Do a freewrite, focusing on an idea or cluster of ideas you create in this process.

    d. Read your freewrites to each other.

    e. Brainstorm a list of words that you would use to describe your experience of clustering, and discuss why you would use these words.

Interviewing

When you *interview*, you hold a conversation—much as television talk show hosts do—to learn more from and about another person. Prepare for interviews by formulating some questions. During the interview, take notes or record the interview itself, depending on the situation.

There are many different purposes and audiences for interviews. For example, in a job interview your prospective employer meets with you to tell you about the requirements of the job and to assess whether you would meet those requirements. In other interviews you can learn about a famous person, your family, how to perform certain tasks, where to find information, and so on. Follow the suggestions in the sidebar on interviewing.

Explorations

1. *Together.* For his paper "An American Tragedy," Maurice Lozzi used some of the strategies listed in the sidebar on interviewing to collect insights from a Vietnam veteran. Read Lozzi's paper on pages 97–98 and identify the strategies that he was able to use in conducting his interview. Which strategies could he not use?

2. *Together.*

    a. Brainstorm a list of people you would like to interview, and discuss why you would like to interview them.

    b. In small groups, create a list of questions that you would like to pose to a famous person. Which questions do you think would lead to the most interesting answers? Which questions would be too broad? Which questions would lead only to one-word answers?

    c. Conduct a mock interview. Let one person or a group of people assume the role of the famous interviewee. If you can, focus on a particular ability or experience. Notice which questions just can't be answered by anyone other than the actual person for whom the questions were designed.

Interviewing

1. *Choose* the most appropriate and available person to interview. Because they are such valuable resources, focus on older people when you can.

2. *Tape* the interview, if at all possible, so that you don't distract yourself or your subject by having to take notes. But as a matter of courtesy, ask for permission *before* the interview. Honor your subject's wishes. If permission to tape is denied, take notes and ask the person to repeat statements if necessary.

3. *List questions* you want to ask. Don't ask for information that you could and should have gotten elsewhere. For example, if you are interviewing an author, find his books ahead of time. Don't ask him what he has already published: you should know. Focus on those questions that are most important to you. But know that questions that arise during the interview may be the best ones to ask.

4. *Use the question star* (Figure 5.3, page 118) to stimulate questions during the interview.

5. *Be patient and compassionate.* Let your subjects tell their own stories. Know that silence during the interview may help them to remember. Let them take tangents. Don't stop them just so you can ask another question.

6. *Observe* the person you are interviewing. Notice her or his actions, voice, and facial and hand expressions, and be aware of the environment.

7. *Acknowledge* the person you interview in three ways. First, thank the person in a letter. Say what you learned and what it means to you. Second, acknowledge the person in your writing when you include ideas learned during the interview. Use a format such as one of these:

- In an interview with *(name)*, I learned _____.

- In a conversation we had on *(date)*, *(name)* said "_____." (Note the quotation marks.)

- I am indebted to *(name)* for telling me that _____.

Third, if you plan to publish what you write, allow the person to read and adjust what you attribute to him or her.

8. *Conduct follow-up interviews* to consider questions that arose while you wrote.

3. *Together or Solo.*

   a. List the talk shows that are aired in your vicinity either on television or radio. Include not only big network and syndicated shows but also shows that include interviews between lesser-known people. Watch or listen to one of these shows (if possible, together), and record the questions asked by both the host and participants. Which questions lead to the most interesting answers? How does the host keep the conversation moving? Notice which questions aren't fully answered.

   b. Watch or listen to a second talk show whose topic or host is very different from the topic or host in the first show. Discuss the differences you notice between these two programs, focusing on the questions asked and the strategies used by the hosts.

   c. Watch a live or videotaped debate between political candidates. Which questions lead to the most interesting answers? Which questions do the candidates dodge, and how?

4. *Solo.* Choose a person in your family or circle of friends who you know has experienced some important historical event, such as a political march, involvement in a war, political imprisonment, meeting an important person, the events surrounding an assassination, or the creation of an institution or church. Focusing on this event, brainstorm a list of questions that will lead the person into telling you stories about the event. Interview the person and write an essay about what you learned.

Chapter Review

1. *Solo.*

   a. Create a sidebar, listing the collecting strategies mentioned in this chapter. Write and underline "Collecting Strategies" to get started.

   b. Using the sidebars on Freewriting (page 14) and interviewing (page 85) as models, create sidebars for other collecting strategies you listed in 1a.

   c. Write one of the collecting strategies in the middle of a piece of paper and circle it. Create a cluster around this term, incorporating what you learned about the strategy from this chapter, and how you used it yourself.

   d. Choose a segment of your cluster from 1c and freewrite for ten minutes, describing the strategy to a new writing student.

2. *Together.* Read and discuss with each other your results from Exploration 1d. What would you have added to or deleted from each description to help the new writing student?

Chapter 5

Focusing I

Strategies

This chapter offers opportunities to

—Explore the dynamics of *focusing*

—Create *unity* in your writing

—Write for *purpose* and *relevance*

—Distinguish *repetition* from *redundance*

—Learn how to *choose, specify, quote, illustrate,* and *question*

—Practice writing *thesis statements*

Keep to one thing and concentrate.
—*Virginia Woolf, Novelist, Essayist*

The pleasure of writing is that the mind doesn't wander.
—*Donald Hall, Poet, Essayist*

You can't eat everything you see.
—*Bessie Delaney,*
101-year-old retired dentist

The Dynamics of Focusing

You can dribble a basketball all over the court for days, but sinking it into the small center of the basket is what makes the game. A lawyer can divide her attention among five trials, but she is more likely to win in court if she devotes her energies to one case at a time. People create and achieve in sports, in medicine, in law, in academics—in most human endeavors—by focusing their energies.

Writing focuses the mind. Part of the mind's survival instinct is to be constantly scanning for pleasures, dangers, and novelties. When the mind doesn't have a focus outside itself, it starts scanning itself— rehashing yesterday, rehearsing tomorrow. If nothing holds the mind's attention, this scanning can turn into either a scattered, bored state or a spinning, confused one. Without a focus for your writing, you can become bored, confused, and discouraged. Your mind goes into a blur, like an unfocused photograph. You won't know what you're looking at, and after a while you will be too frustrated to care. In this chapter, you will have opportunities to learn how to focus and thereby to engage yourself and your audience.

When a piece of writing is focused, it is said to have *unity.* The word *unity* comes from the Latin word *unus,* which means "one." Unity in writing means that all the parts of a piece fit together to form a whole, a oneness. The writing has a clear purpose and point. There are sufficient examples and evidence to support the main purpose or point of the writing. Everything is *relevant:* nothing distracts from the main purpose of the work. When a point is repeated, it is to good effect. That is, it doesn't belabor an idea (the way this sentence is starting to do): it isn't *redundant.*

Your mind is focused by writing and reading pieces that have unity. Reading such works focuses your mind by clearly showing you something about yourself, the world, the author, or how to use words. Often, pieces that focus your mind are written in such a way that you feel you are learning something new and interesting. Learning to focus in the writing process offers you even more benefits than reading because you are fundamentally learning how to focus and refocus yourself.

Do one or more of the following Explorations to recognize the dynamics of focusing in your own life.

*E*xplorations _____

The purpose of these Explorations is to notice where you need to develop focus. The audience can be you and your classmates or some other interested persons.

1. *Solo and Together.* Write about a time when you had *too much* to attend to at the same time. List all the things you had to do and how this affected your performance in each area. What benefits did you experience from writing about this? What did you learn? Read what you wrote to others and discuss it. Write a letter in response to one of the papers you hear in class.

2. *Solo.* Write a paper recommending an activity to others because it both steadies your mind and seems healthy. Some examples include gardening, model building, sewing, and running.

3. *Solo.* Write about how you use an addiction to retreat from a scattered or confused mind. The addiction may be something serious (it makes you lose control over important areas of your life) or relatively harmless (just fun). These are some examples of addictions: shopping, drugs, cigarettes, chocolate, television, sex, speeding, gambling, arguing. Describe your experiences in as much detail as you can to clarify for yourself exactly how the addiction controls you. Your paper may be serious or humorous, depending on your experience.

Focusing and the Writing Process

Rita Williams, a student writer, said, "I find the focus by wandering." Just as there are many ways to sink a basketball and many places where the ball can land, there are many ways to focus and many things on which to focus.

Every writing project begins with some *working* focus followed by some early scanning for ideas. Early freewrites and drafts are exploratory. Sometimes you're lucky and find a clear direction right away. This usually happens with topics that you know well and have lived with for a while. Often you will focus and refocus as you revise and redraft. There's always some point you can clarify. Sometimes you will find a new, more exciting focus and start all over again. It's worth it: focusing steadies your mind and creates a clear message.

Focusing and Purpose

Often the *need* to write helps you to focus on a purpose and audience. For example, you need to pass a course. Your history professor assigns a paper on a contemporary issue in America. You collect some possible ideas, and you focus on Vietnam because it fascinates you. Or, you need to recover from hand injuries, so you write about some of the beneficial lessons you learned to inspire others. You need to sort out the ending of a relationship, so you write about the poems your "ex" sent you. When you make a commitment to satisfy such needs through writing, you find your purpose.

Relevance

Throughout this chapter, you will be invited to practice focusing strategies: choosing, specifying, quoting, illustrating, questioning, and stating. The most satisfying focus for a piece of writing will be a focus that *means* something to you, that *interests* you, or that serves some *purpose:* in short, something that is *relevant* to you. The more meaningful the purpose on which you focus, the more you will have to say.

The concept of relevance is crucial to focusing, in another way. Often new writers are reluctant to offer details, quotes, and illustrating examples because they are afraid of adding monotonous and irrelevant points. But to focus is not merely to collect details at random: it is to choose details, quotes, and examples that are *directly relevant* to the purpose of a work. For example, Roy Smith was attempting to write an essay about his fiancée:

First draft

> I am writing about my fiancée. She is the youngest in her family
> and always had people there for her, doing things for her, making
> decisions, solving problems. And that was because they would
> always think she wasn't able to make her own decisions or solve
> her own problems. Her parents were loving and caring, so she was
> always protected by them. In reality, she was never alone.

In responding to this draft, Roy's peers asked him to be more specific about his fiancée's family: How many siblings did she have? How old were they in comparison to her? What was his fiancée's name, anyhow? So Roy wrote this draft in response:*

Second draft

> I am writing about my fiancée. Her name is Anita Soares. She
> is 24 years old. She was born in the United States, in Newark, New
> Jersey, at St. James Hospital. Her parents are from Brazil. She
> has five sisters and two brothers. Their names and ages are as
> follows: Marco Soares, age 38 (male); Maria Soares, age 36
> (female), born in Brazil, married with three children, living in
> Newark on 100 Blank Street . . .

---

*Names and locations in this essay have been changed to protect privacy.

Roy continued giving such details for every one of Anita's seven siblings. Although Roy was being very thorough, he soon lost the interest of his readers. (Even here, it doesn't make much sense to quote his paragraph in full.) He himself found the listing task tedious and irrelevant to his main purpose: to show how he helped Anita to break the ties of dependence. Details such as the hospital where Anita was born or where her sister Maria currently lives seem to not have a purpose in this essay. Roy revised his paper using illustrations that were more relevant to his purpose. We will return to his revision later in this chapter.

Repetition and Redundance

Dr. Martin Luther King, Jr., inspired a nation and the whole world with his speeches. One of the strategies he used for fulfilling his purposes was *repetition*. For example, we all remember the words "I have a dream." Each time those words resounded in his speech, they gained power and momentum and helped to make him an immortal figure in our history.

Repetition is the very essence of advertising: hear it often enough, and you might buy just to shut the pressure off. Repetition is the heart of humor and the delight of children. Repetition is a basic tool of learning. For example, *The Flexible Writer* offers you reminders, sidebars, and re-statements of important points. Even this paragraph employs repetition to make its point. But repetition, when it becomes repetitious, can bore and distract.

Looking back at Roy's second draft, notice how all seven sentences start with a pronoun: *I, She, Her, Their.* Three of the seven sentences start with *She.* This feels repetitious. The mind naturally seeks more variety.

A writer may also repeat the same idea with different wording. Unnecessary repetition is called *redundance.* For example, the following two sentences say the same thing without adding any new information or insight:

Serious traffic accidents are caused by drunken drivers.

Drunken drivers cause serious traffic accidents.

Notice how Roy was starting to restate himself in his first draft:

She . . . always had people there for her . . .

. . . she was always protected by them.

. . . she was never alone.

Such repetition is natural in language. But without further details, such repetition is redundant. Redundance is like superimposing images on a photograph slightly out of register with each other: even if they are the same image, they blur. Blur is the opposite of focus.

Focusing and Collecting

Even as you identify your purpose and audience, you begin to *collect* information, ideas, experiences: you list the effects of the Vietnam War named in an encyclopedia; you recall experiences and consequences of an injury; you reread letters that someone sent you.

Focusing and collecting are complementary processes. As you collect information, you focus on what interests you and is relevant to your purpose. When you focus, you create a center much like a magnet, which helps you to collect more relevant information. Especially in the early stages of writing a particular piece, there are several strategies you can use to focus and to collect relevant information, ideas, and insights: (1) make choices, (2) identify patterns and repetition, and (3) look for surprise, power, and interest. These strategies are especially helpful if a particular piece of writing requires the planner's style of composing.

1. *Make choices.* Some writers subscribe to "the myth of plenty," the belief that the more things you try to write about in one paper, the more you will have to say. In fact—although it seems inside out—the more you try to write about at once, the less you have to say. Too much chocolate makes you too sick to eat; too much oxygen leads to hyperventilation, so you can't breathe; and you might like lobster, cheesecake, pizza, and spicy sausage—but would you ever put them into a casserole together? As architect Ludwig Mies van der Rohe wrote, "Less is more." The more you try to write about at once, the less you'll have to say. The less you try to write about at once, the more room you will have to develop and expand upon your chosen focus.

The basic way to create unity in your writing is to limit the amount you try to write about in any given piece of writing. *The process of focusing means to choose one person, place, time, event, idea, or thing to write about at a time.* For example, you would choose which one effect of the Vietnam war you can write about to fulfill your assignment, which single experience is most directly relevant to your injury, or which specific letter best captures the experiences of a relationship. If you include other effects and experiences, they must be directly relevant to your chosen subject. You may want to use a slogan to remind you, such as "Choose one" or "One thing at a time." Remember the image of the magnet.

2. *Identify patterns and repetition.* Suppose you list the experiences you remember from working through an injury and notice that some of

> To focus, look for surprise, power, and interest.

them are very positive and some very negative. You can focus your paper by dividing it into positive and negative experiences. You could write first about the positive and then about the negative. Or suppose you were writing about a series of crimes in your neighborhood, and you noticed that certain seemingly innocent persons seem to be involved in many of the cases. Focus on those persons. You may formulate some crucial insights.

3. *Look for surprise, power, and interest.* Remember, what focuses *your* mind and holds *your* interest when you read will focus your readers' minds as well. Choose to write about the most appealing, unusual, or dramatic thing that will help you focus and capture your audience's attention. If you're bored, your audience will be too. To engage your audience, engage yourself.

Focusing and Organizing

Organizing helps you maintain your own and your readers' focus on what you are writing. Even if you have focused on the most dramatic and interesting ideas, if you don't organize and pace your presentation, you can confuse and thereby lose your reader. In organizing, you pay attention to how you (1) start a piece of writing, (2) develop it for unity, and (3) end it in a memorable way. The beginning, or lead, of any piece of writing is a crucial place to focus yourself and capture the attention of your audience. The body should develop from the lead and expand upon and support claims with relevant examples connected in clear ways. The end should reinforce the lead and leave a unified impression on your audience. Organizing helps you to maintain focus in your writing.

Focusing, Consulting, and Revising

The writing process is especially conducive to focusing your mind. Therefore, don't expect yourself to find a clear, powerful focus at the very start of a writing project. The model of the writing process in *The Flexible Writer* developed *as* I explored and developed the first draft of the first edition. Even as I revised *The Flexible Writer* for the second edition, I learned and developed new perspectives on the model. Therefore, I decided to revise Chapter 2, which summarizes the writing process, *last*—so that the chapter would reflect all I learned during the revision process.

> ### *Signals to Focus*
> - Too many topics at once
> - Too many general terms and ideas
> - Treating the reader as a mind reader
> - Not enough specific details or examples
> - Too many questions unanswered
> - Redundance
> - Irrelevant details

To revise the textbook, I consulted with instructors and students, asking them what was helpful and what was not. Using their responses, I was able to expand, delete, and reorganize *The Flexible Writer* so that it would better serve its purposes: to help *you* to become a flexible writer.

Consult with your instructors, tutors, co-workers, family members, and peers to help you develop your focus not only at the start of a project but also during the revising phase. Consult this and the next chapter of *The Flexible Writer*, which offer you a variety of specific strategies for focusing.

Explorations

1. *Together.* Read the following student paragraph. Identify a purpose for it. Notice repetitions in writing style and redundancies in ideas. Discuss whether there are details. Revise the paragraph for greater purpose, focus, relevance, and correctness.

> The projection I have toward my life in the future, is that I want to be formaly educated acadmicly and in life events so I won't have some of the struggles my parents have had through there careers. My projection also holds a more fulfilling life in pleasures, where my parents were so job oriented through my early years that they never seemd to be able to take a break and just enjoy, the life they had created. My life would be greatly enhanced by having a college diploma because seein the struggles my parents have had to contend with in there careers, I can now see the advantages of being educated, in that advancement comes easier to those with a college education. I also feel that with

having advancement came a little easier I would have more time to
fulfill other aspects of my life, where my parents have not
traveled or have no real hobbies.

2. *Together.* Read the following student paragraph. Identify a purpose
    for it. Name and discuss which details are irrelevant to this purpose.
    Revise the paragraph for greater purpose, focus, relevance, and correct-
    ness. Expand the essay, using your own experience to elaborate. Try
    to incorporate and make relevant some of the details you at first
    would want to delete from the student's paragraph as irrelevant.

> I am in my dorm room. The room is square, white, and made of
> cinder blocks. There are two closets. The floor is made of
> linoleum. There is a bathroom that we share with another room.
> There are two windows. The room used to be tidy. That was before
> my roommate settled in. My roommate is a sloven. He infested our
> room with his junk. He possesses some basic characteristics one
> would expect from a college roommate, such as laziness and
> untidiness. He is a chemistry major. His father owns an automobile
> shop. His mother sends him food. He also has some of the most
> unusual bad habits I have encountered.

3. *Together or Solo.*

    a. Consider the following list, generated by student Risca Bowman
        in response to this assignment:

        Assignment: Write about a television personality you admire,
        with the purpose of convincing someone who doesn't watch televi-
        sion to tune in to this person.

        Oprah Winfrey

        A positive black woman

        Successful

        Admired by many people

        Talked about a lot by jealous people

        Concerned about people and tries to help them through her talk
        show

        A book is published about her life and her struggles in life

        Praised by many for losing so much weight

        Put down when she started gaining some weight again

        She seems like a person who didn't let success go to her head

Which item on her list most interests you? Why? Do any of the items on her list go together? Which ones and why?

b. Generate your own list in response to the assignment. Notice which items go together. Choose an item or a closely related group of items. Write an essay in response to the assignment. Strive to incorporate relevant details.

4. a. *Solo.* As a working focus, choose a writing assignment (from this book, another class, or work). Collect ideas by freewriting, listing, brainstorming, or clustering.

b. *Solo.* Choose the most interesting, surprising, or powerful idea that emerges in your collecting. Draft a paper using your chosen focus.

c. *Together.* In small groups or as a class, read your papers to each other. Identify a purpose for each paper. Discuss which details are relevant. Notice any distracting repetitions and blurring redundancies. Suggest ways to improve the papers.

Choosing

Students are surprised at how much more they have to write when they limit the number of topics they try to cover. They find that when they limit their choices, writing is more satisfying and enjoyable. They are eager to revise. Notice what happened when student Maurice Lozzi tried to cover too many topics at once in the first draft of a paper:

First draft

America, home of the free and the brave. A place where you can work hard and attain a good life. A government that is willing to help foreign nations in financial need. Our government who sends out agents to other countries to keep their governments in check. While our poor starve in the cold city streets. A kind and gentler nation? The U.S. has an identity crisis in that it must perceive to the world it still is a world power. It is a problem that we citizens must help to cure ourselves before we hurt ourselves. A good example was Vietnam, a country under colonial rule for 500 years, and before that nearly a thousand under Chinese rule. So you see a country under foreign rule for all its history. So when they have a chance for independence who steps in to stop them? A nation who itself has fought for its independence that started over tea. Can you think why the U.S. has a problem of involving itself in matters it has no business in? We are still active in plots in countries around the world that poor American citizens must pay the price.

*R*eflection _____

Together. Notice how Maurice's sentences jump. Which ones are incomplete? Number the different issues he tries to cover in a one-page paper. Notice how little space he devotes to any one issue.

_____

Notice how Maurice expands on his first draft when he *chooses* one topic: how he learned about what the Vietnam conflict meant to one person who was there. Here are two pages of excerpts out of the eight pages he wrote several drafts later:

An American Tragedy

I was walking around the library looking for information on Vietnam when out of an aisle, a hand grabbed me. "You're still too slow on the dribble," he said. It was my old basketball coach from grammar school. When I told him what I was working on, he looked at me strangely and said, "That's interesting." It was then that I noticed a small black and gold patch on his shoulder with the letters M I A. It stood for "Missing In Action" for missing soldiers. Many of these men were fighter pilots who were kept in prison so they could sign documents admitting that their bombing raids were terrorist actions and claiming that America's involvement was that of the aggressor. . . .

It was weird to meet him just then, but it was like a puzzle with a missing piece. Everything started to fall into place. He was quiet for awhile and I asked him if he knew anyone who went to Vietnam. He said, "Yeah. I know someone who went but came back a different man." I asked who that was and he said, "I was that man."

Maurice's coach then told him about how the recruiting officers persuaded him to join and how he qualified for the Green Berets.

He began talking about his training, on how they put him in a forest for two weeks with no rations of food. He ate tree bark and wild mushrooms. "I lost ten pounds in that two weeks," he said. "I can still taste the bark and the mushrooms I consumed while in survival training. During those few weeks I had thought about my first kill (Commie) and thought in a funny way how I could pose with the 'kill' like a hunter. My training had subtracted the humanity from me. I truly was a killing machine hungry for the kill."

While he talked his eyes looked like a cat's climbing trees like it had a tenth sense. He was using an angry voice during the whole conversation as if he wished he could turn back the clock. He said, "I wished I had not signed my destiny away to that recruiting officer."

I asked him if he had killed anyone by mistake. He said, "No. But a buddy of mine knew a guy in a battalion that had sprung a cartridge of bullets into a hut killing an entire family because he thought he saw a gun. That man had nightmares of guilt and was placed into psychiatric confinement. . . .

"Accidental murder in Vietnam was like a parking ticket at home. But the worst type of killing is of your own. In Vietnam, 10,000 soldiers were killed by their own men or by accident. Some men were killed by improper cleaning of their rifles or stepping into their own booby traps." He stopped and glared at me and said, "It could happen at night. Your turn to keep guard and you doze off and suddenly in the bush you hear noise. You fire and hear a scream. But you hear someone call 'Help' in English. Your own man is lying in the latrine with so many holes in him that he grabs the end of your rifle and places it in his mouth and begs for relief by shooting him like a sick horse."

. . . He began talking about the traps he and his troop set up for South Vietnamese officials who were to be eliminated. . . . These men were to be killed because of ties supposedly with the enemies (Viet Cong): No photographs, just written claims were offered saying that these men were suspected of trading with the Viet Cong officials. "Actually," my coach said, "We killed these men to place U.S. favored people into power, if we were to win the campaign."

. . . May I quote his famous line, "It was a rich man's battle and a poor man's war." My earlier approach to Vietnam was that of a rich man. I only saw the profitable side of the war, what was in the history books, or, in plain English, the good side and not the bad side. I know those two hours I spent with my coach gave me the insight to say, "Don't trust what the textbooks say because dreamers have fictionalized American History." History books shorten events and don't spend enough pages telling the truth because it would be too expensive.

How to Choose

1. **Number** the topics, ideas, time periods, people, or experiences you try to cover in a particular piece of writing. Use the same number for closely related topics that belong together.

2. **Choose** the topic, idea, time period, person, or experience that is most relevant to you. Begin your next draft focused on that.

3. **Remember,** less is more.

4. **Save** your early drafts until you are satisfied with your paper. Keep a "great things said by me" file. You will feel more secure about letting go of irrelevant or distracting work.

*R*eflection

Together. Compare Maurice's two drafts. Point to specific expressions as you contrast them. Here are some suggestions and questions to guide your discussion:

   a. Compare the lengths of the two drafts.

   b. What choices did Maurice make from one draft to the next?

   c. Did limiting his topic improve his writing? If so, how?

   d. Which draft do you like better, and why?

   e. What other topics could Maurice have chosen for his focus?

   f. What choices would he have had to make in order to further focus his treatment of these other topics?

*E*xplorations

1. *Together.*

   a. Read the following student journal entry and number the topics on which the writer touches.

   October 13, 1990

   My car stalled on the way to the bridge, and steam was coming out of the hood. What a time I had coping with it. Jake Bizby had the most bizarre reaction, at my interview and left me wondering whether or not I want to join the company. John couldn't pick Karen up and she was probably waiting for me out in the cold. Couldn't find her by the school. I'm reading *The Scarlet Letter* for my novel course.

b. In small groups, choose one of the events on which the writer touches and write an expanded fictional account of it.

2. *Solo.* Write a journal entry listing significant events of the past week (either personal or public). Choose one event and write about it in more depth.

3. *Solo.* Choose a paper on which you are working, and list the topics or ideas you try to cover. Are there any you could eliminate so as to focus on the more important portion(s) of your paper? If so, write a revised version, focusing on what's most important, interesting, or engaging for you.

Specifying

Another version of the myth of plenty is the belief that the more generally you write, the more room you allow for readers to interpret as they need. Language allows you to refer to many objects, persons, activities, experiences, and events at once. This is very efficient. You wouldn't want to have to reinvent the word *chair* every time you wanted to refer to a chair. If you were to tell me you sat in a chair yesterday, and if I know what *chair* means, I would understand, in general, what you meant. But I wouldn't know *exactly*. I would be left to interpret for myself. Maybe it wouldn't be important that you sat in a chair yesterday. But suppose you sat in an *electric* chair yesterday—that would change everything. If you told that to me, my attention would be instantly focused. I would probably want to know why, how you got there, how it felt. It would *mean* a lot more to say you sat in an electric chair. Our interaction would be stronger and more satisfying.

This applies to everyday topics as well. Think of a student writer, Sam, sitting at his desk, chewing the end of his pen until it looks like taffy. Sam has been assigned to write a paper on the importance of love. But the word *love*—even more than the word *chair*—applies to so many situations, people, animals, and things over the entire history of the world, that he can't figure out where to start, let alone what to say. He's so bored and confused that he can't even remember what focuses *his* attention, what he loves:

A thing—the thick wool carpet he's curling his toes into as he sits

A person—his brother, who drives out of his way to take him to work in the morning

A place—an old oak that he used to climb when he needed to be alone

Instead of writing about what he loves specifically, he writes:

> Love is something everyone wants in life. It makes you feel special and good. We should all strive to be loving.

The way Sam uses the word *love* is not very engaging. His readers end up asking, "So what else is new?" Their minds start scanning, and he's lost his readers. It's no surprise: *he's* lost, too.

Aside from being bored, how can you tell that what Sam wrote says nothing? You could replace the word *love* in his three sentences with almost any other word and still be learning as much. If you replace *love* with *hope,* this is what you get:

> Hope is something everyone wants in life. It makes you feel special and good. We should all strive to be hopeful.

Or try *money:*

> Money is something everyone wants in life. It makes you feel special and good. We should all strive to have money.

The more a word can apply to, the less it says. Words such as *love, hope, special,* and *good* are only a few words that leave you scanning for something to *hold* your attention. The ultimate general word is *thing.* It applies to everything and nothing. It doesn't say anything much to anyone. If you assigned numbers to words to reflect how many situations they applied to, there would be no number for *thing* because there are an infinite number of things. *Love* could get a number because it is used to refer to fewer situations, but the number would be very high. *Fuzzy* applies to fewer persons, situations, and things than *love,* so *fuzzy* would get a lower number. *Fuzzy* says a lot more than *love. George,* a proper name, would apply to fewer persons than the word *person,* which would apply to anyone. *George Orwell* applies to still fewer persons, places, or situations and therefore means more. The more you specify exactly what you mean, the more engaging your work will be.

To *specify* means to *create specifics.* Figure 5.1 shows you a portion of a tree diagram that creates specifics from a general term such as *love.*

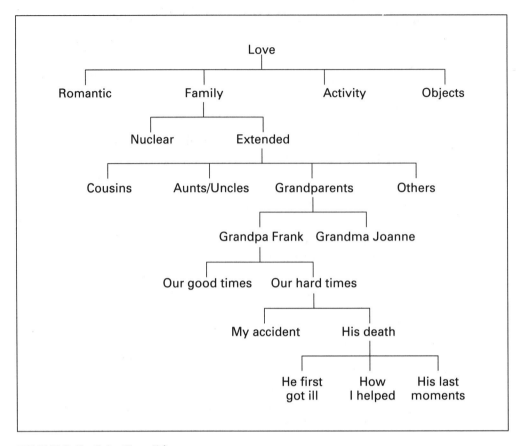

F I G U R E 5.1   Tree Diagram

Notice how the farther you branch from the top, the more there is to specify about your subject. Each item could lead to further branchings.

Read these two paragraphs student David Brzezinski wrote about his grandfather Frank. Although David never uses the general word *love,* he says more about love than does Sam, who uses the word.

> I remember visiting him one evening, upon his request, as he lay on a hospital bed fighting to stay alive. He was moving from a lying to a sitting position, unable to find comfort from anything. He pulled off the oxygen mask and asked for help. The nurses kept giving him shots to calm him, but he could find no rest. I think he knew he was going to die, and he was fighting like hell to stay alive. I could not bear to watch him too long and upon returning to the waiting room I burst into tears. I knew he was going to die.

My dad, sister, uncle, and I returned home while my aunt and mother remained at the hospital throughout the night to be with my grandfather. He died around 2 A.M. peacefully and calmly, surrounded by members of his family. My aunt called from the hospital with the sad news. That morning, I remember looking outside, and I hurt so badly, deep within myself. I wondered how the sun could be shining so brightly, the sky be so blue, the birds chirping so happily, and the trees and grass be so beautiful. It didn't seem right, this lovely day; he wasn't here anymore. It's been more than two years since my grandfather died, but his pain and suffering and his death will be in my memory forever.

Reflections _____

1. Discuss how David makes choices to focus his writing.

2. Point to specific words, phrases, and sentences that best capture David's love for his grandfather.

3. Share experiences that come to mind as you read and consider David's paper. Focus on experiences with death.

4. Write about a specific experience that you remembered while reading David's paper.

_____

One indication that a piece of writing is focused is that readers will be reminded of their own particular experiences. Most people who read this passage find themselves recalling such intimate experiences with a member of their family. Depending on each reader's experiences and inter-

---

How to Specify

1. *Identify* an important word in your topic or paper. Ask yourself, "Could I replace this word or expression with any other word and still say as much?"

2. *Create* a tree diagram similar to the one in Figure 5.1. Focus on an interesting portion.

3. *Choose* a more specific word, expression, or topic.

4. *Avoid* using **thing** words such as **something, anything, everything,** and **nothing.**

5. *Use* **proper names** for people, places, and things.

est, this essay can be interpreted to be about love, or grief, or yearning, or any number of human responses. Few people are left untouched.

Explorations ————————————————————

These Explorations help you to discover how specifying enlivens communication.

1. *Together.* Notice how the items in the following portions of tree diagrams become more meaningful and interesting as they become more specific:

   a. vehicle
       \
         car
           \
             station wagon
               \
                 1989 slate gray Taurus station wagon
                   \
                     my 1989 slate gray Taurus station wagon that was broken into one night when . . .

   b. home
       \
         house
           \
             stone house
               \
                 175-year-old brownstone
                   \
                     175-year-old brownstone that Abraham Lincoln visited when . . .

   c. love
       \
         mother love
           \
             Sam's mother's love
               \
                 Sam's mother bringing him apple cobbler
                   \
                     Sam's mother bringing apple cobbler when he's suffering over writing a paper about love

   d. abortion
       \
         abortion for rape victims
           \
             my cousin's story

In what ways do the more general terms differ from the more specific expressions?

2. *Together.* Following the example of Exploration 1, create portions of tree diagrams that lead to meaningful specifics. Start with one of the following general words:

courage   conversation

furniture   event

person   product

3. *Solo.* Write about courage, trust, responsibility, *or* envy without using the word itself. Choose a specific person, situation, and time on which to focus. Rely on stories, conversations, sights, and sounds to relate your experience of one of these human characteristics.

4. *Together or Solo.* Review pages 63–66, which show you how to distinguish stronger, and therefore more specific words from weaker, more general ones.

Quoting

Most readers aren't *mind* readers. Even if you know someone well, you can't be certain that what you notice is what he or she will notice. Look at Figure 5.2 on the following page.[10] What do you see? Some people see a profile of young woman with a ribbon around her neck; some people see an old woman with a large chin and a slightly opened mouth. Try to see both for yourself.

Do the following Exploration to discover how this dynamic of shifting focus works with language.

E*xploration* _____

Solo. Quickly read the following sentences:

a. Cilantro is a spicy herb to include in avocado dip.

b. Babies should not suck pacifiers, which can cause tooth deformation.

c. It's important to use a moisturizer to counter the effects of heat curling.

d. Major league baseball today is much more politically run than it was in the time of Willie Mays.

e. Studies show that vitamin B6 may be effective in reducing the growth of tumors.

FIGURE 5.2 Focusing

f. Windup watches have been entirely replaced in stores by battery-driven quartz timepieces.

g. Without a proper recovery program, an addict may go from one addiction right into another.

h. To protect your iris garden, cut rot off the roots, separate the plants, and replant them with ample space for new shoots.

i. Floppy disks should never be exposed to magnets or cigarette smoke.

j. Use premium gasoline every fourth tankful to keep fuel injectors clean.

Without looking back at the list, write down what you remember of the sentences you just read. What you remember is an indication of what interests you, what you know the most about, or perhaps what you experienced most recently, just as whether you see a young woman or an old woman in Figure 5.2 is determined by the perspective you take. Your choices reflect your point of view.

Together. Compare what focused (or captured) your attention in doing the Exploration with what others remember. Discuss what you think accounts for the differences and the similarities. For example, you might remember that cilantro is good for avocado dip because you are a gourmet cook.

When you write, you need to focus your readers' attention in the same way that certain sentences focused yours. You cannot assume that what you notice is what your reader will notice. If you could be certain, then there would be no reason for language or communication. We would just all know the same thing. You can't even assume that what you notice today is what you will notice tomorrow. It's possible that sometime in the next day or so, you will remember one of the sentences listed above (that you can't recall right now) because some experience will remind you of it.

Consider how student Michelle Willabus began a first draft in which she is trying to understand why an old relationship ended:

First draft

> After I broke up with my boyfriend I never thought that I would ever meet someone with his charm, looks, or sense of humor. He meant the world to me. I never thought anyone else in the world could turn my frown into a smile, or think of me as his sunflower girl. Harry always made me feel special. He would write me special poems expressing the way he felt about me or send me flowers. Out of the five poems that he wrote to me, I have two favorites.
>
> The title of the two poems that I favor so much are ''My Sunflower Girl'' and ''Forever.'' The first one means a lot because it truly expressed what our relationship means to us. And the second also expressed what we felt when we were saying goodbye for college. Harry always wrote poems that related to special or not-so-special events that occurred in our relationship. . . .

Notice that Michelle *tells* us that Harry wrote her wonderful poems. But we don't know what he wrote or which parts of what he wrote captured her. We don't even know if we would agree with her evaluation of him. Notice how much more we learn about what she valued (and how much she herself learns) when she actually quotes and requotes Harry's words. Here is her fourth draft:

Fourth draft

Forever You and Me

> After Harry and I broke up I never thought that I would ever meet someone with his charm, looks, or sense of humor.

Harry always made me feel special. He would write poems expressing the way he felt about me or bring me red carnations when there wasn't even a special holiday to celebrate. Out of the five poems that Harry wrote to me, the one that I favor the most now is "My Sunflower Girl" because it seemed to truly express how he felt about our relationship. He wrote:

<u>My Sunflower Girl</u>

You are so beautiful,
my sunflower girl.
How could there be anyone
but you?
How could a rose be red enough
to make me blush and look away?
How could a daisy be bright enough
to catch more sun
than you?
How could a violet make me stand so tall
as when I'm standing
with you?

When Harry first read this poem to me, we were saying good-bye for college. I always thought that we would be together. I now realize that he wasn't sure, even back then. This whole poem was about all the other flowers that could attract his attention: the "rose" that could make him "blush and look away"; the "daisy" that could "catch more sun"; the "violet" that could make him "stand so tall." When I look at it now, I see that all those flower names, except the one for me, are names for girls. Eventually Harry and I broke up because when I went to surprise visit him in his dorm, there was a young lady in his room. She was a lot shorter than I am.

*R*eflections ──────────────────────────────

1. What does Michelle change in the redraft? Point to specific words, phrases, and sentences.

2. Does Michelle quote effectively?

3. Does Michelle requote when appropriate?

How to Quote

1. ***Assume*** your reader won't know *exactly* which portion of what you heard or read is important to you, even if your reader said or wrote it.

2. ***Choose*** the relevant excerpt of what you heard or read and write it down. (An ***excerpt*** is a chosen portion of what was said or written.)

3. ***Quote*** your chosen excerpt by putting quotation marks before and after the exact words you are mentioning. (Review the use of quotation marks on pages 481–485 in Chapter 16.)

4. ***Indent and single-space*** quotes that are longer than four lines of printed material.

5. ***Acknowledge*** the person and the work you are quoting. Use such expressions as these: ***according to (person or title), (person) wrote, (person) said, in (title) (person) says.***

6. ***Explain*** exactly what the quote means to you and how it is relevant to your purpose. When appropriate, requote smaller portions of the work.

4. Does Michelle explain what her quotes mean to her in sufficient detail? If so, how? If not, what more should she write?

5. What is your reaction to Michelle's drafts?

6. What additional questions arise for you as you reflect on the two drafts?

*E*xplorations

1. a. *Solo.* Read the following letter that retired public librarian Marvin H. Scilken wrote to *The New York Times.* Write a letter in response to him, saying exactly

- To which letter you are responding,
- Where the letter first appeared, and
- Which of his points were meaningful to you, and why.

Be sure to quote and requote words, phrases, and sentences as you refer to them. Whenever you use his exact words, place them in quotation marks.

To the Editor:

As a retired public librarian I would like to comment on your Sept. 9 article that shows that many Americans cannot read.

People do what gives them pleasure and avoid doing what gives them pain. Regular library users told me that just after learning to read they read hundreds of pleasure-giving books. This intensive period of reading for pleasure honed their reading skills and enabled them to read with ease for the rest of their lives.

I believe children who don't experience this early coupling of reading with pleasure rarely become facile readers as adults. Learning to read, like learning foreign languages, is best done early in one's life.

Schools usually cannot "teach" reading for pleasure because, in their desire to measure a student's progress, they couple reading with the "pain" of tests and book reports. This coupling of reading and "pain" turns many people into aliterates. They can read but don't like to. People who don't read apparently lose some of their ability to read. This may account for some of the shocking literacy figures.

The public library plays a major, but unrecognized, role in the creation and nurturing of America's good readers. Fortunately, public libraries are very inexpensive, perhaps America's greatest education bargain. New Jersey, for instance, spends about $1,000 per capita (about $7,000 per student) for public schooling while it spends a minuscule $26 a year per capita on public libraries.

If we are to have a more literate population, the public should see to it that their public libraries are open when children and adults can get to them and that libraries have a sufficient supply of books that kids and adults want to read when they want to read them. Because libraries are so inexpensive this "keep reading alive" program is within the means of most communities.

Mayor David Dinkins, when he came to office, gutted the libraries. Apparently seeing that this made him unpopular with many voters, he recently gave the libraries money to open six days a week, but he "forgot" to give them more money for books.

It is easier to watch TV than to read. If we want to be a reading country, we have to make desired books and other reading matter easily available.

—Marvin H. Scilken
New York, Sept. 16, 1993[11]

b. *Together.* Read your response letters to each other in small groups or as a class. What point was each letter trying to make? Decide whether the letter used quotes effectively. Were all the quotes relevant? What relevant information, if any, was left out? How would you revise the letter?

2. a. *Solo.* Choose something you have read recently that was important to you, such as a passage from the Bible or the Koran, a newspaper item, a personal letter, a poem, or a book. To clarify what it means to you, and to convince others of its relevance, write an essay in response to your chosen passage. State what it means to you. Assume your readers will not be familiar with your chosen passage or source. Quote and requote words, phrases, and sentences to keep your discussion focused for yourself and for your readers. State the person or the source you are quoting.

b. *Together.* Bring your chosen passage to class along with your essay in response. In small groups, read your essays to each other. Then show each other your passages. Discuss whether you have used relevant quotes. Did you quote sufficiently? If not, what more could you have quoted or requoted to make your essay clearer to readers who won't be reading your chosen passage as you did?

Illustrating

Could you imagine reading a Dr. Seuss book without drawings or a *National Geographic* article on tropical fish without underwater photographs? Of course not. Such drawings and photographs help readers to more fully enjoy and understand what they are reading.

This past century has brought us a carnival of visual and audio media to delight and educate us all. Business professionals often support their presentations with graphics. Music videos are helping to solve social problems such as bringing runaway children home. Medical diagnoses can be made via satellite telecasts. Video games and of course television and the movies have made us all dependent on visual media.

As a writer, you participate in a long tradition of transforming and re-creating the world through words so that others will be able to see it *as you do.* The old saying goes, "A picture paints a thousand words." But just a few words illustrating your points can enliven not only your readers' experience but your own, as writer. Strive to illustrate your ideas in words as visual media illustrate in pictures.

An effective way to focus your work is to offer examples— *illustrations*—of exactly what you mean. In the first paragraph of this section, I could have just written this sentence:

Illustrations help to enliven books and magazines.

Instead, I stopped to think of some examples that are relevant to my point and that you might recognize as well. So, I chose to write:

Could you imagine reading a Dr. Seuss book without drawings or a *National Geographic* article on tropical fish without underwater photographs?

By way of another example—to show you how to transform your work through using examples—here is another look at Roy's first attempt to describe his fiancée:

First draft

I am writing about my fiancée. She is the youngest in her family and always had people there for her, doing things for her, making decisions, solving problems. And that was because they would always think she wasn't able to make her own decisions or solve her own problems. Her parents were loving and caring, so she was always protected by them. In reality, she was never alone.

Roy knows his fiancée well. But in workshop, his peers did not feel they knew her as an individual. He was not specifying how she is different from everyone else. There are many people who are overprotected. But each one has her or his own special experience. To enliven his paper, Roy illustrated his points by offering a few representative examples:

Third draft

My fiancée, Anita, is the youngest of eight children, with five sisters and two brothers. She had always had people doing everything for her: for example, they combed her hair in the morning and decided which movie she could attend on which weekend night. All through her education someone was telling her what to do. For example, they would say, "Take the biology course this year," "Try out for basketball next year," or even "Don't wear jeans to your piano lesson." Everyone was always fixing things for her, so she wouldn't have to confront things herself. For example, when she came home from first grade complaining that a classmate bit her, her father put her in a different school. When she came home not liking a teacher, her father got her into a different class.

Although it helped him to incorporate examples, Roy found his use of "for example" too repetitious. Consulting with others during workshop, he was able to reword his first paragraph in his next draft:

Fourth draft

My fiancée, Anita, is the youngest of eight children in her family. She had always had people doing everything for her from combing her hair in the morning to deciding which movie she could attend and on which weekend night. All through her education someone was telling her things such as "Take the biology course this year," "Try out for basketball next year," or even "Don't wear jeans to your piano lesson." Everyone was always fixing things for her, so she wouldn't have to confront things herself. For example, when she came home from first grade complaining that a classmate bit her, her father put her in a different school. When she came home not liking a teacher, her father got her into a different class.

In the rest of his essay on his fiancée, Roy chose one story to illustrate, in depth, about how Anita made a breakthrough and asserted her independence:

The turning point in Anita's life happened when her mother started getting very ill. It turned out to be cancer. The doctors tried to operate on her, but it just made matters worse.

My fiancée stayed with her mother. She took care of her night and day. Her father was there too. It was so painful for my fiancée because she was seeing her mother in so much pain, and there was really nothing she could do. Anita was really very close with her mother. Sometimes she wouldn't even go to sleep, because she would be afraid of losing her mother while she was sleeping.

In May of 1984, my fiancée's mother become worse then ever. She was at the stage that she just didn't feel any more pain. She was acting like a child. She couldn't really remember all her sons and daughters or others she knew in the past. The only daughter she could really remember was my fiancée. That was because she was with her most of the time.

On May 8, 1984, it was Anita's mother's birthday. The very next day, Anita and her father were in the room at home where her mother was lying down. They were just there, holding her hand, when all of a sudden Anita's mother couldn't breathe anymore. Anita just didn't want to let go. She couldn't believe that she would have to lose the person that meant so much to her. It was very difficult for my fiancée. She thought that losing her mother would mean that she couldn't make it through life, herself.

Fortunately when she was at that point in her life, we met and started seeing each other. I told her that I was the kind of guy that is full of life, independent and likes to take chances. I explained to her that anyone could be that way: you just have to think and do things for yourself. Don't let people run your life for you, because that's your job and no one else's. I told her that anyone who could nurse a mother through such a terrible sickness could take care of herself.

I really encouraged her to go out and get what she wanted in life on her own, which was to be independent and have her own things. For instance, I helped her open a savings account for her to save enough money to move out of her sisters' house and get her own place. I helped her get a better-paying job, and showed her how to budget her money and other minor things she wasn't familiar with.

Today Anita has her own apartment in Elizabeth, a 1992 Plymouth Laser, and a good-paying job at Newark airport. She is going to Kean College to get the career she wants, which is to be a physical therapist. Every time we talk about this experience, she tells me she really appreciated me being there for her, encouraging her to get her life together, and not depending on anyone but herself. She told me that all she needed was someone to tell her that she could do anything she put her mind to, someone who really believed in her and helped her realize that she could make it on her own.

*R*eflections

1. Compare Roy's first and fourth drafts. Which one do you like better, and why?

2. What claims does Roy make about his fiancée in his first draft?

3. Which phrases and sentences does Roy offer in his fourth draft to illustrate the claims he made?

4. Are Roy's illustrations relevant?

5. On what major story does Roy focus?

6. How else does Roy improve his essay?

7. How else could Roy improve on his fourth draft?

To form the habit of using examples, do as Roy did after writing his first draft: write "for example" or "for instance," and offer some relevant

How to Illustrate

1. *Ask* yourself, "What illustration would enliven this writing?"
2. *Use expressions* such as *for example, for instance, from* _____ *to* _____ *, such as,* and *as in* to launch yourself into illustrating.
3. *Rewrite* your draft to reduce unnecessary repetition of words or expressions.
4. *Illustrate* your writing with examples without using suggestion 2.
5. *Focus* on one major illustration or story whenever possible.

illustrations. As you can see, you don't have to write every example that makes your point. One or two examples will offer your readers a good idea of what you mean. Once you have collected and chosen your examples, reword your draft to remove the words "for example" or "for instance" so that you don't sound repetitious. Use expressions such as these instead:

from _____ to _____

such as _____

as when _____

as _____

You might be tempted to use the words *like when* instead of *such as* when offering examples. But the word *like* is more appropriately used when you are comparing two things that are different from each other. Chapters 7 and 13 offer you strategies for using the word *like* to make comparisons. When you are illustrating with examples, use *such* instead. Sometimes, as in the last sentence of the first paragraph of Roy's fourth draft and as in the first sentence of my discussion of illustrating, you won't have to introduce your examples with any expressions. Your readers will know that you are illustrating your writing to make it clearer and more interesting for them.

*E*xplorations _____

1. *Together or Solo.* Read the following sentences. Illustrate the claim made in each. If you are so inspired, write a short essay further illustrating the claim with relevant examples and stories.

   a. The United States has waged many wars.

        b. Many music videos address social problems in a responsible way.

        c. Car manufacturers are creating safety features that are saving lives.

        d. Exercise can be dangerous to your health.

        f. Modern civilization is ruining the planet.

  2. *Solo or Together.*

        a. Read the following student paragraph. Mark portions that could have been enlivened by illustrations.

> Our governor is the best thing that's happened to the state. Before she got in, we had all sorts of social problems that nobody paid attention to. Now we're getting action. Some people are saying mean things about her. All I know is that my problems are not being overlooked anymore. Maybe she's had to change things around to make things happen. But it's worth it. I'm going to help her get reelected in any way I can.

        b. Revise and expand the student paragraph in 2a into an essay. Use your imagination and illustrate the claims with relevant examples and stories.

  3. *Together and Solo.* Bring essays in process to class. Read them in small groups. Mark portions that could have been enlivened by illustrations. Revise your work to include more examples. If possible, choose one example or story to tell in detail.

Questioning

So far in this chapter, you have had opportunities to explore four focusing strategies: choosing, specifying, quoting, and illustrating. All these strategies help you to achieve these objectives:

- Relate *exactly* what you want to relate.
- Create a flow of words.
- Take care of your reader.
- Learn while you write.
- Enjoy writing.

Questioning helps you to practice these four strategies more fully.

    Let's consider here an example of how questioning helped student Jennifer Carter focus and expand her writing. Jennifer made several unquestioned claims in her first attempt at writing about a meaningful experience:

First Draft

A Bad Experience

I was very active and everyone said how I could do everything. I graduated high school and got a day job. I wanted to work hard all summer so that I could go to school and not have to work while I had fall classes. So I got an extra night job because I always thought I could do more.

Then it happened. Both my hands got hurt bad. Everything changed. I couldn't do all the things I was good at. I had to quit both jobs. I thought it was the end of the world. But I worked hard to get better that summer, and it taught me a lot. My family and friends helped a lot. I will never be the same again.

In her first draft, Jennifer was writing more for herself than for her readers. She makes claims that readers have to take on faith:

- She was very active.
- Both hands got badly hurt.
- Everything changed.
- Jennifer couldn't do all the things she was good at.
- Jennifer's family and friends helped a lot.
- Jennifer will never be the same again.

But what proof does a reader have to believe all these claims?

When you write, you have to offer your readers enough evidence so that they can understand what you are claiming. By offering readers this evidence, you not only bring your readers into your experience, you also become clearer about it yourself. It's much like bringing a view into focus when you are photographing: You move from a blur into a clear picture. Anticipate questions that would arise for your readers. Even if your reader is familiar with your topic, you need to focus his or her attention on *exactly* what you mean.

Students helped Jennifer *prove* her claims by asking her questions in class. Questions were asked as they naturally occurred to the readers on hearing the paper read aloud. To boost the process, students referred to the question star (Figure 5.3), which arranges the eight *wh* question words.* It helps to go back to the question star, pick a word, and see if a question forms in your mind.

---

*All the *wh* words were originally spelled with an initial *hw.* Only *hwuo (how)* was not respelled with an initial *wh.* Because *how* comes from the same family of words as the other *wh* words, *how* is included here as an honorary *wh* word.

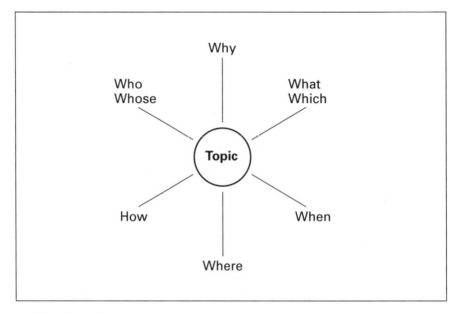

FIGURE **5.3** *The Question Star*

Here are some of the questions that students asked Jennifer about her experiences with her injury:

- What were all the things you could do?
- How were your hands hurt?
- When were your hands hurt?
- Why couldn't you do things anymore?
- Where did you go for treatment?
- How did your family and friends help out?
- Which ways has your life changed most?

Taking these questions into consideration, Jennifer revised her paper and added further details and evidence as they occurred to her. This is her fourth draft:

Fourth Draft

<u>Learning from Injury</u>

My grandmother always told me to believe that I could be a success. So I worked hard to do everything. I didn't like asking for help either. I was the fastest typist in my high school class. I grew vegetables and flowers. I played tennis and piano. I even

figured out a way to knit and do almost anything at the same time:
read, watch television, talk on the phone, and ride my father's
exercise bike. Sometimes I got tense doing everything, but
everybody admired me.

So when I graduated from high school and was waiting to go to
college, I got myself two jobs because I wanted to earn enough
money so I wouldn't have to work during school in the fall. These
jobs were typing during the day and waitressing at night. The
first sign that anything was wrong was when halfway through July
I woke up in the middle of the night feeling my thumbs were going
to explode.

I woke up my mother for the first time since I was a kid. She
put ice on my hands because they looked red. Even though she said
I should stay home I went in to work because I always felt I could
beat anything. I sat down at the word processor and figured I would
just not use my thumbs. In a little while my fingers started to
tingle and then they started to get numb. I took a break and when
I was trying to comb my hair I dropped my comb. My boss sent me
home and I never went back to my typing job or my night job again.

That night I woke up again feeling even worse. The next day
Dr. Smith told me I had acute carpal tunnel syndrome. What was
happening was that the tunnels in my wrists that held the nerves
going to my hand were all swollen. My doctor explained it was an
injury like tennis elbow that people get when they use their hands
a lot. Piano players, supermarket checkout people, hair
dressers, and butchers get it a lot. The bad news was that typists
at computer keyboards were getting this injury a lot, and I was
making it worse by bending back my wrists carrying heavy trays at
night. Now when I looked at all those things I could do that
everybody admired and made me feel I was such a success, I realized
that I had been hurting myself all along.

My doctor said I could take care of the injury by surgery or I
could do it the hard way by changing my life-style. Well, you know
me by now, I figured I would do it the hard way and be a success.
So I stayed home. I had to put ice on my wrists for fifteen minutes
out of every hour. I had to wear wrist braces all the time,
especially at night. I even stopped eating foods like tomatoes
and sugar that make joints feel worse.

Changing my life-style was not easy, but I had to do it. You
see, I couldn't garden, or play tennis, or play piano, or knit. I
had to learn to live with not being able to do all the little things
that anyone else could do: drive a car, open a doorknob, comb my

hair, flip pages in a magazine, cut my food, or even eat popcorn. Believe it or not, I couldn't even hold a phone. From being super active, I got to the point where all I could do was take walks. Then both my knees started to hurt because we live in a very hilly town and I was overdoing it by walking too much. My doctor started to think maybe we should check out if I had some worse diseases than just an injury. Luckily, nothing was wrong with anything else. But I was getting depressed. I wasn't used to not being able to do everything.

The hardest but best part to learn was that I didn't have to do everything by myself. I had to ask my family and friends to help me out with everyday things. I got a headset phone so that I could talk on the phone without hurting my hands. My father found me a job where I could stay at home and make calls on the phone selling magazines.

Later, when school started, I found a person nearby to car pool with. I talked my papers into a tape recorder for my teachers. Then my brother typed them for me. He even retyped when I had to make changes and let me dictate extras. My mother made a reading stand for me so that my books could stay open with a rubber band.

It took me over a year to get to the point where I could take care of everyday little things and not wear my braces all day long. But what I learned was that I could slow down and didn't have to be such a success at everything. Now I take things slower and enjoy life more. I have more friends and lots more caring in my family. I don't recommend that anyone get carpal tunnel syndrome. But I can say that since I had to have it, it has taught me to be a better person. Now when I remember what my grandmother taught me, I realize it's not about outdoing everybody. It's about learning to care for ourselves and each other.

*R*eflection _____

Together. Compare Jennifer's fourth draft with her first one. Refer to specific words, phrases, sentences, and ideas to support your claims. Here are some questions to help stimulate your discussion:

a. What was unclear in Jennifer's first draft?

b. What became clearer in the fourth draft?

c. What did Jennifer do to clarify her experiences?

d. What questions do you find yourself asking in response to the fourth draft that could lead to further clarity?

e. Are all the details relevant? If so, why? If not, why not?

How to Question

1. *Identify* claims that readers could question.
2. *Ask* questions, using each point of the question star (Figure 5.3).
3. *Consult* with other readers.
4. *Choose* questions to answer.
5. *Answer* important questions, including any questions that occur to you as you revise. Push yourself to answer *exactly* what, which, who, whose, when, where, how, and why.

Explorations

1. *Solo and Together.* Choose papers on which you are working right now, and make four copies of each. In turn, read each of them aloud in small groups. Using the question star (Figure 5.3), ask questions of the writers to help them clarify their points with examples and details. Revise your papers by answering these questions and others you anticipate may arise.

2. *Solo and Together.* For an in-depth discussion of questions, turn to pages 324–331. Do the Explorations that follow.

Thesis Statements

Just as questions invite answers, some statements invite further questions, explanation, examples, quotes, and discussion. These statements are called *thesis statements* or *key statements.* They open your mind as well as your reader's. Key statements assert your main purpose or point in your letters, freewrites, and essays.

In the writing process, good thesis statements can focus your mind, trigger your memory, and guide you to collect whatever you need to support your claim. In considering your audience, the purpose of writing a thesis statement is to stimulate interest in your idea, focus the reader's attention, and inspire confidence in your grasp of the subject. Thesis statements are especially geared for academic and professional papers and examinations.

A good thesis statement does this for you:

- Gets you started and keeps you going
- Helps you remember what you know
- Helps you discover that you know more than you thought you knew
- Helps you use and create new knowledge
- Reduces writing anxiety
- Inspires, in your reader, confidence in your knowledge and abilities
- Helps you focus your collecting activities
- Helps you organize your work

Consider these examples of thesis statements:

I have always been afraid to speak.

Burger Barn was a disgusting experience.

Almost everyone has felt like an outsider at one time or another.

These thesis statements embody the main or key idea the authors want to relate. They are good thesis statements because they meet some or all of the following standards:

- They are focused.
- They lead to focused questions.
- They lead to other statements.

The first statement—"I have always been afraid to speak"—meets the three standards. The statement is focused on a particular fear and doesn't attempt to account for aspects of the writer's life that would be irrelevant. The statement readily invites questions such as these: Why have you been afraid? Who made you feel uncomfortable? What were you afraid of saying? Did you ever get over it? The thesis statement leads to a long discussion of the person's fears.

Strong and Weak Statements

To stimulate your own mind and earn the attention of your readers, you need to adopt or formulate strong statements that invite further elaboration and thought. To say, "Milk is good for you" may not stimulate you to write or your readers to read on. Currently, most people believe the statement as a matter of course and have stopped wondering whether it's true or not. The statement "Milk is the only food that can sustain life indefinitely" is much stronger. It invites questions, such as "What makes it so ideal?" "Aren't there other foods that can sustain you as well?" "Are there some deficiencies that adults could develop from consuming milk alone?" "Who could use this information about milk?"

A much stronger statement, because it runs against current popular beliefs, would be, "Milk is dangerous to your health." In fact, many studies question whether milk is good for your health. Some important insights have been developed about the connection between milk consumption and respiratory diseases, cysts, and digestive disturbances. This research occurred because people were willing to adopt a controversial thesis and pursue the questions it raised. Major breakthroughs in all the disciplines start with someone being willing to say something new and controversial. A responsible thinker (further defined in Chapter 12) is able to create new standards and adjust and correct old beliefs.

Strong statements do the following:

- Respond to some important human need
- Make you think
- Lead to good questions
- Give you an "aha" feeling
- Make you say "That's a strong statement."
- Question common beliefs
- Take a stand
- Assume a new point of view
- Stimulate strong reactions
- Form the basis for further research and discovery
- Aren't instantly popular
- May meet with resistance from others
- Have the potential for creating breakthroughs
- Require strong supporting evidence
- Lead you to work together with others who are ready for a breakthrough.

Sometimes you don't want to commit yourself to an extreme statement because you don't feel confident about collecting or synthesizing enough evidence to support it. You can weaken a statement such as "Milk is dangerous to your health" by using the words *can be, could be,* or *may be* instead of *is* or *will.* You can weaken the statement "Milk is the only food that can sustain life indefinitely" by crossing out *only* or by starting it with *sometimes, maybe,* or *some people claim.* You can turn the statement into a very strong statement by crossing out *indefinitely* but may find yourself unable to support the statement. "Milk is the only food that can sustain life" can also be irresponsible because there is too much real evidence against it: namely, all the foods that sustain people, and all the people who survive without milk.

Sometimes you want to commit yourself to an extreme or controversial position to prove a point. For example, in "A Modest Proposal," Jonathan Swift proposed that infants should be used as food. He proposed this outrageous solution to starvation in London to emphasize how people were negligent in solving the crisis. This is a challenging strategy that often leads to effective satire.

Unless you are prepared to take up the challenge of writing satire, be careful of trying to support extreme statements. Some statements, such as "Milk is the only food that can sustain life" or "Women shouldn't be allowed in the workplace," are strong but irresponsible. These statements lead not to the betterment of life for all people and our environment but to possible destruction and sustained misery. Because strong statements invite further discussion and proof, and because (as you will see in Chapter 14, "Writing for Power") most any position can be made convincing to unthinking people, irresponsible statements—assumed and acted upon by people in power—are dangerous. The standard that a responsible thinker will always endeavor to meet when making a strong statement is this:

> The statement must be made in the spirit of preserving or bettering human relations and the environment.

In the past, most writing courses required that you write a thesis statement to focus *all* your essays. But writing a thesis statement is only one way to focus a piece of writing. Many effective pieces of writing do not depend on a thesis statement. Whether you use thesis statements in your writing will be determined by your purpose, your audience, and your thinking style. If you are a planner, you are more likely to favor thesis statements. A good thesis statement allows you to plan ahead. If you are an explorer, you are more likely to favor other strategies for focusing. Freewriting and choosing, illustrating, and questioning are more conducive to exploring.

Whether you think of yourself as a planner or an explorer, learn how to use thesis statements. If you do, you will be able to write them when you need to. You might find yourself using a thesis statement in an early draft of a paper, only to discard it altogether in later drafts. You might find yourself writing early drafts without a thesis statement, only to begin your later drafts with thesis statements you developed in the process. A thesis statement is the roof under which the building must be built. You might start your final draft with a thesis statement. But you might have written it later in the process, as you "built" the essay itself. Be flexible. (For a discussion of where to place thesis statements in your essays and how to further develop essays in response to them, turn to pages 190 and 348–351.)

Writing Thesis Statements

If you are a planner, you are more likely to formulate your thesis statement first and then to write your first draft in response to it. If you are an explorer, you may be more likely to cluster or freewrite first and discover a thesis statement in the process. The planner's and explorer's final products may be identical in structure. How they get there will differ.

For many of your academic and professional writing tasks, you will have an initial assignment that begins the process of focusing for you. Suppose your assignment is posed as a question:

Assignment: Do men or women have it easier in your home community? You have these options:

1. *Record the question* as your introductory sentence and respond to it. This response may serve as your thesis statement:

   Do men or women have it easier in my home community?

   or

   My first answer to the question would be that men have it easier.

2. *Turn the question into a statement* of your position. Use the language of the question so that any reader would know what your purpose is without reading the assignment:

   Men have it easier in my home community than women.

3. *Question the assignment* and how it is worded:

   I don't believe that either men or women have it "easier" in my home community.

or

> It's no longer fair, in the 1990s, to ask whether men or women have easier lives in my home community.

4. *Quote a key statement* by someone else on the subject, and then state your position in response to it:

> It has been over a century since Susan B. Anthony said, "Woman must not depend upon the protection of man, but must be taught to protect herself." There have been many changes since women couldn't vote. But it's still true: men have it easier than women. One way or another, women have to protect themselves against men.

Suppose the assignment is posed as a directive:

Assignment: Write an essay on whether you think honesty is the best policy. You have these options:

1. *Turn the topic into a question* and then proceed with it as if it were a question:

> Is honesty the best policy?

2. *State your position* on the subject. If you are stuck, use one of the following formats to boost you:

> *I agree that* honesty is the best policy.
>
> *I don't believe that* honesty is the best policy.
>
> *Let's consider whether* honesty is the best policy.

3. *Question the assignment* and how it is worded:

> It's always hard to claim that something is "best," because circumstances change. Rather than exploring whether honesty is the best policy, I'd like to ask when honesty is helpful and when it is not.

4. *Quote a key statement* by someone else and state your position in response to it:

How to Write Thesis Statements

1. **Read** your assignment.
2. **Ask** a question and state a response to your own question;

   or

3. **State** whether you agree or disagree;

   or

4. **Question** the assignment and how it is worded.

   or

5. **Quote** someone else on the topic and state your response.
6. **Adjust** the strength of your statement to satisfy your purpose and reach your audience.
7. **Revise** your thesis statement as you write your paper.

> Miguel de Cervantes said, "An honest man's word is as good as a contract." Honesty is the best policy not only in personal relationships but in business and political relationships as well.

You may revise your thesis and key statements completely any time before you finally hand it in. Ideas are triggered and developed in the writing process, and you may change or strengthen your position as you proceed. You may remember or discover a quote you can use. Don't hesitate to revise. Part of the benefit of developing thesis statements is to discover that you know more than you thought you knew.

*E*xplorations _____

1. *Together and Solo.*

   a. Turn the following assignments and questions into thesis statements:

      - Discuss whether television commercials are exaggerated, unrealistic, or even harmful.
      - What values should be taught at home and which should be taught in the schools?
      - Is art a strictly human activity?
      - Should there be mandatory testing for AIDS?

- Compare and contrast the classic English country garden with Japanese tea gardens.

   b. Discuss whether the thesis statements you formulate meet the standards for thesis statements listed earlier in this chapter.

   c. Choose one of the assignments in 1a and write an essay supporting a thesis statement.

2. *Together and Solo.* Write or discuss your reactions to the statements "Milk is dangerous to your health" and "Women should not be allowed in the workplace." Ask as many questions as you can in response to these statements. Discuss what you learn from this process.

3. *Together.*

   a. Rank the following statements on a scale of 1 (for weakest) to 5 (for strongest) according to the strength of the statements for you.

   - Electroshock therapy is cruel and unusual punishment for people who are already in great mental anguish.

   - Toxic waste dumps exist in the United States.

   - The diet of the average U.S. teenager is about as healthy as skydiving without a parachute.

   - Communities can reestablish a sense of unity by organizing social events together.

   - Drugs are a problem in the world today.

   b. For practice, revise the weaker statements into stronger statements and the stronger into weaker. Whenever possible, do so by adding or crossing out a few words.

   c. Discuss which statements from 3a and 3b would be most effective in stimulating further research and discussion.

4. *Together and Solo.* Collect statements from the editorial page of a college or city newspaper. Discuss whether the statements are strong, weak, responsible, or irresponsible, and why.

5. *Together and Solo.* Choose a strong statement from something you have read or heard that you only half-believe. Write an essay in response to it with the purpose of convincing yourself and your audience of the claim. Notice how one statement leads to another and what you learn as you proceed.

6. *Solo.* Revise a paper with special attention to the strength and relevance of your statements.

Reading for Focus and Meaning

Ask these questions to test a piece of writing:

1. Could almost anyone have written this? (This is a measure of how general it is.)
2. Does the writer try to cover too many subjects?
3. Does the writer use strong, specific words and expressions?
4. Can I replace an important word or expression with any other and say as much or more?
5. Does the writer illustrate the claims?
6. Are all the details relevant to a main purpose?
7. Is any of this redundant?
8. Is any of this false or unclear?
9. Are any important questions left unanswered?
10. Are the statements appropriately strong?

*C*hapter Review _____

1. *Together.* Read the following student essay. Notice your own reactions. Are you interested? Are you bored? Are you being forced to make up examples yourself to enrich your experience of the essay? Use the questions in the sidebar on reading for focus and meaning to discuss the essay. Notice what happens, for example, if you replace *drug* with *exercise* or *diet.* Using the strategies developed in this chapter, offer suggestions for how the writer could have focused. What risks may the author have to take?

<u>Drug Abuse Today</u>

In recent years drug abuse has been increasing at a rapid rate in the United States and throughout the world. The practice occurs mostly among young people who are looking for new sensations or who think that drugs will increase their mental functioning or their ability to understand themselves.

Some young people begin to take drugs while they are still in elementary school, particularly if their friends have persuaded them to do so. During high school and early in college, more and more people take drugs. By the middle of their college years, most of this group realize that the practice is dangerous. Most young people who try drugs soon stop, but some find that they cannot, even if they want to. Even among preteenagers, alcohol is now a problem. It seems that the earlier the use, the more likely a young person is to become an alcoholic.

Sometimes people use a doctor's prescription for a drug unwisely. A person takes too much of the drug or fails to check with the doctor about stopping its use. But very often one person introduces another to drug abuse. The newcomer, in turn, introduces others to drugs. In this way, more and more people, unaware of the dangers of drugs, begin to take them. This is the situation today.

2. *Together and Solo.* Develop your own focus on the issue of drug abuse. Write an essay in response.

3. a. *Together.* Consult with each other about essays you are now writing. Focus on focusing. Refer to specific strategies offered in this chapter.

   b. *Solo.* Revise a paper according to questions and suggestions that emerged in your discussions.

Chapter 6

Focusing II

Sense Appeal

This chapter offers opportunities to

—Give your writing **sense appeal**
—**Describe** persons, places, things, and events
—Distinguish **showing** from **telling**
—Balance **objective** and **subjective** writing
—Use **comparisons** to enliven your writing

I learned to love the small details until they
were large.

—*Mark Rubin, Poet*

. . . touch and taste and hear and see the
world, and shrink . . . from all that is of the
brain only, from all that is not a fountain
jetting from the entire hopes, memories, and
sensations of the body.

—*William Butler Yeats, Poet*

Writing is a mind-taxing process. Using
sensory detail makes it more enjoyable.

—*Jen Levine, Student*

The Dynamics of Sense Appeal

Life depends on the ability to perceive everyday sensations such as the color of a traffic light, the texture of rain, the smell of breakfast cooking. Without the senses of sight, touch, hearing, motion, taste, and smell, you would be locked in emptiness. You would not be able to develop your mind or have common sense, good sense, or a sense of humor. In every human endeavor—from noticing the skin texture of a sick person to observing the flight patterns of aircraft, from listening for prowlers in a danger zone to appreciating how light shifts on a landscape you are photographing—the quicker and sharper your senses, the more fully you can live. At times, you may shut off your senses if your environment is unpleasant. At other times, even pleasant stimulation such as music, television, junk food—or the more dangerous experiences of fast driving, alcohol, and drugs—can numb you. You find yourself reaching for more stimulation and so get even more numbed. The antidote is to calm down and start focusing your attention on small sense details that surround you every day.

The greatest achievements in art, science, business, education, sports, and human relations require sharp senses. One of the most powerful ways to develop your senses is to learn how to focus them in the writing process. As you enliven your writing with sensory images, you increase its *sense appeal:* it becomes *sensational.* You thereby engage your audience to focus on your writing and your purpose.

Chapter 5 showed you strategies for focusing your writing. To further develop your ability to choose, to specify, to quote, to illustrate, to question, and to make statements, give your writing sense appeal. The more sense appeal your writing has, the more likely you are to enjoy writing and engage your readers' interest. This chapter is devoted to helping you appreciate, focus, and develop your senses through the writing process.

Start with the following Explorations to become aware of what your senses mean to you in everyday life and how you may be taking them for granted.

Explorations

1. *Solo and Together. Without referring to the real thing,* draw one of the following to test your awareness and memory:

   - The front of a dollar bill
   - A familiar cartoon character
   - A modern pay phone

- A particular campus building

- The hallway outside the classroom

- The lines in your palm (don't look)

Compare your drawings with the real thing. How accurate were you?

2. *Solo.* If you have had, or currently have, a disability involving a sense or body part, write about your experiences. Relate experiences before, during, and after the disability occurred. You may also write about another person's way of coping with a disability.

3. *Solo.* If you wear glasses or a hearing aid or experience your senses of smell, taste, touch, or motion reduced from time to time, write a description of the difference between having your senses fully functioning and having them impaired.

4. *Solo or Together.* Imagine you had to live forever in the same place and could arrange every detail in that environment. Write a description of this place. What would you be sure to include? Which senses would be most stimulated by the environment you create?

Collecting: Your Six Senses

The five senses you've heard about since grammar school are *sight, hearing, smell, taste,* and *touch*. These senses are focused mostly in your head and fingertips. But you live in more than your head and fingertips. When you ride on a roller coaster, dance, fall, or feel muscle pain, you are experiencing what it means to live in a body. Therefore, *body sensations* have been added to this discussion as the sixth sense.

The sensations you notice reflect your *point of view*. If you are angry, you will focus on things in your environment that make you angry. If you are in a pleasant mood, you are more likely to focus on pleasant sensations. A cook will notice the edible mushrooms on a nature walk. An environmentalist will notice how pollution bleaches the bark on maple trees. Since point of view determines how you sense the world, it is placed at the center of the model of the senses in Figure 6.1.

Here is a list of the kinds of phenomena related to each sense with specific examples:

Sight: color, shape, size, light/dark, perspective, movement

Specific Examples: neon pink T-shirt, flickering glints from a heart-shaped diamond, a green river snaking through a valley

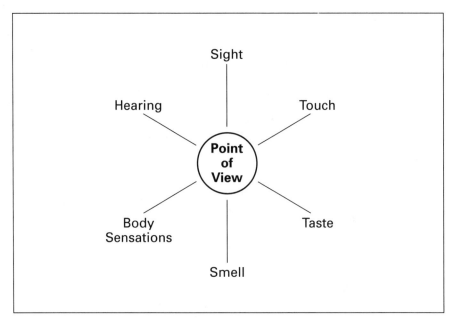

FIGURE 6.1 The Sense Star

Touch: texture, itching, heat/cold

   Specific Examples: prickling wool slacks on a hot day, juiciness of a ripe peach, warm sand trickling through your fingers

Taste: single and combined tastes of sweet, sour, salty, spicy, bitter (taste is closely related to smell)

   Specific Examples: tang of lemonade, sweetness of watermelon, metallic taste from smelling silver polish

Smell: single and combined smells of sweet, sour, salty, bitter (smell is closely related to taste)

   Specific Examples: smell of old sneakers, aroma of brewing coffee, salty smell of ocean breeze

Body Sensations: motion, movements, balance, pressure, pain, tension, pleasure, weight

   Specific Examples: sensations of riding in a roller coaster, release of tension from a massaged muscle, heft of a basket of apples, stabbing toothache, throb from bass speakers felt through the body

Hearing: pitch, tone, loudness, frequency, rhythm, sound imitations

   Specific Examples: shrill of a lifeguard's whistle, scraping and sloshing sounds of autumn leaves being raked, basso of a Mack truck's horn, hum of bees, quiver of a complaining voice

How to Collect Sensations

1. *Cluster.* Draw the sense star in the center of a piece of paper. As you observe, record sensations for each of the senses at the appropriate rays.
2. *Brainstorm* sense impressions.
3. *Draw.* An effective way to stimulate your memory is to sketch your subject.
4. *Prime your senses.* Don't try to remember sensations. Get your subject in front of you. Go to the place you are describing.
5. *Use prompts.* If you can't prime your senses directly, use photographs and audio and video tapes. Collect objects that can help you recall sensations.

Read the fourth draft of a paper written by student Meir Benjamin Burton (Ben). Notice how he collects imagery for most of his senses. Notice, as well, how his choices reflect a particular point of view.

The Gym

I raise my arm, grasp the handle, and pull open the door. When I or anyone else enters the gym, everyone temporarily stops doing what he's doing to see who it is.

The air is cold, stale, and stagnant. The smell of sweat slaps you in the face as you take your first breath. You hear the hum of several fans straining to circulate the thick air, and the clanging of weights. At times the gym sounds like a zoo full of animals, with everyone grunting, groaning, and some screaming to get in that last burning repetition.

I make my way to the counter and stumble over a piece of slightly torn blue carpet. I look at the tan walls and notice a new picture of some guy I don't know. I throw down my belt on the poorly made wood counter. Making a large thud, it attracts the attention of my friend Bob.

Bob, who manages the gym in the morning and afternoon sessions, is always up for a good conversation about lifting and is always eager to give advice. I sit down next to him on an old plastic crate, and without fail, he starts a conversation. This time it is about one of the most commonly talked-about subjects in the gym: steroids--drugs that are worshipped in the gym because of the incredible size and strength results they can help produce. He informs me of a new oral drug that has come out on the black market, but I disappoint him when I tell him I already heard of it. So, with the conversation ended, I decide to go lift.

I slowly make my way over to the side of the gym saying ''Hi'' to a few friends on the way. I notice that the lat pulldown machine is still broken and thank goodness that I wasn't using it when it broke. Bob told me that the man who was using it was pulling the bar down to his chest so hard that when the chain snapped he almost broke his sternum. I have an urge to get a drink when I remember this, but it suddenly disappears when I get a look at the dirt-infested fountain.

I go over to where the flat benches are. I am lucky that the gym is relatively empty so I don't have to use the bench with the ripped upholstery. I lie down and start preparing for my lift. I'm slightly distracted by a spider working on a web in the corner. I grasp the bar and the cold steel stings my hands as if I were holding a hive of bees. A truck rumbles by and the gym vibrates slightly. I look toward it to try to catch a glimpse of it, but a ray of sun escapes through the blinds and hits me directly in the eye. Being temporarily blinded and not being able to see anything distracting, I decide to begin my set. I complete 10 reps and by this time my sweat starts to drip on the bench. This gives the black vinyl upholstery a shine like a newly waxed car--the kind I could buy if I ever won a championship.

After completing most of my workout, I look at the clock mounted on the wall and notice it is earlier than I thought. So, having a few extra minutes, and thinking that I might find something of value, I decide to go downstairs and check out the lockers. As I make my descent into the basement, the wooden stairs start to squeak and groan. By the time I reach the bottom, the stairs seem as if they are howling. Perhaps because I know I am doing something wrong, I really notice the noise.

As I enter the locker room I notice that it is extremely dim. I suppose that someone knocked some of the bulbs out. I look to see if someone is coming and then furiously start to open every locker I can. I am very disappointed to not find anything.

Suddenly one of the overhead lights flickers on as if an idea is popping into my head. That is when I notice that some of the ceiling tiles are missing. I take my arm and start feeling around in this dark space. My hand comes across dirt and many other things that are too old or mangled to describe. Finally, my hand comes

across something that is hard and vial-shaped. I grab it and pull
it down to see it is an empty vial-shaped bottle of testosterone
with the label still intact. Now that my search is completed, I
go back upstairs, bid my friends farewell, and with my newfound
discovery go home to examine it.

On reading "The Gym," students remark that they feel they almost
become Ben, going through the gym. Ben's paper offers *immediacy*—the
you-are-there feeling that focuses you into a particular experience. He
manages it by using:

- The pronoun *I*
- The present tense
- All his senses
- Human interactions
- A meaningful purpose
- A clear point of view—his position in the scene

These techniques are not the only ways to achieve immediacy and
sense appeal, but they worked for Ben. Reflect further on "The Gym,"
using the following questions and suggestions as guides.

Reflections

1. Why do you think Ben wrote this? What purpose could it serve him
   as a writer? What purpose could the paper serve for his readers?

2. Who is Ben's likely audience? Who would he want to read "The Gym"?
   Who would he not want to read it?

3. Underline parts of "The Gym" where Ben appeals to a sense.

4. Which senses does Ben tend to favor?

5. What words would you use to describe Ben's attitudes and feelings
   toward the gym? Point to specific parts of his essay that lead you to
   using these words.

6. Which parts of "The Gym" are the most interesting? Why?

7. Where and how does Ben use human interactions to give meaning to
   his description?

8. Are all of Ben's details relevant? How or how not?

9. State what you believe is Ben's point of view on the gym.

10. Are there any questions and suggestions you would offer Ben if he were to revise his essay?

Explorations

1. *Together.* Revise Ben's paper from the point of view of a new weight-lifter eager to convince a woman friend of the lure of the gym. Compare your revision with Ben's version and discuss the kinds of changes you needed to make and why. What do you emphasize? What details become irrelevant or counterproductive to your purpose?

Each person tends to favor some senses over others, depending on her or his physical constitution, culture, and training and the purpose at hand. The following Explorations invite you to notice which senses you favor and to develop senses you may have ignored.

2. *Solo.*

   a. Go to a place that is significant to you in some way—it could be a room, a natural setting, a store, a restaurant, a laundromat, a library, a sports area, a transportation depot, or even your writing classroom. Draw the sense star on a page. Choose a sense you tend to ignore. First, collect images for that sense. Then record other images that occur to you for that or any other sense. Use more paper if you need to. Here are some places and activities that may stimulate the three senses people tend to ignore:

      Smell: Place yourself in a busy bar or restaurant, garden, bus depot, or hospital, or by a river or lake.

      Hearing: Sit where you can eavesdrop on conversations and write or record exactly what you hear, including nonhuman sounds. Or describe the sounds in a nightclub, at a ballgame, in a library, or in your car as you drive.

      Body Sensations: Moving at a tenth of your usual speed, tie or untie your shoes, brush your teeth, or comb your hair. Record what it feels like to lift a particular weight, hit a tennis ball, take a ride in an amusement park, or knead dough.

   b. Freewrite in your journal about the experience. What did you notice that you hadn't noticed before? How does focusing on your senses and looking for images affect what you actually experience? What lesson can you learn from this Exploration about finding what you need?

   c. Write an essay about your chosen place or activity, focusing on some human interest as Ben did. Give your reader a you-are-there experience.

3. **a.** *Solo.* Write two sets of directions from school to your home for the purpose of directing your choice of two different audiences: a child, a physically or perceptually disabled adult without a car, a teenager with a car, a trucker, a helicopter pilot.

    b. *Together.* Read and discuss your descriptions with each other. Use the following suggestions and questions:

- Point out sense cues that the writer offers.
- To which senses does the writer appeal?
- Which sense does the writer favor?
- Compare and contrast directions offered to different audiences.
- Are the directions tailored to the needs of the chosen audiences?
- Take the point of view of these audiences and ask questions to help clarify the routes.

    c. *Solo.* On your way home, stop to observe your route closely and make notes. When you were looking for cues, what did you notice that you had forgotten or not noticed before? What did you learn about your perceptions from consciously observing your route home? Revise your first draft, or write new directions using as many sense impressions as you can.

    Variation: Write a route to a certain place using only one sense (e.g., a smell route or a touch route).

4. **a.** *Together.* Each person is to bring a piece of the *same kind of fruit* to class, such as an apple, strawberry, or peach (preferably fruit that is in season). After taking a close look at your piece, place it on a table with all the others so that you can get a sense of the relative sizes, colors, shapes, textures, and markings of the fruit. Then retrieve yours.

    b. *Solo.* Write a description of your own piece of fruit in as much detail as possible so that you can distinguish it from all the others. Without actually eating the fruit at this point, call on as many of your senses as you can. Include any stories and memories that occur to you. Be imaginative. Name your fruit. Imagine a life for it.

    c. *Together.* Have someone collect all the pieces of fruit, place them on a table, and assign each piece a number, written on a slip of paper. Exchange your written description with someone who didn't identify your piece of fruit as yours. Identify the number of the fruit that you believe fits the description written by your partner.

    d. *Together.* Discuss which descriptions worked and why, and which didn't and why. List what you learned about yourself, writing, others' perceptions, and fruit.

5. **a.** *Solo.* Either in class or at home, decide to spend at least a half hour eating some of your favorite food. (If you do Exploration 4, you may want to eat the fruit you all brought.) As you eat, record all the sensations, emotions, and ideas that occur to you. Try to include all six senses. When you are done, freewrite for ten minutes about what the experience taught you about the food, ways of eating, yourself, and writing. What memories did the food stimulate?

   b. *Solo.* Create an essay, story, or poem inspired by your favorite food.

   c. *Together.* Share your drafts.

Showing and Telling

Anton Chekhov, one of the world's greatest playwrights, once said, "If you bring a cannon onstage, you have to fire it." In early drafts, you might find yourself *telling* your readers about your subject instead of *showing* them your subject. The benefits of telling your reader about your subject are these:

- Telling helps you to clarify your feelings and attitudes.
- Telling helps to focus your reader on your point of view.

But when all you do is tell about your subject, you ask your reader to read your mind and do the work of filling in the details for you. This is a sure way to bore your reader and to find yourself misunderstood. You also bore yourself and hurt your writing, because you are just stating what you already know and feel. This is like bringing a cannon on stage and letting it rust.

Instead of just telling you about the difference between showing and telling, I'm going to show you the first draft of a student paper that does more telling than showing. Read student Jen Levine's first draft:

First draft

   A fear that I would like to over come is my fear of spiders. My fear of spiders is severe because the sight of a spider causes me to flee the area where the spider is. A way that I can overcome my fear is to expose myself to spiders. I can do this by gradually working my way up to becoming able to handle a live spider. This gradual exposure is a way to cure myself of the fear of spiders. It takes a lot of courage to face my fear. However, I should give

```
it a try because the fear is a nuisance. It would be a relief when
and if my fear of spiders becomes destroyed.
```

Jen's peers noticed that she was merely repeating herself, saying over and over that she would like to get rid of her fear of spiders. They also had questions:

- "What makes spiders so scary for you?"
- "What happens to you when you see a spider?"
- "How does your fear show up in your life?"
- "Exactly how would you cure yourself of the fear?"

Students noticed as well that Jen did not use any specific sensory details, a strategy that would be very effective in writing about spiders.

Jen focused her work by first recognizing statements that merely told instead of showed:

```
My fear of spiders is severe because the sight of a spider
causes me to flee the area where the spider is.
```

```
A way that I can overcome my fear is to expose myself to
spiders. I can do this by gradually working my way up to becoming
able to handle a live spider.
```

In the first statement, she *tells* that her fear is severe, but she does not *show* us what makes spiders frightful. She does not *show* us how severe her avoidance is. In the second and third statements, Jen *tells* us that exposing herself to spiders would help her overcome her fear, but she doesn't *show* us how she would do it and how it would help her to overcome her fear.

Jen referred to the sense star and illustrated her statements with specific sensory images. Here is Jen's third draft, revised with special attention to sense appeal:

Third draft

```
    A fear that I would like to over come is arachnaphobia.
Arachnaphobia is the fear of spiders. My fear of spiders is severe
because the sight of an atrocious, eight-legged spider gazing at
me with it's devilish ruby eyes, screams at me to flee the webbed
territory as if the spider was ten times bigger and towering over
me. In response, I dash away from the creature. Whenever I
encounter a spider I become very tense and nervous, my heart pumps
a ''hundred beats per second.'' Sometimes I think I see a spider
```

when there isn't one. For example, When I sat at the T.V. and saw a small black dot on the screen, I involuntarily dashed away from the T.V. This example demonstrates the severity of my fear. Another example of when I demonstrate fear is when there is a spider nesting in my bedroom: I cannot sleep unless someone squishes the remains of the venom-sucking predator.

A way that I can overcome arachnaphobia is to expose myself to spiders. I can do this by gradually working my way up to becoming brave enough to handle a live spider. I would begin by looking at pictures of all types of spiders: black spiny ones, poisonous red spiders with bulging abdomens, and charcoal gray spiders with long dental floss legs. I can also cut out pictures of spiders and display them around my room. I would do this until I felt I could handle observing a decayed spider. While observing, I would have to relax my body. The next step would be to closely observe a live spider by capturing one in a small jar. This is not an easy step. By exposing myself to a live spider, first I would place it on a table and gradually walk up to the jar and hold it until I felt relaxed. The last step would be to touch the hairy, spindle-legged spider with my bare hands.

This gradual exposure is a way to cure myself of the fear of spiders. It takes alot of courage to face my fear. However, I should give it a try because the fear is a nuisance, and I have been faced with the fear ever since I can remember. It would be a relief when and if my fear of spiders becomes destroyed.

Not only did Jen's later draft interest her readers much more, but writing it helped her to better face her fear of spiders. By writing about spiders, she was literally pinning her fear to the page. *Telling* only superficially engages you and your reader. *Showing*—focusing with sense images—engages and empowers everyone.

*R*eflections ⸻

1. Underline the sensory images in Jen's third draft.

2. Which senses does Jen favor?

3. Are there any questions that Jen has left unanswered?

4. What more could Jen write to show you about her fear of spiders?

Showing and Telling

To recognize the difference between showing and telling, ask these questions of your own and others' writing:

1. How many sense details are offered? (Sense details tend to *show.*)

2. Which words and expressions carry evaluations and preferences? (Evaluations and preferences tend to *tell.*)

3. Does the writer make any claims without illustrating them? (That is, does the writer tell and not show?)

4. Will readers know what is meant without having observed what the writer observed?

5. Are any of the sense details irrelevant?

*E*xplorations _____

1. *Together.* Consider the following pairs of statements. Which of each pair tells more than shows? Which of each pair shows the reader what the writer has in mind? To which senses is the writer appealing in the "show" statement?

   Pair A

   Nursing homes are sometimes run by people who care only about money, not their clients' comfort.

   The cafeteria in Shady Rest Nursing Home reeked of urine and disinfectant.

   Pair B

   Twenty-five people linked arms in front of "Girls, Girls, Girls" to bar businessmen in gray suits from entering the nude show.

   Lots of people dislike nude shows.

   Pair C

   My roommate is a terror.

   Old styrofoam cups with moldy food in them, socks that trip me like puppies, weird music squealing from his headset at night, and magazines with leather and chains in them—my roommate is a terror.

   Pair D

   There is nothing worse than taking a class you don't want to take, with a teacher you can't understand, in a subject area that has nothing to do with your major.

I took the last open gym class, Fencing, with Mr. Zsolt, who sounded like Count Dracula and made me wonder what pushing a sword in someone's face had to do with studying nursing, my major.

2. *Solo.* Describe a person who is important to you for some reason—pleasant or unpleasant. Be clear as to why this person is important to you. Show your reader why you feel as you do. Let your reader experience this person in detail, using as many senses as seem appropriate to support your point of view.

3. **a** *Together.* Read papers in progress to each other. Point out statements that, like rusty cannons, tell without delivering. Suggest ways in which the writer can show the reader what's happening by using sensory images.

   b. *Solo.* Revise your paper to show more of what you mean. Use the sense star in Figure 6.1 to encourage yourself to use sensory images.

Subjective and Objective Modes

To focus your writing and your reader's experience of it, you have to discover and relate what your subject means to you. In other words, you have to *make sense* of your subject:

- Why is it important?
- How do you feel about it?
- What questions do you have about it?
- How do you evaluate it?
- What do you need to do with it?

The answers to these questions reveal your *subjective* attitude toward your topic.

Recognize that you will tend to choose images that reflect your purpose, attitudes, ideas, intuitions, and experiences; the audience you anticipate; and your emotional states—in short, you will reveal your point of view. Unless you consciously strive to take another point of view, you will tend to ignore images that don't reflect your current point of view.

For example, think of a red rose. Most people think of it as a symbol of love. If you limit yourself to the popular point of view, you won't notice that it can mean many more things. You can look at the same red rose and have many different reactions at the same time. You may feel despair because the rose reminds you of the funeral of a loved one. You may feel proud because you grew the rose from a bush you revived. You might be fascinated by the pattern of the rose's petals as you analyze it for a botany class.

The writing process gives you an opportunity to become aware of many points of view and to sort out what each means to you. It also gives you an opportunity to recognize other points of view. Learning how to take other points of view can help you grow as a person and thinker.

Your point of view may be relatively subjective or objective. An *objective* collection of sensory images is meant to avoid biases and prejudices. Objective statements are often used to illustrate and support subjective statements. Notice the differences between these three descriptions that education major Amy M. Puzzo wrote about a high school class she observed:

> *Objective:* The students were calling out answers to the teacher's questions as soon as she asked them. Many students answered without raising their hands. The teacher did not pause but proceeded from one question to the next as soon as the correct answer was given.
>
> *Subjective (positive):* The students were eager to respond to the teacher. They obviously wanted to please her. Many of them were so eager that they answered without raising their hands. The lesson was energizing.
>
> *Subjective (negative):* The students in this class were anxious about their grades. They competed for the teacher's attention and competitively cut each other off. It was a tense class.

The relatively objective description avoids emotional and evaluative terms such as *eager, please, energizing, anxious, competitively, cut each other off,* and *tense.* The objective description focuses on describing events that anyone would agree upon, no matter what attitude, feelings, biases, or prejudices the person may bring to a situation.

However, it is possible to write descriptions that *seem* objective but that leave out important details that the writers either don't recognize or don't want to recognize because of their particular attitudes or biases. For example, the following two descriptions may *seem* objective—others would see the same details—but they show a biased attitude:

The sky was filled with bright flashes of lights against a red sky.

The bombs were bursting over the burning city.

Both of these sentences seem to objectively describe events, and most viewers on the scene would agree that both descriptions are accurate.

However, the first description, if taken alone, shows the bias of someone who may be glad that a city is being bombed. The details the writer chooses sound much like the details that someone would choose during a beautiful fireworks display at sunset. The second description, if taken alone, is more likely to be made by someone who mourns the events. The details focus on violence and destruction. Your choice of images determines the relative objectivity or subjectivity of what you write as much as your choice of words does.

Here are some relatively objective and subjective statements:

Objective	Subjective
The bus went 60 mph.	The reckless driver pushed the school bus to go 60 mph on the dirt road.
The governor wrote the budget.	The governor slashed public programs to cut taxes and please the voters.
Only women bear children.	Women are the best caretakers of children.

Neither objectivity nor subjectivity is, in itself, better than the other. A subjective statement may, in the long run, be far more accurate and true than a seemingly objective one. An objective statement may take things out of context and miss the larger scope of what is being described. It is important to describe situations objectively, in ways that others can also perceive them. However, much can be said for the subjective hunch, felt sense, gut feeling, or intuition that often precedes and inspires breakthroughs in human endeavors. The more you develop your senses, the more accurate your intuition will become and the more fully you will be able to support your subjective reactions with objective observations.

Using the Reflections suggestions listed below, compare the following two starts of student Leslie Cox's paper on the homeless:

First draft

There are three homeless individuals who sleep in the train station depot in our town. One is a man with long gray hair and a beard who smokes cigarettes. Another is a lady who pushes a Big Deal shopping cart. Then there's a tall skinny man who talks to himself and walks back and forth on the platform all day. Something has to be done to offer them a decent place to live. They are causing problems in the station.

Second Draft

> No one seems to care about the three homeless individuals who
> sleep in the train station depot in our town. One of them is a
> gentle man who looks a lot like Santa Claus with long gray hair
> and a white beard. He looks so lonely sitting on the bench, looking
> at all the children who go by. I tried to talk to him once, but I
> got scared. He started to talk in a language I didn't understand.
> Then he reached his hand out to me. I felt like screaming and crying
> at the same time. I didn't know what to do. He looked into my eyes.
> Then he just slid away on the bench and walked to the next one. I
> felt terrible.

*R*eflections

1. As a whole, which draft is relatively more objective? Which is more subjective? Why?

2. Which draft do you prefer? Why?

3. Consider the first draft. Point to specific words, phrases, and sentences that are relatively more objective. Point to portions that are relatively more subjective.

4. Consider the second draft, using instructions in Reflection 3.

5. What purposes and audiences would best be addressed by the first draft? The second draft? Why?

Finding Meaning and Purpose

Unless your readers find meaning and purpose in what you write, you will not engage them. Read the following paragraphs from Michael's* first freewrite about his basement:

First draft

> The basement has two sections that form the letter T and my
> desk is in the inside corner of this shape. The section I'm in is
> about thirty feet long by twenty feet wide and is the newer of the
> two, it is about fifteen years old. As I scan the section I'm in,

---

*Michael, a student writer, preferred that his last name be withheld.

I see the wood-burning stove along the same wall in the far corner that we use in the winter to keep the heating cost down. The basement is unfinished so the floor is concrete and not painted. In the middle of the floor there is a pile of masonary red bricks, that are to be used around the wood stove for decoration.

As I walk in this section of the basement, I can tell this side is much older. This section is about sixty years old and you can tell because the beams in the ceiling are a dark brown in color and the pipes that run along the ceiling are also dark in color. I smell soap and detergent which comes from the washer and dryer at the north end to my left.

If you are like other readers, you may wonder what the point of Michael's description is. Although he does provide sensory details, they are almost purely objective: his description lacks enough human interest. Now read the last paragraph of his five-page first draft:

This room is only about twenty feet wide and ten feet deep and always cool never getting any warmer than about seventy-five degrees. I think it was used as a coal cellar, to hold the coal before you used it in the old coal stoves. The room has no windows and the walls and floor are a flat dark gray brick color, which reflects almost no light. There is no light switch on the wall when you walk in, you have to go to the center of the room and reach up and tighten the light bulb in the socket. There is almost no light and you can't see anything. As my brother and I were growing up, we would avoid this room at all costs. If my brother came down the stairs and saw the door open, he would run up to the door and kick it closed. He would swear to have nightmares if the door was left open. I bet my parents hid our Christmas presents in that room because they knew we would never look in there. Even though the basement is dark and cool it is still very quiet and peaceful, and easy to work here.

In this paragraph, Michael introduces *human interest*. He tells us what the basement has meant to him and his brother. We learn how he experiences the basement, so that we become more engaged in his life, his point of view, and his writing about it. We learn to experience the world with him, as he does.

In his second draft, Michael refocused his description by starting with the end of his last first draft paragraph:

Second draft

The Basement

When my brother and I were growing up, we spent every rainy day in the basement playing. My brother and I are only two years apart with me being the oldest. Our mother would tell us to play in the basement when it rained. With all the questions and noise, the two of us probably drove my mother crazy. My brother and I never really minded playing in the basement, because all of our toys and games were down there. But there was one room of the basement that terrified us.

As I walk into that section of the basement today, I can tell this side is much older. This section is about sixty years old and you can tell because the beams in the ceiling are a dark brown in color and the pipes that run along the ceiling are also dark in color. This section of the basement is dark and dungeon like because the ceiling is low, and the floor is painted a dark gray. All of this, combined with the fact that it's poorly lit, makes it look like a dungeon. Around the edges of the basement are tables that have old clothes on them. At the end of the basement opposite the door to the outside and to my right is another door that looks like it could have come from an old horror movie. This door is painted dark gray and squeaks loudly when you open or close it. This door is also in the most poorly lit part of the basement.

This room is only about twenty feet wide and ten feet deep and always cool, never getting any warmer than about seventy-five degrees. I think it was used as a coal cellar, to store the coal before you used it in the old coal stoves. The room has no windows and the walls and floor are a flat dark gray color, which reflects almost no light. There is no light switch on the wall. When you walk into the room, you have to go to the center of the room and reach up and tighten the light bulb in the socket. The basement is poorly lit. When you enter the room there is almost no light and you can't see anything. The room is full of shelves and the shelves are full of electrical tools like drills, sanders, and circular saws.

Once we got to an age where we were allowed to watch horror movies, my brother and I started to see the resemblance between the two. We were probably about eight or nine years old when we stopped playing with the toys in the basement. I think not being in the basement a lot made the back room even more scary. When we came down the stairs and turned the corner, the first thing we would see is ''the door.'' This room became off limits to us, by our own choice. My brother and I would avoid this room at all costs.

If my brother came down the stairs and saw the door open, he would run up to the door and kick it closed. There was no way my brother would spend one second in the basement if the door was left open. He would also swear that he would have nightmares if the door was left open overnight. I would run past the room and try not to look at the door when I went by. I would never look in this room even if the door was left open. My parents probably hid our Christmas presents in this room, because they knew we would never look in there.

I started feeling more comfortable in the basement when I bought my weight lifting equipment, at about age thirteen. It was then that the basement became a place to be alone, and work out in peace. Now it's a place where I can work without being disturbed and in total quiet. In the summer it's always the coolest place in the house, and a relief to be there. In the winter, the basement becomes hard to work in because the dry heat from the wood-burning stove is very relaxing. The occasional crackling of a log burning can put me to sleep in minutes if I'm not keeping busy. It may be torture to some. To me it is the only way I can totally relax and concentrate on my work.

*R*eflections

1. What does Michael's basement mean to him?

2. Which statement serves as a key or thesis statement in his essay?

3. Which sensory details show the reader what the basement meant and means to Michael?

4. Are there any details that aren't relevant to Michael's main purpose, to show us what the basement means?

5. How could Michael improve his essay?

You can find your meaning and purpose in writing by either of these approaches:

1. *Explorer's approach:* Collect your sensory images and notice what you choose. Discover what these images mean to you, in the process. Then you can start your next draft with a thesis statement that embodies your subjective mood, attitude, or meaning.

2. *Planner's approach:* Write a thesis statement about how you already feel, and collect sensory images that illustrate your statement.

Michael originally used an explorer's approach by collecting images until his meaning emerged at the end of his first freewrite. He then used a planner's approach and started his next draft by stating what his basement meant to him and his brother.

Ben did not directly state what the gym meant to him. He took an explorer's approach throughout. He showed us his attitude by carefully choosing negative or suspenseful images. By introducing the subject of steroids, he showed his readers one of the reasons it was important for him to visit the gym that day and what it meant to him.

Here are some examples of thesis statements that embody the writers' meaning and purpose. Notice that sometimes more than one sentence is needed:

> My favorite place in the universe is a small cave I found near my house when I was four years old.
>
> —*Jackson Joyce, Student*

> A great majority of our nine million college students are not in school because they want to be or because they want to learn. They are there because it has become the thing to do or because college is a pleasant place to be.
>
> —*From "College Is a Waste of Time and Money" by Caroline Bird, Writer*

> All shrews are particularly difficult to keep.
>
> —*From "The Taming of the Shrew" by Konrad Z. Lorenz, Scientist*

> I don't know what I would do if I didn't have my car. It's better to me than any friend.
>
> —*Guy Percy, Student*

> My grandfather owned this watch. Every time I hold it, I think of all the good times we had.
>
> —*Marion Kowalski, Student*

*E*xplorations

1. *Together.* Compare the following sets of statements. Decide which statement in each set is relatively more objective or subjective.

Focusing Your Senses

1. *Choose your subject.* To focus your mind, be sure to choose and design situations that will help you to keep focused on your subject. (Review suggestions for collecting sensory images.)

2. *Clear your mind.* To focus your senses, clear your mind of static. Sit comfortably and focus your eyes on a spot in front of you. Take a deep breath. Without moving, notice three sights, then three sounds, then three body sensations. Notice how your breathing changes and if some tensions release. Then notice two more sights, sounds, and body sensations. Then notice one more sight, sound, and body sensation. Close your eyes for a few minutes. Return to your project by opening your eyes and stretching. Be receptive.

3. *State or show your meaning and purpose.* If you *state* your meaning and purpose, use either the explorer's or the planner's approach to formulate a subjective statement of what your topic means to you. If you *show* your meaning and purpose, choose your images carefully so that your readers will know exactly what your subject means to you. Develop and maintain a mood.

4. *Develop human interest.* Whenever possible, include human interactions in your descriptions so that your readers can identify with what is happening.

Which subjective statements are more positive or more negative? Which statements could serve as thesis statements? Which statements could serve as illustrations of the thesis statements?

a. Winter is the cruelest time of year.
    In New England, snow can fall from October to April.
    Other people may dislike winter, but for me it is a wonderland for sports and parties.

b. His lips quivered and his upper lip sweat.
    The president looked agitated and guilty.
    His speech was full of passion and sensitivity.

c. MacEnroe wound up his racket and fired a bomb.
    Once again, John was slamming at the ball.
    The serve was clocked at 120 mph.

d. The police nearly bludgeoned the man to death.
    The police restrained the perpetrator.
    The police hit the man with a club.

2. *Together.* Consider the following collections of images. For each, name the feeling, mood, or attitude of the writer who collected these images.

Write a subjective thesis statement that the writer could use to show the meaning and purpose in the images.

a. This baby never stops screaming, crying, whining, demanding. Then there are all those smells, mostly from the diaper, but also the spit up. And you never saw such squirming in your life. He's always snatching at everything, breaking dishes, crawling around things, kicking people, and yanking off their jewelry.

b. Black tubes hang from the wall of the auto repair shop. They look like elephant trunks. Next to them are hammers, wrenches, and screwdrivers carefully arranged like trophies. In the corner is the old dog, grease on his paws and muzzle, always sleeping. In the background, the radio is usually mumbling. With all the clanking and drilling and all the engines growling or screaming, it's hard to make out any music.

c. This ring is nearly 150 years old. The band is 18-karat gold with filigree carvings. The diamond in the center is round and multifaceted. Exquisite ruby chips surround it. It was made for my great-great-great grandmother's wedding.

d. First I get to the parking lot about ten minutes before my class and choose a particular aisle. I stop my car and wait. The trick is to look at people coming toward the lot. If they look like they're trying to see their car, get ready. Notice the direction their bodies are turned to as they walk. But don't be fooled. Unless they start fumbling for their keys in their pockets or have them in their hands, they're probably just going to the next building. The worst, of course, is when you are all set to take a space and the person is just getting something from the car.

3. a. *Solo.* Write a description of a child you know well. Write it from one of the following points of view:

   - A loving grandparent
   - A stressed parent
   - The child itself
   - An artist
   - A jealous sibling
   - A dentist
   - Your special relationship (e.g., as a neighbor)

   Be sure to relate your subjective experience of the child. Write a thesis statement and/or relate your feelings with images that clearly carry your attitude. Enliven your description by appealing to all the senses. In addition, relate how the child talks, and quote him or her.

   b. *Solo.* Write another description of the child, using a different point of view.

    c. *Together.* Read and compare your pairs of descriptions.

- What does the child mean to the writer in each description?
- How does the writer relate these subjective attitudes?
- Which senses are favored in the descriptions?
- How do the selections of sensory images relate the writers' points of view?
- How could the writer revise these descriptions to more fully reflect the intended meaning?

Variations. Do Exploration 3 using either of the following subjects:

a. Write about a pet or a neighborhood animal.

b. Write about a television or movie personality.

4. a. *Together.* Bring papers in progress to class. Read each aloud. Help each other discern what the subject means to the writer. Ask questions such as these:

- "Why did you write about this?"
- "What does it mean to you?"
- "Who else is or was involved in this with you?"
- "What interests you most about this subject?"
- "What are your attitudes, feelings, and opinions on this subject?"

Help each other formulate some subjective thesis statements for each paper.

b. *Solo.* Revise your paper with a clear focus on what your subject means to you. Choose and create more sensory images that will clearly relay your attitude to your readers.

Organizing Sensations

So far in this chapter, you have explored how to collect, focus, and find meaning and purpose through your senses. In order to keep your readers' interest and to most effectively present your observations, you will have to organize and develop your work. Notice the difference between James Wong's two descriptions of his roommate:

First draft

<u>My Room . . . mate</u>

    I am in my dorm room. The room is square, white, and made of cinder blocks. There are two closets. The floor is made of

linoleum. There is a bathroom that we share with another room.
There are two windows. The room used to be tidy. That was before
my roommate settled in. My roommate is a sloven. He infested our
room with his junk. He possesses some basic characteristics one
would expect from a college roommate, such as laziness and
untidiness. He is a chemistry major. His father owns an automobile
shop. His mother sends him food. He also has some of the most
unusual bad habits I have encountered.

In this first draft, James focused on how his roommate treated their
living quarters. Early on, he clearly states his attitude and collects images
to show what he means. But James jumps from one idea to another, one
sense to another, and one area to another. Although his peers found his
essay humorous and engaging, they also found it somewhat hectic to read.
So, James decided to reorganize his description:

Second draft

<u>My Room . . . mate</u>

I am in my dorm room. The room is square, white, and used to be
tidy. That was before my roommate settled in. My roommate is a
sloven. He infested our room with his junk. He possesses some
basic characteristics one would expect from a college roommate,
such as laziness and untidiness. He also has some of the most
unusual bad habits I have encountered.

We shall start with his laziness. He seldom washes his
laundry, so you can imagine the exquisite foul smell of his
clothes, especially his socks. They smell like rotten eggs even
if I'm ten feet away from them. Pheew! Thus, even if he does wash
his clothes, he never irons his shirts until the day he has to wear
them. He just puts most of them on the chairs.

As for untidiness, his clothing is all over the place. I almost
can't walk anywhere without stepping on them, since they're all
over the floor. Luckily, I still have my bed and desk or else I
wouldn't be able to sit. My roommate is very sloppy and dirty. His
desk is the perfect breeding ground for insects and rodents. Some
of the items he has on his desk are empty soda cans and uncapped
juice bottles, a bottle of uncapped ammonia, some disseminated
notebooks, and dining leftovers. He also leaves behind a trail
of food crumbs everywhere on the floor. Oh, I forgot to mention
that our room currently smells like ammonia. On the chairs and

dressers (his and mine), he has his ironing board, sweat pants, towel, notebooks, bodybuilding magazines, and garbage.

Some of the bad habits my roommate possesses are that he enjoys sleeping with his shoes on and has a tendency to keep bottle caps in his pocket. Other bad habits of his are that, in the bathroom, he leaves his razor and shaving gel on the shower floor or in the soap dish. Someone is going to slip and get hurt one of these days. He also uses everyone's soap and shampoo when he showers.

Whenever I get back to my room, I feel like I just entered the city dump. That's what our room looks like. If I tidied the place today, tomorrow it would turn into a dump again. I think nobody can get a worse roommate than mine.

Reflections ————————————————————

1. Point to specific transitions in James's first draft that seem illogical or abrupt.

2. How did James reorganize his paper for his second draft?

3. Mark the sensory details in James's second draft.

4. How did reorganizing help James find more sensory details to include in his description?

5. Could James reorganize or expand his essay? If so, how? If not, why not?

Just as you can take either an explorer's or a planner's approach to focusing, so, too, you can take either approach to organizing:

1. *Explorer's approach:* Collect your sensory images and notice how you are starting to organize them. Then you can decide on a strategy for organizing and revising. As you revise, you will collect more images to fill in the skeleton structure that your strategy provides.

2. *Planner's approach:* Decide on a strategy for organizing your paper. Write a thesis stating how you already feel. Collect sensory images to fill in the skeleton structure your strategy provides.

As always, strive to be flexible. You might write your first draft using a planner's approach, only to decide that you want to loosen up with a freewrite. As you freewrite, you might find another strategy that will be more effective for organizing your observations.

After reading the suggestions for "How to Organize Sensations" in the sidebar, do some of the Explorations that follow.

How to Organize Sensations

1. **Start and end** your work with the most interesting images that will engage your audience and fulfill your purpose, and/or start and end your work by stating what your subject means to you. State your attitude, feeling, or purpose. Use human interest.

2. **Shape** your description of the object, place, person, or event to best orient your reader and relate your sensations. When appropriate, tell your reader which strategy you are using. Use one of the following strategies:

   Thesis and Support. Make a claim about your subject and support it with sensory detail. If you make *additional* specific claims about your subject, support these claims as well, preferably one at a time.

   Spatial. Use *one* of these strategies: top to bottom *or* bottom to top; left to right *or* right to left; one corner to the other; clockwise *or* counterclockwise; here (where you are) and there.

   You-are-there. Give your readers a you-are-there feeling by leading them through an experience as it happens.

   Before and After. Describe your subject as it was before and after a significant event.

   Senses. Describe your subject by appealing to one kind of sensation. Then describe it again using another sense.

   Chronological. Relate an experience as it happens or happened in time.

   Comparison or Contrast. Compare or contrast your subjects by describing one completely and then the other. Or compare or contrast your subjects by zig zagging between them on each point of comparison or contrast.

*E*xplorations

1. **a.** *Together and Solo.* Describe the drawing of the women in Figure 5.2 for a reader who hasn't seen it. Choose an organizing strategy that will help engage your reader and accurately describe what is happening and how it feels to you.

   b. *Together.* Read your descriptions aloud. For each paper, notice:

   - The organizing strategy.
   - Which sensory details were included or ignored.
   - How the writer felt about the picture.
   - How aware the writer was of the reader.

Point to particular words, phrases, and sentences in your responses.

2. **a.** *Solo.* Choose an interesting and unusual object. List sense images about it, *or* freewrite your observations. Discover what the object means to you. Choose an organizing strategy and describe the object in writing. Use as many sense details as you can. Engage your readers' interest with sense appeal, so that they will want to own such an object as well.

   b. *Together.* Bring your descriptions to class. Bring your objects in a *closed bag or box.* Read the descriptions to each other in small groups. Then reveal your object. Discuss details that might have been included in the written descriptions to better engage readers. Were the organizing strategies effective?

3. **a.** *Solo.* Describe a person or a relationship between two persons. Be clear about your feelings and point of view. Show us the person(s) in action and use quotes. Focus on sense appeal. Organize your essay so as to engage your readers.

4. **a.** *Solo.* Choose an event or activity in which you plan to participate in the next few days, such as a particular concert, sport, theater event, dance, or hobby. Referring to the sense star in Figure 6.1, take careful notes either during or soon after the event. Freewrite about the event to explore what it means to you. Choose an organizing strategy. Write a description of the event or activity, using sense appeal.

   b. *Together.* Read your descriptions to each other. Point to your favorite words, phrases, and sentences. Discuss the organizing strategy. Ask questions to help the writer revise.

Comparisons and Clichés

How do you describe the taste of coffee to someone who has never tasted it, or the colors in a sunset to someone who has always been blind? How do you describe a pain to the doctor who could never feel your pain? How do you describe a knock in your engine to the mechanic when your car just won't do it when you're at the service station? The best way is to compare what you experience to something that someone else can experience too. Drawing comparisons enlivens your writing and engages your reader.

Read student Lydia Gordon's description of a trip to a hamburger restaurant. Notice how she uses comparisons to relate and enliven her experiences for her reader:

Never Again

Going to Burger Barn was a disgusting experience for me. As soon as my sister April and I walked to the door, the smell attacked us. It smelled like an old underground subway station that hadn't been cleaned for years. I wanted to turn around and get out, but my sister grabbed me by the arm and insisted that I stay until she ordered.

As I waited, I looked around at my surroundings and felt my nose and lips curl as if someone were shoving cod liver oil at me. It was terrible. There was a length of toilet tissue curled on the floor like a snake that had been wrestled to death by a hungry lion. The floor itself was supposed to be white (as it was under one of the tables) but instead it was yellowed like a set of rotting teeth. Ketchup was smeared on the walls as if someone had tried to wipe his or her hands on it. There was dirt and tartar sauce on the tables that reminded me of soap scum in a polluted pond. I don't know how April could have put up with the smell, either. I think she was too hungry to care.

When we entered, I had also been struck by the noise inside. People around us were either arguing amongst themselves or with the cashier. The phone was ringing and babies were crying.

April received her order and sat next to me. I told her, ''It took long enough.'' She took the burger out of the box and felt it. She asked me to touch it. It was soggy and felt like the grease was stuck to the bread making it look like pink dough. She wanted a refund, but I wouldn't let her get it. I didn't want to spend another moment in there.

April finally tasted it. From the expression on her face I knew it wasn't good. I laughed and asked her for a bite. I spit it back into the plate. It tasted like the dog food I once tried on a dare. It was half cooked, the meat still red, the grease oozing out, and it stuck to my hands. I lost my appetite. Burger Barn is a great place to start a weight loss program.

*R*eflections _____

1. What is Lydia's main purpose in writing the paper? What mood is she trying to create? How does she communicate this?

2. To what senses does Lydia tend to appeal? Point to particular images in Lydia's paper.

3. Are there any parts of "Never Again" that could be expanded to appeal to the senses that Lydia doesn't emphasize?

4. Underline portions of Lydia's paper where she uses comparisons to communicate her experiences. Are they fresh and new, or have you heard them before?

5. Are there any questions and suggestions you would offer Lydia if she were to revise "Never Again"?

Many comparisons—such as "white as snow"—have lost their zest because they have been overused. Overused expressions are called *clichés* after the sound made by a stereotyper (a printing machine) as it moves monotonously back and forth: *cliché, cliché, cliché*. Because they are too general, clichés do not help you either to develop your senses or to communicate your purpose to your audience. Clichés may feel safe and familiar: "Everybody knows what I'm saying." But clichés suggest lazy thinking by the person using them. Thoughtful listeners and readers lose respect for someone who relies on clichés.

Take, for example, "white as snow." Snow can take on many shades of color from blinding white to slush brown. Because most people have heard it before, the expression is an invitation for them to tune out. Compare "white as snow" with "white as a drift of new snow against a red barn." The contrast of the snow against the specific red barn focuses the mind and offers something you can imagine. Or consider the phrase

---

Reading for Sense Appeal

When you review a piece of writing for sense appeal, ask these questions:

1. What is the meaning and purpose of this piece?
2. To which senses does this writing appeal? (Point to specific words, phrases, and sentences.)
3. To which senses does this writing *not* appeal? Would it improve the paper to add more sense appeal?
4. Does the writer tell too much without showing?
5. Is the writer relatively more subjective or objective?
6. Does the writer enliven the work with fresh, new comparisons?

Whenever possible, with someone else observe the subject you are trying to describe. Another point of view may help you become aware of images that you take for granted.

"white as the skull of a dead vampire." The comparison is startling and humorous, so it forces you to form a picture in your mind. By either giving more details or forming fresh, new comparisons, you enliven your mind, engage your readers, and communicate your purpose.

In Chapter 13, you will have opportunities to write extended essays in which you compare and contrast. Here are some Explorations to help you start enlivening your work with fresh, new comparisons.

Explorations

1. *Solo or Together.* For the next week, collect at least twenty-five comparisons from what you read or hear. Note that comparisons are often signaled by words and expressions such as *like, as, reminds me of,* and *as if.* Country and rock songs are especially filled with them. Bring these lists to class and consider which comparisons offer vivid, new images and which are overused and clichéd.

2. **a.** *Together.* Add some overused expressions to the following list of clichéd comparisons that refer to qualities. Use adjectives and nouns.

Smooth as silk	Cold as ice
Quick as a wink	Stiff as a board
Green as grass	Quiet as a mouse

   b. *Solo or Together.* Choose adjectives from the list of clichés you develop and either revive them with specific details or write vivid, new comparisons. As you write, note the kinds of audiences that your comparison would engage, the attribute it could communicate, and the purpose it could satisfy.

3. **a.** *Together.* Add to the following list of clichéd comparisons that refer to activities and experiences:

Work like a dog	Sweat like a pig
Sing like an angel	Run like the devil
Sleep like a baby	Walk like a man
Feel like a wreck	Look like death

   b. *Solo or Together.* Choose verbs from the list of clichés you develop and either revive them with specific details or write vivid, new comparisons.

4. *Together and Solo.* Review for sense appeal some of the essays you are writing. Discuss whether any of your descriptions might be enlivened with comparisons. Revise the essays, incorporating fresh, new comparisons. Identify and replace clichés.

A STUDENT MODEL FOR DISCUSSION

Using the following questions and suggestions, read and reflect on student Debbie Bober's paper, "Meeting Protocol."

*R*eflections _____

Support all your remarks by pointing to specific words, expressions, and other aspects of the paper.

1. What is Debbie's purpose and audience?

2. What is Debbie's point of view and focus?

3. What mood is Debbie trying to convey, and how?

4. Is Debbie relatively more subjective or objective in this paper?

5. Which part of the paper do you find most memorable, and why?

6. Which senses are being appealed to, and how?

7. Which words and expressions bear strong connotations?

8. Does Debbie show enough of the situation?

9. Is the organization of the paper effective? The title? The lead? The body? The ending?

10. Would you offer some questions and suggestions for revising the paper?

11. Write a letter to Debbie discussing the subject and commenting on how her paper was written. Notice your own purpose, point of view, and level of subjectivity or objectivity.

Meeting Protocol

Debbie Bober[12]

Monthly staff meetings are a necessary evil at every company. So one might ask, "Why are they held?" Ostensibly, they create opportunities for departments to communicate and, hopefully, solve problems. But do they really achieve this purpose? Let's take a look at a typical staff meeting and judge for ourselves.

9:15—This is the scheduled start of the meeting but the conference room chairs sit silently in the darkened room awaiting their occupants. The first manager arrives and turns on the lights. Seeing that no one else is there, he drops his pad on the table and heads out back for a cup of coffee. Two more managers arrive with their coffee. As other members stroll in, the usual jokes and innuendos are tossed about the room. They don't even stop when the only female member arrives. Instead, she tosses back a few remarks of her own. The chatter quiets noticeably as the president, a.k.a. "King Cliché," enters the room. Scanning the room, the president notices that Marmack hasn't arrived. He reaches for the phone to have the receptionist page Marmack just as he rushes in and takes his seat.

Let's take a closer look at the seating arrangement. There are no labels on the chairs nor are there assigned seats—yet month after month each manager takes the same seat. The president sits at the head of the rectangular table, his second-in-command sits on his right, and the rest of the managers divide up evenly on either side of the table. No one dares to sit directly across from the president. Could it be that no one has the guts to face him throughout the meeting? A curious note—the president's seat is closest to the door—his escape route if the staff mutinies—not that the idea would ever occur to them. Ah . . . a more creative bunch couldn't be found.

9:30—The president cues Marmack, the manager to his left, to begin. Marmack straightens his glasses, opens his planner, and reads about the various activities being performed by his department. As Marmack drones on, various members can be seen stifling yawns and checking watches. Marmack finishes in less than 15 minutes, yet it feels like an hour.

9:42—The next manager, Mr. Blue, tentatively begins his report. His delivery brings to mind a young child seeking parental approval—always trying hard to please, but never succeeding. Mr. Blue tries, sometimes too hard, to please the president by never saying anything offensive or contrary. As soon as the slightest hint of disagreement is broached by any member, especially the president, Blue's defense mechanisms click into place like a surrounding glass wall.

9:55—The president calls on Mr. Bleak, whose voice carries the message to all present that he is above this, and that he merely tolerates everyone. On technical points, Mr. Bleak deems it necessary to clarify his terminology so Ms. Rebob will understand. Mr. Bleak feels that since Ms. Rebob was born a female she couldn't possibly understand the technical terms he uses. Since Mr. Bleak assumes his intellect is higher than the others', he tempers his words so that all, especially Ms. Rebob, will understand—an annoying habit that Ms. Rebob does not appreciate. Consequently, she does not give her full attention to Bleak's words. During Bleak's dissertation, there's a timid knock on the door. No one moves, even though everyone knows it's Robin with the coffee cart. When the president says, "Why don't we stop here and get some coffee?"—an audible sigh is heard.

10:15—Everyone is once again seated. Mr. Bleak finishes, and "the baton" (one of "King Cliché's" favorite sayings) is passed to Ms. Rebob. Often, Ms. Rebob has little to report on, since her area of responsibilities include the support service departments rather than the product departments. But occasionally, she comes up with something exciting—like the date of the blood drive or the next softball game. Even though Rebob does not add much to the proceedings, her pad is covered with notes—taken to keep her attention focused—and lots of doodles. Things like "smiley faces," linear designs, comments such as, "I'm hungry, I'm thirsty, and I'm bored" are found scattered in the margins of her pad.

10:30—Mr. Stab opens his planner and recites his department's activities. Ms. Rebob shifts in her seat trying to relieve the pressure on her bladder. Mr. Blue can be seen making similar movements. Marmack's eyelids come down and would probably stay down except that Blue kicks him in the leg.

10:38—As the long-winded Mr. Harmony begins, remarks about not being able to get out before lunch are soon heard. Others groan. It all washes over Mr. Harmony. Nothing deters or quickens Harmony's report as he plods along as if no one has said a thing.

11:00—Harmony keeps humming along. Except for the president, it seems Harmony has lost everyone's attention. Rebob continues her doodles and Marmack's lids are once again dropping—another kick administered by Blue.

11:10—Mr. Roberts's opportunity arrives, and as usual he says, "Nothing today." Someone asks about medical insurance, but before Roberts gets a chance to open his mouth, Mr. Big jumps in with the answer. Is it any wonder Roberts never has anything to say when his own boss continually upstages him?

11:15—With the meeting nearing its end, the managers begin to think that maybe they'll get to salvage some of the morning. But first, Mr. Big must give his usual dour news on the budget. The president backs him up with, "We all must tighten our belts."

11:20—Finally, the president runs through a few items and concludes the meeting at 11:30 A.M.

Bleaks leads the way, as everyone heads straight for the bathrooms.

Chapter Review

1. *Solo.* Choose three specific strategies from this chapter that you want to remember, such as using the sense star (Figure 6.1) as a reminder while you write. For each strategy, do the following:

    a. Record the strategy at the top of a page.

    b. Describe the strategy.

    c. Write about why this strategy is important to you. Offer examples from your own writing to show how you have experimented with it.

    d. Using your own words and insights, write advice to a new writer on how to use this strategy.

    e. Wherever it is appropriate, quote directly from *The Flexible Writer.* Acknowledge your source and use proper punctuation.

2. *Together.* Share the results of Chapter Review 1.

Chapter 7

Organizing

This chapter offers opportunities to

—Explore the dynamics of ***organizing***

—Explore strategies for writing ***leads, titles,*** and ***endings***

—Learn when to use ***thesis*** and ***topic*** statements

—Develop the body of your work for ***coherence*** and ***unity***

—Learn how to ***shape*** and to ***outline***

—***Organize*** writing to satisfy different purposes

Good form is whatever keeps the reader
feeling at home.

—*Martin Joos, Writer*

The Dynamics of Organizing

Cartoonist Gary Larson drew a "boneless chicken farm" with chickens draped on stones, fences, and the ground, as if they were rags and not fowl. A chicken without bones is just not a chicken. A human without a skeleton can't survive. A building without beams and girders is just a pile of rubble. So, too, each piece you write needs some *structure* to keep you and your readers focused and secure. You create the structure of what you write by *organizing.*

Applications and other forms are structured to direct you to do specific things such as record your name, list previous jobs, and offer references. How a piece of writing is formed or structured directs your audience in how to read and what to do in response. If a letter of application is well written, for example, it directs your audience to offer you an interview. If the letter is carelessly written, it directs your audience to set your letter aside.

In this book you know when a new chapter is beginning because the words begin lower on the page, there are summaries of what to expect, and there is a quote or two. You come to know that the words *Chapter Review* signal that it's time to stop, reflect, review, and perhaps take a breather from reading. At the end of this book there is an index. You would not read through the index from beginning to end the way you would a chapter. You just dip into it when you want help in finding a certain topic in the book.

Chapter breaks and the index are only two examples of the organizational structures that help establish relationships between you and your topic and you and your readers. Organizing devices steady the flow of ideas and support your learning. This chapter outlines many more strategies that help you organize short as well as long pieces of writing.

Organizing and the Writing Process

Organizing, Focusing, and Coherence

As you focus a piece of writing, you need to develop an organizing principle that you and your audience will experience as *flow.* The technical terms for this flow are *unity* and *coherence.* When a piece of writing has unity, all the parts work together to maintain the focus of the piece. If any details or information were introduced that didn't help maintain the focus, it would be clear that something was irrelevant. When a piece of writing has *coherence,* the *arrangement* "holds together" the whole piece, just as glue adheres two pieces of paper. If any given part were taken out, something would clearly be missing.

Chapters 5 and 6 help you to understand how to create unity in your work. This chapter offers you strategies for developing coherence. You will learn how to begin your writing, structure its body, and create transitions leading to an effective ending.

Organizing and Collecting

When you organize your writing, you may discover that you have not collected enough information or ideas. For example, suppose you were writing about the effects of the Vietnam War on a particular veteran and decided to organize your essay in chronological order. If you were missing information on the year following the veteran's discharge, you would want to interview him about that time. Or suppose you decided to write about your experiences working through an injury and organized your essay to represent the full range of your experience from positive to negative. If you had forgotten to write about negative experiences or had written only about the pain and not the lessons you learned, you would want to collect more experiences to fill the gaps in your structure.

Organizing, Consulting, and Revising

Different readers may notice different patterns in your writing. When you consult with others, note carefully the parts of your essay that confuse or disorient your readers. You may need to reorganize your work or move back to another phase of the writing process. Revise your work with your purpose and audience in mind.

When to Organize

Some writers prefer the planner's style and organize their ideas and information *before* they begin to write. Other writers prefer the explorer's style and freewrite until they notice a plan developing *through* their writing. Most writers combine both styles, sketching a plan, writing, identifying an emerging structure, reorganizing, and so on. You will develop your own strategies for when to organize any given piece of writing.

Leads

Newswriters call introductions "leads." This term reminds us that introductions are meant to *lead* the reader to read on. Effective leads—in any kind of writing—focus the reader's mind as quickly as possible by offering something familiar and something new. Especially in a world where television pictures flicker away in five seconds, you need to find ways to sustain your own and your reader's attention. Effective leads do four things at once: (1) focus; (2) familiarize; (3) interest; and (4) immerse your reader in your writing. In addition, writing effective leads helps you to focus, familiarize, interest, and immerse yourself, as the writer.

Fourteen Strategies for Leads

There are many ways to focus yourself and engage your reader. Here are fourteen of the most-used strategies for doing so. Writers often combine them. To show you how flexible these strategies are, one subject has been chosen to illustrate them.

Leads that familiarize

1. Illustrating.   To familiarize your reader, you can focus on particular examples that illustrate your topic. Here is the lead from Ellen Goodman's article in a 1979 issue of the *Boston Globe*, "Checks on Parental Power." In it, she considers a law that allows parents to put children into mental hospitals:

> First, consider the stories.
> An eleven-year-old retarded boy was brought to a mental hospital with a teddy bear under his arm. His parents were, they said, going on a two-week vacation. They never came back.

In her lead, Goodman offers a clear illustration of the topic of her essay. Similarly, the lead for Chapter 8 of this book, "Consulting," illustrates what a writing community is like. Both give you a "you-are-there" feeling.

2. Imaging.   A picture, a sound, a taste, a smell, a touch, or a movement can give your readers a you-are-there experience that leads them to read on. The image of the boy with a teddy bear under his arm makes a strong impression on Goodman's readers. Student LaDonna Kiley began her paper on child abuse with a strong image:

> My friend Shelly and I heard a moaning, like a cat, coming from the old boarded-up building we found. We thought maybe we could find a kitten to take home. When we found the door where the crying was coming from, we didn't know what we would see. We opened the door. A terrible smell came out, like a bathroom that's never been cleaned. There on the floor was a little child, naked with his hair all matted against his face. His hands were tied to the corner of the bed with a piece of clothesline. Around his wrists were all these bite marks. He had been trying to get free.

In this lead, LaDonna offers us detailed sensory images to involve us as her readers. She kept the most powerful image for last.

3. Quoting.   A time-honored way to begin academic essays is to quote an expert in the field. You will notice that each chapter in this book begins with such quotes. Included, as well, are quotes by students like yourself, with whom you may identify. The purpose of quoting is to lend authority to your writing. Using effective quotes shows that you are familiar with others who have spoken well on the topic. Therefore, you are already a part of the community to which the audience wants to belong. Your quote may be from known people, books (such as the Bible), or the news. If your source is not likely to be familiar to your audience, offer some indication of the person's credentials. This is how a student began an essay about children's rights:

> In her essay "Checks on Parental Power," Ellen Goodman states: "Parents obviously have and must have a wide range of decisions over their children's lives. But they don't have absolute power and never have."

It is also effective to quote persons *about* whom you are writing. This gives your reader a feeling of knowing the person, too. So, for example, if you knew a child who was hospitalized unjustly, you could quote her or him. If you were writing about a grandmother, you could quote her favorite piece of advice to you.

4. Stating Your Thesis.   Writing a thesis statement—a statement of your main point—is *only one* of the ways to begin an essay. Usually, this is the strategy used in essay exams, legal documents, news reports, business memos, and other pieces of writing in which the purpose is to quickly relay information or argue an interpretation. (This strategy is further explored in Chapters 5, 12, and 13.) The following lead states the thesis of a student paper:

> All children should have lawyers to protect their rights, even against their parents' wishes. Today, the judicial system in the United States is allowing parents more rights over their children's lives. This means that parents can put their children into a mental institution even if there is nothing wrong with the children. Children, in turn, have taken their parents to court.

5. Stating Your Purpose.   You may find it helpful to state your purpose in writing. Sometimes you will leave this statement in the final draft. Sometimes the purpose of your writing will be so clear from your lead that there will be no reason to state that purpose. Here is an example of a lead that states the writer's purpose and method:

In this paper I will argue that children have the right to decide where they want to live. By considering several situations, I will show that parents who don't respect this right are being abusive.

6. Defining.   The word *defining* literally means to show the limits of a word, subject, or problem. The purpose of defining words and expressions is to establish a common understanding with your reader and to clarify your position on a subject. You can define your subject by what it is or by what it is not. Here is one possible way to define the expression *children's rights:*

> We can define children's rights according to the United States Declaration of Independence as the right to life, liberty, and the pursuit of happiness. Parents who do not honor these rights for their children are breaking the law.

7. Telling a Story.   Humans are, by nature, storytellers. Children love bedtime stories, and gossip is all too popular. Telling a story can be a very effective way to focus yourself and involve your readers. Notice how this strategy is used in the following example:

> When I was a child, my father always told me to stick up for myself. However, there came a time when I had to stick up for myself with him. It was a Saturday morning and I had an extra soccer practice; my father had other plans for me. He expected me to clean out the inside of his car for him because he was going to Penn Station to pick up an important client that day. This was the beginning of an ongoing battle in my teens that culminated in our landing in court one day.

8. Showing Relationship to the Subject.   To give readers a reason to read your paper, show them what it means to *you:*

> The most difficult thing a parent can ever do is to place his own child in an institution. Soon after my older son turned sixteen, I took him to a county hospital that would be the first stop on a long journey for both of us. For him it was almost a relief. He knew what was happening; nevertheless, I was filled with fear and anxiety. Even now as I write I can feel the tightness in my chest that I felt when I saw him standing in the corridor as I walked away.

You can also show relationship to a subject by *reflecting on your current writing process,* as the parent above does.

9. Offering History. You can help orient your reader to your topic by offering historical background:

> In ancient Greece when a child was born with a deformity or if the child was an excess female, the child would be placed on a mountaintop to die. Throughout history, children have been forced to do work that even adults found difficult. Child abuse, in some countries, has been considered to be the best way to discipline the child. It is only in this century that we are coming to understand the need to legally protect children's rights.

10. Using the News. Student Jill Minor was very concerned about child abuse. She started her essay by reporting a current local news event:

> On March 14, 1987, Susan Greenville from Somer, New Jersey was stabbed 23 times in the upper chest and received a fractured skull from a 33-year-old man. Susan Greenville was a four-year-old child. The 33-year-old man was her father. This occurred after repeated beatings that nobody reported. My argument begins here. How could the people living near the Greenville family have let such a thing happen?

Leads that surprise

11. Asking Questions. Asking a question, you invite your readers to read on for the answer. Asking a question, you inspire yourself to discover an answer through writing—a strategy that is further explored in Chapters 5, 12, and 13.

Especially in academic settings, it is appropriate and helpful to begin essays with a question or questions as student Dina Singer does in her essay "For Our Children's Sake?":

> Are we going back to previous times when children had no more rights than cattle? Some migrant children still work fourteen hours a day picking fruits and vegetables on farms. Can we afford to spend money on putting people into space? Countless children live on the streets with no place to call their own.

The questions do not have to be asked in the first lines of the essay but may be asked after some other introductory remarks. Notice how Dina Singer works her title as a question and uses questions in her lead, as well.

12. Stating Something Controversial or Contradictory. Dina considered starting her essay by saying something controversial:

Let's take food from homeless children and with the money saved, send another person to the moon. That's what the government seems to be saying every time they make cuts on food budgets for children. But children have a right to expect to be fed so that they can grow into healthy adults.

13. Surprising with Statistics.   Student Adam Joyner used startling statistics to rivet his readers' attention:

This year over 40% of the homeless are under the age of eleven. Of these children 30% won't reach the age of eighteen, and 70% will have had experiences with drugs and/or prostitution.

14. Using Humor.   Put your readers at ease *and* encourage them to read on by leading with a joke or a touch of humor. Of course, not all topics lend themselves to humor. The following is a humorous lead to an essay about everyday negotiations between a parent and child:

When I was a child my father would punish me by telling me he would put me in a Macy's bag and return me. Whenever I complained he said, "So, sue me." Well, I just received my law degree, and guess what my first case is going to be?

Writing Leads

Leads are written first and they are written last. With practice and luck, you sometimes devise a lead that works the first time. Most of the time, however, you will revise your lead many times, often finishing it last.

Fourteen Strategies for Leads

1. Illustrating
2. Imaging
3. Quoting
4. Stating your thesis
5. Stating your purpose
6. Defining
7. Telling a story
8. Showing relationship to the subject
9. Offering history
10. Using the news
11. Asking questions
12. Stating something controversial or contradictory
13. Surprising with statistics
14. Using humor

Writers have problems with leads during the writing process for two reasons: (1) they adhere too much to early attempts, or (2) they overdo strategies. Leaving in failed attempts or freewrites is like having dancers do their warm-ups during a performance on stage or like tossing the leaves and vines in with the tomatoes for sauce. Overdoing a familiarizing strategy can bore or irritate the reader. For example, telling the twentieth-century reader that William Shakespeare wrote plays is giving too much background information to readers. Overdoing a surprising strategy can confuse or turn away the reader. Several jokes in a row can wear thin, for example, and saying something too controversial can make you sound unreliable. Here are three strategies to help you write and revise your leads:

1. *Find a lead.* Working as an explorer, find your favorite sentence or paragraph from a freewrite or early draft, and bring it to the top of your piece. Repeat this in your next drafts as often as necessary until you commit yourself to a final draft.

2. *Choose a strategy.* Working as a planner, choose a strategy from the sidebar on page 173 on leads. Create several leads using that strategy, and choose the best.

3. *Cross out false leads.* A true lead engages and interests both the writer and the reader. A false lead gives the writer and reader the feeling that the writer is running in place, getting nowhere. A humorous image of this is cartoon character Fred Flintstone trying to drive off in his car: he spins his feet and goes backward before he takes off.

   One of the most useful ways to find a true lead is to learn how to cross out chunks of early attempts. Writers often cross out two and three pages of writing to get to a lead that is right. Three chapter-length attempts at the first chapter of this book were set aside in favor of the current version.

Just as Michael had to write five pages to find a suitable focus and lead for his essay on his basement (see pages 147–150), you may have to freewrite and draft several times before you find a suitable lead. The lead

---

Writing Leads

1. Find a lead.
2. Choose a strategy.
3. Cross out false leads.

for this chapter, describing Gary Larson's cartoon, didn't occur to me until four years after I first started writing this book.

You may feel reluctant, at first, to let go of false leads. There is a certain amount of satisfaction in completing a project. But experiment. Cross out false leads. Place that later paragraph up front. You can always reorganize and reincorporate the dropped portions in another part of the paper or in another paper. Crossing out false leads will improve your writing and give you greater freedom and flexibility.

Explorations

1. *Together.* Most writers combine strategies in a given lead. Return to the examples listed for the fourteen strategies. For each, notice if the writer is combining the strategy with another. Which leads both familiarize and surprise the reader?

2. *Solo and Together.*

   a. Read through a magazine or a newspaper. Choose three leads that interest you from three separate pieces of writing. Choose three leads that you find *un*interesting. Bring all six to class.

   b. In small groups, read your leads and discuss how they affected you and why. As a group, choose one lead that you all find very effective. As you decide, discuss why you agree or disagree on certain leads. Read the favorite leads to the whole class. How did the writers offer something familiar and new at the same time?

The purpose of Explorations 3 through 5 is to develop flexibility in writing leads.

3. *Together.* Consider the following beginnings of student papers. For each one:

   - Decide whether you think the writing is effective;
   - Cross out false leads or parts of the leads that seem to be leading nowhere;
   - Either find a better lead in the paper itself or write a new one.

   Experiment with different strategies or combinations of strategies for leads.

   a. Living on campus compared to living at home is different in many ways. There are advantages and disadvantages when you are living on campus. The same holds true when you are living at home. In this paper I will discuss the different aspects of living on campus and living at home with your parents.

      When you are dorming you have freedom that you never had when you were staying home. You can basically do what you want when you want to.

b. "The more things change the more they stay the same." Last semester at Kean College parking was virtually impossible and this semester, as expected, the situation has not changed.

My first day at Kean College in the fall semester I found out that parking was going to be a problem. I thought if I would come early I would get a parking space right up front. Apparently everyone else had the same idea. . . .

c. Snow is one of nature's weapons in fighting excessive heat waves. It is not found in every part of the world. My country in particular sees no snow even though the temperature would remain comparatively low. Some months of the year are hotter than others.

Between September and March, Nigeria is crossed by the Northeast Trade Winds. During this time, dusty winds blow from and across the Sahara Desert bringing dusty winds and sand throughout the inland.

My first experience with snow didn't come until I came to the United States from Nigeria. What I saw was a dream come true.

d. "Union is strength." We witness this constantly throughout our everyday lives from the machinists of Eastern Airlines, to the anti-apartheid movement in South Africa, from the teamwork of athletes on the gridiron, to the cohesiveness of a championship basketball team on the hardwood floor. Two experiences I have had which truly demonstrated the power of a union to me were in the United States Army, and a speech delivered by the Reverend Jesse Jackson.*

e. Happiness and anger is in one's inner self. It is the personality that makes me a person. Happiness in my opinion brings out joy that is held in my feelings as well as the anger that lies deep inside me.

Happiness at one point can bring laughter among myself and others. It is a sign of a smile. Being happy doesn't mean having everything like money, houses, and cars. There's a saying, "Money can't buy happiness." But happiness is the feeling of enjoying.

Anger is one aspect of my personality that brings the devil out of me. There are many times I have gotten angry at myself and others. Muscles flare, body tightens, and my body temperature rises. I can remember getting into a particular fight recently.

4. *Together.* In small groups, choose one of the following topics and develop a series of possible leads. Use as many of the fourteen strategies for leads as you can, either singly or in combination.

a. Can prisons rehabilitate criminals?

b. Is joint custody good for children?

c. Who should decide which artists should be supported by federal grants?

---

*By student Alan T. Russell.

    d. Should women be in combat?

    e. Would it be worth letting go of some luxuries for a while to reduce dependence on nuclear energy and to transfer over to solar, wind, and hydro power?

5. *Solo or Together.* Read over the leads of papers you are writing. Develop different possible leads. Use the instructions for Exploration 3.

Titles

Titles must do in a short space what leads do: both familiarize and interest. Whether the stress is on familiarizing or interesting readers depends on your purpose and audience. The chapter titles in this book are designed to help you find specific aspects of the writing process that you want to explore. For example, instead of being called "Landing the Helicopter"—a title that might have surprised and amused you—Chapter 5 is called "Focusing." This reflects a main purpose of this book: to help you to find what you need for yourself. If the chapter were being written as an article for a writing magazine, the title "Landing the Helicopter" might capture the reader who is more interested in being entertained than having an easy reference.

Writing Titles

Some authors wait until they are finished with their stories, poems, essays, chapters, or books to title them. In the writing process, though, always

---

Ten Strategies for Titles

Strategies for titles are similar to those for leads.

    Naming your topic: Children's Rights

    Quoting: Suffer the Little Children

    Stating your thesis: Children Have Legal Rights

    Addressing your audience: Save the Children

    Showing relationship to subject: My Son's Life in an Institution

    Offering history: Child Abuse: From Ancient Sparta to New York

    Asking questions: For Our Children's Sake?

    Stating something controversial: Let's Starve Our Children

    Surprising with statistics: Forty Percent of the Homeless Are Children

    Using humor: Bagging Dad

have a *working title.* The process of writing and rewriting a title helps remind you of your focus, purpose, and audience. As you develop your title, more ideas may occur to you for the body of your piece, as well.

Explorations

The purpose of these Explorations is to help you become aware of the characteristics of effective titles.

1. *Together.* Read the following titles and decide which ones interest you and why. Discuss whether each title is meant to familiarize or to surprise the reader. Which titles do both? Name the strategy(ies) the writer uses. What does each title suggest about the nature of the piece it heads? Which titles are not engaging, and why? How would you revise them? What do you learn about yourselves as readers from this Exploration?

Mother

Crocodile

How to Cram

College Is a Waste of Time and Money

But What If I Need It Some Day?

When Nice People Burn Books

Write On

Challenging My Fears

Ducks on Corrigan's Pond

Jealous

Dusk in Fierce Pajamas

Living with Death

Amusing Ourselves to Death

Writing Titles

1. **Brainstorm** as many possible titles as you can, preferably with the help of others.

2. **Choose** for your title a favorite phrase or sentence from a freewrite or draft.

3. **List common or popular expressions and quotes** that relate to your topic. Adapt the language of your choice expression to suit your purpose and audience. For example, "Suffer the little children" is from the Bible. Check reference books of quotations, such as *Bartlett's Familiar Quotations.* The book is organized according to topics and authors.

4. **Use** one of the fourteen **strategies for leads.**

5. **Model your title** on ones you find in books, magazines, and newspapers. To prime yourself, do some browsing.

6. **Revise** your title. Make it brief and specific.

2. *Together.* Bring your favorite magazines to class. In small groups or as a class, collect and record titles that interest you. Discuss them, using the suggestions offered in Exploration 1.

3. *Solo.* Choose your favorite title from Exploration 1 or 2. Freewrite for fifteen minutes in response to it. If you find you are engaged, develop this freewrite into an essay.

4. *Solo and Together.* Choose some papers you have been writing and develop titles for them. Use strategies suggested in the sidebar. Discuss how your sense of your paper changes with different titles. Revise your paper to reflect your best one.

Endings

A tightrope walker steadies her eyes and her steps by focusing on a point at the end of her rope. Similarly, you can keep yourself focused during the writing process by keeping your eyes on a *working ending.* A working ending not only steadies you, it helps you decide what you need to reach your goal. Once you reach that goal, you will have a certain sense of completion and satisfaction. So will your reader.

The purposes of effective endings are (1) to leave a lasting impression on the reader, (2) to frame the paper for a sense of completion, and (3) to keep you focused in the writing process.

Eight Strategies for Endings

1. Use a Lead.   In general, the same strategies that work for leads work for endings. In some cases, you may choose to use an ending from an earlier draft as the lead in a later one, and vice versa.

2. Full Circle.   By referring to the lead, you fulfill the purpose of forming a frame for the whole piece. You can refer to the lead using the same strategies as Goodman does in her essay "Checks on Parental Power":

> Chalk one up for the folks who dropped off the boy with the teddy bear.

3. Resolution.   You can solve a problem or answer a question that was posed in the lead. The father concluded his paper about his institutionalized son in this way:

Today my thirty-year-old son is living in a group home with five other adults. He has a job folding boxes which he enjoys. He has always loved working with his hands on things he can do over and over again. Every day he goes to the pool and dazzles everyone with his 100 laps of perfectly smooth strokes. When I visit him, we go shopping for clothes just as we did when he was a little boy. But now when it's time for me to go, he's the one who walks away as I stand there in the corridor.

4. Meaning or Lesson. Formulate what your subject means to you. This will help you to better understand and revise your writing. It will also help to complete the experience of it for your readers. Here is how one student summed up the meaning of an essay:

I learned that some things are more important than family pride. If a trusted parent is abusing a child, the child's pride must be saved first.

5. Quotation. You can offer your reader a short memorable quote or a phrase with which he or she may be familiar. This establishes a common bond at the end of a piece of writing. However, avoid overused quotations that seem clichéd (see pages 158–161 for further discussion of clichés). Write variations on them so they sound new. Here are several endings that would be appropriate for papers on children's rights. Some are direct quotes. Others remind us of quotes:

Suffer the little children so they won't have to.

The child shall be father to the man.

Keep the cradle out of the trees.

6. Image. You can leave the reader with an image to remember just as Goodman ends her essay with the image of the teddy bear and the father leaves us with the image of his son walking away.

7. Questions or Problems. Writing is a process not only of exploring questions but of posing new ones for further consideration. Many scientific papers end up with more questions than they started with. It's effective to end essays and papers with questions and problems. Here are two examples of such endings:

Do we have a future if our children remain homeless?

How can we identify at-risk children and the families that they come from? What can we do to help them heal?

Eight Strategies for Endings

1. Use a lead
2. Full circle
3. Resolution
4. Meaning or lesson

5. Quotation
6. Image
7. Questions or problems
8. Summary

8. Summary. If your essay or story is long and your purpose is to clarify or stress your main points, sometimes it is appropriate to summarize them in your last paragraph. To summarize is to collect the main points that you want to remember or that you want remembered. This summary may take the form of a thesis statement.

Use this strategy *very carefully.* Readers may skim over it: they've seen the strategy before. In very short essays, avoid writing anything that sounds like "This is what I have just said." Here is an example of a summary ending:

> It is clear that there are many issues to be considered in deciding the line between children's and parents' rights. Not only safety and welfare are important but so is the quality of the life of the whole family. It is hard to develop a good balance. It must be adjusted daily, hourly in some families. In this paper I have considered some of the major court cases in recent history in which this delicate balancing either didn't occur or was too late and not enough.

Writing Endings

The clearer your lead is, the more easily you will be able to find a suitable ending. The best way to develop an effective ending is to fully write and

Writing Endings

1. *Record* attempted leads. The second choice for your lead may serve as your ending.
2. *Choose* and use a particular strategy for endings.
3. *Repeat* your actual lead with an interesting twist.
4. *Signal* your reader if you are ending with a summary by using an expression such as *in conclusion, to summarize, let's review, so then, reconsidering, essentially,* or *in sum.*
5. *Focus* on and *revise working endings* throughout the process.

revise the body of your paper. Use the strategies listed in the sidebar to develop and leave a lasting impression on your readers.

*E*xplorations _____

1. *Together.* Choose a section from a chapter in this book or from one of the essays that are printed in entirety. Is the ending effective? What strategy is being used? Could the ending be more effective? If so, what strategy could the writer have used?

2. *Solo and Together.* Choose some papers you have been writing. Develop endings for them using strategies suggested to you in this section. Discuss how your sense of your papers changes with different endings.

3. *Solo.* For your next paper, develop a working ending to help you focus as you write the first draft. Revise the ending as new ideas develop in the process.

The Body

Depending on your purpose and audience, there are many ways you can develop the main body of your writing between your lead and your ending. The following is a discussion of ten main strategies of development. Notice that they all start with some focus. Each strategy also depends on certain transitional words that enable you to maintain coherence, guide your reader from one idea to another, and show your reader how your ideas are related. To save space, the examples used to illustrate the strategies are paragraphs. Whole essays and books are developed using these strategies either singly or in combination. The illustrations range over a variety of subjects.

Ten Strategies of Development

1. Chronological Order.   When your purpose is to relate a series of events, whether personal or professional, you can follow them as they occurred through time—chronologically. Describe events *forward*, as they happened. Or, use *flashback:* start with an event in the present and reflect on events that led to it. The following two paragraphs (written by student Bruce Inge) use these strategies:

Forward

During my early teens, cars were very attractive to me. I spent all of my time finding work so I could buy a red Oldsmobile two-door coupe. Once I bought it I spent all of my time washing it, caring for it, and riding it around the neighborhood.

Flashback

As I sit in my new Mercedes Benz 500E I look back at all I've experienced in order to get where I'm sitting. Not only the past five years, but my whole life seems to have led to this. Five years ago I was driving my third red Oldsmobile two-door coupe.

Transitional words for maintaining chronological order include these: *first, later, finally, next, as soon as, suddenly,* and *earlier.*

2. Spatial Order. When your purpose is to familiarize your reader with how a place, an object, or a person looks or acts, develop your description focusing on space. You can describe your subject from *left to right, right to left, top to bottom, bottom to top, clockwise or counterclockwise, diagonally, to or from a particular focus,* or *from your particular perspective.* Here is student Loretta Durning's description of a sculpture for an art assignment. She uses a particular perspective to anchor her observations:

> One of Cuevas's works was of "wood, ceramic clay, found objects," which could describe the day-to-day acquisitions of these people wandering the streets, gathering discarded treasures. There was a body made of clay reclining on a bed of wood. The eyes and mouth of its gaunt face were gaping holes. A television mounted on the wall across the room showed bright colors. The person on the bed looked away. A chair stood in the corner, and hovering above it was a rope knotted into a noose. It seemed as if the body on the bed was so hopelessly depressed by his situation that he was gathering the courage to end it.

Transitional words for maintaining spatial order include these: *under, over, around, in, out, beside, next to, left, right,* and *through.*

3. Statement and Illustration. To engage your readers, illustrate your claims. You can develop your entire essay by using a series of examples that amplify and elaborate on your statement. Here is a statement supported by an example:

The grading system of pluses and minuses has proved to be very discouraging to students. One student who received minuses on all his grades decided to switch out of his major. He said, "I always thought I was an 'A' student and that my professors in my major considered me a candidate for a scholarship. Now with all these minuses, I think I'm going to switch. I'm too discouraged."

Transitional expressions that link statement and example include these: *for example, for instance, as, such as,* and *to illustrate.*

Your illustration may also take the form of sensory images, as in this paragraph:

My bedroom is a warm and cozy place. The soft orange walls are complemented by a deep brown shag rug. Large paisley and striped pillows nestle into the lofty goose down comforter. Bayberry potpourri scents the air. And if that doesn't beckon you in, the soft lights or the classical guitar music will.

Transitions for sensory images are most easily managed either by using spatial development, by appealing to one particular sense, or by choosing a variety of images to create a mood (as in the illustration).

4. Statement and Argument. If your purpose is to convince someone to adopt your point of view and to accept your claims, or if you want to show your grasp of information, you can develop your writing by focusing on a series of statements followed by supporting arguments: reasons why readers should believe you. This is a strategy often used in academics. Here is a statement supported with arguments:

The college should not change the grading system to include pluses and minuses because it is unfair to those students who have been under the old system and haven't yet graduated. The change in calculating their grade point averages would put them at a disadvantage in comparison to students who will now be receiving pluses. You may argue that the pluses would be balanced out by minuses. However, in an informal survey of instructors, it was found that though they appreciate being able to award pluses, most of them are reluctant to add minuses. Students much prefer the clarity that whole grades provide. The old system also is a check on any unfairness in grading that may come from personality differences between instructors and students.

Transitional expressions that link statement and argument include these: *in order to, therefore, hence, because,* and *in sum.* Strive to anticipate others' disagreements and counterarguments. Use transitional expressions such as these: *you may argue that . . . , one objection could be . . .* , and *on the other hand. . . .*

5. Question and Answer. If your purpose is to question an issue or explore alternatives, you can develop your paper as a series of *questions and answers*. This is an especially effective strategy for developing and connecting ideas (as Chapters 12 and 13 show), because questions, by their very nature, lead you from one idea to the next. You can proceed in two directions (or move back and forth): *statements to questions* and *questions to statements*. For an example of this procedure, turn back to page 172 where student Dina Singer develops her lead with a series of questions and answers.

Transitional words for the question and answer strategy include these: *who, whose, what, which, when, where, how, why,* and *in response to.*

6. Problem and Solution. If your purpose is to solve or propose a solution to a problem, you can organize your work by focusing on *problems and solutions*. You can state a problem, list possible solutions, explore the consequences of those solutions, and suggest further problems that may arise. Here is a statement of a problem with proposed solutions:

> Small rodents destroy crops and invade grain supplies. There are several approaches to solving the problem: poisons, traps, and natural forces. Poisons are effective in destroying rodents but can affect the water supply and endanger other animals. Traps are not effective in handling a large infestation. In exploring the balance of nature, it has been found that a population of certain kinds of owls may be helpful in controlling rodents and protecting the environment at the same time.

Transitional expressions for the problem and solution strategy include these: *one solution is . . . ; another approach to the problem is . . . ; one way to think about . . . ;* and *if this doesn't work, then . . . .* You can also use process analysis and cause-and-effect transitions.

7. Process Analysis. When your purpose is to understand how something is done or should be done, you can focus your writing by describing or analyzing a process. Chapter 2, "The Writing Process," is organized as a process analysis.

Transitional words that help you develop process analyses include words for chronological and spatial ordering and words used to establish cause and effect.

8. Cause and Effect.   When your purpose is to explain why something happened, you can develop your paper by focusing on the links between causes and effects. A cause is connected by time and space to its effect. Your task is to fill the relevant gaps in time and space. The distinction between a mere chronological or spatial development and one that establishes cause and effect is that the events have to be carefully and logically linked. Here is a paragraph that links causes to effects:

> Sherlock Holmes proved that Beppo stole the rare, expensive pearl of the Borgias and hid it in a plaster bust of Napoleon. He proved this by showing that Beppo had all the resources for stealing and hiding it. A sister of a friend worked for the countess from whom the pearl was stolen. A cousin was a sculptor. Beppo's store sold plaster busts of Napoleon. The one in which he stashed the pearl was accidentally sold. He went around breaking these busts at customers' houses. He was the one who engineered the theft because he had the motive and the means to do so.[13]

Transitional words for establishing cause and effect include these: *because, since, hence, therefore,* and *if . . . then.*

9. Classification.   When your purpose is to more fully understand the differences and similarities between persons, places, objects, or events, you can develop your writing through classification. This chapter and this section classify types of organizing strategies. *Classification* is a process of finding different types within a group. For another example of classification, refer to Chapter 8, pages 215–217, which offer you a classification of different kinds of workshop personalities. To develop your classifications, use the comparison or contrast strategy.

Transitional expressions that help you classify include these: *There are _____ ways to categorize X, there are _____ kinds of X,* and *X is a type of _____ .*

10. Comparison and Contrast.   When your purpose is to make connections or distinctions between two or more ideas, people, places, objects, events, or ideas, develop the body of your work by using strategies of comparison and/or contrast. When you focus on *similarities,* you write a *comparison.* When you focus on *differences,* you draw *contrasts.* You can devote a whole paper either to comparison or to contrast, or you can write a paper in which you both compare and contrast. For this strategy, begin by creating lists under your subjects that match points of comparison and contrast. Here is an illustration of corresponding lists comparing and contrasting cats and dogs as pets. In process, these lists will be much messier as you cross out and draw arrows to match points:

Cats	**Dogs**
Easy	Take time
Litter box	Need to be housebroken
Naturally clean	Need to be bathed
Food reasonably priced	Food expensive
Affectionate	Pals
Good lap sitters	Learn tricks

To develop your essay, use either the block or the zig-zag method. In the block method, you describe each subject fully before considering the next. In the zig-zag method, you move back and forth between the two or more subjects you are considering. The following paragraphs, contrasting cats and dogs as pets, illustrate the block and zig-zag methods:

Block method

Cats are the easiest pets to have and enjoy. Kittens can be trained to use a litter box in one or two days, and they are naturally clean. Supermarkets sell many cat foods at reasonable prices, so the cost of feeding them is low. Most cats are affectionate, just wanting to curl up with you and make you feel good with their purring.

Dogs are a lot of fun and a lot of trouble. They take patience and time to housebreak, and they need to be walked frequently, whatever the weather. Some of them are messy with food and water, scattering it all around their feeding bowls. As companions, they can't be beat. They love to run and play and greet you as soon as you come home.

Zig-zag method

Cats are the easiest pets to have, but dogs are more fun. All cats can be litter-trained in a few days; however, dogs can take weeks to housebreak. While cats are naturally clean, dogs need regular baths or they smell terrible. Feeding a cat is easy and inexpensive. Dogs eat more than cats. Cats are good lap sitters, but dogs are more affectionate. There is no greater fun than running with a dog or throwing a stick for the dog to retrieve.

Transitional expressions that help you *compare* include *similarly, the same as, just as, also, not only . . . but also, like,* and *and.* Transitional words that help you *contrast* include *whereas, on the other hand, but, although, however, while,* and *although.* When you attempt to both compare and contrast in an essay, be especially careful to use transitions that clearly state when you are focusing on similarities and when you are focusing on differences.

For further discussion of comparison and contrast, turn to Chapter 13, pages 354–362.

Ten Strategies for Developing the Body

1. Chronological order
2. Spatial order
3. Statement and illustration
4. Statement and argument
5. Question and answer
6. Problem and solution
7. Process analysis
8. Cause and effect
9. Classification
10. Comparison and contrast

Matching Leads and Development

Some leads naturally call for certain kinds of development. Here are a few possible matches:

Lead	Development
Telling a story	Chronological
Offering history	Chronological
Imaging	Spatial
Quoting	Statement and argument
Stating a thesis	Statement and illustration
Stating your purpose	Problem and solution
Asking questions	Question and answer
Using the news	Cause and effect

Shaping

Deduction and induction

Even within a particular strategy for developing the body of your paper, you have different options for how you arrange your examples and evidence. In this section you are offered seven shapes to help you structure what you write. You can use the planner's style and decide on a shape for your writing before you begin, or you can use the explorer's style and develop your sense of the shape in process.

There are two directions from which you can develop the body of a piece of writing. For example, you can state your thesis and provide illustrations of it or arguments for it. This is called *deduction.* Or, you can shape your essay by offering a series of examples concluding with a summary thesis statement. This is called *induction.* You can combine deduction and induction in a given essay as well.

Your thesis statement can come in different places in your essay:

1. The first sentence
2. The last sentence of the first paragraph
3. The first sentence of the second paragraph, following a description, example, or story told in the first
4. Part of your ending

Whether you use deduction or induction, and where you place a thesis statement, depend on your purpose, audience, and style. Experiment with both deduction and induction. You may find that in revising a paper you will want to switch completely from one to the other. In either case, focus on the lead and the ending. These are strategic points for engaging your audience. The sidebar shows some options you have with deduction and induction.

Diagrams

Some writers who are visually and spatially oriented find it helpful to diagram—draw—the structure of their work in process. Here are seven visual shapes that your writing may take:

1. The V. The *V shape* reflects the funneling effect of collecting specific experiences, ideas, and information and then focusing down to an important point. Mysteries are often written in this pattern. You get many different clues until one clue ties it all together and solves the mystery at the end. Reports of scientific data that take a V shape illustrate *inductive reasoning.* You collect many observations and notice that they

Deduction and Induction

Deduction

Options for the Lead

1. State the problem.
2. State your position (key or thesis statement).
3. State your purpose.
4. Define any key words.
5. Ask a question.
6. Establish common ground.*

Options for the Body

1. Present the first main point, example, or supporting evidence.
2. Continue to present more points, examples, and supporting evidence.
3. Anticipate and respond to possible objections.
4. Organize your supporting materials either from least important to most or from most important to least.

Options for the Ending

1. Restate the problem, your position, and your purpose.
2. Suggest further action or discussion.
3. Reestablish common ground.
4. Use a striking example.
5. Ask a question.
6. Summarize.

Induction

Options for the Lead

1. Engage your reader by providing a striking illustration of the issue or problem.
2. Establish common ground.

Options for the Body

1. Add more evidence and examples illustrating the issue or problem
2. Anticipate and respond to possible objections.
3. Organize your evidence and examples from least important to most or from most important to least.

Options for the Ending

1. State the problem.
2. State your position (key or thesis statement).
3. Establish common ground.
4. Use a striking example.
5. Ask a question.
6. Summarize.

* For a discussion of establishing common ground see pages 378–381.

all come down to one common pattern or law. When you are writing, you can use the V shape by offering a number of *specific* examples and then tying them together with a *general* statement (see Figure 7.1).

2. The Inverted V.   The *inverted V* shape starts with a general statement, theory, or rule and then offers examples, evidence, stories, and other illustrations in support of it (see Figure 7.2). This is *deductive reasoning.* Many scientists have explored problems deductively: they start with a general statement of theory and test whether it holds true for the available evidence.

3. The Hourglass.   Sometimes a piece of writing will combine the V and the inverted V strategies. So, for example, a scientist who decides that all swans are white and then finds a black swan will have to broaden the theory to include black swans (see Figure 7.3).

4. The String of Pearls.   Events and processes told from beginning to end as they happened, or in exact reverse order, without any emphasis

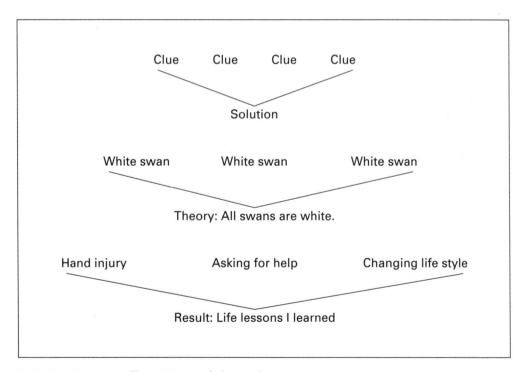

FIGURE **7.1** *Illustrations of the V Shape*

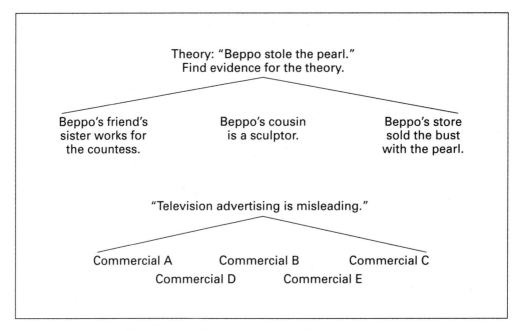

FIGURE 7.2   *Illustrations of the Inverted V Shape*

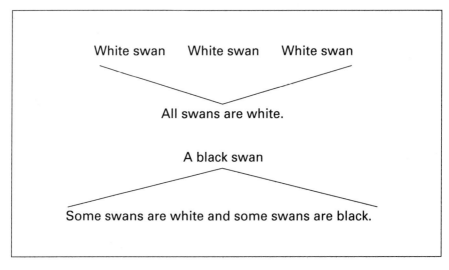

FIGURE 7.3   *Illustration of the Hourglass Shape*

or distinction between them, are referred to by newspaper writers as "strings of pearls" (because in most strands, one pearl is usually meant to match all the others). If you describe a person, place, or thing from top to bottom, left to right, or vice versa, without emphasizing or developing a point of view on your subject, you are also using a string-of-pearls shape. In some contexts this strategy may be adequate. In general, avoid the string of pearls; without emphasis, the reader will not know your meaning or purpose. Also, you, as writer, will miss an opportunity for developing a more meaningful sense of your subject for yourself (see Figure 7.4).

5. The Scales. You can organize your evidence and examples to show the relative importance between them. You can start with the most important and end with the least. The problem with this balance is that you may lose your reader's interest and leave a weak last impression. You can start with the least important examples and build to the most interesting. The problem with this balance is that you may not capture your reader's interest soon enough. In general, use one of your most interesting or representative examples for your lead and either reflect on it or use another interesting example for your end. Then organize the other examples in the body of your writing as seems most appropriate to your purpose and audience (see Figure 7.5). This principle applies to individual paragraphs, as well.

Expressions that will help you provide emphasis include the following: *and, too, actually, indeed, more than, especially,* and *without a doubt.* Another strategy for providing emphasis is repetition. Recall how Dr. Martin Luther King, Jr., repeated "I have a dream" and how effectively the repetition helps us to remember his words.

6. The Block. When you compare or contrast two or more things, you can shape your essay by fully describing one side and then fully describing the other. This works, as well, if you are telling a history in which you focus on only one character or event at a time. In a block structure, you present your material so that the reader will be able to see

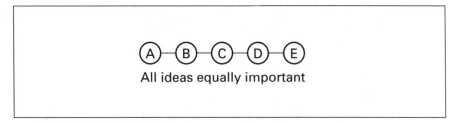

FIGURE 7.4 Illustration of the String of Pearls

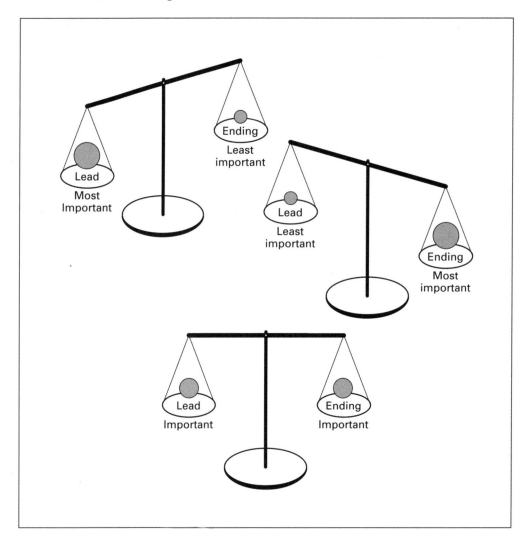

FIGURE 7.5   Illustration of Scales

what makes your points of comparison separate but equal. It is also helpful to summarize the main purpose and points of your comparison and/or contrast (see Figure 7.6).

7. The Zig-zag.   When you compare or contrast two things, you can do so by zig-zagging between them on each point. For example, in comparing two cars you can compare their gas consumption, their suspension, their price, and so on (see Figure 7.7).

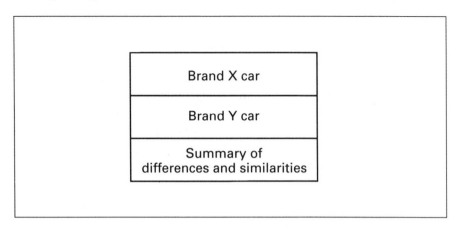

F I G U R E   7.6   Illustration of the Block Shape

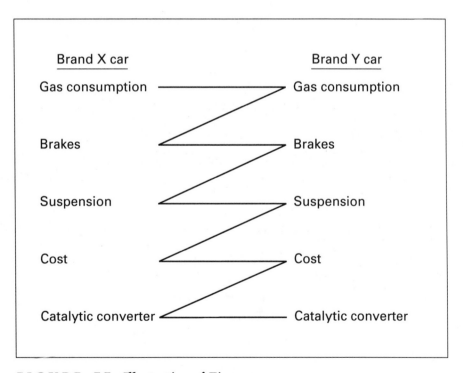

F I G U R E   7.7   Illustration of Zig-zag

Writing the Body

In the writing process it is helpful to keep a *working plan,* or outline. This outline may be as simple as a few words on a scrap of paper, noting what you want to include. Or, the plan may be as formal as the table of contents of this book. In general, the larger the work, the more planning there is. Hammering two boards together doesn't take much planning. Raising a house requires an intricate design. In any case, the plan often changes as you develop a piece of writing, just as your title, leads, and endings change in the process.

1. Collecting. As you work, jot down points you want to cover on notecards, on a piece of paper, or, as some writers do, at the point in a computer file where you anticipate using an idea. You can shuffle your cards into piles for "Lead," "Body," and "Ending." Or you can divide a paper into three columns and jot down notes for lead, body, and ending in them. Plan and replan throughout the process: before (to help you focus), during (to help you keep track), and after (for final polishing).

2. Outlining. An outline is an arranged list of topics and ideas that guides you through your drafting and redrafting. If you are working as a planner, list what you want to include in your paper *before* you start drafting it. If you are an explorer, freewrite, experiment, and draft your paper. Then review what you have written and write an outline of it. Most often, you will find yourself working both as a planner and an explorer, as I did with this book. The first draft of this chapter was written to fill in this planned working outline:

I. Leads
II. Body
III. Endings

As I wrote, I discovered and developed further ideas for how to detail each section. I rewrote my outline. Here is the more fully developed outline for Leads:

I.   Leads
    A.   Fourteen strategies for leads
    B.   Sidebars
    C.   Writing leads
    D.   Explorations

    . . .

Because one of the purposes of this chapter is to offer you opportunities to discover ideas for yourself, this description helped me to check whether I was offering enough Explorations in each section. You may have noticed that this chapter includes comments on the process of writing leads, titles, endings, and bodies of papers. The idea to do this occurred to me while I was writing about leads. I wrote it into my working plan, which reminded me to offer such sections on the process of writing endings, titles, and bodies, as well. Putting "Sidebars" into the outline reminded me to formulate them for each section.

3. Analyzing. Review your work and decide which strategies of development are most appropriate for your purpose and audience. Experiment with drafting your paper using these strategies. Choose the one that provides the most unity and coherence of the topics you want to cover. Write a working outline. Revise it as necessary.

4. Diagramming. Writers who are visually oriented often find it helpful to diagram their work in process. Decide what shape you want to use, ahead of time or discover your shape as you freewrite and explore. Draw your diagram on a sheet of paper (see Figure 7.8). Then write your topics into the diagram. Revise the topics and the diagram as you write and develop your piece.

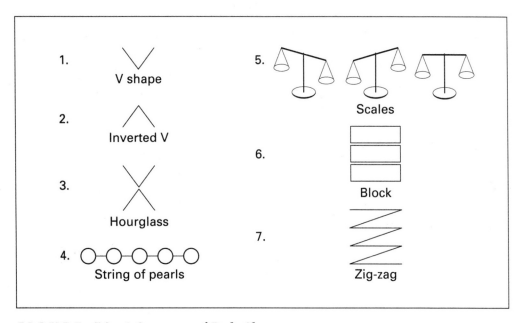

FIGURE *7.8* *A Summary of Body Shapes*

5. Pacing.   Pacing is especially important in writing. Too much too soon, or too little too late, and you lose your focus and your reader. It's helpful to notice how long you spend on each section of a piece of writing. If you claim that your paper is a strong argument in favor of AIDS research but you spend only three sentences on it in a three-page paper, you will have to readjust. If you find that you only offer one brief focused example to support your point, you may want to add more. (Or you may want to revise your whole purpose and approach.)

To pace yourself, count your sentences, paragraphs, examples, and sometimes even your words in particular portions. Use these calculations to help you decide whether you could speed up or slow down your paper by subtracting or adding. So, for example, if you claim to be writing about the difference between poisons and medicines but don't devote equal space to them, you may want to readjust the balance. These are some questions that may help you in pacing:

- Am I trying to do too much?
- Could I spend more time on any parts?
- Do I spend too much time on things that are not important to my purpose or audience?
- Does the order make sense?
- Are there some sentences that belong to another paragraph?
- Do I try to cover too much in any paragraph?
- Am I leaving out any relevant steps?
- Do I get bored with writing any of the portions, myself? Why? How could I make it more interesting for me to write them?
- Should I remove any section?

Draw blocks to indicate the relative amount of space you devote to each idea or topic (see Figure 7.9). This will help you visualize your pacing.

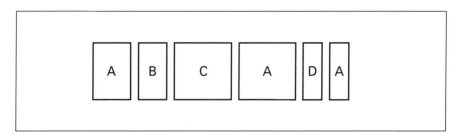

FIGURE 7.9 Drawing Blocks for Pacing

Writing the Body

Use the following strategies singly or in combination:

1. **Collect** your ideas on notecards, pieces of paper, and in computer files. Organize them before and during the drafting process.
2. **Outline** your topics and ideas before and during the drafting process.
3. **Analyze** strategies of development. Choose those that best apply to your current purpose and audience.
4. **Diagram** your work, using the shapes in Figure 7.8.
5. **Pace** your writing by asking yourself the questions on page 198. Draw blocks to visualize your pacing.

*E*xplorations

The purpose of these Explorations is to provide you practice in developing and shaping your writing.

1. *Together.* In the following paragraphs, the sentences have been placed out of the order in which the author arranged them. Reorganize them using these suggestions:

   - Find what you believe would be a good lead sentence.
   - Reorder the sentences so that they make sense to you.
   - Decide what the purpose and audience could be.
   - Decide which strategy of development your version follows.
   - Decide which shape your version takes. Draw a diagram.
   - If you work in small groups, compare the results as a class. How do different orders change the meaning?

   a.   Perhaps a center will emerge. If that is not the final center, then go on to another way of writing. Keep up this burst of writing—this attempt to figure out what your writing is about—as long as you can. Keep this up for a while. If not, go on to the step of standing back and looking for a center. Give your writing more time in a drawer unlooked at. If this doesn't work, you may simply have to stop and rest. Some complicated and important reordering of things is trying to take place inside you. Anything that takes this long simply to emerge is probably important.[14]

   b.   But how much TV does one have to watch to qualify as a heavy TV watcher? Try to create a mental picture of what these phrases represent. Look closely at her reasoning. Also, what does it mean to overestimate the danger of physical violence, or to become desensitized? She argues that heavy TV watchers "overestimate the danger of physical violence in real life" and "become desensitized to violence in the real world." You can see that if you accept this writer's argument without requiring her to clarify these ambiguous phrases, you will not have understood what you agreed to believe. If you can't, the phrases are ambiguous.[15]

c.   Not you. And although we're taught that it is bad to boast, that it is trashy to toot our own horn, that nice people don't strut their stuff, seek attention, or name-drop, there are times when showing off may be forgivable and may be even acceptable. No one is completely immune. Indeed everyone, I would like to propose, has some sort of need to show off.[16]

d.   Helping women to disguise their pregnancy so that it will not interfere with "business" has itself become big business. This ensemble presumably provides her the male dress she needs to navigate in a man's world even while she manifests what Robert Seidenberg has called the irreducible of womanhood—pregnancy and birth. Working women who gather the courage to have families despite the culture's dismissal of mothering find themselves subject to corporate standards even in this female process. Here again women have been coerced by "male" values, the professional overtaking the personal and blotting it out. One of many ads for stores with this intent, titled "Today's Maternity," pictures a woman dressed in a dark suit, complete with stiff white collar, "softened" by the usual corporate tie at the neck. Franchised chain stores with names such as "Mothers Work" specialize in supplying pregnant women with the obligatory corporate uniform.[17]

2.   *Together.* Choose a short newspaper or magazine article or a paper on which you are working. Cut it into paragraph segments and number the original order of each paragraph on the back of the paper with a pencil. Shuffle the paragraphs, and in small groups or as a class, decide the order in which you would put them. The group may have different ideas of the best order. You may decide that some paragraphs are not necessary. Then compare your version to the original order and note differences. (Resist the temptation to just fit the pieces back as if they were parts of a jigsaw puzzle.)

- Which order do you prefer, and why?

- What shapes would you assign to the different versions?

- Create a list of phrases describing what the author is doing in each paragraph.

- Create a list of the topics the writer covers.

3.   *Solo and Together.* Choose a paper on which you are working either for your writing class or some other purpose. Photocopy it. In pairs

or groups of three, help each other order paragraphs (or sentences), while reflecting on the purpose and audience of the paper.

4. a. *Solo.* Revise a paper you are writing, with special attention to coherence. Develop a working outline. Diagram the shape of your development. Notice whether you are using a planner's or explorer's approach. Decide whether to organize deductively or inductively. Monitor your transitions.

    b. *Together.* Read and discuss each other's papers, with special attention to organizing strategies.

Chapter Review

1. *Together.* Discuss how this chapter is organized, using the following questions and suggestions:

    a. Read the table of contents for the chapter.

    b. What are the major sections of the chapter?

    c. For each section:

        -   Outline what is included.

        -   What strategy is used for the lead? Why?

        -   What strategy is used for the title? Why?

        -   How is the body developed? Why?

        -   What strategy is used for the ending? Why?

    d. What charts and diagrams are used?

    e. Would you reorganize the chapter? If so, how and why?

2. *Solo.* Revise a paper with special attention to writing a title, lead, body, and ending that provide unity and coherence. Develop a working outline for the paper as well. Diagram its shape.

Chapter 8

Consulting

This chapter offers opportunities to

—Create a **community of writers**

—**Respond** to each other in **writing workshop**

—Become a better **reader**

—Learn how to **grade** writing

> Company is better than will power.
>
> *—Amrit Desai, Artist and Educator*

> No passion in the world is equal to the passion
> to alter someone else's draft.
>
> *—H. G. Wells, Novelist*

A Community of Writers

You open the door to a noisy classroom and hear bits of speech: "I like . . ." "Maybe you could . . ." "You need . . ." "I meant . . ." Students are clustered in small groups of four or five with papers, dictionaries, magazines, scissors, and tape spread out on their desks and on the floor. They are leaning toward each other, gesturing, pointing to each other's papers, and calling out. Several other students are writing by themselves in a corner. In the middle of the classroom is a wastebasket; around it are crumpled papers that missed. In one group, two students are discussing what happened during a nationally televised court case: "You can't say the woman was guilty without evidence. It makes you sound sexist." In another group, there's a burst of laughter and someone says, "There I go. Can't stop talking about my favorite person: me." A student stands up to consult with another in the next group. "You're the comma expert," she says, pointing to a paper. "Do we or don't we put a comma here? Marsha says it weakens the sentence. I say it makes it clearer." An older man dressed in a suit (who seems to be the teacher) walks over to a group silently focused on the papers before them. "Come back later," says one of the readers. The man raises his hands and calls for attention. But people are just too involved to notice. He smiles and shrugs his shoulders. Welcome to a community of writers.

This scene may be different from what you have come to expect in a writing classroom. Perhaps you have written most of your papers with only teachers as audience. You would try to figure out what they wanted and write accordingly. They would mark and grade your papers. Maybe you would revise the paper once, just changing what was marked. That would be that. The teachers would end up doing *for* you what they were hoping you could do for yourself. You wouldn't feel as if your papers were your own.

In the real world of writing, writers consult frequently with other writers, colleagues, family, friends, and members of their prospective audiences. For example, writers of children's books regularly gather children to listen to a reading of their work in progress. These children tell them what they like, both directly and indirectly. In response, the authors revise their own writing. Business executives consult with each other on proposals, and often their support staff will edit and reword memos for them. Scientists, journalists, and textbook writers—among others—often write together. Hundreds of people have been directly involved in giving suggestions and ideas for the development of *The Flexible Writer.* Some of these people are listed in the acknowledgments section in the Preface of this book and in footnotes.

One of the most important characteristics of practicing writers is that they know how to talk about writing. This chapter offers you a variety of ways in which you can develop your own community of writers so that you can discover how to talk about writing and revise your work.*

---

*For ideas that inspired this chapter, I am indebted to Peter Elbow, Pat Belanoff, Dixie Goswami, Nancy Sommers, Mimi Schwartz, and the New Jersey Center for the Study of Writing, which granted me a Fellowship for Research in the Classroom.

Writing Workshop

One of the most exciting parts of learning to write is consulting with others in *writing workshop.* In writing workshop, writers discuss their own and others' papers. Writers benefit because they hear a broader and deeper range of responses than if only the teacher were "marking" their work. Teachers feel refreshed because they learn more about and from their students and are freed of having to be error-hunters. Everyone is in charge. A sense of belonging develops. As one student said at the end of a workshop session, "Wow! We're so great together."

The following are some practical considerations to negotiate with each other and your instructor as you discuss papers. Experiment to suit your needs and resources.

Names. Names on papers can be included, deleted, or replaced by made-up names. Remaining anonymous, writers may be spared some self-consciousness and can speak about papers as if they belonged to someone else. Writers can start out anonymously—to get comfortable—and can identify themselves at any point. The benefit of identifying yourself as the writer is that you can more fully discuss your work, ask questions, and request specific responses. You can guide the discussion toward issues that concern you. Often, you may not realize that the idea that seems too obvious or familiar to you is, in fact, very engaging and interesting to others. If you identify yourself as the writer, others can help you recognize the value in what you have to express.

Size. You can respond to papers as a whole group, in small groups of four to five writers, or in pairs. Workshop with the whole group helps you develop a common understanding and new points of view. You collect more responses to your paper, and you build on each other's ideas. Small groups can offer more freedom of expression and more time for more papers.

Choosing and Copying Papers. Ideally, all papers should be typewritten when you consult others about them. Although you may not want to consult over every paper, as part of the community you will want *some* of your work considered. In the beginning, you may want to entrust teachers to choose and copy papers anonymously. Later, you may be asked to bring in three or four copies of papers for small group workshop. If you bring copies for the whole class to share, one copy for every two persons is enough. If you are working in a computer lab, you can sometimes generate copies on printers.

For quick response in a regular classroom, you can use carbon paper to create multiple copies of first drafts that you can discuss in small groups right away. How much you will cover of any given paper may vary, too. Many of the most fruitful workshops are focused just on those important first paragraphs or first pages.

Timing. Decide on how many papers you want to discuss in a given time and what levels of responses you want to give. Appoint a timekeeper whose job it is to make sure every paper is given a fair share of time. A half hour is usually enough for a one-page paper, although a focused fifteen minutes may accomplish as much.

Recording. Make a habit of writing comments on all copies of papers in workshop, for several reasons. First, writing on all copies protects the author's anonymity: If everyone is recording comments, questions, and corrections, the author is not singled out as the only one taking notes. Second, it's good practice to make adjustments in writing: You learn to write better. Third, writing workshop can be lively, and you don't want to forget your point by the time it's your turn to talk.

Sometimes one person will record all comments and read them back to the class as a review. This is a useful exercise in writing notes. Sometimes two people will record comments and you can notice the differences in their perceptions. If identified, the writer may be the best one to tell the group what she or he has learned. The recorder gives the notes to the writer.

Order. If possible, arrange seating so that participants can face each other. For example, as a whole class, you can place your desks close to the walls to leave a central area open. In small groups, you can arrange your desks so that everyone is equally included: the front edges of the desks in a group of three will form a triangle, four will form a square, five a pentagon.

Responses can be managed by your instructor or a designated student. Above all, be *flexible.* You may want to open up your workshops so members can speak to each other without first raising hands. Sometimes there will be periods of silence while you consider your responses. That is perfectly all right.

Usually in writing workshop, a writer, if identified, will stay silent while participants discuss his or her paper. Later in the process, the writer may ask and answer questions. At that time, direct responses to the writer.

Reminders.   On bulletin boards and chalkboards, post photocopies of diagrams, charts, and sidebars from *The Flexible Writer*. Choose those that are most relevant to your needs and processes.

Networking.   Post papers and letters you would like to "publish" for others to read. If your class uses a writing lab, you can develop a mailing system. Partners can read and respond to papers in a file at their individual convenience. If, in addition, you are working with computer systems, you can leave electronic mail messages and responses concerning your papers and workshops.

Responding to Writing

Most students find writing workshop to be the most productive and enjoyable activity in their writing courses. But how you respond is important. Read the purposes of writing workshop listed in the sidebar. Writing workshop is a supportive, not a competitive activity. The better reader you become of other people's writing, the better reader you can become of your own. Respond to writing first by looking for the person and purpose behind the words. Identify strengths. Then reach for ways to build on these strengths.

There is *no absolute sequence* for how to conduct a workshop, because each session is a unique—often surprising—experience with different people focusing on different things at different times. The following basic sequence, however, is designed to ensure you notice writers' *strengths first.* It makes no sense to correct punctuation in a section of a paper that will be deleted because it doesn't fit anyhow. Skip certain kinds of responses until a draft is ready for them. *You don't have to take every step for every paper every time.* For example, the discussion may focus on the issue of audience. Stay with what seems most relevant and helpful. *Always point to specific parts of the paper as you respond.*

Purposes of Writing Workshop

1. To help each other find *meaning and purpose* through writing
2. To be the *ideal audience* for each other
3. To develop flexibility with *phases of the writing process*
4. To develop *honesty and confidence* in both reading and writing
5. To develop *commitment* to excellence

Offer suggestions. Look at the model of the writing process and suggest the phases to which the writer needs to pay more attention. Perhaps the writer hasn't collected enough information or needs to reorganize or refocus. Perhaps the writer is using words with unwanted connotations. Suggest models of writing you have read that the writer might find useful.

Offer alternative ways to write the paper, but don't argue them too strongly. Avoid the temptation to rewrite others' papers for them. Writers need to have final say on their own papers. Writers also need time away from workshop to consider suggestions.

For your first few workshops, you may want to respond to each other in the order in which the "Twelve Responses to Writing" are offered here, just to practice; then develop your own flexible procedures. As with anything else, the more you practice responding to writing, the better you will be at it.

Twelve Responses to Writing: A Model Workshop

To illustrate writing workshop, we will be considering the first draft of student Mery Vinas's paper, "The Mall." She decided to identify herself as the writer of the paper so that she could participate more fully in the workshop process.

First draft

The Mall

```
    The place I find significant, where I enjoyed spending my
time, is the Franklin Mills Mall. It was only the first time I was
there but I would love to make it a habbit.
    The mall is about a mile and half long. This makes the biggest
```

Workshop Reminders

1. Find strengths first.
2. Be specific.
3. Point to words, phrases, sentences, and punctuation *in* the writing.
4. Suggest changes, but don't rewrite for others.
5. Skip certain kinds of responses until a draft is ready for them.
6. Be honest.
7. Writing workshop is supportive, *not* competitive.

mall on the east coast. There is a lots of great outlet stores.
The prices were incredibly low. A lots of people go to this mall
from all over. You can tell by the many difference license plates
from the tri-state area and beyond on a lots of different make of
cars. There is plenty of space to wander around since the mall is
so big and they expect a big crowd every day. Walking around the
mall is the best way I could relax myself and think about different
things such as imaging being with your boyfriend holding hands,
getting the wedding dress. Buying the clothes for the honeymoon
or even relaxing to get your problems away; and see different
thinks that will bring attention to forget about your problems.

1. Read Aloud.   Someone other than the writer reads the paper aloud
exactly the way it appears on the page. As a reader, read slowly. Don't
add, delete, or otherwise correct as you read. When you read so precisely,
you help the writer recognize what does and doesn't sound right. Where
a reader hesitates, has trouble pronouncing a word, seems confused, or
fumbles over whether to raise or lower the voice, there may be a problem
with the writing. Circle those portions. In some workshops, you may
decide just to read everyone's paper aloud without commenting. This is
what authors do when they offer readings of their works in gatherings at
libraries, schools, and other forums. You can learn much about writing
just by listening and reading along without comment.

Read Mery's first draft aloud before you read further here. What do
you notice?

*When her paper was read aloud in writing workshop, Mery said she
noticed that the paper was short. She also felt that she bounced around
from one topic to another. The class laughed when the reader said "being
with your boyfriend." Mery realized that her sentence could be misunderstood as meaning a desire to be with someone else's boyfriend.*

2. Remember.   Start your responses by saying what you remember
specifically from the paper (without looking back at it) and why you
remembered it. This will show the writer what "sticks." People tend to
remember what they heard first and last, what they liked, and what caused
them trouble.

Before reading beyond this paragraph, jot down what you remember
of Mery's paper. This is a test of the paper, not your memory. Compare
your list with the workshop list.

*On first reading, workshop participants remembered these portions
of Mery's paper:*

- *Franklin Mills Mall (because it was specific)*
- *License plates (because they were interesting)*
- *Holding hands with your boyfriend (because it was funny)*
- *That the mall is a mile and a half long (because that was surprising)*

3. Express Likes.   Looking back at the paper, focus on what you like about it. Point to specific sentences, words, and ideas on the page. Place check marks by them as you notice them. Read them aloud. Or perhaps you appreciate the way the paper is shaped. Say so. Be sure to say *why* you like what you like so that the writer can understand how you are reading the paper. For example, if you like a paper because it's about a grandmother and you like your grandmother, say so. Understand, though, that this is not a reflection on the writing. The writer needs to know what the paper, itself, does for you.

Before reading on, place checkmarks and write about what you liked in Mery's paper. Then compare your reactions to those of Mery's workshop peers.

Students said they especially liked Mery's topic because some of them had been to the Franklin Mills Mall, too. One person, who was getting married soon, said he liked the idea of the mall as a romantic place to buy honeymoon clothes. Another student was interested because she liked buying at outlets.

4. Name Purpose.   Name what the writer's purpose in writing the paper may be. Was it written, for example, to:

- Express a feeling? Name it.
- Argue a certain point? Name it.
- Clarify a problem? Name it.
- Find an answer?
- Cause trouble?
- Get an assignment over with?

Does the writer try to fulfill too many purposes at the same time?

Write down what you believe to be Mery's purpose. Then compare it with the purpose Mery's peers identified.

For most students, the purpose of the first paragraph was to state that the Franklin Mills Mall is significant to Mery. The second paragraph was meant to show what the mall is like. No one was sure, reading this first draft, **why exactly** *that mall is significant to Mery. So Mery's overall purpose was unclear.*

5. Assess Audience Appeal.   Discuss who the audience of the paper seems to be. For example, does the paper sound as though it's written to a government official or a next-door neighbor? Discuss whether a paper in progress pays attention to the needs of the audience. Does the paper offer enough information for you to understand what is happening? If not, what more do you need to know? Has the writer made an effort to make the paper interesting, engaging, and clear? How? What more does the writer need to do? What point of view is being taken? How much is the reader asked to fill in?

Write your reaction to Mery's paper. Were you engaged? If so, why? If not, why not?

Workshop members felt that Mery had anticipated a limited audience: the instructor. The first sentence seems to be a response to a question posed in class. The second paragraph was more interesting because it included details with which readers could identify. A few students felt they couldn't focus on the paper because they didn't understand the point of it. Readers who weren't interested in shopping were not engaged with her draft. Readers who were interested in shopping felt she could have written much more.

6. Find Focus.   Identify the focus of the paper as a whole, and look for sentences that capture it. Help the writer identify whether she or he needs to further use any of the focusing strategies: choosing, specifying, quoting, illustrating, questioning, and/or stating. Are all portions of the paper relevant to the main focus? Are there shifts in the purpose and focus as the paper proceeds? Do these work? Help the writer decide the most promising focus and which portions throw the paper off center. Could the writer delete early portions of the paper and begin with ideas discovered later in the writing?

What do you think is Mery's main focus for the paper? Compare your response to the workshop responses.

Discussing Mery's needs, purposes, and audience, students wanted Mery to focus more clearly on what the mall meant to her. Some students were sure that Mery liked the mall because she was feeling very romantic. Some students were certain that Mery was a recreational shopper. They recommended that Mery write a working thesis statement to focus her paper so she wouldn't bounce around so much.

7. Ask Questions.   Ask questions to help the writer focus the paper. The writer doesn't have to answer right away. Use the question star from page 118 to help you develop questions.

What questions do you have concerning Mery's draft?

Workshop members asked Mery these questions:

- *"Which state is the mall in?"*
- *"When did you go to the mall for the first time?"*
- *"Did you go with someone? Who?"*
- *"Are you engaged to be married?"*
- *"Why did you choose the Franklin Mills Mall?"*
- *"How did you learn about the mall?"*
- *"Which outlets are at the mall? What are their names?"*
- *"Did you buy anything? What? For how much?"*
- *"Just how low were the prices?"*
- *"What was the farthest license plate?"*
- *"Did you have anything to eat there?"*
- *"How long did you stay?"*

8. Assess Sense Appeal.   Notice if the paper has enough sense appeal. Does the writer use specific images that bring the focus to life? To what senses could the writer appeal to better engage the audience and fulfill the purpose of the paper? Use the sense star from page 134 to help trigger ideas for imagery.

Does Mery's draft have enough sense appeal for you? If so, where? If not, where could she incorporate more images?

Workshop members felt that Mery missed opportunities to give her first draft sense appeal. For example, weren't there any interesting features to the building? Lights? Archways? Domes? Fountains? Weren't there any inviting food areas? Tastes? Smells? Were there comfortable lounges?

Readers who didn't like malls wanted to be shown why the Franklin Mills Mall was worth visiting. Mery told them mostly about its vast size. She assumed others would find this to be as attractive as she did. Some readers said that size was not enough to interest them: they actually preferred smaller, and therefore perhaps safer, shopping areas.

9. Describe Organization.   Notice if and how the paper is organized. Sketch an outline of the paper as it is now, naming what the purpose of each paragraph or portion seems to be. Draw a diagram of how the ideas are or aren't connected. Draw boxes to determine the balance and pacing of ideas. Discuss the effectiveness of the title, the lead, the body, and the ending. How is Mery's draft organized?

Mery's draft shifted so much from one aspect of the mall to the other that students felt it was more important, at this point, to refocus and expand the paper. Once Mery's purpose and focus were clearer, she could consider how to organize. The instructor recommended that Mery write a working title that better specifies what the mall means to her.

10. Find Repetitions and Redundancies.   Note and circle repetitions. For example, you may notice that the word *neat* appears five times in a paragraph or that five out of six sentences start with the word *The.* Does this help connect ideas, or is it distracting? Can the writer offer more variety to maintain the reader's interest? Sometimes a writer may repeat the same idea but with different wording. Distinguish unnecessary or uninformative repetitions from effective ones.

Do you notice repetitions and redundancies in Mery's paper? If you do, note them here:

Workshop members noticed that Mery used the words different *and* a lots *a lot. She repeatedly referred to the size of the mall, but that didn't seem redundant. However, the last long sentence, referring to problems twice, did seem redundant.*

11. Copy-edit.   Spend time silently circling portions of the paper where you have questions or concerns about grammar, punctuation, style, or spelling. Notice if there is a pattern of difficulties. Look for repetitions and decide whether they are effective or distracting. Then, as a group, decide which parts deserve the most attention and how the writer might change these features of the paper.

What grammar, punctuation, and spelling changes do you think Mery needs to make?

Although it seemed clear that Mery would have to substantially revise her paper, students made a few suggestions:

- *" 'A lots' doesn't make sense. Use 'a lot' instead."*
- *"Stay in either the present or past tense. Don't switch."*
- *"Use 'different' before 'license plates.' "*

- *" 'Imaging' should be 'imagining.' "*
- *"The last sentence is a fragment. It starts with an 'ing' word and doesn't finish as a sentence."*

12. Reflect.   To clarify and emphasize the benefits of writing workshop, summarize what you learned from discussing a certain paper. Discuss how the workshop went. Make plans for next time. What did you learn about yourself as a reader? If the writer has been identified, this is the time for him or her to respond, say what helped, and ask questions.

What did you learn about yourself as a reader of Mery's paper? How did your insights compare with those made by members of Mery's workshop?

In this case, Mery was eager to respond to what was said about her first draft. She said that as she wrote, she felt that her paper didn't really tell the whole story. When she heard it read aloud, she realized just how short it was.

Mery said she loved the mall but hadn't quite figured out why. She told workshop members that their questions gave her some ideas. Yes, she had gone to the mall with a male friend, but that's not why she enjoyed her experience. It was because she was celebrating her ninth anniversary of coming to the United States. What she loved about the mall was how international it was. Workshop members were surprised. Many more of them became interested in how Mery would revise her paper.

Mery's resulting revisions are shown on pages 235–236 and 243–244 in Chapter 9, "Revising." Experiment with writing workshop yourself, using the following Explorations as a guide.

Twelve Responses to Writing

1. Read aloud.
2. Remember.
3. Express likes.
4. Name purpose.
5. Assess audience appeal.
6. Find focus.
7. Ask questions.
8. Assess sense appeal.
9. Describe organization.
10. Find repetitions and redundancies.
11. Copy-edit.
12. Reflect.

Explorations _____

1. *Together.* In turn, read aloud a choice of your papers in process, without making comments. Discuss your experiences of doing so. How did you feel? What did you learn about your own and others' papers?

2. *Together.* Discuss the student draft given here. Focus on one step at a time. If you find that it's too soon to make a particular response, skip it. Discuss your experience of workshop: How did you feel? What did you learn about each step? What are the benefits of each step?

> Living on campus compared to living at home is different in many ways. There are advantages and disadvantages when you are living on campus. The same hold true when you are living at home. In this paper I will discuss the different aspects of living on campus with living at home with your parents.
>
> When you are dorming you have freedom that you never had when you were staying home. You could basically do what you want, when you want You will be able to come home at any time you want and nobody will be there screaming at you, that you came home too late. But that freedom could break a lot of people, because they never go to there morning classes.
>
> At home you don't get the same freedom that you get when living on campus. You will always have you parents telling you what to, and do when to do it. If you come home later your parents tell you lectures on, ''why you shouldn't come home late.'' Also, you always have you brother or sister going in and out of your room.
>
> When you are staying on campus you have all your necessity at your very own reach. If you need a library all you have to do walk a few building over and you have a library to do your work in. Some campus even have little supermarkets in them if you need groceries. Basically, everything you need you will find it on campus.
>
> When your at home almost everything you need you have to go out of your way to get it. If you have to go to the library you have to jump in car and head towards your local library. If you don't have groceries at home you have to jump in your car and head towards the nearest supermarket.

When your living on campus you will never get bored.
You always have something to do. There is a game room were
you can meet a lot of people. If you want you can throw a
little party, if someone else is not throwing one. There's
a little diner in most campuses where you can go and
hangout. If you don't want to do that you can always study.
So you have to be a real dead head not to have fun on campus.

At home you get bored very easily. You are use to the
same old stuff. When you turn on the TV there giving the
same old stuff. You also get bord of seeing the same old
people. Of course you could do different things but that
means you have to jump in your car and money.

Campus life is hard as well. When you sick mommy isn't
there to take care of you. That means that no one is there
to wash your clothing. So that means when your dorming you
have too take care of your self.

3. *Together.*

   a. Conduct a workshop to discuss a paper. Use the "Twelve Responses to Writing" in the order in which they are offered in this
   chapter. Or, develop your own flexible procedures.

   b. List words you would use to describe your experience of this
   writing workshop. Why do these words describe your experiences?

   c. Plan your next workshop. Discuss which phases of the writing
   process you would like to explore further, and refer to the appropriate chapters in Parts II and IV to refresh and refine your skills.

4. **a.** *Solo.* Before others respond to one of your papers, write a statement
   of your intentions: Why are you writing this paper? What is your
   purpose and audience for the paper? How do you hope specific
   parts of your paper will affect others? What questions do you
   have?

   b. *Together.* Conduct a workshop on these papers. After others respond, read them your statement of intention and compare their
   responses. How do they compare? What could you change in your
   paper to better reflect your intended purpose? Would it be more
   satisfying to adopt a different purpose or audience?

5. *Together.* One of the ways you develop a sense of how to write is to
   read and reread models of writing that you admire. Choose a piece of
   writing from this book that you admire, and discuss it using the
   relevant steps in the list of "Twelve Responses to Writing." Suggest
   how the writer could revise the piece to tailor it to you as a reader.

Workshop Personalities

In writing workshop, you will find yourself at different times defending a point, cleaning up, wondering, questioning, appreciating, laughing, and puzzling. You may have a preferred approach to workshop. From time to time, step back and notice what role you are playing and if it is helpful. The difference between someone who is new and someone who is practiced in writing workshop is that the *practiced* person can move flexibly among different roles. In a workshop, these are the roles that people may assume at different times:

The *Judge* is interested in following rules and what she or he interprets as "correctness." The Judge asks important questions about whether something makes sense, contradicts itself, or is true. This can be very helpful when you are editing and proofreading and keeping a piece of writing organized. But the Judge may be too impatient and hard on a piece of writing that is still in an early draft and may try to rewrite the paper for the writer prematurely. You can tell when the Judge is overdoing it because people will tense up, and the writer will become very unhappy.

The *Free Spirit* is very energetic in brainstorming and creating new ways of looking at a topic and will often discover strengths that others may not see. The Free Spirit is fun in a workshop and may offer interesting and valuable points of view. But the Free Spirit may also pull the discussion too far away from the paper and onto something that may turn out to be irrelevant. You can tell when the Free Spirit is overdoing it because no one will be looking at the paper in question or writing anything down.

The *Social Worker* wants peace, good will, and cooperation. Often the Social Worker will be the one negotiating between opposing viewpoints. However, the Social Worker may try to force everyone to agree on everything. One of the best features of writing workshop is that you realize that there are many points of view and many ways of reading a paper. The writer has to decide what will serve the purpose of the paper. You can tell the Social Worker is overdoing it when people stop being willing to disagree.

The *Doer* is very helpful in organizing the workshop so that it runs smoothly, papers are thoroughly reviewed, and the focus stays on how the paper is actually written. But the Doer may be so task-oriented that he or she forgets that sometimes going off on a tangent may be helpful to the writer and that laughter and flexibility smooth the process. You can tell the Doer is overdoing it when people look distracted, uninvolved, or overwhelmed.

The *Rebel*, unlike the Social Worker, doesn't like to be just "one of the crowd," and may resist the whole process of group interaction or try to undermine it. This resistance may show up in two extremes: sullen silence, withdrawal, chronic lateness, and absence; or active objections, distractions, griping, and hostility. The Rebel can be a very important member of a community, pointing out problems that need to be addressed. It's often the Rebel who initiates positive change. After all, the United States has developed into the nation it is because it allows for opposing viewpoints and styles. However, if the Rebel is disruptive or too much of a damper on the group process, she or he will have to negotiate with the group about whether to stay. Someone will have to address the Rebel directly. Keep in mind that rebellion may be temporary and minor—at some point, everyone feels like withdrawing out of fear, hurt, or just having a bad day.

The *Silent Partner*, rarely talking or interacting with others, may seem to be a Rebel. The difference is that the Silent Partner listens carefully and is alert to group process. The Silent Partner offers support by his or her presence and is a welcome balance in a group of talkers. Often the Silent Partner is the one who formulates *the* insights for which others are grappling aloud. However, the Silent Partner may recede so much that he or she seems bored or judgmental, which reduces the group's energy. When the Silent Partner gets too silent, draw the person out by asking, "What do you think?"

The sidebar titled "Checklist for Writing Workshop" can help you assess how you are working together in writing workshop.

Problems and Opportunities in Writing Workshop

To revise your writing is to revise your language. To revise your language is to revise your beliefs and yourself. Revising may, at times, be uncomfortable and embarrassing. Most of the time it is empowering and energizing. The more you notice how others respond and the more generous you are in responding to others' writing, the more *flexibility* and *strength* you develop as a writer. Here are some problems you may encounter in response to writing workshop and ways you can turn them into opportunities:

Problem: You don't understand the response.

Opportunity: Ask your responder to rephrase the comment and point to more specific examples in your paper.

Problem: You disagree.

Opportunity: Restate the purpose and audience of your paper and use these as a basis for discussing how the paper is written. If your responder still disagrees, consult with other readers.

Checklist for Writing Workshop

On a scale of never (0) to always (5), rank yourself and/or your group on the following kinds of participation:

The Writing Process

_____ Read aloud

_____ Remembered

_____ Expressed likes

_____ Identified purpose

_____ Assessed audience appeal

_____ Helped find and create focus

_____ Pointed to specific parts of papers

_____ Asked questions

_____ Helped develop sense appeal

_____ Suggested ways to organize

_____ Noticed repetitions and redundancies

_____ Discussed grammar, punctuation, style, and spelling

The Workshop Process

_____ Found and supported strengths

_____ Acknowledged others' ideas

_____ Offered honest reader reactions

_____ Voiced disagreements

_____ Involved quiet members

_____ Listened to suggestions

_____ Kept the group focused on writing

_____ Monitored time for papers

_____ Reflected and summarized particular lessons learned

Workshop Personalities

Assign yourself a low of 0 to a high of 5 for playing each of these roles in the workshop:

_____ The Judge

_____ The Free Spirit

_____ The Social Worker

_____ The Doer

_____ The Rebel

_____ The Silent Partner

Problem: You don't know how to change.

Opportunity: Ask for suggestions. Consult with resources such as this textbook and handbooks. Reread examples of writing that you admire.

Problem: You get conflicting responses.

Opportunity: Ask your responders to further clarify the reasons for their comments. Evaluate for yourself who you believe (1) has more relevant experience (this may be a peer instead of your instructor), (2) understands your purpose and audience best, and (3) is the kind of reader you are most interested in capturing.

Problem: You feel resistant to change.

Opportunity: Take time off from your paper until you can gather the proper resources to return to it. Reconsider which phase of the writing process you may have neglected, and relax with Explorations in the relevant sections of this book. You may find a way to maintain your approach in a way that other readers can accept, you may figure out how to use their responses in a way that satisfies you, or you may be satisfied with others' not accepting your paper.

Problem: Others won't take your suggestion.

Opportunity: Find another way to state your suggestion. Refer to the purpose and audience and point to specific parts of the paper to support your claim. Point out what you like and be encouraging about the strengths of the paper. If someone still won't listen to you, ask why, or drop the issue. The person may need some time to reflect. You may be missing something, yourself.

Explorations

1. *Together.*

    a. To sharpen your awareness of the dynamics of workshop personalities, choose six people who feel they tend to (or would like to) assume one of the roles described above. These people will form a workshop group (either at the front of the classroom or in the middle of a circle formed by the rest of the class) and conduct a workshop on a paper. The rest of the class will take notes on what the different personalities do and say.

    b. Discuss:

    - Which personalities people assumed
    - If people changed personalities in process
    - What kinds of words and expressions different personalities used
    - What did or didn't work
    - How the workshop could have been more effective

Allow the discussion to develop its own direction. What role did you assume in the discussion of the workshop?

2. *Solo.* Write a journal entry discussing which workshop personality you tend to assume, what your special contributions can be, and how you could use your tendencies to learn more from working with others. In your journal entry, discuss the roles you take in other classes, as well. How do you expect to be the same or different in your writing class? Why?

3. *Together and Solo.* Conduct a writing workshop (either as a whole class or in small groups) and evaluate your involvement using the "Checklist for Writing Workshop."

4. *Together or Solo.* Discuss or write a letter about any problems you have with writing workshop. How could you turn these problems into opportunities?

Five Variations

The benefit of conducting writing workshop as a whole group is that more people can offer a greater range of perspectives and insights. However, working as a whole group can be time-consuming. Fewer papers can be reviewed, and not everyone will be able to say all that she or he wants to say. Some people feel more comfortable talking in small groups of peers than talking with a whole class (including the instructor) listening. Here are five variations on writing workshop that will enable you to respond to more papers, more often, and to become more familiar with the work and development of particular writers. Most important, these variations will help you to become more confident in your own ability to read and revise your own work.

1. Self-review.   Before you submit a draft of a paper, do a workshop of it yourself. Fill in the cover sheet offered in the sidebar, or write a letter to your instructor or workshop members answering the suggested questions. Workshopping your paper for yourself is an effective way to take a reader's point of view. Writing a cover sheet or letter further attunes you to audience and purpose.

Often you may write something in your letter or cover sheet that you could have written into your paper. Your instructor and workshop members can encourage you to use that idea. Also, by practicing self-review, you learn to revise your own writing and speed your development.

Here is the letter Mery wrote about her paper on the mall. Notice how some of what she says in her letter anticipated comments and revisions in the model workshop:

Dear Readers,

    I'm writing this letter to let you know that I like the mall a lot. I was very happy to go to the mall. Never before did I feel like a little girl again. There was so many different things at the mall that is hard for me to know where to say. Every time I think on something, something else comes to my mind and I want to talk about that. Because I didn't know where to start the paper took me a long time to write. This is a problem I still feel. There's a lot more I want to tell you but I feel I don't know how else to get it all there.

    I hope you can all see that the mall is my favorite place. My favorite part of my paper is when I told how big the place was. I also hope you can see why I could relax myself at the mall.

    The question I have is do you see why I like the mall? Is there anything you would like me to tell you so that I can know what to write into my paper? Also, is my English OK? I was grew up in Spanish speaking environment. As a result of that I learn very little about how to express my thought a different language. I need help and don't be afraid to tell me. I like it when someone helps me to speak better English.

    My benefits in this paper: I got to talk about something I like and that made memories come back that I love. I feel I can give to other people an experience I had so that they can have it too.

    Thank you for being my workshop.

    Mery

2. Writing Partners.   Exchange papers with your partner. Note parts you like, circle areas of concern, and then write a letter to your partner about his or her paper. Then read the letters, make adjustments, and discuss them. If others (such as your instructor or tutor) have already commented on your paper, show these responses to your partner. Discuss what changes to make and how to make them.

3. Networking.   Develop a system by which you can support each other through a network. Two different sections of writing courses can respond to each other. Or perhaps you might want to develop a letter-writing relationship with some members of the community such as seniors or schoolchildren. Respond to each other's letters saying what was helpful and what you need clarified.

If you have a writing lab, arrange for a file system by which you can review each other's works at convenient times. If you have a computer networking system, you can respond to each other's works on disk and

Letters and Cover Sheets

For each submitted paper, write a letter or cover sheet on the following points. Use as much space as necessary.

Why did you write the paper?

Who is your audience?

What benefits did you experience in the process?

What do you like about your paper? (Highlight, checkmark, and quote directly.)

How did you organize your time, your collecting activities, your writing space, and your writing tools?

What specific problems in your paper do you want others to address? (Circle these portions. Ask specific questions in the margins. Refer to phases of the writing process.)

How have you developed as a writer while writing this paper?

leave electronic mail messages. As always, when working with computers, make backup copies in case of technical failures.

4. Power Groups.   Studies have shown that more often than not, students who succeed work and study together. Students who isolate themselves slow down their progress toward joining the language communities to which they want to belong. Create a writing power group with other students and meet regularly. Do timed freewriting together and workshop the results. Discuss papers in process. This is how many professional writers develop and refine their skills.

5. Conferencing. Plan to work with your instructor or tutor regularly. Prepare by reviewing and reflecting on your own paper. Choose which aspects of it you want to discuss *specifically*. Your instructor or tutor will negotiate with you when and for how long to conference. After a conference, share what you learned with your writing partner, network, or power group.

Acknowledgments

Acknowledge each other's contributions to papers, especially when submitting them for grade evaluations. Practicing writers know that they are a part of a community of writers, whether in person or through reading. As a member of a workshop or network, each of you has committed time and energy to others' papers, as others have to yours. Always express your thanks when receiving help. Write your acknowledgment of workshop members, name them, and say exactly how they helped you. (Your instructor might want you to submit earlier drafts and some of your letters and notes.) Showing your appreciation in this way shows that you know how to belong to an academic community. Not to acknowledge others' support can result in what is called "plagiarism"—stealing others' ideas. Plagiarism places you outside the community of thinkers and writers and may have serious consequences such as expulsion.

*E*xploration _____

Together and Solo. Plan a system for consulting with others regularly. Develop a power group or a network for the term.

Making the Grade

A *B* or an *A* on your paper can give you a real surge of confidence, whereas a *D* or an *F* may deflate you. In either case, it can be very frustrating to feel you have no control over the process by which you are evaluated. The whole process of grading may seem unfair, biased, or hit-or-miss.

In this section, you will have the opportunity to explore how papers are graded from an instructor's point of view.

Holistic Scoring

Sometimes you have received two grades on a paper: one for content and one for "mechanics." But, most often, people who evaluate your work will do so on the basis of a general impression of the whole paper. If your ideas are well developed, mechanical distractions are easier to tolerate. However, your ideas and your audience's confidence in your believability can be much compromised by errors or confusions in grammar, punctuation, style, and spelling. When you evaluate a paper as a whole, you are grading *holistically*. If, for example, you were judging the performance of figure skaters, you would consider many factors: speed, endurance, the difficulty of the jumps, grace, choreography, number of falls, and so on. The same is true for a boxer or a gymnast. Wine tasters evaluate holistically, as do job interviewers. Similarly, when you score a paper holistically you consider many factors: sense of purpose and audience, focus, organization, consistency, interest, persuasiveness, use of examples, grammar, punctuation, style, spelling, and so on.

Learning to Score Holistically

Step 1.   While reading the following set of short student essays, rank them as best, next-best, and so on down to the essay that you feel needs the most revision. Decide with your instructor which scale you want to use: A to F, a high of 6 to a low of 1, a scale your instructor gives you, or a scale you design with your instructor. You may be giving some of these essays the same score. It's possible, too, that on a scale of a high of 6 to a low of 1, you will find none meriting a full 6 or a full 1.

Dive in. By the second or third essay you will find your bearings. You may want to readjust your assessment of the first few after you have read other essays. Remember to rank the essays on general impressions.

This was the topic for the essay:

Assignment: Who have it easier in your home community—women or men?

Essay AK

Do men or women have it easer in my home community?

Women, black, and jews need not apply. This sign could be hung on any post in my home town of Union, New Jersey. Yes, I know it is 1993, but how many others know?

The Union little league baseball association is one that doesn't. In the association, women can be the "team mother", or they will be asked to sell hot dogs and sodas at the games. Men are not allow to sell these item, because it will interfered with their watching the game. When the leaders was asked why their reply was, "Women, don't know the finer point of the baseball game, so they can make themselves useful by selling and cooking the food for the "men".

Women are not allowed to be coaches. They don't know the finer points of the game. They can sell tickets for "fifty-fifty" or be a "team mother", and leave the coaching to the "men".

I know that the Union little league baseball association is not the world, but if the men in charged of this small group are put in charged of a company, then where are the women going to be?

Do men or women have it easier in my home town? Last year we had two black coaches and one jewish coach, but no women as coaches.

In the town hall, there is one woman on the city council with six men. How many sentors and governors are women? How many times have a woman run for the president? Yes, women have it easier in my home town; if they only want to raised the kids and keep the house clean. Women, who try to be the equal of men, find it hard just to get a foot hold.

I am glad that I was born a man; I don't know if I could cope with the pain of rejection that women goes through.

Essay RQ

In my personal opinion men has it easier in the home community. The reason that make me say that, is the following: For example men work at a regular job they have. Their responsabilities is only to work for their convenience and to give their paycheck to the housewife if they have any marry.

Women responsabilities is totally different because they only don't work outdoor but also in the house. Once a woman marry she commit herself for many other responsabilities they didn't have before. For example they have to think they have do the laundry, cook, iron, and take care of the children while the man party or go to a reunion. Marry is not only to have a person who a women can share the feeling and just be happy for the rest of your life. It is also to do the house work.

Men are very unpatience because they do things their way. Since their life is easier they look at women that way. When a marry man come from work his food is already on the table warm enough to eat it, while the woman come from work and in order to eat her food warm she has to cook it. Some of the examples I gave is what make our community easier for men than for women.

Essay CM

In most communities men have difficult jobs in most homes. Women are in today times have the most lengthy job.

In my household my father has the most strenuous job yet my mothers' job has the most decisions. Day and night my mother's job is never done. In the morning when she gets up and she starts her day off wakeing everybody up. Once everybody is up and starts to get dress then my mother starts breakfast. Before she starts to dress herself, she irons my nephew clothes for school. Then she takes me to work. When she arrives back home then she will dress herself for work. It takes her one hour and thirty minutes to drive to work. She deals with the everyday traffic. She deals with the confusion of trucks cutting in front of her. Even though, at times traffic is so backedup. When she arrives at work just traveling to get there has been a job.

Now at work, she has to make decisions, since she's the supervisor. The work of that day, that has to be done is up to her. She has to plan the structure of that day. She has to deal with the people who work under her. She has to deal with the people who work over her. For eight hour she has to decide what would work to get out the days work.

After the day is over then it is time to drive home. Now its dark and the traffic is much more congestive. After a long day the only thing on her mind is to get home and to relax.

Once she gets ome, she has to decide what to cook for dinner. She has to decide what the children are going to wear for school the next day. She has to help her children with their home work. Once the homework is done then the dinner dishes has to be washed. After the dishes has been washed and put up, now the children has to be bathed. After the children have been washed then they are put to bed. Now after a long day, she can relax. So I would say women jobs are harder and men jobs are easier.

Essay VO

In my home community the women of the ninety are finding it less difficult for them, when compared to that of my parent. One primary reason for this feeling in my home would be the choice's of opportunity that were present for my mother, versus my sister.

During my mother early years their was less opportunity for her as a high school graduate, who went on to vocational school to received a certificate as a beautician, then their is for my sister, who received a degree from college as an early childhood educater, this was possible for my sister because unlike the time of my mothers, their was financial aid to help her pay the tuition.

Essay SG

In my community, I've witnessed alot of men versus women situations. I must say that I strongly feel that men have it much easier than women.

There are numerous reasons I can give to back up my statement. For one, if you go to any supermarket or wholesale store, you'll always see that the cashiers are mostly women. The men mainly do stock work. Why is that? You see society feels that all the manual labor has to be done by a man; whereas the women do the easy job waiting on customers--WRONG!! Customers can be the most ignorant, and annoying people. Cashiers have to go through alot some times just to make the customer happy. You see, it's been known that women have alot more patience than men. So that's why they're so quick to stick women in the front to be cashiers.

Now, I can use my Mom as an example. She works a full time job; comes home to cook, clean, and supervise the kids. There has been many nights when my Mom has stayed up to help finish a project or do their homework.

I'm not saying my dad doesn't do anything because he does. What I'm saying is that his responsibilities mainly require money. Whereas my mom's responsibilities demand her money, time, patience, and domestic skills.

Last but not least, who's responsible for the population of our world? Why the women of course. The men play a small part in it, but it's the women who carry the child for nine months sometimes very painfully. We go through menstrual cramps, miscarriages, abortions, and cesarean operations. Honestly, I don't think men hauling heavy cargo, can even compare to the heavy loads we have to handle.

So in conclusion, men and women both do their part in society. Nonetheless, women go through mental, emotional, and physical activities much more often than men ever will.

Step 2. With your instructor, tabulate how the group scored and ranked the essays, using the scoring grid in Figure 8.1. It's helpful to use a grid. You will notice that although you disagree widely on some essays, many of you will agree on which you thought were the most and the least accomplished. Once you have tabulated your scores, your teacher can report on how a group of experienced readers scored the essays and how she or he would have scored them.

As you will see, there will be a full range of responses. You don't have to agree on the scores; other experienced readers didn't. The true value of this exploration is in your discussions and in the insights you will draw from them.

Step 3. As a class or in smaller groups, choose the essay you liked best and list why you favored it. Since this is holistic scoring, all impressions—small and large—are relevant. These impressions may be in response to anything from depth of insight to length of essay and grammar. Be certain to highlight what you noticed specifically. Strive to say exactly what you liked and why. Discuss your reactions.

Code Names

Scores	AK	RQ	CM	VO	SG
6					
5					
4					
3					
2					
1					

F I G U R E   8 . 1   Scoring Grid Using a Scale of 6 (High) to 1 (Low)

Step 4. Choose the essay you liked the least. List and discuss the reasons you had trouble with it.

Step 5. Choose the essay on which you disagreed the most, and list and weigh the reasons for your impressions.

Step 6. Together, formulate and rank in order of importance ten features of a successful essay.

Explorations _____

1. *Together and Solo.*

   a. Invent a new name (pseudonym) for yourself to identify your work anonymously. Write a timed essay, illustrating why you agree or disagree with one of the following morals from *Aesop's Fables.* Use printouts or carbon paper. An original and a copy of your essay can be shared among four people.

      Morals from *Aesop's Fables*

      Appearances are often deceiving.

      Slow and steady wins the race.

      Union gives strength.

      It is not fine feathers that make fine birds.

      People often grudge others what they can't have themselves.

   b. Your instructor will gather your papers and distribute them either to other groups or to another class. He or she will also collect your pseudonyms.

   c. Holistically score these essays and discuss your impressions using the steps outlined above. Have one person record the scores and group impressions of these essays.

2. *Solo.* On a separate sheet of paper, score one of your own essays and offer reasons for your score. Honesty is what is important here, not a high grade. Record, as well, your experience of writing the essay. The more conscious you are of your strengths and concerns, the more empowered you will be. Then compare your assessment with reviews offered by your peers and your instructor. Notice if you were either too easy or unnecessarily hard on yourself.

3. *Solo.* Write a letter to yourself or your instructor about what you learned about effective writing from your experience of holistic scoring. How will you apply this experience to your writing?

Chapter Review _____

Together.

1. Write a one-page manual about the writing process for new writers. Choose the ten points from this chapter that you feel are most important. One benefit of this project is that, it provides you further practice in consulting with each other and negotiating decisions. Another benefit of discussing this chapter is that, in the process, you will rehearse and thereby better remember it.

2. Reflect on the problems of writing this one-page manual and on how you created opportunities and benefits in response.

Chapter *9*

Revising

This chapter offers opportunities to

—**Revise** your own papers

—**Help others** to revise

—Distinguish **revising** from recopying, readjusting, and copy-editing

—Develop **strategies for copy-editing** your papers

Error marks the place where education begins.
—Mike Rose,
Author of Lives on the Boundary

When you revise, the writing becomes good to you.
—Kyle Davis, Student

Excellence is millimeters and not miles.
From poor to good is great.
From good to best is small.

—Robert Francis, Poet

Why Revise?

The word *revise* means to "see again," to "have a new vision." To revise means to use others' comments on your work to inspire you to develop new ideas. Revising means taking charge. It is an act of generosity. When you revise you not only change your paper according to what others suggest, you also take the risk of trying out ideas that occur to you as you return to your current draft. You develop and relate your own new "vision." You find new and better ways to change what you write so that you can better reach your audience and fulfill your purposes. Many writers claim that they learn the most and enjoy their writing best while they revise.

In practical terms, when you revise you reconsider which phase of the writing process you need to re-enter. Perhaps you have to refocus your beginning or reidentify your purpose and audience. Perhaps you need to reorganize or to collect more materials. In some cases, you may decide to start all over again. The biggest breakthrough is being willing to let go of a large portion of your work in the service of expanding on that *one* sentence that really matters. Revising takes courage, work, humility, flexibility, and a sense of humor.

Revising Strategies

When you revise, you follow some of the same procedures as you do when you consult with others.

1. *Read aloud.* Throughout the drafting and revising process, read your paper aloud as often as you can. Voicing the words will help you notice for yourself what you want to keep and what you want to change.

2. *Mark your own paper.* Using colored pens, cross out what you want to delete; draw arrows to reorganize the order of words, sentences,

---

Purposes for Revising

- To learn more about your purpose and how to satisfy it
- To further sensitize yourself to your real or anticipated audience
- To discover and create meaning
- To enjoy the benefits of creating something new
- To develop courage and generosity in the writing process

and paragraphs. Check or underline main points and favorite passages. Cut anything that distracts from them. If you want to add something, note it and place a wedge (∧) where you want to insert the additions. Circle portions of which you are unsure.

3. *Pace yourself.* Time is one of the most important factors in revising. You need time off between drafts to let ideas surface, to collect more information, to write other pieces—in short, to distance yourself from identifying with your paper. Sure, those are your words. But you aren't your words. That's why it is so important to start writing projects early enough to give yourself the necessary time and space to explore, experiment, and have enough work from which to harvest your best. It's like this—the larger the school, the better the basketball team, because the larger school has more candidates from which to choose the best. The more you write and the more time you have to write, the better your final product will be. You will have more from which to choose your best.

4. *Be efficient.* Sometimes using scissors and tape in the revising process is easier than recopying. Cut out large sections of your paper that don't belong. If you need to expand, either tape the additions to the side of the paper or cut your paper where the addition needs to be taped in. You can also reorganize by cutting, reshuffling, and taping sections.

If you are working with a computer, learn and use commands that let you add, delete, insert, and move letters, words, phrases, sentences, and paragraphs. Be sure to open a new file and copy in your previous version. This will let you save versions so you can choose portions that best satisfy your purpose.

5. *Be organized.* Use a revision to-do list or a writer's journal (both described below) to help you benefit the most from other's responses and make the most effective revisions.

Revision To-Do List

If you know exactly how you want to start revising, just go to it. But when you're at a stopping point, you may want to create a revision to-do list. A *revision to-do list* helps you focus on and remember suggestions offered by others. It helps you develop a plan for revising. It will remind you of the aspects of writing that you need to attend to, yourself. You can organize this list in several ways. The first is to organize your list by referring to the phases of the writing process. Here is an example of such a revision to-do list. Mery Vinas compiled it, using the responses made to her paper featured in Chapter 8.

The Mall

1. *Purpose.* Become clear about what the mall means to me.
2. *Audience.* Write it so that my readers can see the place. Remember

that some of my readers don't like malls so I have to make it look good to them.

3. *Focus.* Write a thesis statement about what it means to me.

4. *Collect.* Go to the mall. Write down many sense appeal things to include in my paper.

5. *Organize.* Organize the paper after making the focus. Write a new title.

Another way to write a revision to-do list is to list all the questions you and others ask about your paper. To guide her revision process, Mery used the list of workshop questions shown on page 211.

Explorations _____

a. *Solo.* Choose a paper for which you have received responses from your instructor, your peers, or both. Write a revision to-do list focusing on phases of the writing process. Then write another revision list in the form of questions.

b. *Together.* Read these lists in small groups with the purpose of expanding or shortening the lists. Pay special attention to purpose and audience.

Writer's Journal

Your writer's journal helps you discover how to revise. If you write even a short note about a draft, you are already experiencing what student Michelle Willabus calls "semi-revision." Other students have mentioned these benefits of reflecting on their own writing:

- It opens a door.
- It develops a relationship with your first reader—*yourself.*
- It gives you ten times more confidence.
- To think and talk about writing is to start revising.

Mery developed ideas for revising her paper while writing in her writer's journal. Here is one of her entries:

Today people did my paper in workshop. First I was disappointed that they didn't think it was finished. But I guess I knew it was too short. I guess I just really like the mall and didn't know other people might not like shopping. I learned a lot that other people think different from me.

This time my group helped me to see that I didn't use my sense appeal. They all had a lot of questions. Now I'm going to find a way to show them that it is a place like the whole world.

*E*xplorations _____

1. *Solo.* Write in your writer's journal about a paper that you have been revising or that you plan to revise. Include all your concerns and develop your plans.

2. *Together.* Read to each other from your writer's journals and discuss what you learned by writing in them.

_____

Mery revised her paper, taking the advice of her workshop:

Second draft

The World at Franklin Mills Mall

Mery Vinas

The place I find significant, where I enjoyed spending my time, is in the Franklin Mills Mall in Pennsylvania. After my first visit I had a feeling that I would love to make it a habbit. The reason was because of the beutiful water fountain in the lobby. The water spurted out of the top of the fountain very high. I was excited to explore the mall atmosphere.

On a sunday morning September 5, 1993 was the day I visited the mall and also the ninth anniversary of being in the United States. After coming from my original country Dominican Republic, I went to Franklin Mills Mall with my best friend Lee Rodriguez. This was an experience that I'll never forget. Lee took me to eat at one of the nicest places in the mall. The places were all nice and the foodcourt was decorated with different cultural traditions. One place was Italian, the other was chinesse, and the other one was mexican. Every place in the mall was international. We went to a chinesse place where we had delicious seafood. The name of the place was called Ocean Pacific. When we finished eating, we went to take a look at the mall and every store we looked at, was different. Many people who worked at the stores were dressed in different styles of clothing. For example, I saw a lady who had a Hawiian flowered print blouse. I also went to another place where they sale shoes. The sales person had a big mexican hat and big boots with a handkerchief on his pants. Lee and I went to a store name Banana Republic this people were dressed like the people in the 50s from the Dominican Republic. I like the clothes they sales there because they had old fashion which are now on style. From Banana Republic Lee bought me a lot of nice clothes, some of which I still wear today. He bought me a beutiful tight red dress. He must of known that red was my favorite color. He also bought me a champion jacket which I saw at the woodbridge mall for $80 and at Franklin Mills Mall was for $40. We went to all the stores at the mall even the expensive ones. My friend Lee made me feel so secure and important on that day .

The mall is about a mile and half long. This makes it the biggest mall on the East Coast. There are a lot of great outlets stores, the prices were incredibbly low. A lot of people go to this mall from all over the tri- state area. You can tell this by the licensed plates, not only from New Jersey but also from Rhode Island, New York, and Pennsylvania. Even from out of the United States I saw people I could tell by the way people dressed, talked and walked. Every store I went I heard different kind of music. For example the song of John Secada "Otro Día Mas" I heard it in spanish in the Banana Republic.

There were many import products for example kids toys from Korea and instruments for kids such as piano. Everything was cheap and the kids imported items were only $1 each.

Time definetly goes fast when touring at the Franklin Mills Mall. Both the crowd and the cozy atmosphore tend to make the time just fly. I wish I could go to this mall more often. I'll never forget the Franklin Mills Mall because it was a beautiful place and I still have a pretty nice warddrobe from them.

Reflect on Mery's second draft, using the following questions and suggestions:

*R*eflections _____

1. Read Mery's second draft aloud. What do you notice?

2. What do you remember without looking back at it?

3. What do you like about Mery's second draft?

4. Is Mery's purpose clearer? What does the mall mean to her?

5. Has her audience appeal improved? Are you better engaged? If so, where in the paper does she engage you?

6. What specifics does Mery mention in this draft?

7. What is her thesis statement?

8. Where does Mery make a sense appeal in this second draft?

9. Does Mery place her thesis statement in an effective place? If not, where could she place it?

10. Is Mery's title effective? Does it both familiarize and surprise her audience?

11. Are there ineffective repetitions or redundancies?

12. Circle any problems with grammar, punctuation, spelling, or style.

Copy-editing Strategies

To copy-edit is to adjust grammar, punctuation, spelling, and typing. As the Handbook chapters (15 and 16) in this text show, grammar and punctuation are crucial to the creation and communication of meaning. Often copy-editing leads to deeper revisions: reformulating purpose, re-addressing audience, refocusing, recollecting, reorganizing. Notice if copy-editing leads to deeper revisions for you.

Mery's class did a workshop of Mery's second draft, addressing questions you were invited to consider above. They had some further concerns about focus and organization, which she addressed in writing a third draft.

In reading Mery's second draft, you may have noticed, as she and her classmates did, that there were problems with grammar, punctuation, spelling, and style. So, at this point, when Mery had better established her purpose, audience, and focus, students offered copy-editing suggestions she could incorporate into her next draft. The eight strategies that follow will help you to copy-edit your own writing.

1. Read Backward. You can look at your own work for so long that it's hard to see it after awhile. One sentence leads to another, and the flow of ideas takes over. When you read aloud forward, you tend to punctuate with your voice instead of on the page. So one of the most useful strategies for editing your paper is to read aloud backward, sentence by sentence. This helps you recognize grammatical structures, punctuation, and spelling.

2. Mark Your Paper. Use these symbols:

Insert— ∧ Reverse— ⟨AU⟩ Connect— ⟝

Cut— ℓ New paragraph— ¶ Space— #

Capitalize— ≡

Circle any parts of the paper where you feel uncertain about something or wonder if a punctuation mark is needed. If you have an idea of what to do, write it in. Use these helpful abbreviations:

Fragment— *frag* Comma splice— C-S

Misplaced modifier— *mod* Parallel construction— ||

Run-on— *RO* Verb shift— V-sf

Subject-verb agreement— S-V Pronoun shift— P-sf

Pronoun agreement— *pro* Spelling— Sp

Make up your own marks as you discover patterns of concern in your work or in that of others. Sometimes a particular portion can be marked with several editing notes. However, remember this: *You don't have to name what's wrong to be able to copy-edit a portion of your paper effectively. If you know what to change, just change it.*

With the help of some of her classmates, Mery circled and marked parts of her paper that she needed to copy-edit for grammar, punctuation, spelling, or style. Mery and her group focused on editing her paper so that her meaning would be clear to her readers. The marked version is shown here.

Marked second draft

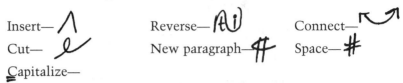

<u>The World at Franklin Mills Mall</u>

Mery Vinas

The place I find significant, where I enjoyed spending my time, is in the Franklin Mills Mall in Pennsylvania. After my first visit I had a feeling that I would love to make it a habit. *Sp* The reason was because of the (beutiful) water fountain in the *Sp* lobby. The water spurted out of the top of the fountain very high. I was excited to explore the mall atmosphere.

On a (sunday) morning September 5, 1993 (was the day) I visited the mall (and also) the ninth anniversary of being in the United States. After coming from my original country, the Dominican

Republic, I went to Franklin Mills Mall with my best friend Lee
Rodriguez. This was an experience that I'll never forget. Lee
took me to eat at one of the nicest places in the mall. The places
were all nice and the food court was decorated with different
cultural traditions. One place was Italian, the other was
chinese, and the other one was mexican. Every place in the mall
was international. We went to a chinese place where we had
delicious seafood. The name of the place was called Ocean
Pacific. When we finished eating, we went to take a look at the
mall and every store we looked at, was different. Many people who
worked at the stores were dressed in different styles of clothing.
For example, I saw a lady who had a Hawiian flowered print blouse.
I also went to another place where they sale shoes. The sales
person had a big mexican hat and big boots with a handkerchief on
his pants. Lee and I went to a store name Banana Republic this
people were dressed like the people in the 50s from the Dominican
Republic. I like the clothes they sales there because they had
old fashion which are now on style. From Banana Republic Lee
bought me a lot of nice clothes, some of which I still wear today.
He bought me a beutiful tight red dress. He must of known that red
was my favorite color. He also bought me a champion jacket which
I saw at the woodbridge mall for $80 and at Franklin Mills Mall
was for $40. We went to all the stores at the mall even the expensive
ones. My friend Lee made me feel so secure and important on that
day.

The mall is about a mile and half long. This makes it the
biggest mall on the East Coast. There are a lot of great outlets
stores, the prices were incredibly low. A lot of people go to
this mall from all over the tri-state area. You can tell this by
the licensed plates, not only from New Jersey but also from Rhode
Island, New York, and Pennsylvania. Even from out of the United
States I saw people I could tell by the way people dressed,
talked, and walked. Every store I went I heard different kind of
music. For example the song of John Secada "Otro Día Mas" I heard
it in spanish in the Banana Republic.

There were many import products for example, kids' toys from Korea and instruments for kids such as piano. Everything was cheap and the kids imported items were only $1 each.

Time definetly goes fast when touring at the Franklin Mills Mall. Both the crowd and the cozy atmosphore tend to make the time just fly. I wish I could go to this mall more often. I'll never forget the Franklin Mills Mall because it was a beautiful place and I still have a pretty nice wardrobe from them.

3. Make Easy Changes First. If you know how to edit a particular portion of your paper, do so right away. There is something satisfying about reducing the task of editing in this way. So Mery corrected her spelling, quotation marks, and typos first.

4. Experiment. Consider portions of your paper that need more careful attention. These will include phrases or sentences that are difficult to understand or that contradict what you want to say. Experiment with different ways of rephrasing or punctuating these portions.

Mery tackled her lead, because she wanted to establish exactly what the mall meant to her. This had been her first lead:

> The place I find significant, where I enjoyed spending my time, is the Franklin Mills Mall. It was only the first time I was there but I would love to make it a habit.

Mery realized that she was being redundant: she was telling her readers she liked the mall without saying why or making a sense appeal. Mery wanted to establish what the mall meant so that people would like it through her description. Her first attempt was to add a sense detail:

> The place I find significant, where I enjoyed spending my time, is the Franklin Mills Mall. It was only the first time I was there but I would love to make it a habit. The reason was because of the beutiful water fountain in the lobby. The water spurted out of the top of the fountain very high. I was excited to explore the mall atmosphere.

Consulting with a peer, Mery realized that the fountain would still seem like a romantic interest. She wanted to establish that she loved the mall because it helped her to celebrate her ninth anniversary of being in this country. Her first three sentences were still redundant. After her second draft, she completely revised her lead:

> On a Sunday morning, September 5, 1993, it was my ninth
> anniversary of being in the United States. After coming from my
> original country, the Dominican Republic, I went to Franklin
> Mills Mall with my best friend, Lee Rodriguez. This was an
> experience I'll never forget. Every place in the mall was
> international, like if the whole world was in one place. It was a
> beautiful place to celebrate my anniversary.

When Mery showed this version to her classmates, they agreed that she had made a breakthrough. The purpose of her paper, and what the mall meant to her, had become very clear. She was no longer just repeating that she liked the mall. She was showing her readers why.

5. Make a Checklist.   All writers have habits that they need to develop or break. Identify comments and suggestions that people often make in editing your papers. From these, create a *checklist* of notes on grammar, punctuation, spelling, and style that apply particularly to you. Keep it on the inside cover of your writer's journal where you can easily refer to it or on a sheet tacked up in front of you where you write. On this list, record those things you want to double-check for yourself. Organize your checklist according to grammar, spelling, punctuation, and style. Use the sidebar to format your own copy-editing checklists.

6. Use Computer Checkers.   If you can use a computer for your writing, you may find that spelling and grammar checkers are valuable learning aids and time-savers.

7. Reread Changes Aloud.   Do so to ensure that you don't leave both old and new versions in your papers, especially if you use a computer. If you change a sentence in any way, read out the whole sentence. If you add new sentences or paragraphs or reorganize larger portions, read the new versions in the context of what precedes and follows.

Mery compiled a checklist of the particular copy-editing concerns her workshop noted:

Copy-editing checklist

Grammar

- Verb tenses--don't skip back and forth.
- Fragments--check for sentences starting with an *-ing.*

Punctuation

- Quotation marks
- Apostrophes

Spelling

- a lot
- sell
- imagining
- beautiful
- must have
- definitely
- Hawaiian
- Chinese

Style

- Don't use *different* so much.

8. Revise Yourself. Don't feel as if you must always rely on others to help you revise. The purpose of writing workshop is to help each

---

Copy-editing Checklist

Grammar

Punctuation

Spelling

Style (including repetitions and redundancies)

other so that you will be able to read and revise your own work more independently.

Third draft

The World at Franklin Mills Mall

Mery Vinas

On a Sunday morning, September 5, 1993, it was my ninth anniversary of being in the United States. After coming from my original country, the Dominican Republic, I went to Franklin Mills Mall in Pennsylvania with my best friend, Lee Rodriguez. This was an experience I'll never forget. Every place in the mall was international, like if the whole world was in one place. It was a beautiful place to celebrate my anniversary.

Lee took me to eat at one of the nicest places in the mall. The places were all nice and the food court was decorated with different cultural traditions. One place was Italian, the other was Chinese, and the other one was Mexican. We went to a Chinese place where we had delicious seafood. The name of the place was Ocean Pacific.

When we finished eating, we went to take a look at the mall and every store we looked at was different. Many people who worked at the stores were dressed in international clothing. For example, I saw a lady who had a Hawaiian flowered print blouse. I also went to another place where they sell shoes. The salesperson had a big Mexican hat and big boots with a handkerchief on his pants. Lee and I went to a store named Banana Republic. These people were dressed like the people in the 50s from the Dominican Republic.

Copy-editing Strategies

1. Read backward.
2. Mark your paper.
3. Make easy changes first.
4. Experiment.
5. Make a checklist.
6. Use computer checkers.
7. Reread changes aloud.
8. Revise yourself.

The 50s are now in style again. This made me feel very much at home again.

From Banana Republic Lee bought me a lot of nice clothes, some of what I still wear today. He bought me a beautiful tight red dress. He must have known that red was my favorite color. He also bought me a Champion jacket, which I saw at the Woodbridge Mall for $80. At Franklin Mills Mall it was $40. We went to all the stores at the mall, even the expensive ones. My friend Lee made me feel so secure and important on that day.

The mall is about a mile and a half long. This makes it the biggest mall on the East Coast of the United States. There are a lot of great outlet stores. The prices were incredibly low. A lot of people go to this mall from all over the tri-state area of New York, New Jersey, and Pennsylvania. You can tell this by the license plates. Even from out of the United States I saw people. I could tell they were not from this country by the way they dressed, talked, and walked. It was like everyone from the world could be at home at the Franklin Mills Mall.

Every store I went I heard different kinds of music. For example, the song of John Secada, "Otro Día Mas," I heard in Spanish in the Banana Republic. There were many import products, for example, kids' toys from Korea and instruments for kids such as pianos. Everything was cheap, only $1 each.

Time definitely goes fast when touring at the Franklin Mills Mall. I'll never forget the Franklin Mills Mall because it was a beautiful place to celebrate my ninth anniversary of coming to the United States. The whole international world was there with me and Lee.

*R*eflections _____

Compare Mery's marked second draft and her third draft. Answer the following questions for each draft. Point to specific parts of her papers to focus your Reflections.

1. Are her verb tenses consistent, or does she bounce between present, past, and future?

2. Are all her sentences complete?

3. Does she use quotation marks appropriately?

4. Does she use apostrophes appropriately?

5. How is her spelling?

6. Does Mery repeat herself? Is this effective or ineffective?

7. Which draft do you like better, and why?

8. Are there any other suggestions you would offer for revising or copy-editing the third draft?

Explorations

1. *Solo and Together.* Copy-edit the following paper as a whole class or in small groups. Use the first five editing strategies. Notice how different people will focus on different aspects of the paper. Discuss what you learned about yourself and others as editors.

My family sees me as a negative person. My family feels that I'm not a responsible person. for example keeping my bedroom clean, clothes neat and doing my homework. My family also feels I'm not serious in life. As in being prompt in doing things for example, doing housework when asked to by a certain time or going to the store when asked instead of going the next day; and they believe I am always clowning around. For example laughing when the family stated how junky my room looks and I reply I'm run a second hand store, would you like to by something or should I bring a cow home instead of going to the store for milk everyday because it would save time and money. My sister's repeat the same saying ''you're not smart you're a stupid backward of a human being.'' I think my family believes I'm treating them badly by the way I express my feelings and actions to them by the way I ignore them at times by walking away or turning my back to them when they are criticizing me, I also tell them to get lost because I didn't invite you to my home to inspect me or evaluate my body or my sleeping quarters.

I feel that I am trying my best to do things (ex. go to school or be neat ect.) To make my family proud of me. I try to earn thur respect and love along the way. I will not try to be someone I am not. I feel if my family can't accept me for who or what I am then they are the losers, not me because I feel deep down inside I am changing daily, trying to stringten my weak points and because

```
my own individual person instead being a person molded by other
people.
```

2. *Together.* Team up with someone who has copy-editing strengths where you have weaknesses and vice versa (or create groups where a student expert in some aspect of writing presides). Copy-edit papers together and notice what you learn.

3. *Together and Solo.* Copy-edit one of your own papers. How does copy-editing alone differ from doing it with others?

Levels of Changes

Many people use the word *revise* to talk about different ways you can change your writing by cutting, adding to, or reorganizing it. In the process of making changes, you will find yourself moving among four levels: (1) recopying, (2) readjusting, (3) copy-editing, and (4) revising, the most satisfying level. Revising and copy-editing have already been discussed in this chapter. This section distinguishes revising and copy-editing from recopying and readjusting so that you will not mistake one level of change for another.

Recopying

The purpose of recopying is to create a clean reading surface. A paper cluttered with marks and changes can be overwhelming. Furthermore, a typed paper is easier to revise than one that is handwritten. A clean paper is an act of respect to yourself and your readers and a first way of establishing good writer-audience relations. If you write with a computer, it will be much easier to generate clean copies.

Remember that recopying is not *revising*. When you recopy, your main concern is neatness and typos. These are surface concerns, and anybody can manage them. Your attitude may be to "get it over with." That's no wonder. Humans need to be intellectually and emotionally engaged in their work to want to devote energy to it. Unless you enjoy typing or handwriting, recopying is not as satisfying as revising.

During an early stage of writing your paper, sometimes it is more effective to use scissors and tape to reorganize and clean up your copy than to spend time recopying. *Don't avoid revising by settling for recopying.* Recopying is effective if it is your way of warming up for a writing session. If you find that recopying inspires you to revise, then start your revising sessions with recopying. Never avoid revising for fear of messing up a clean copy. Making changes shows you know how to read and to revise.

Readjusting

The purpose of readjusting is to satisfy the readers who have read your work. Readjusting your work is responding to only specific comments others have offered. Sometimes this may be enough on a given paper. However, in readjusting, others are still guiding your process. The most satisfying way of changing your work is to use others' comments mostly as springboards for developing new ideas. Never settle for merely doing what others say: Be your own person.

Revising in the Writing Process

Keep the following ten points in mind as you perform different levels of revising:

1. Make a commitment.   Commitment is most important in the revising process. *Sometimes a piece of writing seems to get worse before it gets better.* The more you develop as a writer, the higher your standards will become for yourself. There can be a period when you are not satisfied with what you have written, but you haven't yet found a better way. If you give up at this point, you may be shortchanging yourself. Remember that there's a valley before every mountain. If you are discouraged, give yourself a specific amount of time to feel discouraged: "I'll feel bad about this until noon." Then, move on. Consult with others. Experiment. Use the strategies offered in *The Flexible Writer* to keep going.

2. Choose your level of changes.   Be aware of which level of change you are performing. Don't settle for recopying, readjusting, or copy-editing when you have opportunities to revise.

3. Don't revise too soon.   Be aware that you may need more time and space to collect ideas, focus, draft, organize, and consult before you revise.

4. Revise as many times as necessary.   Someone once said that you don't finish a piece of writing, you abandon it. Writers report doing anywhere from 0 to 600 revisions of poems, stories, leads, articles, plays, memos, proposals, and so on. Most practiced writers will look at their own published work and want to change it. If you feel there's more you want to do, do it. But, at some point, something—a deadline, the end of a semester, a new writing project—will signal that it's time to let go. Know this: Every bit of writing you do, whether you save it or not, helps make the next bit of writing better.

5. Let new ideas emerge at all stages of revising.   It's tempting to settle for recopying or readjusting. It may be frustrating to finish copy-editing only to find more ideas and insights that might help you more fully *revise* your paper. But, ideas come as a result of making changes. Note the new ideas, take a break, and revise when you can.

6. Keep a clean copy.   As you move from one level of the revising process to another, a clean copy invites you to develop new ideas and make effective changes. Whenever possible, create a clean copy of your paper. Using a computer or memory typewriter can help you to do this easily. Mark several photocopies in different ways. This will help you experiment with ways of revising and reorganizing your work.

7. When you can't solve a problem, come back to it later.   Sometimes you may not be able to solve a particular problem right away. Leave it, even if for only a few minutes, turn to some other task, and in the meantime a solution for the first problem may emerge.

8. Study the strategies of the writing process you need to learn. Sometimes you can't solve a problem in revising, because you don't know what to do. In the revising process, you will discover which phases of the writing process and which points of grammar, spelling, punctuation, and style you need to focus on. Use this book to help you develop the strategies you need to learn. Refer to the index and the table of contents and consult with your instructor and peers to find the sections of the book that address your particular needs. Post photocopies of sidebars from *The Flexible Writer* that respond most specifically to your writing concerns. Post your revision and copy-editing checklists.

9. Develop your own copy-editing style.   Just as some writers prefer to compose according to a plan, and other writers compose by exploration, different writers follow different copy-editing procedures. You may prefer to copy-edit your papers line by line. Or, you may prefer to address a particular problem throughout your paper before turning to another problem. You may switch between the two styles.

10. When in doubt, try without.   If you struggle and struggle with a particular portion of your paper but never seem to get anywhere, try crossing out that phrase, sentence, or paragraph. Maybe it just doesn't belong. Read your paper without that troublesome part. Are you still making sense? If so, and the paper is better, you have successfully revised. If not, try writing a whole new replacement. Developing the ability to cross out what doesn't work will give you freedom and strength in the writing process. Why hang on to false starts and stubborn words that get in the way?

Revising in the Writing Process

1. Make a commitment.
2. Choose your level of changes: recopying, readjusting, copy-editing, revising.
3. Don't revise too soon.
4. Revise as many times as necessary.
5. Let new ideas emerge.
6. Keep a clean copy.
7. When you can't solve a problem, come back to it later.
8. Study writing strategies.
9. Develop your own copy-editing style.
10. When in doubt, try without.

Reflecting on the Revising Process

Just as writing about early drafts helps you to prepare for revising, writing about the revising process helps you to name and understand what you learned *through* revising. In turn, writing about revising can prepare you for further revisions. Here is what Mery wrote about revising her paper on the Franklin Mills Mall:

In the process of revising my paper ''The World at Franklin Mills Mall,'' I had to get focused about why I went there and why it was so beautiful for me. I looked over the suggestions of the class workshops (we did two on me!) and decided to work on my start the most. My workshop really wouldn't let me stop until I got the start right. I also was very happy because we brainstormed and figured out a title that sounded just right.

Once I got what the mall meant to me, I remembered many parts of it. I remembered many international things. Before I wrote this paper I never knew why the mall was so beautiful to me. Just because it was big would not be enough to my readers. But they liked my sense appeal on the second draft. Then we worked some more on my grammar, punctuation, and spelling. And then my paper got better again.

The benefit of doing this revising is that I know I can do it. I never did any better on my papers before. Now I know I can.

Progress Review

Check areas that need improvement. Focus on those portions of *The Flexible Writer* that address your particular needs. Checklist 1 is for the beginning of the term, 2 is for midterm, and 3 is for final evaluation.

Process	1	2	3	Punctuation	1	2	3
Sense of purpose	___	___	___	Apostrophe	___	___	___
Audience awareness	___	___	___	Comma	___	___	___
Drafting	___	___	___	Semicolon	___	___	___
Focusing: Strategies	___	___	___	Colon	___	___	___
Focusing: Sense Appeal	___	___	___	Period	___	___	___
Collecting	___	___	___	Question mark	___	___	___
Organizing	___	___	___	Quotation mark	___	___	___
Consulting	___	___	___	Hyphen	___	___	___
Revising	___	___	___	Dash	___	___	___
				Parentheses	___	___	___

Grammar and Usage	1	2	3
Fragments	___	___	___
Run-ons	___	___	___
Comma splices	___	___	___
Verb agreement	___	___	___
Verb tense shifts	___	___	___
Pronoun agreement	___	___	___
Pronoun shifts	___	___	___
Spelling	___	___	___
Vocabulary	___	___	___
Other	___	___	___

Progress Review

To help you monitor your progress during this class, use the sidebar called "Progress Review." Check the points of process, grammar and usage, and punctuation on which you most need to focus.

*E*xplorations

1. *Solo and Together.* Compare the following two drafts of student Maria DaFonseca's paper on drugs.

First draft

Drugs and Related Issues

Maria DaFonseca

The use of drugs turned to be an epidemic rather than an addiction, not only in the United States but all over the world. This is so because, at first people use drugs to feel good or because drugs were new in society and at the time people were not so violent as today, where they kill for pleasure or to get back at someone that hurt them before.

From studies that have being done shown that people that use drugs are more likely to get the aids virus, especially those who use injected drugs and then share the needles. This is the type of a person that do not have the sense of responsibility to protect themselves as well as others.

I am a parent that are really concerned with all of this, now my daughter is only three years old but once she gets to her teen-ager years I do not known if I can impress her enough to stay away from it I will do anything to keep that from happen but this do not depend only on me, also depends on the type of society and environment which she will in.

It is time for the governments worldwide to do something that could make a difference, like create programs to educate people to make people aware that drugs only destroy lives and the society itself.

Third draft

My First Experience with Drugs

Drugs scare me. Even though they do not come directly into my life on a daily basis, I always know that they are there. I have never used illicit drugs, neither has any member of my family. My brothers and I come from a conservative family that raised us to be strong in any situation and to try to find cures or remedies for problems as they arrive, not to turn to something like illegal drugs to help us forget about them.

My first experience with drugs was not a direct one but close enough to get me scared. It happened last summer where I live, in a nice clean neighborhood. One night my husband and I heard voices and loud music so we looked through the window and saw a group of kids talking. Some of them were very young.

We thought they were our neighbors' kids, so we ignored the noise. On the following night the same group came doing basically the same thing. We were watching them for a while and saw them passing things among themselves. Not only that, they were hiding things in an abandoned car.

That same night I called the police and asked them to come because the kids were disturbing us, and it was past midnight. But the cops never came. This sort of thing went on for several nights, and I was calling the police every night, more than once, until they appeared on location. The next night things got worse; there was not only one group but two. They entered into some kind of argument and started fighting. One of them was stabbed and critically injured, but did not die. The police were there saying that they were disputing over the neighborhood as a market for illegal drugs.

Since then, the police patrolled the area almost every night, but it did not prevent the kids from coming back. Summer was over: dealers and buyers went back to school. Everything got back to normal, and may remain normal until next summer.

Every time I called the police, I got scared that if the kids found out or suspected who was calling the police, they would do something to me. But at the same time, I could not just sit back watching them destroy our neighborhood by exposing our kids to the drugs and the violence that went with them. At the same time, I was upset that the police were treating me in such a manner, as if I were the criminal. They made me give my name, and my address, and my phone number, as if I were some kind of crazy person using the phone and they had to make sure I wasn't making it up. Not only was I afraid of the fights, I felt afraid to call for help.

If this happens again, I will do the same thing--no matter how uncomfortable I feel--to keep them away from my backyard and to protect my daughter from these people. Maybe it will get to the point that if they keep coming back, we will have to leave the town, or even the country.

- What changed from the first draft to the third draft?

- Which phases of the writing process did she move through to transform the first draft to the third?

- Would you suggest further revisions?

The following Explorations invite you to revise and to reflect on your revising processes.

2. *Solo.* Revise a paper to which you have had responses. Write a letter reflecting on the changes you have made. You may want to respond to the following questions and suggestions:

   a. How did you actually organize your time so that you could revise?

   b. What problems did you have?

   c. What were the benefits of revising your paper? You may want to start with expressions such as these:

      "I realized . . ."

      "I remembered . . ."

      "Before I wrote this paper I never knew that . . ."

      "I see _____ in a whole new way."

   d. Draw arrows to portions of your paper you want others to notice. Your instructor may want you to highlight portions in your revision that represent changes.

3. *Together.* Read your revisions to each other, and reflect on them using the questions you considered on pages 236–237 in response to Mery's work.

4. *Together.* Discuss what makes you proud about your revisions. For example, students report being proud of noticing what they needed to change on their own, having revised a paper three times, or even having placed a specific semicolon. Discuss what more you could do with your paper.

Chapter Review

Together.

   a. Write a one-page manual for new writers, choosing the ten points from this chapter that you feel are most important. One benefit of this project is that it provides you further practice in consulting and revising with each other. In the process of discussing this chapter, you will rehearse and thereby better remember it.

   b. Reflect on the problems of writing this one-page manual and on how you revised it in process.

Chapter **10**

Writing to Remember

This chapter offers opportunities to

—Develop ***memory*** skills

—***Write*** to remember

—***Find meaning*** in past experiences

—Create ***personal and family histories***

> The version we dare to write is the only truth,
> the only relationship we can have with
> the past. Refuse to write your life and
> you have no life.
>
> —*Patricia Hampl, Novelist and Educator*

> You have to own it before you can leave it.
>
> —*Carletta Joy Walker,*
> *Writer and Broadcaster*

The Dynamics of Memory

"Fame!" says the song from the hit movie. "I want to live forever." Writing down memories helps people "survive" in the minds of others. William Shakespeare captured this idea in a sonnet he wrote to his beloved:

So long as men can breathe, or eyes can see,
So long lives this, and this gives life to thee.

As long as people can read Shakespeare's sonnet, his loved one will live through their readings. As long as people read his works, Shakespeare, as the writer, survives as well.

Writing memories not only helps you survive—it also helps you to understand and therefore live your life more fully. Richard Rodriguez captured the essential need for remembering in the title of his memoirs, *Hunger of Memory.* We all need to remember, to tell and be told stories, to learn and to teach through them. Before there was writing, traditions and knowledge were passed down through storytelling and singing. But if you have ever played the game of telephone or found yourself at the wrong end of gossip, you know that stories can change with each telling. Writing brought a new dimension to storytelling. Because the written word is a physical object—like a painting or an arrowhead—it can outlast the writer. We are still deciphering and enjoying the memories that ancient civilizations carved into stone thousands of years ago.

Most people are unable to retain more than four things in their conscious minds at the same time. Through writing, you can access thoughts without having to strain to keep them in that narrow corridor of consciousness. By turning thoughts, feelings, and ideas into solid objects—written words—you can inspect your thoughts, arrange and rearrange them, and hold a conversation with yourself. You can communicate with people in the past and those in the future. You can, in short, own your life.

This chapter focuses on accessing and finding meaning in personal and family memories.* Chapters 11 through 14 offer you further strategies for accessing the memories of the community that are embodied in books, newspapers, tapes, and other documents.

Meaning and Purpose

The purpose of writing memories is not merely to record them but to make sense of them—to discover why those flowers or that first car were important to you, why the groom was chewing on his cuffs during the wedding or why you weren't wearing a cap at your graduation. When you read through your memoirs, you can discern patterns in your life and recapture or discover meaning. At the very least, if you record your memo-

---

*For ideas that inspired this chapter, I am indebted to Morton D. Rich of Montclair State University.

ries, as the ancients did, others might be able to discover these meanings for you.

Writing to remember may mean different things at different times. You might write about a hand injury, sustained from computer use, to learn a spiritual lesson from your body. Or, you might write about the injury to help put safety regulations on computer design into the law. In a play or a poem, you might write about your injury to make, as one poster put it, "lemonade out of lemons." These purposes are, respectively, self-expressive, interpersonal, aesthetic, or a combination of these.

Some general *self-expressive* purposes for writing to remember include the following:

- For relief
- To relive an experience
- To own your life
- To learn life lessons
- To make sense of, come to terms with, or find reasons for what happened
- To savor good times and find strength from them
- To ask important questions
- To formulate plans of action
- To create at least one sympathetic reader: yourself

Some *interpersonal* purposes for writing to remember include the following:

- To be heard
- To gain sympathy from your audience
- To help you forgive and forget
- To reach out to others
- To create changes
- To inform
- To connect with the past
- To create a record for future generations

Some of the *aesthetic* satisfactions of writing memories are these:

- To fit pieces of your life into a meaningful whole
- To create a sense of order that brings meaning and purpose to your experiences
- To move others with emotion
- To make something beautiful

Finding Meaning and Purpose in Memories

1. *Choose* topics that are meaningful to you, that carry emotion, drama, conflict, or surprise.

2. *Assume a sympathetic audience.* The more you anticipate being heard without judgment, the more honest and thorough you can be.

3. *Strive for balance.* Few people are all good or all bad. Add dimension to your work: Consider different angles.

4. *Find humor* in what you are writing, whenever you can.

5. *Connect memories to the present.* Note changes in your own and others' attitudes, personalities, and expectations.

6. *Ask questions* to help you focus on meaning. Here are some that you might find helpful:

   - Why is this important?
   - How did I feel it about it then? How do I feel now?
   - What am I learning by writing this memory?
   - Who would benefit from reading this memory? Why?
   - What would my audience want to know?
   - How can I gain the sympathy of my audience?
   - What does this memory mean to my life?
   - How did this experience shape my life?

Deaths, accidents, illnesses, divorces, abuse, and other losses—these are events in your life you may want to forget. But they are often the events that hold the most meaning. Therefore, we will start our exploration of memories with these more difficult experiences. Often you can't leave them behind unless you express and learn lessons from them. As Carletta Joy Walker puts it, to leave them you have to *own them.*

Read Michelle Willabus's paper about a childhood accident that affects her to this day. Notice how she uses attention to sense details to help recapture the event so she can better understand and learn from it.

My Earliest Childhood Memory

It all happened during school vacation back in my hometown, Georgetown, Guyana, a brilliant tropical island located in South America. I was six years old at the time and a very mean and disobedient child. I was every parent's nightmare. They wouldn't let me play with other kids because they thought I was a bad influence. I would beat up some of the kids and take their toys or make them do something that would get them in trouble. I remember once I made a girl named Nicole ring one of the neighbors' doorbells and run. She didn't want to do it, but I told her if she didn't do it, I would break both of her doll's legs off.

So on July 12, 1976, when it was raining, I couldn't go to anyone's house to play, and no one would let other children come play with me. So I asked my mom if it would be OK if I rode my tricycle around the kitchen while my aunt washed the dishes. She replied, ''Yes, but be careful.'' Mom used that phrase a lot around me but I never paid any attention to her. Once, I was climbing a mango tree and it was still slippery from rain the night before. Mom saw me and warned me that I could slip and hurt myself, but I didn't listen: I kept right on going. I really don't remember how it happened, but yes, I did slip and fall and broke one of my legs.

Anyway, I went to the closet, got my raincoat and boots on, and went out to the shed to get my trike. I carried it into the kitchen so I wouldn't get the wheels dirty. Mom would have changed her mind, otherwise. I started riding around the breakfast table and chairs. I bumped into a few of them and turned them over. After awhile even that bored me and I was making my last lap around the table when something caught my eyes. It was a bottle cork lying in the doorway. I decided to make one additional lap and hit the cork with the front wheel so that it would go rolling down the stairs. But that's not the way it turned out, because I lost control of the bike and everything went helter-skelter. The last thing I could remember was calling for help.

Upon hearing the rest of the story from my mother, I learned that when they found me at the bottom of the stairs I had bruises and cuts all over my face and a concussion. I was rushed to the hospital to be treated. The doctor told my parents that I had more serious injuries than just the ones they had found. I'd hit a nerve over my left eye which would lead to sight problems and would probably develop into a tumor later on in life. I was given fifteen stitches in my head and had to stay in the hospital for a month. After semi-recovery, I was sent home and told to return for a checkup every three weeks. It was a terrible experience because to this day I suffer from horrible headaches and also have to wear glasses.

Because of this experience I never learned to ride a two-wheeler, and I am very scared of the idea of even trying to learn.

```
I'm also afraid of getting behind the wheel of a car. I've become
an 80 percent careful person at long last, but at what price? Kids
sometimes think that their parents don't always know what they
are talking about. We also think that we know what's best for us
but that's not always true. Listen when others warn you to be
careful. Others may know what's best.
```

*R*eflections _____

1. What details does Michelle use to help re-create the events of her injury?

2. Which words, phrases, or sentences create a feeling of suspense mounting?

3. What does the incident mean to Michelle? What did she learn?

4. What benefits do you believe Michelle gained from writing about this incident?

5. What questions would you ask to help Michelle expand and revise her paper?

*E*xplorations _____

These Explorations offer you opportunities to write about experiences for which you want to discover new meaning. Each time you do one of these Explorations, reflect on what you have learned and gained.

1. *Solo.* Write about a difficult experience in your life, such as an accident, a death, an illness or injury, a divorce, a lost relationship, an incident of abuse, a troubling sight, or a "close call." Describe what life was like *before* this event and *during the event* and how your life is affected by it *now*. What does it mean for you to be writing about the experience?

2. *Together.* Write a letter to a person (alive or dead) in politics, sports, music, or education. Choose a person for whom you have some strong feelings. Address the person directly, clearly state the events to which you are reacting, and express your collective reactions. State the purpose of your letter and ask any questions that arise.

3. *Solo.* Write a letter to someone (alive or dead) saying, at last, what you have needed to say. This letter may express grief, curiosity, fear, anger, love, regret—whatever. Notice if there are any changes in you as you write. Reflect on what it means to you to write this letter and on what you have learned. You may want to write more letters to

this person and see if there are changes from letter to letter. Freewrite in your journal about the experience of writing each letter.

4. *Solo.* Describe a recurring nightmare. What do you learn about your-self from having written about it?

Focusing Memories with Statements

A memory can become meaningful to both you and your readers by the mere act of stating clearly why it is or was important to you. Notice how focusing these statements are:

It was the worst experience of my life.

My first kiss changed me forever.

I never want to do that again.

My last conversation with my father was very healing.

Such statements of meaning are like magnets that invite you to write more. They draw readers to you—engage and interest them. Notice how the following paragraph by student James Wong is transformed from the first to the second draft when he clearly states what his father's restaurant means to him:

First draft

> Upon entering my father's restaurant, I can see its title in big red letters ''Wong's Garden.'' Once inside the restaurant, the first thing I notice is a forty gallon fish tank. The tank was recently added into the establishment in mid-August. My father and grandfather thought it would be attractive for the restaurant. The tank has nine gold fish with decorations of plastic weeds and different color rocks. The next thing I can see is that one side of the wall is covered by mirrors that ran the length of the restaurant. The mirrors made the restaurant look larger.

In this first draft, James describes the setting without offering his subjective point of view. He doesn't tell us what the setting means to him or why we should be interested in it. In his second draft, he finds a focus by stating what the place means to him and his family:

Second draft

> My father's restaurant, Wong's Garden, has meant different
> things me. He has made it beautiful as a garden with a fish tank,
> chinese works of art, mirrors, and chandeliers. But the garden
> sometimes felt like a jungle to me with all the problems that are
> involved when you work in a busy restaurant.

When James stated that the restaurant sometimes felt like a jungle because of problems, he not only focused his discussion but also engaged the interest of his readers. They wanted to know more about how the restaurant was beautiful. They also wanted to know how it felt to work in the restaurant and what problems James had.

Fires, accidents, sudden lights, strange sounds—people tend to gather around the unusual. Strong words and statements, problems, conflicts, fears, feelings, surprises, and unusual things and events capture attention like a couple bungee jumping at their wedding. Whenever it is appropriate, endeavor to engage your readers with clear statements.

The following Explorations are designed to help you trigger and interpret memories using strong words, phrases, and statements. The Explorations assume that you create who you are—your identity—by what you favor and what you choose.

Explorations _____

1. *Together and Solo.* Emotion is usually a signal that something is meaningful to you. Fill in this blank to create a working title for an essay: "A Time I Felt Most _____." Here are some feelings you might want to choose:

Embarrassed	Shy
Angry	Loving
Afraid	Joyful
Frustrated	Confused
Surprised	Harassed
Silly	Amused

    Create a working title and start writing. State your subject clearly and show what it means to you. Be sure to illustrate your discussion with significant details, quotes, examples, and sense impressions. Write so that your audience will empathize with you. What purpose

Focusing with Statements

1. *Choose* topics that are meaningful to you, that carry emotion, drama, conflict, surprise, or humor.

2. *Specify.* Write about particular events and particular times.

3. *State* what your subject means to you. Here are some sample formats with examples that can help you focus:

"I [feeling verb] [subject]."

> "I feel disgusted with Burger Barn."

"My [adjective] [subject] was _____ ."

> "My favorite baseball game was the Little League match between the Cubs and the Jays one summer."

"The [subject] is just like a [noun]."

> "During the holidays, the convalescent center is just like a carnival."

4. *Commit* yourself to strong words and statements that clearly capture what your subject means to you.

5. *Illustrate* your statement. Show what you mean by offering specifics, quotes, examples, and sensations. Use the question star (Figure 5.3 on page 118) and the sense star (Figure 6.1 on page 134) to ensure that you have included all significant details.

6. *State* at the end of your paper what it was you learned through writing your story. Here are some formats to help you focus:

"From this experience I learned that _____ ."

> "From this experience I learned that sometimes it's better to stay silent than say what you're really thinking."

"I'll never [action] again because _____ ."

> "I'll never ski in muddy snow again because the price Jane paid for doing it will always haunt me."

"I'll always remember [subject] because _____ ."

> "I'll always remember Mimi because I never want to lose a friend that way again."

does it serve you to write and others to read this piece? State what you learned from your experience. Share and discuss your essays.

2. *Together and Solo.* You are reflected in what you choose and what you favor. Therefore, your favorite things are meaningful to you. List some ways to fill in the blank in this working title for an essay: "My

Favorite _____ ." When something inspires you—start writing. Here are some favorites that others have used to fill in the blank:

Uncle	Car
Ice Cream	Mall
Sweater	Beach
Pastime	Book

Notice as you write who your likely audience(s) might be. Write so that your audience will appreciate what you favor, as well. Share and discuss your results.

3. *Together and Solo.* First impressions, first romances, first times at most anything are significant. Brainstorm some ways to fill in the blank in this working title for an essay: "My First _____ ." When something inspires you—start writing. Here are some "firsts":

Basketball Game	Failure
Day at School	Childhood Memory
Date	Car

Be sure to offer your audience a you-are-there feeling. Formulate what this "first" means in your life. How does this experience affect you today? Share and discuss your results.

4. *Together and Solo.* Last impressions can be the lasting ones. Brainstorm ways to fill in the blank in this working title for an essay: "My Last _____ ." Here are some "lasts" that may inspire you:

Time with My Sister	Cigarette
Day in High School	Child
Skiing Trip	Hamburger

Choose a lasting last event and start writing. Why will this event be the last one of its kind for you? How has this event affected you in the past and today? How do you project it will affect you in the future? Share and discuss your results.

5. *Solo.* Write an essay with the following working title: "I'll Never Do That Again." Follow this format to get started:

- State what you did.

- Explain why you did it.

- Report the results.

- Clarify what the events meant to you.

- State why you won't do it again.

Collecting Memories

You have probably had experiences in your life that you want to relive and savor. So you may photograph or videotape weddings, graduations, and other important events. Perhaps you save objects:

- Statues
- Postcards
- Printed buttons
- Dried flowers from wreaths or corsages
- Letters, cards, and other documents
- A hood ornament from an old car
- An old baseball glove

Such objects are called *memorabilia* or *souvenirs.* Memorabilia and souvenirs are memory aids. But what they mean—just like whispered messages—can change and be distorted over time. As *you* change, your memories can change, too. It's fascinating to collect memories and see how their meanings vary over time.

Because photographs and videotapes are such powerful aids to memory, we will focus on how to use them to collect memories that will enliven your writing. Most of the same principles will apply to how to use other objects, as well. Susan Mitchell's "Meditations on a Photograph" offers many clues as to how to "read" meaning from pictures. Read the poem through twice, the first time for the experience of the poem, the second to notice how she approaches her photograph:

Meditations on a Photograph[18]

Susan Mitchell

"When you look at me that way
you look just like my mother. . . ."

This said by my own mother.
But in this last photo taken of my grandmother
she looks like someone we'd never known,
as if at the last moment
she's realized another possibility and become it
without warning or the least hesitation.
Whenever mother looks at the picture she says
"You can see she is dying there."

Can you? Can you see it?
The picture was taken August 23, 1965
at my aunt's beach house overlooking Conscience Bay.
The time is a little after lunch,
a long lunch that must have gone on until two or three.
Some of what we were eating is in the photo—
bread, ham and a bunch of green grapes.
Grandmother should have been sitting between
me and two of her daughters. But at the last moment
she leaned forward, reaching out of the picture,
as if she wanted to stop the photographer
or had something urgent to say.
She blurred part of the photo. The leaves are smeared.
I could be looking at them through a rain-streaked window.
And for whatever eternity a photo has
there will be a silver streak
where she elbowed a knife off the table.

"Look at the eyes." That's mother again.
One of grandmother's eyes is rheumy, enflamed,
the eye of an old and decrepit bird,
a maddened eye,
fixed, staring out at the world, angry
at what it can no longer see.
I follow it back
into the skull, pulled inward, sucked
into the brain where the anger burns aimlessly,
a blind hole
beyond the reaches of us whose eyes
swing lightly over trees, houses, hands and other eyes.

Then there's the mouth—smiling, open, working
against the eye, denying the meaning of the eye, insisting
that the eye, like the hand lifting
the grapes, only wants—what? What does it want?
The hand lifts out of the photo, the eye
leads back in. I weave in and out, sometimes
thinking the eye must have been caught unawares,
before it could compose itself
into the weakly tearing eye
Grandmother always wiped with a white handkerchief.

Perhaps the problem with the photo is my expectations.
For example, I've always been surprised
by my pale skin, the almost overexposed cheeks
and the purple shadows deepening
under the eyes, even surrounding my face.
There is something latent about them
as if they had always been just under the skin
waiting for this photo to bring them out
the way air brings out the blue of potatoes.

Or take the grapes. Are they really grapes?
They could be a green skull. See
where some grapes are missing—
you have the eye sockets.
And there, where we must have eaten quite a few,
a gaping hole that could be a mouth.
The longer I look at it
the more clearly I see inside
each grape a tiny skull. . . .

Maybe the picture isn't important.
After all, grandmother didn't choose to be in it.
She hardly touched any of the food.
Her legs hurt her all afternoon. Perhaps
her hand is pointing to what the photographer left out—
the wind, salty and fresh, the buzz
of a seaplane and the beach tilting slightly
upward, where only that morning I had picked mussels.
Grandmother spotted them. The shells,
purple-black under the water, were opening,
the orange tongues sticking out.
We sat on the beach and ate them out of their shells.
Then we watched the wake of a boat.
One wave came in to the shore. The other wave,
lifting like the fin of an enormous fish,
continued out to sea.

From reading Mitchell's poem, some students developed the following guidelines for "reading visuals," such as pictures, photographs, paintings, drawings, and videos:

- *Notice faces.* What are the eyes doing? Blot out different portions on a face and notice if the expression of the eyes matches the expression of the mouth. Notice the differences between upper and lower portions and left and right sides of faces. Is the person putting on a false face? What feelings are being expressed?

- *Notice relationships.* How are people relating to each other? In what positions are they relative to each other? Who's touching and who isn't? What attitudes are you noticing and from what details?

- *Notice perspective.* What attitude or position is the photographer/artist taking? (This is especially interesting and sometimes humorous when you look at photographs taken by professionals who are strangers to the persons they are photographing.)

Notice who or what is left out of the photograph.

Notice the attitudes people in the photograph have toward the photographer.

The following guidelines apply to objects as well as to photographs:

- Ask yourself what emotional state or attitude you bring to the picture or photograph. (You can figure this out as you see what ideas come to you as you read along.)

- Relate the sense data to human events.

- Reintroduce motion, smell, taste, and touch in whatever way you can.

- Notice what significant person or thing is left out.

- Treat all "errors" or "irregularities" seriously.

- Treat every detail as significant.

- Use your imagination (as Mitchell does with the grapes).

- As you read, notice how you feel in relation to the picture or photograph. Notice what you learn and what it means to you.

*R*eflections

1. Find specific portions of Mitchell's poem that illustrate each guideline.

2. Formulate further guidelines that you discover as you read the poem, and point to the specific portions of Mitchell's poem that illustrate the guideline.

3. What did the photograph mean to Mitchell? How did she feel about what it portrayed?

4. What do you believe were Mitchell's main purposes in writing the poem?

5. Who would be included in Mitchell's chosen audience for the poem? Who might not?

6. How would the poem change if the grandmother were the main audience?

7. Draw the photograph Mitchell is describing. Compare your drawing with others' drawings.

Explorations

The purpose of Explorations 1 through 3 is to practice using photographs and objects to recollect memories. The purpose of Explorations 4 and 5 are to practice writing for different audiences and purposes.

1. a. *Together.* Bring photographs of family and/or friends to class. In small groups, discuss these informally. What do other people discern about the relationships they see in your pictures?

   b. *Solo.* Freewrite about a meaningful event or relationship the photograph(s) bring to mind. You can write about something in the photograph or something else that you remember as you look at it. Apply some of the guidelines developed above.

   c. *Together and Solo.* Read some of these freewrites to each other, and discuss what you learned. If you find an inspiring focus through freewriting, plan to write an essay from it. Help each other notice interesting focuses for further writing. Be clear about what purpose you want to serve in writing about your chosen topic. Discover and state what your memory means to you.

Collecting Memories

1. **Collect** memorabilia, souvenirs, and photographs to help you recollect meaningful events and feelings.

2. **Visit** significant places and participate in activities that will help memories surface.

3. **Brainstorm, freewrite, and cluster.** Your basic source of information and meaning is you.

4. **Draw** pictures of your topic. This will help you to visualize and recall details.

5. **Interview** significant others who can remember with or for you. (For guidelines, turn to the sidebar on page 85.)

2. *Together and Solo.* Bring some treasure to class—an especially important object that you could never discard (and that you can carry into the classroom). Talk with each other about what these objects mean to you. When you find yourself focusing on some meaningful event or relationship that this object represents, start freewriting. Some of the objects that have inspired others are these:

   - A mouthpiece from a saxophone
   - An heirloom ring
   - A membership card
   - A personal Bible
   - A teddy bear

3. *Solo and Together.* Look through attics, drawers, and files to find documents that are very meaningful to you. Look for materials such as these:

   - Checks
   - Diaries
   - Letters
   - Health reports
   - Certificates (marriage, birth, death, achievements)
   - Diplomas
   - Passports and immigration papers
   - Tickets

   Bring some meaningful documents to class. Discuss what they mean to you. Read them as detectives, noticing the paper, the form of writing, the ink, the date, and of course, what is written. Consider, as well, if any significant documents or portions of them are missing, and why. Freewrite, and then read to each other what you wrote, looking for an interesting focus for further writing.

4. a. *Solo.* Choose a paper you are writing about a memory. Think of an audience (a family member or friend) who would find it difficult to read what you wrote. Revise the paper so that this new audience would be able to read it. What do you change? What do you leave out? What do you introduce? How does the purpose of your paper change? How do you feel about making the changes?

   b. *Together.* Discuss the differences that occur when you write for different audiences. How do purpose and meaning change as a result?

5. a. *Solo.* Choose a paper you are writing about a memory. Revise it for one of the following audiences:

A doctor	A psychologist
A lawyer	A film director
A member of the clergy	A banker

b. *Together.* Do Exploration 4b for this revision as well.

Focusing Memories with Sense Appeal

Seeing a photograph of a forgotten friend or touching the worn leather on a baseball glove can trigger a whole range of memories. Sometimes, even a simple sensation like a few notes from an old song or the smell of mothballs is enough. In one episode of television's "M*A*S*H," Hawkeye relives the whole experience of his cousin's drowning when he smells mildew. His cousin had smelled of it when they pulled him out of the water.

A research study reported in *The New York Times*[19] showed that college students who smelled chocolate during a word exercise and again the next day were better at remembering their answers than others who did not use the chocolate smell to help trigger their memory. The article also suggested that smell could be a more powerful trigger for memories than could any of the other senses. We will focus on the sense of smell in this chapter on remembering. Many of the insights you gain apply to other senses, as well.

Student Rena Cobrinik started an essay by focusing on the smell of pickled herring. It triggered a series of memories she wrote into an essay that was eventually published in *The New York Times:*[20]

Let's Hear It for Pickled Herring!

Rena Cobrinik

Late at night, my father would sit at the kitchen table reading a Hebrew text or working on a chess problem. On the table was his glass of tea and sometimes a dish of herring.

When I was little and got up to go to the bathroom, he would be there. When I was older and came home from a date, it was the same.

I never thought about it, the way I never thought about the constant hum of the refrigerator.

Ours was a noisy house. Everyone had an opinion to express. Although most of the arguments were of only passing interest, views were vehemently and loudly defended—except at night, when it was quiet.

So my father's reading then made sense, as did the salty herring, because herring was at the heart of an enduring battle between my parents: My father loved it, my mother hated it.

As soon as my father sneaked a little herring for himself, my mother would begin her assault. Scraping carrots for a salad or cleaning a chicken at the sink with her hand in its belly and the water running—it made no difference. She would attack.

"Look," she would say, "he's eating the herring with pleasure!"

Then, trying to pull us to her side, she would explain:

"His father used it in his cafe to make the customers thirsty. He used it to sell the wine."

My father didn't try to defend himself. What was the use? It was true; he did like herring even though it was a lowly peasant fish. And anyway he'd heard it before.

Yet my mother took his silence to mean he needed more convincing. She would try to shame him.

"You're a scholar! In Hebrew you read Socrates! And you eat herring? Herring's for peasants!"

We later found out that my father had low blood pressure and without the salt, he'd be out on the couch. My mother, on the other hand, had high blood pressure.

"For me," she'd whisper, "it's poison." And rested her case.

I have low blood pressure, too, and a love for herring. This is not something I usually own up to. And not because I am afraid to take a side in an old family argument. I know that that smell does not invite kisses.

It is pungent. Herring smells of the sea. If I had to describe it to someone who had no sense of smell, I would say it feels like a fingernail running down your arm.

Now, on mornings when I have breakfast alone, I leave the insipid Danish my husband has kindly left. I take my bit of herring, gray and wet—no cherry in the middle. On the table is my cup of black coffee.

My day has begun.

---

*R*eflections

1. Point to portions of Rena's essay where she uses her senses to offer us immediacy—that you-are-there feeling.

2. Where and how does Rena use the following focusing strategies?

   • Choosing
   • Quoting

- Questioning
- Specifying
- Illustrating
- Stating

3. Referring to the sense star (Figure 6.1 on page 134), note the senses to which Rena appeals. Where are these appeals in her essay?

4. What do you learn about Rena and her family through her essay? What did Rena do to help you learn each thing?

5. How did Rena feel toward her father? Her mother? Herring? How can you tell? Point to particular portions of her paper for examples of what you claim.

6. How does Rena describe the smell of herring to bring it more to life for the reader?

7. Who is and isn't a likely audience for Rena's article? Why?

8. What did it mean to Rena to write this article? What did she learn about her family and herself?

---

*E*xplorations ⎯⎯⎯⎯⎯⎯⎯⎯⎯⎯⎯⎯⎯⎯⎯⎯⎯⎯

The purpose of these Explorations is to help you stimulate memories through sensations.

1. *Together or Solo.* Do you agree with the claims of the *New York Times* article that smell can be a more powerful trigger for remembering

---

Focusing Memories with Sense Appeal

1. ***Choose*** a meaningful memory.
2. ***Specify*** particular people, actions, events, and objects related to your memory.
3. ***Draw the sense star.*** Cluster sense images related to your topic around each ray.
4. ***Prime your senses.*** Use souvenirs to stimulate sense memories.
5. ***Offer a you-are-there description*** for your reader.
6. ***Appeal to the sense of smell,*** whenever appropriate, to help both you and your reader experience your memory most fully.

than the other senses? Refer to specific smells and their effects on you.

2. *Together and Solo.* Brainstorm two lists of specific smells—one of pleasant smells, the other of unpleasant. Choose one smell that is particularly meaningful to you, and freewrite about the memories it stirs for you. Share these freewrites. If a freewrite inspires you, write a memory essay from it.

3. *Together and Solo.* Bring to class bottles and boxes of things with distinctive odors. You can include specific perfumes, foods, flowers, spices—and, if you must, old sneakers. Be creative in your choices. Have a "sniff-around" and write about what the smells mean to you, what memories they trigger. If you are one of those people who has little or no sense of smell, write about a smell you *do* remember, or what a world without smells means to you.

4. *Solo.* Spend a day recording smells you perceive in your environment and how you feel about them. If any particular smell stirs a memory, freewrite about the memory.

5. *Together and Solo.* Do a choice of Explorations 1 through 4, focusing on either the sense of touch or the sense of hearing.

6. *Together and Solo.* In small groups, discuss freewrites or essays you are writing in order to remember. For each paper, refer to the sense star (Figure 6.1 on page 134).

   • To which senses does the writer appeal? Where exactly is the appeal made in the paper?

   • To which senses does the writer *not* appeal? Would it enliven the paper to appeal to these senses? Where?

   • Does the writer offer a you-are-there feeling? If so, how? If not, how could it be done?

Organizing Memories

You have access to an enormous store of memories. But most memories lie in clutter in the mind. By organizing memories through the writing process, you gain greater access to them, just as organizing objects in an attic helps you to retrieve them when you need them.

Personal and family histories are exciting to organize and write. In exploring and writing personal and family histories, you can connect not only with past but future generations as well. Because memories and histories are meant to last for a long time, you will want to fill in all the missing pieces you can and to anticipate questions that may be of interest to future readers. Also, you will want to polish drafts to show your writing to its best advantage. Bind your memories and histories in attractive covers, and include photographs and drawings where appropriate.

Personal History

When you construct a personal history, you develop a sense of order or meaning. To write a personal history, you need to divide the task into smaller sections so that you don't end up saying something so general that it can be the history of *any*one and so *no* one. Student Kenneth Lavy wrote a series of papers focusing on different childhood memories that would be a treasure for his whole family. He organized his essay on "The Fishing Trip" by using a flashback strategy. He started with a significant event in the present and connected it with another significant event in the past. Read and reflect.

The Fishing Trip

Kenneth Lavy

Three years ago on a hot August day my son, Chris, and myself were fishing at my parents' farm. He glanced up at me and asked, "Dad, why do you like fishing so much?"

I peered down at him, and wiped a bead of sweat from my forehead. I then gave him this reply, "Because it keeps me close to my father." A frown appeared on his round inquisitive face. The glare in his eyes was asking me, "Are you crazy? Your father is dead." I reached down and touched his young face and responded to his unasked question. "My father loved to fish." This appeared to satisfy his nine-year-old mind.

He then inquired, "Dad. Are you crying?"

I choked out a one-word reply. "Yes." I looked into his tear-filled aqua blue eyes and started to reminisce.

I was no longer on the farm. It wasn't hot. It was dark as my father and I tried to start the old cold boat motor. The deep Canadian lake mirrored the dark, overcast, grizzled predawn sky as the engine sputtered to life. We climbed into the diminutive skiff and sent delicate ripples across the surface of the water. This was our time alone: no words were needed, just a pole and a jig. We fished the whole morning without a bite. As noon approached, my father said, "Well, the biting was not very good, but the fishing was excellent. Let's go back to the cabin and get something to eat."

I tried not to hear him as I cast my lure out again. I had not brought my father fifteen hundred miles to eat, but to catch fish. Then my line snagged something. I pulled, but the line did not move. I said, "Dad, I think I hit a log. Can you help me?" The line started to move so I told him that I was bringing up the bottom of the lake. My father started toward me just as two cold black eyes and a toothy jade green face appeared from the misty deep. I appealed for the net.

My father's reply was, "We don't have a net that big." Before I could say anything he reached into the frigid water with both arms and pulled out my thirty-two pound pike. The look on my father's face was worth the price of the week. He could not have been more elated if he had made the cast himself.

My mind returned to my son as he pulled in his half-pound bass. The joy in his face was the same ecstasy I saw on that overcast Canadian lake some years earlier. I knew that my father was reaching into that murky green water and pulling out another fish.

I hope that one day Chris's child can look into what will still be my baby's blue eyes and ask, "Dad? Why do you like fishing so much?" I hope his reply is with a tear or a smirk or a grin. I hope he answers, "Son, it keeps me close to my father: my best friend."

*R*eflections

1. What is your reaction to Ken's essay?

2. Point to portions of Ken's essay where he uses sense appeal to offer readers a you-are-there feeling.

3. Where and how does Ken use the following focusing strategies?

Choosing	Illustrating
Specifying	Questioning
Quoting	Stating

4. What do you learn about Ken and Chris through this essay? How does Ken help you learn each thing?

5. What did the fishing experience mean to Ken?

6. Where does Ken make transitions between the past and the present? Are they effective? Why or why not?

7. What are the likely purposes and audiences of Ken's essay?

Read the sidebar on "Organizing Memories." Do some of the following Explorations designed to provide you with ideas to help you start and

Organizing Memories

1. *Lead* your essay with a clear focus, using one of these strategies:

   - State your memory and what it means to you.
   - Tell a story.
   - Describe a person, place, object, or event.

2. *Develop* your essay with special attention to time. Use one of the following organizing strategies:

   - *Chronological.* Report your memory as it happened through time.
   - *Flashback.* Start with some present event and then show how events led up to the present.
   - *Before and after.* Focus on a significant event that created changes. Show how conditions were before and after the event. Show how the event created the changes.
   - *Zig-zag.* Move back and forth from the present to the past.
   - *Backtrack.* Start with some present event and move backward in the exact order of events to the first event you want to consider.

3. *Create transitions* that show how events are related.

4. *Avoid* details that are not relevant to either fulfilling your purpose or showing what your memory means to you.

5. *End* your essay using one of these strategies:

   - State what your memory means to you.
   - State what changed.
   - State what you learned.
   - Describe a person, place, object, event, or image that sums up the experience best.

6. *Construct* a special album in which you collect photographs, memorabilia, notes, ideas, and essays.

organize writing personal histories. Each Exploration gives instructions on how to shape an essay with time sequence in mind.

Explorations ──────────────────

These Explorations invite you to write personal histories. Find opportunities to consult with each other on your essays and writing processes.

1. **a.** *Together.* List some ideas for filling in the blank in the working title "A History of My _____." Some ideas that others have used include these:

Name	Hair
Soccer Career	Strudel Recipe
Shoes	Jobs
Illness	Writing

   b. *Solo.* Create a working title by filling in the blank in "A History of My _____." List crucial events or scenes that you would want to include in the history. If you prefer, create a cluster around the title. Organize the events you want to write about by using one of the strategies offered in the sidebar. Focus on one event at a time and enliven your essay with sense impressions, quotes, and examples. These questions may help you to draw meaning from this history:

   • What do you learn about yourself as you write?

   • What do the events mean to you?

   • How did events in this particular history affect other aspects of your life?

   • Who would be your likely audience(s)?

   • Who would *not* be a likely audience, and why?

3. *Solo.*

   a. A turning point in your life is when you go through a significant change. This change may be as simple as starting to wear make-up or taking a road test, or as complex as going through a divorce or moving to a different country. Because turning points bear so much meaning, they provide a strong focus for memories. Choose a turning point in your life and create a cluster around it (for instructions on clustering, see pages 82–84). Include the following:

Sense impressions	Events	Persons
Objects	Places	Feelings

   Choose one item from your cluster to start a freewrite. As you develop an essay on this topic, consider these questions:

   • What did your turning point mean to you?

   • Who would be your likely audience for this essay?

   • How did your turning point change your life?

b. Create a personal history by writing a series of papers about other turning points. Create transitions between the papers by finding similarities between events and changes.

3. *Solo.* Imagine that you could change something that happened in your life. Rewrite some special aspect of it. In developing your paper, use any of the following questions that you find useful:

- What would you change?

- Why would you change it?

- How would you change it?

- What do you regret?

- With whom would you like to make amends?

- What would you gain or lose in the rewritten life?

- Who would you want to read your revision of your life?

- What do you think the likely response would be?

- What do learn from rewriting your personal history?

To get started, you might want to fill in this sentence: "If I could change one thing in my past, it would be _____."

Family History

To know where you are going, you have to know where you have been. Becoming more aware of your family patterns can help you practically, emotionally, financially, physically, and spiritually. For example, it can be very encouraging to you to learn that—although your family may be experiencing difficulties now—you had a courageous great-grandmother who single-handedly raised ten children. Knowing the history of family illnesses can save your life: You can monitor yourself for warning signs. In constructing a family history you may discover relatives who can become a resource to you emotionally. And so on.

Many of the strategies for writing personal histories apply to family histories, and vice versa. An essential tool for constructing family histories is the interview. When you interview someone, you hold a conversation— much as television talk show hosts do—to learn more from and about another person, a time, an object, or an event. Read the strategies for interviewing listed in the sidebar, and do some of the Explorations that follow.

Interviewing for Family Histories

1. **Review** the instructions for interviewing on pages 84–86.

2. **Interview older people** when possible, because they are such valuable resources for family histories. If you can, interview family, friends, and other people who know the family, such as doctors and merchants.

3. **Ask focused questions.** Here are some questions that are especially helpful in writing family histories. Think of your own questions, as well.

   - When and where were you born?
   - How were you named, and what is the significance of your name?
   - Whom did you live with as a child?
   - Where did you live, and what were your accommodations?
   - What was the most important turning point in your life, and what did it mean to you?
   - What was the most difficult time in your life, and why?
   - What was the happiest time in your life, and why?
   - What was _____ (name another family member) like as a child or teenager?
   - What kinds of foods did you eat as a child?
   - What were holidays like for you? (Choose a specific one that reflects your culture or religion.)
   - What are the most important changes in technology, culture, or the economy that you've experienced? How did they affect your life?
   - Who was the most important person in your life, and how did she or he affect you?
   - Am I like anyone else in my family? Who? How?
   - Do you have any regrets?
   - What advice would you give me?

*E*xplorations _____

These Explorations invite you to write personal and family histories. Consult with your family, if possible, to collect and refine details and insights. Consult with your writing community to help you to develop perspective, to discover ideas, and to revise your resulting essays.

1. *Solo.* Write a tribute—a statement of gratitude, respect, and admiration—to a significant family member. To balance your tribute, write

not only about positive traits but about how this person managed difficulties, problems, and personal flaws. Collect information by interviewing.

2. **a.**   *Solo.* Choose an interview question from the sidebar and respond to it yourself. Freewrite until you find yourself focusing on a particular person, place, object, or event. Using this focus, begin writing a chapter from your own history with the purpose of leaving important information for future generations. How would this history be different if your audience were your parents and grandparents?

    b.   *Together.* Ask the question you chose in Exploration 2a of a family member. Compare your freewrite with the family member's response.

3. *Solo and Together.* Look through family albums and discover people that you don't know. There are often family members or friends of whom little or nothing is spoken. Interviewing different family members and family friends, construct a history for the person. Note any resistance. Reconstruct this person's life, and write about some specific turning point in it. Record and write about any mysteries that surround this person.

4. *Solo and Together.*

    a.   Choose a relative or family friend whom you would like to interview. Select three questions you would like to ask. Star the one question you want answered most. Conduct an interview at this person's convenience. Start with your selected questions. Allow other questions to emerge in the process.

    b.   Choose the most interesting portion of the interview and write it down. Write about why it is useful or meaningful to you. Organize it so that it will engage other readers. Write about how you benefited from interviewing and writing about your family memory. What more do you want to learn about your family, and why? Do you think you can get this information? Why or why not?

    c.   *Variation.* If possible, interview a relative, focusing on a family photo album. Focus on photographs that interest you or that your relative finds especially meaningful.

    d.   *Variation.* Ask a relative to show you his or her treasured objects. Interview him or her, asking, "What memory does this object hold for you?" or "What stories does this object have to tell?"

5. *Solo.* Family members have different—often conflicting—perspectives on family stories. Choose a family story that you have heard from different points of view, and try to sort out the different versions on paper. What accounts for the differing points of view? How do they agree and disagree? Whom do family members remember with affection? Toward whom do they express negative feelings? What is your sense of what is true? What further information would you need to settle the story better? How could you find this information?

STUDENTS WRITING TO REMEMBER

Read the following essays by students writing to remember. Choose your favorite essay. Reflect on it, using the following questions and suggestions. As you reflect on your chosen essay, be certain to point to particular words, phrases, sentences, and sections that illustrate your points.

1. Why is this your favorite essay?

2. How does the writer engage you?

3. Who is the anticipated audience for the essay? Who is not?

4. What focusing strategies does the writer use?

5. What collecting strategies does the writer use?

6. What organizing strategies does the writer use?

7. How would you revise the essay?

8. How does the paper compare to the other papers?

9. Write a letter in response to the paper, relating a memory that it triggered for you. If you are inspired, transform this memory into an essay.

10. What strategies or ideas did you learn from reading this paper? Do you plan to use them in your own writing?

My Eleventh Grade Memory

Tamara Tolbert

As long as I live, I'll never, ever forget what happened during my homecoming in my eleventh grade year. You see, everything was normal at first. The laughing and joking went on all week. There were numerous activities planned for us to participate in. I loved this time of the year. Since I'm a very proud person, I was always in someone's face reminding them how the junior class was the best in everything.

Eventually, I went to my English class. My seat was near the door, so when my friend and class rival Gary Wynne came to the door laughing and making faces at me, I couldn't help but to laugh. He was a sight. He was about 5'10", weighed between 185 and 190 lbs., brown-skinned, had a big head and big brown puppy dog eyes. He was my buddy and we constantly lived just to aggravate each other. He kept on until my teacher politely told him to leave and then shut the door. The rest of the day went on as normal. After school I met up with Gary and we started up again. After a while, we started laughing because we knew we sounded silly.

For the next two days I didn't see Gary. But that wasn't strange, so I never gave it any thought. So I'm sitting in my Spanish class doing an assignment when I hear a voice over the loudspeaker announce: "Gary Wynne was admitted to the John Harris Memorial Hospital two days ago. He had a blackout due to heart failure. He underwent heart surgery but didn't make it. Gary Wynne passed away 8:55 A.M. this morning." For the next couple of seconds it was so quiet you could hear the beating of everyone's heart, especially mine. My head was pounding like the sound of a thousand horses running from a fire. I just knew I heard the name wrong, so I asked another student to repeat the name. I silently prayed I heard wrong, but inwardly I knew I didn't. Sure enough, it was my friend Gary they were talking about. I almost passed out.

I immediately rushed out of class to get some fresh air. That was a big mistake because students were everywhere crying and swearing out loud. One of Gary's closest friends, Jake, was so upset he broke his hand when he swung at the door, missed, and shattered the window. The teachers were trying to get the students under control but it was hard because they were just as upset. My former math teacher, Mr. Simpkins, was in the hallway literally sitting on the floor with his head in his hands. You see, Gary and I used to be his favorite students. He loved us like his children, and up until now, Gary and I used to go visit him after school. So this affected him tremendously.

My brain was flooded with unanswered questions such as, "How could Gary die? Why didn't he tell me he had a bad heart? How could a person so full of laughter be in so much pain inside? How could he just leave me without saying good-bye?" I began to feel nauseated. Luckily they ended school early or I would have skipped anyway. I ran all the way home refusing to cry. Just as I came to my room everything came out. I cried and cried until it literally hurt.

Afterward, I just lay on my bed thinking of the past. At this time last year, Gary was in my math class. We had had so much fun. He was such a liar though. When we were in class together, he used to be in charge of passing out the test results. He would tell me I got an A, and being gullible at times, I believed him. Yet when I got my paper, it was nowhere near an A. I'd be so mad at him for lying, but not for long. He would always find a way to make it up to me. That was good old Gary for you, always getting out of something. Nevertheless, I didn't want Gary any other way.

Once I thought I had gotten myself together, I gathered up the nerve to call his family to offer my condolences. But the phone kept ringing and ringing. As I was about to hang up, someone finally answered. But my voice ran away from me and my eyes began filling up with tears. I began to panic so I just hung up. I cried the rest of the night.

When my mom came home, I told her what happened and she tried to comfort me. But it didn't make me feel any better. I thought she couldn't possibly understand what I was going through.

We had the rest of the week off due to the funeral services. It was like reliving a nightmare. Everyone was crying and literally passing out during the viewing. I finally couldn't take it anymore and left. I felt so guilty because the last words I said to Gary before he died were "Shut up, bighead." Even though I was joking and he knew it, I still felt very bad for not being able to tell him how much I valued his friendship and that I loved him like a brother.

I've learned a very valuable lesson from this experience. First, you should never take anyone for granted for you never know what tomorrow will bring. Who'd have thought an eighteen-year-old boy would die of a heart failure? I sure didn't. This was a very tragic experience for me. It took me a while to accept Gary's death, but I'm older now and I've put that memory behind me. Yet, the funny and serious times we spent together will always stay within me.

A Still Pose

Marta Cuervo

It's incredible how so many memories can be recorded in one still pose. I have a photograph of myself that I treasure. When I look at it, I can remember the exact moment when it was taken. The details are still vivid in my mind. Even a quick glimpse of the image has the ability to transport me to a wonderful moment in time.

Looking at the picture I can still hear the music of Vivaldi's *Four Seasons.* The crescendo sound of the violins consumed the space. We were thirty-two dancers on that huge stage. Our bright-colored costumes appeared to be swirling out of control. We were leaping, twirling, running, and swaying. As the tempo of the music increased and the sounds of the violins became louder, we danced faster and stronger. I could hear the dancers around me breathing hard. We were stomping the floor with our feet and slashing the air with our arms. In essence, we were trying to devour the space with our bodies. The kinetic energy of the group made it feel as though we were all one body, with one connecting heartbeat. That one shared beat had the driving force to keep us united in motion.

Then, in one nanosecond, it happened. Thirty-one dancers exited the stage, all at once. The music was replaced by complete silence and the bright-colored lights gave way to total darkness. Everything seemed to stop. I had been left alone.

What happened next took place in thirty seconds. However, the details I remember make it seem as though the moment lasted an eternity. On a very high and sustained musical note, I stepped into a lit spot on a dark stage. This light came from a huge computer-operated flashlight in the back of the theater. In the business we refer to it as a spotlight. As I stepped into the circle of light, my body froze in a position I had executed many times before. My arms went up in the air to create a V formation. One of my legs extended itself behind me, in the air. The other leg was on the floor, balancing me. My foot was inside a pointe shoe that was drilling an imaginary hole into the floor. My four limbs were reaching in four different directions. I felt like a marionette being held up by a set of strings. I was experiencing the peacefulness and serenity of perfect balance.

As I held this position I became aware of many things that were occurring in and around me. I remember being aware of the pounding beat of my heart. The only other sound, which seemed faint and in the distance, was that of a soft note from a violin. My eyes had been fixed on the beam of light coming from the back of the theater and basking me with glorious warmth. If I looked hard enough I could see the dust particles in the ray of light. They too seemed to be giving me energy.

In the midst of all this, I heard a loud snap. It was then that I realized that a picture had been taken. I knew instantly what the eye of the photographer had captured. This moment would be imprinted in my mind for the rest of my life.

My First Basketball Game

Kennie Rankin

I was the tallest person in the third grade. I was five feet seven inches tall and weighed about a hundred pounds. My uniform was white with a pinstripe going down the sides. My shorts came down about six inches from my waist. My tank top seemed to be painted on my body with a T-shirt under it. My socks were white and had been pushed down to my ankles and my sneakers were untied. I left them untied because I wanted to be cool and didn't want anyone to make fun of me. My legs looked like toothpicks, my body resembled a bird cage, and I had a big head.

I was the tallest and wanted to be the coolest in grammar school. I was very conceited and cocky. I was not worried about what it took to win a championship. I just worried about looking good.

While I attended Our Lady of the Valley, I wore all the new style clothes. I had the super-fat untied multicolor shoestrings and also glasses that didn't have lenses in them, and I had a "shag" style hair cut.

I was not concerned with the game, just the crowd. I looked to see if there was anyone new that I could speak to. I did my pregame checklist—sneakers untied, shoelaces straight, hair puffed out—and I was ready to go.

It was the first quarter and we were getting the final instructions from the coach. We all looked a bit pensive and jittery. I guessed we were wondering what the crowd thought about us. I remembered having butterflies in my stomach as we went through the pregame drills, but I acted like nothing was bothering me. I remember stretching my shorts, trying to make them longer. The coach told the starters to sit down in front of him. While I sat in front of him, I began to daydream. I envisioned myself scoring points, getting rebounds, and blocking shots. Then I came back to reality. I really was going to run up and down the court and make a fool of myself. I wasn't good at basketball in the third grade. I was needed only because I was tall.

As we walked on the court the other team did not look like they could play: they all had their shoes tied up and their hair was messy. In the huddle, the coach was telling us they were good and that we should watch out for them. All the guys looked around at each other with smirks on their faces as if to say, "This guy can't be serious; they're all dressed like punks." After the jump ball, we realized that we were wrong and the coach was right.

After the first quarter the score was something like twenty-five to two. The school's name was Our Lady of Sorrows, but they didn't play like ladies. They seemed to run faster than us and shoot better than us. They were the ones that were scoring all the points and blocking our shots. What it really came down to was they just outplayed us. The final score was seventy to twenty and we were embarrassed. I was embarrassed also. There was more to being cool than looking cool.

The Old '62 Holiday Rambler

Donna Mekita Kuhl

The day my neighbor came to take our old Rambler away was very depressing for me. I could barely handle the situation.

The reason the trailer was out of commission was because the steel hitch which connects our red and white Dodge van to the trailer was rotted with age. My father tried everything he could do to repair the hitch, but nothing could be done. My father also tried getting a professional welder to come and weld plates and brackets to restore the Rambler's back hitch, but it was too expensive to repair. So my father's last decision was to have our next door neighbor Jim (who owns Jack Daniels' Body Shop where he could fix it much easier and cheaper) take it. So, my father decided to have Jim come over to work out a fair price on the Rambler. They both talked for awhile on a price, but they both knew the Rambler was worth nothing. In my heart no other trailer could replace it.

So the last result was that we had to painfully clean out the trailer so our neighbor could take it off our property for free. The reason the trailer would be useful to our neighbor is that it would not have to be moved. It would be used as an office for his business.

The day of cleaning out the Rambler was like sharing the possessions of a dead person. All I kept saying to my mother was this: "I can't believe we're not going to have the trailer any more." Then the memories started flowing. When I entered the trailer I smelled the cedar branch that my father cut off a cedar tree when we went on vacation to Lake George, New York. When walking through the trailer, I felt a sense of security because it was such a dim, relaxed atmosphere.

The day my neighbor came to take our Rambler away was very heart-breaking for me. I could barely handle the situation. Finally, the time arrived. It was 1:30 in the afternoon when my neighbor pulled up in his brand new Blazer 4 × 4 to take our old '62 away. I stood next to the driveway on the side door steps and watched my neighbor back up his Blazer and hook it up to our old Rambler. I couldn't stand it anymore; the tears just started rolling down my cheeks. I felt like screaming at my neighbor, saying "You should at least give us two hundred dollars for our trailer." The reason for this is because I felt robbed that someone just took a particular item from me that is worth more than money, gold, diamonds, or anything. Unfortunately, this did not happen. Jim pulled the time-worn '62 out of the driveway. All I could hear was the creaking of the axle which holds the tires on. I could barely watch, but I had to wave goodbye as he hauled the Rambler up Cliff Hill Road.

Grandpa

*David Scott Woulfin**

Grandpa. I haven't seen him in a long time. He passed away years ago, but occasionally I do see him in my dreams. We're always outside

---

*David Scott Woulfin is instructor Susan Woulfin's son. Her essay appears on pages 22–23.

in the modest backyard of my grandparents' Queens townhouse, playing catch with a tennis ball, or in the warmth of the old-fashioned dining room, playing checkers on the plastic tablecloth.

I am always younger in these dreams because that's when I knew him. But if I were to see him now, I would probably want to just sit and talk with him, maybe at the Old Roma Restaurant or the newsstand/candy store where he bought lottery tickets for himself and baseball cards for me. I would tell him about all my accomplishments, both academic and athletic. He was a man I always wanted to impress. He had such integrity and a strong belief in education. Grandpa wasn't perfect, though.

He was also very stubborn. In his mind he was always right. I remember him saying, "There is no reason not to get a hundred on a math test because there is only one right answer." Somehow I didn't see math the same way. However, because I didn't know enough to debate him, I took his word on education, politics, religion, and sports. If I met him today, just for fun I might ask his opinion about the upcoming election, just to see if I could survive against his logical and formidable mind. Somehow I know I would lose, but we would both enjoy the sparring.

Being thirteen at the time of his death, I never got to face him as his equal. I never had the opportunity to have a truly intellectual discussion with him. This type of philosophical debate would have appealed to both of us. In fact, just spending time with him, seeing him through my seventeen-year-old eyes, would give me such happiness and fulfillment.

I'd like to feel his warmth again. Just by looking at his lively eyes and bright smile, I could tell how much he loved and cared about me. To have such unconditional love is a rare thing. I miss it and him very much.

*C*hapter Review

Solo or *Together* respond to the following:

1. If you were an instructor of writing, what five points from this chapter would *you* stress in teaching student writers? Why?

2. Which strategies offered in this chapter were either new to you or made clearer?

3. Which strategies do you need to further develop? How do you plan to incorporate them into your writing process?

4. What are the benefits, drawbacks, and challenges of writing to remember?

Chapter 11

Writing to Bridge Cultures

This chapter offers opportunities to

—Explore how **cultures** work

—Discover the dynamics of **language** and **dialect**

—Practice taking different **points of view**

—Understand what it means to be an **outsider**

—Focus on issues concerning **ethnicity, gender,** and **age**

—**Bridge cultures** through writing

> If we are to achieve a richer culture, rich in
> contrasting values, we must recognize the
> whole gamut of human potentialities, and
> so weave a less arbitrary social fabric, one
> in which each diverse human gift will find a
> fitting place.
>
> —*Margaret Mead, Anthropologist*

What Are Cultures?

The word *culture* comes from a Latin word that means "to work the soil." You are who you are—to a great extent—because of the culture that offers you the physical, emotional, mental, and spiritual soil from which to grow. This culture, or environment, is made up of people, food, shelter, clothing, objects, customs, laws, and language.

The word *culture*, when used in reference to human culture, most often refers to ethnic or national cultures such as the Japanese, Hungarian, or Jamaican cultures. The United States in the 1990s has within it diverse *national* cultures including, among many others, Navajo, Puerto Rican, Ethiopian, Chicano, Chinese, Greek, and Creole cultures that each have special things in common. In this book, the word *culture* is used more generally to refer to any group of people who have something important in common. So, for example, in the *popular* culture of the United States today, we have things in common that distinguish us from people of the United States in the 1890s, such as television, movies, fast food, voting on the national level, running shoes, the singer Madonna, and personal computers.

Some cultures cut across national lines. Women of all national cultures have things in common that distinguish them from men. Parents share experiences that their childless children don't. Those who were born eighty years ago have lives that are different from those who were born twenty years ago. If your culture has been shaped by slavery, war, or certain illnesses, you will be different from people who haven't been so oppressed.

Finally, there are many smaller cultures, such as those defined by clubs, your workplace, the corner store, a popular eating place where you tend to see the same people, your neighborhood, your place of worship, the recreation hall you frequent, your school, and your writing class. The way people interact with others, the customary way to dress, and the rules of what is or is not appropriate will vary from culture to culture.

This chapter invites you to explore similarities and differences between human cultures, especially those that include people who are different by virtue of ethnicity (nationality, religion, race), gender, and age. Begin with the following Explorations, which help you appreciate how many cultures you already live in every day and how these cultures shape you and your values.

Explorations ————————————————

1. *Together.* List the different environments, or cultures, in which you live in a typical week. Name them specifically: writing class, skating

rink, father's kitchen, mall, school cafeteria. Notice if there is a culture within a culture in a particular place. For example, a recreation center might have different cultures, such as those of weightlifters, swimmers, runners, and spectators.

2. **a.** *Together.* Choose two cultures (such as the writing classroom and the school cafeteria) in which most of you participate: one in which you feel comfortable and one in which you feel less comfortable. Create two columns, and list the dos and don'ts that define each culture and that make them different from each other. What rules are the same for each? Are the rules different for different people?

   b. *Solo.* In writing, compare and contrast your particular experience of two different cultures. Focus on rules, spoken or unspoken, that significantly affect you. Organize your essay by using the block or zig-zag strategy for comparing and contrasting. (See pages 193–195 and 354–362 for guidelines.)

3. **a.** *Solo.* Your values are cultivated by the environments in which you live and grow. Read the following list of values. Place a mark along the continuum (the line) to indicate the importance of each value to you.

	Least	Somewhat	Most
	←	Continuum of importance	→
Ambition			
Cheerfulness			
Cleanliness			
Creativity			
Generosity			
Honesty			
Intelligence			
Love			
Obedience			
Openmindedness			
Patience			

	Least	Somewhat	Most

←————————————————————————————→

Continuum of importance

Politeness _____

Responsibility _____

Self-reliance _____

Successfulness _____

b. Write an essay about your top three values. State your three values. Illustrate each value by describing an incident that shows how you learned the value and from whom. For example, if honesty is your top value, you might illustrate how telling a lie got you into serious trouble as a child.

4. a. *Together.* Many television programs feature members of special ethnic and regional cultures, such as African Americans, Hispanics, Japanese, and Appalachians. List some of these programs. Choose an episode from one of them. If possible, watch a taped version of it together. Discuss how you relate to the portrayals of the cultural group.

b. *Solo.* Describe, in writing, a television program that bridges cultures. Your audience has never seen it. Argue that you believe the program offers worthwhile insights into language habits and bridging cultures. Focus on specific characters, events, and episodes to illustrate and support your case.

Why Bridge Cultures?

Bridging cultures can be as sensitive and difficult as it can be powerful, enriching, and fun. Therefore, it is important to (1) be clear about the purpose of your explorations and (2) know your audience. Here are two lists of purposes to consult during the writing process:

Empowering purposes

- To find meaning in difficult experiences
- To appreciate different points of view
- To enjoy new experiences

- To stretch your world view
- To assert your needs
- To clarify problems
- To negotiate solutions to problems
- To develop compassion
- To develop common values
- To create new cultures that include more people

Destructive purposes

- To stereotype
- To blame without negotiating
- To oppress
- To diminish others
- To pity yourself without dignity
- To inflate yourself at others' expense

By committing yourself to empowering purposes, you discover ways to bridge cultures and grow.

Develop your sense of audience by writing from several points of view. Find values you hold in common with your anticipated readers. Pay special attention to how language embodies attitude.

Language and Culture

Languages are storehouses of shared experiences. To know a language is to know a way of life.* For example, Inuit peoples of Alaska, Canada, and Greenland have many words that refer to different kinds of snow and ice. To know an Inuit language is to realize that the native speakers of the language depend on being able to distinguish different traveling and hunting conditions. To learn the language of a community is to take the most important step in becoming a member.

Language and life-style differences are reflected in the vocabulary, the grammar, the accent, the tone in which the language is expressed, the gestures that people use to support their communications, and the rules of writing. Languages can be vastly different from each other—both in oral and in written form. Notice how different the word for woman is in

---

*From Ludwig Wingenstein, *Philosophical Investigations* (New York: Macmillan, 1953), p. 88.

Writing to Bridge Cultures

As you write to bridge cultures, ask yourself these questions:

1. Why am I writing this? Is my purpose empowering or destructive?
2. What is my point of view? What other points of view are there?
3. Who is my audience? Do I need to adjust my approach?
4. How can I best focus my essay?
5. What point(s) do I hope to make?
6. What sensory images can I use?
7. How can I best illustrate my point(s)?
8. How can I best organize this to fulfill my purpose?
9. What questions do I anticipate others might ask?
10. What am I learning or gaining from writing this?

When you review each other's papers, ask these questions:

1. As a reader, which part of this essay do I identify with the most? Why?
2. What is the purpose of this essay? Is it empowering or destructive?
3. What interests or problems is the writer addressing?
4. What is the writer's point of view?
5. How does the writer organize the work to fulfill the purpose of the paper?
6. Does the writer seem to better understand or bridge cultures from having written this piece?
8. How would I further develop this essay?
9. How have I been changed by reading this work?
10. Write a letter in response to this essay, or write an essay inspired by something in it.

English, Japanese, and Greek—*woman*, 女 (pronounced *onna*), and γυνη (pronounced *gūnā*). Originally, people who spoke these languages were totally separated from each other geographically and culturally. Since these people had no reason to formulate lines of communication, their vocabularies, grammars, accents, and gestures—and therefore their ideas and experiences—were very different.

If people speak the same basic language, such as English, but live apart either geographically or socially, they may develop different forms of the same language, called *dialects,* with some shared vocabulary and grammar. The differences between dialects are often noticeable in accents and emphasis. For example, some American English dialects (as opposed to those of British English) are Chicano, Black, Creole, Southern American, and Brooklynese. These dialects differ from the standard English used in the popular culture determined by schools, television, newspapers, advertising, and other established communities. The different dialects show that the people who speak them have been separated from each other at some point. Whether you tend to say "I don't have any money," "I got no money," "I no have money," "I'm temporarily low on financial resources," or "I'm broke" depends on the cultures you frequent.

Language communities can be grouped according to professions and mutual interests, as well. These differences may be limited to vocabulary or grammar, and accents and gestures may not matter. For example, the dialects of computerese, legalese, militarese, and "writerese" have favored technical terms for *eliminate: trash, strike, terminate, delete.* But the accents in which these terms are spoken don't matter. Professional communities also have varied rules for written communications, as for example academic communities (considered in Chapters 12 and 13). Although many professional languages bind people together, they may also leave other people out. Luckily, there have been moves in different professions—such as law and education—to develop languages that will allow more people the opportunity to learn the terminology of these professions and so become empowered to use the resources of those communities.

Sometimes there are more specialized and even secret languages such as those that mark off a pair of lovers or twins, a club, or a spy ring. You may even have a special code just for yourself, as some people do for writing journals or notes.

Finally, cultures differ with respect to the gestures, or body language, that people in them use to support communication. In Greece, for example, nodding your head means "no." In the United States, nodding means "yes."

The more varied the community using a language, the greater are the gains made by bridging gaps, as can be seen in the case of air traffic controllers and international pilots, who are united all over the world by using English. And the more languages you know, the more easily you can move among different environments.

Read Annie E. Lee's paper "Owning My Words" (on pages 21–22), in which she writes about bridging dialects. Use the following questions and suggestions to guide your Reflections.

Reflections _____

1. Name Annie's audience for this essay.

2. What purpose do you believe Annie is trying to serve for her readers? Point to portions of the paper that lead you to believe this.

3. What purpose do you believe writing this paper served for Annie? Do you think writing this essay could help Annie to successfully bridge cultures? Why?

4. How does she focus her essay to give her readers a you-are-there experience?

5. Have you ever had a similar experience, either from Annie's perspective or from her friend's? Write about your experience and how you feel about it now.

Explorations _____

Try some of the following Explorations to discover how languages serve to either include you in or exclude you from a given culture.

1. a. *Together.* If the language or dialect you speak in your home community is different from the one you use at school, discuss how people at home react if you speak in academic English. How do people react to you in an academic setting when you speak in your home language or dialect? What is your experience of trying to move between your different language communities? If you normally speak academic English, how do you react to people who don't?

    b. *Solo or Together.* Write a basic instruction manual teaching others how to communicate in your home language or special dialect. Focus on a few phrases, words, grammatical habits, and gestures. Include a list of dos and don'ts. Write what it means to you to be relating these codes of language to an outsider.

2. *Together and Solo.* Silence, or absence of words, can speak as powerfully as words themselves. Discuss experiences in which silence was used in a particular culture to include or exclude you or someone else. Focus on one such experience as an illustration. Describe how silence is interpreted in your home community.

3. *Solo.* Between friends, relatives, lovers, club members, and spies, there are often secret codes or "in" languages. Write about a secret language or gesture code that you had with another person or persons. Relate

what these codes were, how they functioned, and what they meant to you. Illustrate with specific examples. Relate what it means to you to be revealing these codes now. If you presently have such a code, write about that—if you are willing.

4. *Together.* In the late-twentieth-century United States, television is the prime medium to which most people have access. List some programs that most of you favor. What words, expressions, gestures, and ways of communicating do they teach us? Which ones have you adopted? Why?

Points of View

People tend to find what they look for, that is, to interpret events in ways that support what they need to believe. When you meet someone who is different from you, who *you* are becomes more obvious by contrast. For example, if you were always with people who are the same height as you, you wouldn't much notice it. However, meeting someone much taller or much shorter will make you aware of the other person's height and your own as well. Having to question the belief that most adults are the same height might be difficult for you. Questions might arise from both points of view: Will this very big person hurt me? Will people ignore me because they don't like craning their necks to look up at me? Am I inferior because I can't walk as fast with my short legs? Won't I seem clumsy in this small conference room?

Meeting someone with a different point of view, who makes you question who you are and what you believe, can elicit many reactions: lack of interest, mistrust, fear, curiosity. Lack of interest may be insulting. Mistrust and fear can lead to anything from rejection to war. But curiosity may lead you to learn more about others and therefore yourself. That tall person and that short one may be able to benefit from their differences. One can sink the baskets while the other runs defense. One can dust those higher shelves while the other does the lower. One can see over the hill while the other can see details closer to the ground. Through writing, you clarify the differences between cultures and learn to take others' points of view. By finding what you have in common, you can learn to honor and appreciate differences, as well. You move more comfortably between environments and don't feel so fragmented. Ultimately, by bridging cultures we create a global culture whose purpose is the survival and enrichment of all. (To support you in this process, you may want to review "Denotations and Connotations" and "Adjusting to Your Audience" in Chapter 3.)

Being an Outsider

If you feel comfortable in a particular culture and have all your needs met, it is easy to ignore or mistrust those who are outsiders. One way to shut others out is to stereotype them. To *stereotype* someone is to make snap judgments about a person because of race, religion, sex, clothing, physical features, or any other clichéd excuse. To stereotype someone is to be locked into old myths about people who may be different from you. It is to be *prejudiced.* When you stereotype someone, you deny the person's individuality and therefore freedom. You lock yourself into your contrasting role. You forfeit your own freedom to learn and grow.

A first step to bridging cultures is to appreciate that everyone has—to a lesser or greater extent—been an outsider. To further appreciate the dynamics of what it means to be an outsider, read Louis Mills's account of being an outsider. As you read, highlight or underline portions to which you have strong reactions.

Being an Outsider

Louis Mills

I'm Black. When I was in seventh grade, I had a friend, a white friend, who didn't know enough to not befriend me. We used to meet on a street corner near my house and walk to school together, but I told him to wait at a corner a block away from school so we wouldn't be seen walking into the school yard together. If we had been seen, there were toughs who would have beaten up on me, or him, or both of us. We used to talk about teachers, the other kids, which high schools we would be going to, and what came after that.

I knew how to take care of myself, but he needed protection. I told the other black kids to watch out for him, because there were kids who threatened him all the time. You see, he was Jewish, and there weren't many Jewish people in our area. I felt good about helping him and he always treated me like I was somebody. He helped me with reading and I helped him with long division so we could graduate together with our class and go on to high school on time.

My mother and I used to go shopping together after school and sometimes we saw my friend with his mother on the street. She was friendly and they talked like mothers do, about their boys, about what produce was fresh today, about the weather. What they didn't say to each other was, "Why don't you drop in for a cup of coffee after you're done shopping?" Or, "We'd like Louis to come over for supper tomorrow." Or, "Let's plan a Sunday picnic together. The men need a break." Why didn't they say those things to each other? It was 1944, in Newark, New Jersey, and the U.S. Army was still segregated. Negroes (that's what we were called back then) went to the same schools as Whites—this was the North, not the South—and shopped in the same stores. But Blacks and Whites did not live on the same block or bowl or picnic together. Surprisingly, some of us went to the same Catholic church, but that's all we did together, except for my friend, who was afraid of the Catholic kids because he was Jewish.

One day our teacher asked me to go to my friend's house with some homework assignments. He had been out sick for a week and this was Friday. She wanted him to catch up on the work he had missed. I took the envelope and went to his house, on a block I never would have walked on. I rang the doorbell and an old woman opened the door, then started to pull it closed behind her as she pushed the screen door out. It was clear I wouldn't be getting into that house. I told her who I was and why I was there. Then I heard my friend's voice calling, "Let him in Bubba, that's my friend Louis Mills." She actually let me in and I saw him in a flannel bathrobe sitting at the head of the stairs. We talked to each other politely— the old woman made sure he didn't come down to me. There was no possibility that I could go up—she didn't even have to say that. He thanked me and so did she, but what we really wanted was to talk as we had every morning and afternoon for most of a year.

Looking back, I realize that he was in pain too. I was not welcome in that house, except as a messenger, as long as the adults were in charge. I wanted to tell my friend that I missed him, our talks, our kidding around. I could tell he missed me, but he couldn't tell me, either.

Years later, when he had just graduated from college and I was a sergeant in the Air Force, we met, briefly. We were in different worlds and we both knew it. We were both proud of what we had become, and somehow, that separated us. I knew I had lost something. Did he know that too?

---

*R*eflections ————————————————

Together or Solo. Respond to a choice of the following prompts for discussion:

1. What words would you use to describe your general reaction to Mills's essay? Point to particular words, statements, or portions of Mills's essay that evoked your strong reactions. Share your reflections in writing or in discussion. Do you believe these are reactions Mills was trying to create in his readers? If so, why? If not, why not?

2. What needs do you believe writing "Being an Outsider" satisfied for Mills, and why? Point to portions of "Being an Outsider" that lead you to believe this.

3. What audience would Mills have in mind for his essay?

4. Which points of view are represented in this essay?

5. How would the essay change if Mills used a different point of view?

6. What purpose do you think Mills is trying to fulfill with his audience?

7. How does Mills focus his essay?

8. Where does he use sense appeal?

9. How does Mills organize his essay to fulfill his purpose?

10. How do you think this essay could help Mills and his audience bridge cultures? How would his friend be affected?

Explorations

The following Explorations help you to explore what it means to be an outsider.

1. *Together or Solo.* List the different possible points of view represented in Louis Mills's essay. Write an essay about the events he reports—from a different point of view. Present the point of view either compassionately or in order to expose its limitations. If you write these essays solo, read and compare them. Use the sidebar on page 294 to guide your discussion. What do you learn?

2. a. *Together.* The following chart lists some kinds of prejudicial stereotyping and the division into dominant and subordinate groups they create. Complete the list of subordinate groups. Can you think of any other kinds of stereotyping?

Stereotyping	Dominant group	Subordinate group
Sexism	Males (in some cultures)	Females (in some cultures)
Classism	Professionals, wealthy	_____
Ageism	21- to 50-year-olds	_____
Racism	Whites (in some cultures)	_____

Physicalism	Body types featured on magazine covers	_____
Fashionism	_____	_____
_____	_____	_____
_____	_____	_____
_____	_____	_____

b. *Solo.* Write an essay about the benefits you have gained from being a member of a dominant group. Write about some of the problems and drawbacks. Focus on specific events to illustrate your experiences. Use sense appeal. Organize your paper by writing first about benefits and then about drawbacks. End your paper by relating what you have learned about being a member of a dominant group.

c. *Solo.* Write an essay about the difficulties you have experienced from being a member of a subordinate group. Illustrate your paper with specific examples. Relate strategies you have developed to cope.

3. *Solo.* Write an essay about a stereotyping belief you formerly held. Relate some incidents that contradicted that particular stereotype. Who was involved? What did you learn about others? What did you learn about yourself?

4. *Solo.* Write an essay about an experience in which you were (or are) an outsider. This may include being part of a smaller culture, such as a club, or a larger national, racial, economic, or religious culture. Respond to these questions:

- How were you different from the other people?
- What particular experience best illustrates how you were (or are) an outsider?
- How were you treated?
- How did you treat the insiders?
- How did you feel?
- Did you put on a social mask, changing your facial expressions, language, gestures, or actions, in order to belong?
- Did a common understanding develop? If so, how? If not, why not?
- What beliefs did you formulate from the experience?
- What, if any, were the benefits of being the outsider?

Variation. Describe an experience in which you were an insider and a newcomer arrived into that particular culture.

5. *Solo.* Write a letter to a person or a group of people with whom you have felt uncomfortable because of cultural differences. As you write, clarify for yourself and your audience what your purpose is in writing the letter. Focus your discussion on particular events. Write this letter with the expressed purpose of creating a bridge between yourself and your audience.

The rest of this chapter is a series of explorations to help you bridge cultures through writing. The points of view represented by differences in ethnicity, gender, and age were chosen because they are general enough to encompass the concerns of all people, regardless of race, economic class, or religion. While considering issues of ethnicity, gender, and age, you will be able to focus on those issues of race, economic class, and religion that are important to you.

Ethnicity

The word *ethnicity* comes from a Greek word meaning "nation" and is usually used to refer to cultural groups that are defined by religion, race, or nationality. Because the United States is so rich with diverse ethnic groups, you can travel the world while staying at home. Your own sense of yourself and your origins deepens as you compare and contrast ethnic differences.

Satellites, air travel, high-speed information networks, and sophisticated television and telephone systems have united the world into a global community. If we can use these systems to bridge cultural differences, perhaps we will eliminate the misunderstandings and wars that belong to a divided world.

Explorations _____

1. a. *Together.* Create a list of the ethnic groups—religious, racial, and national—represented by members of your class. List some special events, holidays, and ceremonies in which these ethnic groups participate. Describe your favorite events to each other and what they mean to you.

   b. *Solo.* Choose one special event and write in depth about a most memorable occasion of it.

   c. *Together.* Read your essays to each other. If class members choose some of the same holidays to discuss, compare and contrast how different ethnic groups celebrate them. What have you learned about yourself and each other?

2. *Together and Solo.* One of the most satisfying and instructive ways to learn about other ethnic groups is to explore food habits. Create a list of foods that are typical of your ethnic group. In writing, describe a special meal, how it is prepared and eaten, and any special ceremonies or meanings associated with the food. Assume your audience is from a different culture. Include any special memories you associate with the food. (You might want to have an international potluck meal together.)

   Variation. Adapt this Exploration by focusing on clothing instead of food.

3. **a.** *Together.* In English, many expressions based on food and eating are used to refer to other aspects of life. For example, *piece of cake* means "easy," and *eat your heart out* means "suffer." Create a list of English expressions with food and eating terms in them. Discuss what they mean.

   b. *Solo.* Write an essay about expressions (in either English or another language) that refer to food and eating. State the words, what they mean, and when to use them. Organize your essay by grouping expressions according to shared meaning.

4. **a.** *Together.* People of different cultures have varied ways of coping with emotions. In some cultures, it is inappropriate to express emotions, and there are complex ways in which people are stopped from doing so. In some cultures, emotions are freely and openly expressed. Consider your own cultural background. Compare notes with each other on how the following emotions are dealt with, in your experience. Consider what facial, bodily, and verbal cues are permitted and how these are either encouraged or discouraged.

   - Anger
   - Parental affection
   - Romantic interest
   - Fear
   - Confusion
   - Inadequacy
   - Envy and jealousy
   - Grief
   - Sadness
   - Mistrust

Write a group essay comparing how a particular emotion is expressed by different cultures. Use either a block or zig-zag organizing strategy (see pages 193–195 and 354–362).

b. *Solo.* Write an essay describing an occasion when you did not follow the rules of a community in expressing an emotion. How did other people treat you? What did you learn about yourself and others?

5. a. *Together.* Find newspaper articles that address ethnic issues and cultural clashes either directly or indirectly. Share these articles with others in class.

b. *Solo.* Choose one of these articles. Write a summary of it for someone who hasn't read it. Then write your reaction to the events and issues raised in the article. Point out prejudicial and violent actions. Suggest solutions to problems and how you would bridge the clashing cultures.

Variation. Do this Exploration by focusing on a television program or film.

6. *Together and Solo.*

a. Discuss and write about specific ways in which you have already committed yourselves to bridging ethnic cultures. What benefits have you enjoyed? What challenges are you meeting?

b. Devise specific ways in which you can further work against ethnic—racial, national, and religious—discrimination in your everyday life. Write about your experience of trying to implement some of these plans. What groups could you join to help you make a deeper commitment to bridging ethnic cultures?

Gender

Cultures determine what roles males and females should have and what is masculine and feminine. These roles and rules determine a person's gender. *Sexual* differences are biological. *Gender* differences are social. Gender roles are meant to define and control a person's activities and sexual preferences.

Gender roles are defined by many cultural influences, including religion, race, ethnicity, economy, geography, age, and historical era. For example, people who insist upon conventional family gender roles for everyone may disapprove of others who prefer careers without parenthood, interracial marriages, or homosexual relationships. People with alternative life-styles may, in turn, be hostile to those who try to impose conventional values on them. The following Explorations provide opportunities for you to discover such variations in gender expectations and the complications they may produce.

*E*xplorations _____

1. *Together and Solo.* Discuss one or more of the controversial statements listed below. For each statement you discuss, brainstorm two lists, one in favor of the statement and one against it. Record supporting examples and reasons for each. Refer to religious, racial, economic, and generational influences. Then write an essay supporting or disagreeing with one of the statements. Focus your essay by presenting your position in a thesis statement. Describe particular individuals who illustrate your point of view. Directly address points that are opposed to your position and argue against them.

   • Women should stay at home to raise their children.

   • Date rape is usually the woman's fault.

   • Wives should be loyal to their husbands. If they are beaten, they've done something to provoke their men.

   • There's nothing wrong with prostitution or pornography. Women get paid well for their services, and they enjoy it.

   • Men are by nature more intellectual; women are more emotional.

   • Playful comments and touches are not sexual harassment.

   • Homosexuals shouldn't be teachers or parents. They will corrupt the children under their care.

   • A man's success depends on his having a woman behind him.

   • Men need more sexual variety than women and so should therefore be allowed more freedom outside of marriage.

   • Sex-change operations are a viable way to improve life-style.

2. **a.** *Together.* Create a list of statements that contrast gender roles. Use one of the following formats for starters:

   Men should . . . and women should . . .

   All men are . . . and all women are . . .

   Men can('t) . . . and women can('t) . . .

   I wish men could . . . and I wish women could . . .

   Be sure to include everyday household roles, work roles, social roles, and personal and language habits. You might want to divide into same-sex groups to create these lists and compare the results. Mark the items on your list that cause the most disagreement.

   b. *Together or Solo.* Write an essay arguing your position on a controversial statement you created together. Pay special attention to what cultural influences—religious, racial, ethnic, economic, or age/generational—determine your position. Read these essays to the whole class. Discuss examples of people who do not fit the prescribed gender roles.

3. **a.** *Together.* Find newspaper or magazine articles that address issues of gender or sex abuse, either directly or indirectly. These articles may refer to such issues as spouse abuse, child pornography, oppression of homosexuals, discrimination in the military, or sexual harassment. Share these in class.

   b. *Solo.* Write an essay in response to one article. Focus your essay by quoting the main points in the article. List the points you would like to make in your response. Organize your points so that your most important ones come first and last. Draft your essay, and then consult with others about it.

   Variation. Do this Exploration in response to a television program or film that addresses issues of gender or sex abuse.

4. *Solo.* Write an essay arguing which sex has it easier in your home community. Focus your essay by describing the lives of two representative individuals. Enliven your essay by interviewing these individuals and quoting them in your paper.

5. *Solo.* Write an essay about a particular man or woman, convincing your reader that the person is the ideal man or woman. This may be a public figure or someone you know personally.

   Variation. Write an essay describing a person who was your model for what is masculine or feminine. What particular gender roles and rules did you learn from this person? Have you patterned your life to reflect this person's influence? If so, how?

6. **a.** *Together.* Discuss a number of people who you believe best bridge traits of both genders in their own lives.

   b. *Solo.* Write an essay about how you, yourself, can develop traits of both genders to become a more well-rounded person.

7. *Together and Solo.* Name or devise specific ways in which you can work against gender discrimination in your everyday life. Write about your experience of trying to implement some of these in your own life.

Age

Age is important in determining how you experience the world. Not only is your body different at different ages, but so are your experiences. Among many other factors, medical care, technology, social roles, economics, world events, and ecology have varied tremendously over time, especially in the last few decades. People born today know a different world from people born sixty to a hundred years ago.

Cultures vary on how they care for children and the elderly. For example, in some cultures, children are raised collectively in a small, close-knit community. In other cultures, children are sent to boarding schools. In still others, children have to fend for themselves, often taking care of younger siblings. Similarly, in some cultures, the elderly are revered and are always cared for in the family. In other cultures, the elderly are sent to nursing homes and institutions and youth is revered. In still others, elderly members are expected to retreat by themselves when they no longer feel they can be active members of the family.

The following Explorations provide opportunities for you to discover the cultural variations experienced by people of different ages.

*E*xplorations _____

1. **a.** *Together.* Create two lists of what you believe parents should be able to expect from their children and what children should be able to expect from their parents. Include such things as long-term care, educational support, and care of grandchildren. If you disagree with other members of the group, state your reasons for disagreeing. Describe particular people and situations to support your position. Notice how your cultural backgrounds influence your ideas.

   b. *Solo.* Write an essay stating what you believe parents and children should be able to expect from each other. Support your position by describing particular people and situations. You might want to relate a situation in which you were in conflict with your parents. To balance your essay, write a section describing what you believe parents and children should *not* expect from each other, and why.

2. *Solo.* List conflicts that you have (or had) with your parents over such issues as money, dating, household contributions, and education. Focus an essay on a particular conflict and any attempts that have been made to resolve it. Was this conflict determined by differences in age? What other cultural and generational gaps helped to create this conflict? How could this essay help you?

3. **a.** *Together.* Some senior citizens have had their rights and freedoms limited by mandatory retirement age, retesting for driver's licenses, discrimination in hiring, low income, medical and insurance inequalities, and nursing homes. Discuss examples of such situations.

     b. *Solo.* Choose a person you know who has had her or his rights and freedoms infringed upon because of age. Tell the story from two or three points of view. Discuss what you have learned from doing this Exploration.

4. *Together and Solo.* Discuss and write about different cultural customs and expectations for treating the elderly. In your individual writing, focus on how the elderly are treated in your home community. Is this treatment a reflection of the traditions of your ethnic origin? If so, how? If not, what cultural influences determine how the elderly are treated in your family?

5. a. *Together.* List names of senior citizens who have made significant contributions in their old age.

     b. *Solo.* Write an essay about someone who made or is making significant contributions as an elderly person.

6. *Together and Solo.*

     a. Discuss and write about ways in which you have already committed yourselves to working against age discrimination. What benefits have you enjoyed? What challenges are you meeting?

     b. Devise specific ways in which you can further work against age discrimination in your everyday life. Write about your experience of trying to implement some of these plans.

7. a. *Together.* Discuss inequalities and pressures that women and men experience because of age. To start your discussion, use the following phrases to generate lists of expectations that U.S. culture has of women and men. Note if your particular home culture has different expectations, and include them in your discussion.

        Elderly women should . . .

        Elderly women should not . . .

        Elderly men should . . .

        Elderly men should not . . .

     b. *Solo.* Write an essay in which you state a strong belief about what elderly women or men should or should not do. Focus your work by illustrating your points with specific examples of elderly persons. To balance your essay, address opposing issues and arguments that someone might raise in response to you. End your essay describing an individual who would benefit from your point of view.

8. *Variation.* Adapt your choice of Explorations 3, 4, 5, 6, or 7 to children's issues and rights. Compare and contrast treatment of the elderly with treatment of children.

STUDENTS WRITING
TO BRIDGE CULTURES

Read the following student models,[21] which were written for the purpose of understanding and bridging cultures. Use the second set of questions on page 294 to guide your reflections. Be sure to point to specific parts of papers to support your views.

Living with Prejudice
Avantika Patel

Almost everyone has felt like an outsider because of prejudice or discrimination at one time or another. Most of the prejudice occurs because of people's physical characteristics and their beliefs. I have been prejudged and discriminated against because of my physical characteristics and my beliefs. From that I have learned that people have different views about people who are from different countries or backgrounds, and that I shouldn't let them get to me.

I experienced prejudice and discrimination when I was in high school, soon after coming to this country from India. When I would walk by American students, they would start talking about me or say something really bad about Indians. They would talk about me because of the way I dressed. I used to wear Indian clothes to school when I first started school in the United States. Most people can tell if you are an Indian or not just by looking at a person or the way he/she is dressed. Once when I was standing in the lunchroom to pay for my lunch, a guy suddenly came and started to say bad things to me as soon as he saw me. He was saying that I didn't belong in this country, and that I should go back to my own country. He also cursed at me a lot, saying words too awful to repeat. The guy even cut in the line and stood right in front of me without asking for my permission. He was pretending that I didn't exist. I didn't say anything because I was always taught to be nice to everyone and not say bad words or fight in public and that's what I still believe.

At first when the lunch incident occurred, I felt very bad and depressed. I said to myself that I didn't belong here, and that there is something wrong with me. But then I thought what if somebody did that to that guy who called me names in the cafeteria and he went to another country and he didn't know the language of that country? I thought, I am a human being, too. I have some rights. So what if I was from another country? The sad part is that he didn't even care how other people would feel when they heard this garbage from his mouth. He didn't care about

309

himself and the impression he made on other people. I was very angry and sad at the same time when this incident occurred.

From that incident I learned that there is such a thing called "prejudice" and that people actually say bad things to each other. When I was in India, I used to live in a small town where everyone was nice to each other. So I really didn't know anything about the outside world. This incident in high school taught me that different people think differently when they meet people from different backgrounds and with different looks. Now I am used to these kinds of remarks and criticisms, so I don't let them get to me. I mind my own business. I smile if some person seems sincere and frank, but I try to ignore a person who looks as if he or she wouldn't feel the same about smiling or saying "Hi." To cope with these kinds of incidents, I try to speak English when I am around Americans, even when I am speaking to an Indian who speaks the same Indian language (not English) that I do. When I go somewhere and see some people who might say bad things or who don't like Indians, I go another way or wait until they leave.

Not every person you meet is prejudiced. Most people are nice, but once in a while you meet or bump into a person who is prejudiced, who makes you feel bad and treats you like dirt. A person discriminates against other people because of their physical appearance and their background. That person might do that to you because it never happened to him or her or that person really likes to make people feel bad, and knows what he/she is doing. Sometimes you learn things from these kinds of incidents. You learn people's feelings and their personality, along with their views. These kinds of incidents teach you how to deal with prejudice and discrimination, and also make you stronger from inside, too.

Respect for Elderly Persons in the United States and Korean Cultures

Dong Shin

When comparing Americans with Koreans, one of the most interesting characteristics is to observe how young people respect the older people of their country. In my opinion, Americans don't show respect for elderly persons as much as we do in my native country, Korea.

When I first came to the United States, I was shocked by the way young students treated their teachers. I saw a movie which was about American high school students. The story showed disorderly students.

They had flunked for the semester, so they had to stay in school during the summer in order to make up their work. A teacher had to punish his students because they didn't want to follow his directions. Then, the students decided to give their teacher a hard time. It was difficult for me to believe that high school students could show such disrespect for their teacher. They locked up their teacher in the bathroom, cursed him, and even punched him. I thought it was just fiction, but the movie was depicting the real world. I realized that today's American's high school students sometimes have terrible behavior. I think this situation could happen in any place in America.

In Korea, a teacher is one of the most highly respected person. Students must obey their teacher whether a teacher is right or wrong. Whatever a teacher says becomes the law. Also, students have to bow every time they see their teachers.

Koreans show respect to their elders in many ways. When Koreans have their meals with a family, children have to wait to eat until their father or any elderly person begins to eat the meal. Also, when children receive something from an elderly person, they have to use both their hands to hold that thing. These are just a few basic manners of respect for elderly people in Korea.

The Korean culture is influenced by Confucian ideas, which emphasize respect for the elderly, filial duty, and patriotism. Although today's Koreans tend to become Westernized, Confucian ideas are still the essential spirit of the majority of Koreans.

I think the uniqueness of languages also makes a difference in respect between Americans and Koreans. The reason for this is that the Korean language has special words which show respect for elderly people, and the English language doesn't. For example, an American may ask a friend, "Do you want to have dinner now?" The American person may also ask an elderly person, "Do you want to have dinner now?" There is no difference between the sentences. However, Koreans don't use the same sentences to speak with elderly persons as they use for their friends. When Koreans speak to an elderly person, the sentence usually gets longer than a normal sentence, or the words are changed into other words. Therefore, Koreans have to be very careful when they speak to an elderly person. If they make mistakes in using words for respect, it becomes a matter for which they are criticized.

In conclusion, Koreans have a higher standard of respect for elderly people than Americans have. I don't mean that too much respect is always good, because sometimes it gets too complicated. I often feel pressure when I speak to a Korean elderly person because I have to think about how I am speaking and how my attitude is while I speak. However, I believe that it would be nicer if Americans improved their respect for elderly people.

Body Language: Focus on Hong Kong

Debbie Chung

As we all know, language is a common form of communication among people, but body language has the same function. What is body language? In my opinion body language is a kind of language that expresses your ideas and feelings through gestures. Sometimes there is no need to speak up, and you can just use some facial expressions or gestures in order to express and indicate something.

Different countries have different forms of body language, but some gestures have the same meanings and are acceptable internationally. For example, if you want to say "yes," you can nod; if you want to say "no," you can move your head from one side to the other side, back and forth. There are few exceptions to these universal gestures. Also, waving your hands toward your body more often than not indicates "come here," and winking means you like somebody. These are all socially acceptable gestures and they have the same meanings.

Because of different cultural backgrounds, some gestures are different. For instance, Chinese people eat rice, and rice is the basic food in China, so when we Chinese indicate we want to eat, we will put our left hand in a horizontal position and put our right hand toward our mouths in order to pretend we are using chopsticks to pick something up. On the other hand, Hispanic people have different gestures to indicate eating. They use their right hand to pretend they are holding a spoon. The whole thing is we have different cultural backgrounds, therefore we have different gestures to indicate certain things.

Some gestures are totally different between China and other countries. Chinese people will show their thumb in order to indicate that people are really excellent and smart, unlike Hispanics, who use their fingers to point at your head to show you are outstanding. It is very funny that in Chinese if you point at someone's head you are saying "that person has mental problems." So I told my Hispanic classmates that they should not point at the head of a Chinese person or they will make someone angry with them. Next, when Chinese people swear that they tell the truth, they will put their middle three fingers up and say something honestly, but Venezuelans put their thumb and first finger up in a circle shape and then kiss them; this means "swear in honesty." It is cute, isn't it?

In short, body language is a way of expressing human feeling through gestures. Some of them are instinctive and so they are universally acceptable. And the others are related to different cultural backgrounds. It is interesting to learn about the gestures of different countries.

Marriage in Ghana, Marriage in America

Fred Ampofo

In Ghanaian society, men and women have certain traditional roles which they perform. My father has been the breadwinner of the family and my mother has taken care of such responsibilities as childcare and housework which are the duties expected of Ghanaian women. If I get married, I will provide financial support for my family similar to my father's and share my spouse's childcare and housework responsibilities because I have realized that such responsibilities shared between husbands and wives in American families have led to very close relationships between spouses.

My father maintains the role of breadwinner of the family and provides major financial support. He has successfully put three of my brothers through college and is still paying for my college tuition and my younger brother's high school tuition. Also, he pays the major bills in the household, such as the medical bills, and he has paid off the mortgage on the house. On the other hand, my mother, who is a full-time school teacher, takes care of the household and childcare responsibilities which are duties Ghanaian women willingly perform. When my brothers and I were younger, she had greater childcare obligations since she had to ensure that we had the proper clothes to wear. She also had to keep a record of our doctor's appointments. She still has to carry out these duties for my brother in high school and has a hectic household schedule which includes cooking the family meals and making sure my father's laundry is done. In addition, she provides money for grocery shopping and ensures that weekly grocery shopping is done.

I would adopt my father's role in the family, if I get married, by providing substantial financial support for my family including paying my children's tuition, if I have any. However, I would change the role of my spouse so it would differ from my mother's responsibilities in the family. Two-career families in both Ghana and the United States have created a situation whereby couples spend less time together at home during the week. In American society, I have noticed that men make up for this lost quality time with their spouses by helping them carry out such household responsibilities as grocery shopping and laundry. This has resulted in close relationships and helps maintain successful marriages. In Ghana, however, men do not help their spouses fulfill such duties because society sees such activities as laundry and grocery shopping as being traditional roles of Ghanaian women, and as a result the relationships between Ghanaian spouses are not as intimate as American marriage relationships.

In Ghana, if I were to perform such duties as grocery shopping and laundry, my friends would be amazed because they see such roles as women's responsibilities. Since my future wife will be Ghanaian, I will encourage her to organize a movement that would change the traditional roles of Ghanaian spouses, whereby they can adopt the American marriage system of shared responsibilities, such as financial and house work.

Gender roles are culturally defined in Ghana. Men are still regarded as the breadwinners of the family, and as such, still earn more income than women. Out of respect to the Ghanaian culture, I would like to maintain the major financial obligations in the family. However, I would alter the traditional role of Ghanaian women and help my spouse fulfill some of her childcare and housework responsibilities, since my observation of American housework shows that when spouses share such duties intimate relationships result.

Generations and Gender

Silvia Trillo

The biggest contrast of the female gender that I have been exposed to happens to be between my generation and my mother's. I feel our differences lie in our opinions on career, home, and sexuality. The responsibility for our differences may lie in our age difference, my age being eighteen and hers fifty. It may also be the difference in the culture we were raised in. I was raised in New Jersey. My mother, on the other hand, was raised in Honduras, Central America.

The differences between my mother's generation and mine are quite broad. For example, my mother went to college to get a husband first and a degree second. My goal is entirely different; my priority is to graduate with a degree and then to go on to a higher level of education. Although I haven't decided what field I want to go into, education is my first priority. Another example is my mother's belief that women should be soft-spoken, demure, and polite. I think a woman has to be aggressive to obtain what she wants in "a man's world."

Another difference between us is the way we feel about roles at home. My mother's generation was quite family oriented: girls were expected to marry young, settle down, and care for a husband and children. My generation is more career oriented and identity conscious. We just don't want to be simply wives and housekeepers or dependent on a man. We want to marry after our lives and roles in the workplace are set; we expect a husband to care for himself and help with the children. Women of my generation do not believe in being subservient to a man and having a husband as the only head of household, wage earner, and decision maker, as my mother's generation did. Although many women of her generation do work for financial reasons, they still allow the man to make most of the decisions in the household.

My mother also seems to believe that there are separate rules in life for males and females. For example, she believes that a man can be sexually promiscuous and have an aggressive attitude simply because of gender; however, a woman who approaches a man for a phone number is a trollop. I feel that every person should have his or her own personal code of ethics and adhere to it. People should interact socially, showing respect for members of the opposite sex and their views on relationships.

The differences between my mother's views on career, home, and sexuality are so different from my own, it is astonishing: it's amazing that I could grow up with such different ideas in the same household. Maybe the differences in my views result from exposure to the concept of women's rights through television, radio, and newspapers, and the sexual revolution that occurred before my birth. I am truly fortunate to be growing up in a more progressive era for women.

Chapter Review

Together or Solo. Write a response to the following questions:

1. What are the three most important things you learned about culture from working with this chapter?

2. What cultural stereotypes did you believe before working with this chapter? Have you modified your view? If so, how? If not, why not?

3. Since working with this chapter, how have you modified your view of yourself and the cultures in which you move?

4. What did you learn about the challenges and benefits of *writing* to bridge cultures?

5. How can you more actively work against ethnic, gender, and age discrimination at home? At work? At school? In your community?

Chapter **12**

Writing to Learn I

Becoming a Responsible Thinker

This chapter offers opportunities to
- —Identify the traits of a **responsible thinker**
- —Compare and contrast purposes and audiences **across the curriculum**
- —Take **effective notes**
- —Distinguish different **kinds of questions**
- —Write **thesis statements** for exams and papers
- —**Summarize** for different purposes

Writing is a learning process.
— *Bruce Inge, Student*

The Need to Learn

Being human, you have a vast capacity for learning. You start to learn even while in the womb and may continue to do so for over a hundred years. Using your senses and intellect, you can design experiences so that you can name and meet your needs. You can store most, if not all of the experiences you have in the storehouse of your experiences—your unconscious. The trick is to recall and utilize information when you need it. Doing so is a matter of survival: the better you use what you know, the better your life can be. Ideally, if you don't know what you need to know, you can find a way to search for it, learn it, and store it.

Writing to Become a Responsible Thinker

If you are like most people, you are able to hold only a few things at a time in the corridor of your consciousness. This is a survival aid. If all you know were to flood your mind at once, you would be utterly confused. In writing, too, you can write only one thing at a time. But usually, as soon as you write something down, you clear the way for more thoughts to follow. Writing is ideal for helping you recall and use information, because, by its nature, writing focuses on and draws things from the storehouse of your unconscious, one thing at a time.

Intelligence can be defined as the ability to make useful and creative connections between experiences. The more you write about what you experience and read, the more of these connections you will develop. The more connections you can make between ideas and experiences, the more quickly you will be able to trigger your memory. Writing helps you to see, organize, and make connections that may be too complex to manage in the small space of your consciousness. For these and other reasons, writing and reading others' writings are the foundations of formal education.

The model of the writing process used in this book and the Explorations in this and the next chapter are designed to help you become more conscious of your educational experiences and to develop the three main qualities of a responsible learner and thinker:

1. Sensitivity to purpose and audience

2. Ability to adopt or formulate standards for coping with different purposes and audiences

3. Ability to adjust and correct oneself*

---

*These three characteristics are adapted from Matthew Lipman's three criteria for critical thinking published in *Inquiry: Critical Thinking Across the Disciplines* 1(2), March 1988— the newsletter of the Institute for Critical Thinking at Montclair State University.

This chapter shows you two tools to help you focus your attention so that you can better learn and remember what you learn: note taking and summarizing. Chapter 13 offers you opportunities to write responses and essays so that you can engage more actively with the materials you study.

To begin your explorations into learning, participate in some of the following activities that are designed to help you become more aware of the need to learn.

Explorations _____

1. *Together.* Read the following illustrations of people who used writing to help them satisfy a need to learn. Discuss how each person displays the three main skills of a responsible thinker. How did the writing process help each person to solve problems? Identify how each writer used specific phases of the writing process.

   a.   Ned, a writer, develops severe pains in his hands from typing. The doctors diagnose it as carpal tunnel syndrome and recommend an operation. But Ned has both personal and religious objections to such intervention. Using the skills he has developed as a writer, he researches carpal tunnel syndrome, consults with others who have the syndrome, and finds alternative ways to heal his hands. Ned writes an article that creates more interest in these alternative methods. Readers write him letters with questions and further suggestions.

   b.   Jocelyn finds herself getting involved in one destructive relationship after another. She decides to start writing a personal journal to notice what these relationships have in common. A course in human interactions leads her to books and articles about such relationships. Using her own experience and the theories that are offered in her readings, Jocelyn synthesizes a plan for developing healthier relationships.

   c.   After years of believing that he just can't handle mathematics, Mark decides to give it one last chance. He has wanted a college degree so he can teach high school sports, but he just hasn't been able to fulfill his math requirements. The class that Mark takes is taught by a teacher who uses writing to help students learn. Writing about what he doesn't understand, formulating questions, and describing his process, Mark finds he is able to articulate the kinds of help he needs from his instructor. Mark steadily breaks through one block after another. By the end of the semester he has gained enough momentum to earn a B. Also, he has come to recognize ways in which mathematics can help him better understand the dynamics of muscle development and how to design a training schedule for athletes. The confidence he gains is helping him to explore difficult new ideas in his physical education courses, as well.

2. *Solo.* Write about a time when you needed to learn something for personal, physical, economic, social, or educational reasons. What steps did you take? What frustrations did you experience? What did you learn? How would you approach the problem if it occurred now?

Purpose and Audience Across the Curriculum

Formal education is divided into different fields of learning called *disciplines.* Some of the current academic disciplines are mathematics, sociology, history, and fine arts. Every discipline is a culture or community defined by certain rules, questions, languages, and procedures. Even within disciplines there are smaller cultures. History, for example, includes the subdisciplines of ancient history, African history, and history of ideas.

Learning a new discipline is like entering a new country or social club. To survive and thrive you have to learn what others expect, what they know, how you can adapt to them, and how you can make them accept you. Throughout this chapter, you will be invited to compare and contrast different disciplines so that you can learn how best to achieve your purposes with specific audiences.

Points of View

The more points of view from which you can approach the world, the richer your experience will be. The various disciplines provide you with different points of view or perspectives, much as looking at a statue from different angles will enrich your experience of it or evaluating a social issue from three points of view will empower you with a greater sense of your options.

How you view a subject will be determined by your purpose. Notice the wide range of points of view from which the subject of laughter can be considered, according to the purpose at hand:

- A physiologist explains the functions of the human body. Therefore, a physiologist would explain laughter as rhythmic, repetitive, spasmodic exhalation controlled by the parasympathetic nervous system.

- An anthropologist explores human cultures. So, an anthropologist could show us that laughter is used in some societies as punishment and in other societies as a way of becoming comfortable with strangers.

- A linguist notices and accounts for language patterns and would collect a series of successful jokes to discern what patterns of vocabulary and grammar they have in common.

- An economist, who accounts for how people earn, spend, and manage money, may research how humor is used in television commercials and compare the sales generated by humorous commercials to those generated by more serious approaches.

- A management science expert, trained in organizing people in work settings, may explore how humor can be used in the workplace to enhance job satisfaction.

- A mathematician, trained in predicting numerical patterns, may tabulate how a certain comedian paces her punch lines.

Exciting new insights are gained when ideas from one discipline are adapted by another. So, for example, the management science expert can use the anthropologist's insights when organizing workers from different ethnic backgrounds. The physiologist can formulate further insights about the physiology of laughter by using the mathematician's tabulations of comic pacing.

To discover for yourself the points of view from which different disciplines approach the world, do one or more of the following Explorations.

*E*xplorations _____

1. *Together.*

   a. Review the discussion of purposes in education on pages 53–55.

   b. Divide yourselves into groups of four. Assign a different academic discipline to each group. If possible, bring textbooks to class from these other disciplines. (One group can be devoted to *writing* as a discipline and use *The Flexible Writer* as an example.) Look through the tables of content and indexes for ideas. Modeling your discussions on the example of laughter, above, formulate how someone in a particular discipline would approach one of the following topics. Create a typical assignment in that course on your chosen topic.

Death	Hunger
War	Love
Racism	Aging

   c. As a class, compare the different approaches academic disciplines take to your topic. Identify the main purpose of each academic discipline as reflected in your assignments: is it information, skills, interpretation, or experimentation?

2. *Solo and Together.* For the next week, notice when ideas from one course or discipline give you greater insights into others. Record these insights in your journal and write about their significance to you. Share what you wrote with each other.

Focusing: Taking Effective Notes

Concepts, information, observations, and memories cluster around key words, questions, statements, and sense imagery the way the spokes of a wheel radiate from its hub, the planets cluster around the sun, iron gathers to a magnet, and fans congregate around a rock star. By learning to identify and focus on key words, questions, statements, and sense imagery, you develop your ability to access what you need from the storehouse of your experiences.

Key Words

A *key word* can literally open the way to whole portions of the storehouse of your own and others' experiences. Learning the key words in a discipline allows you into the community of people who have chosen that way of viewing the world. For example, historians are people who know the various meanings of key words such as *democracy, socialism,* and *fascism.* Lawyers are people who know how to effectively use such key expressions as *tort, habeas corpus,* and *writ.* Knowing the meaning of key words in a discipline helps professionals save time. They don't have to waste energy constantly renegotiating basic ideas. That's why, when needed, professionals will devote so much time and effort to carefully defining and redefining key words to form a firm foundation for communicating with their colleagues.

Focusing on key words in a discipline will help you to learn, retain, and recall information when you need it. The first step is to identify key words. Here are some ways to do so:

- Your instructor or book repeats the word.
- Your instructor or book emphasizes the word. Key words are often used as chapter or section headings in books, just as the key words in this book include *Purpose and Audience, Writing to Learn,* and *Key Words.* They are often italicized, underlined, printed in bold type, or set between quotation marks.
- Key words may be collected in the glossary of a textbook.
- You keep noticing a word *yourself.*

Learning Key Words

1. **Collect.** For each course you take, collect key words and concepts. Here are places to write them:
    - The inside covers of your notebook or textbook
    - 3 × 5 index cards in a file
    - A bulletin board

2. **Define** key words and concepts you collect.

3. **Chart and diagram** key words and concepts.

4. **Write** in a learning journal, using key words for your focus. Record relevant examples that illustrate each concept. When appropriate, note differences and similarities between how a word is used in one discipline and how it is used in another.

5. **Review** key words and concepts for exams and projects. Ask someone to quiz you.

Do one or more of the following Explorations to practice identifying key words.

*E*xplorations _____

1. **a.** *Together.* Each person responds to certain key words that trigger strong reactions. Create two lists of everyday words that are significant to you—the first of favorite expressions, the second of ones you dislike. For example, one person loves to use *relish* as in the expression "I *relish* reading mysteries." Another person feels irritated with the word *share.*

    b. *Solo and Together.* Choose a significant expression and write about what it means to you. Read some of these responses to each other.

2. *Solo and Together.* Underline key words or expressions in the following passages.* Identify the disciplines to which they may belong. Then compare your identifications.

---

*These passages were drawn from the following sources across the curriculum: Joel R. Evans and Barry Berman, *Marketing,* 4th ed. (New York: Macmillan, 1990), pp. 61, 173; Robert J. Foster, *General Geology,* 5th ed. (Columbus, Ohio: Merrill, 1988), pp. 21, 97, 240; Larry Madaras and James M. SoRelle, *Taking Sides: Clashing Views on Controversial Issues in American History* (Guilford, Conn.: Dushkin, 1989), pp. 21, 79; and Charles P. McKeague, *Pre-Algebra* (Belmont, Calif.: Wadsworth, 1987), p. 316. The excerpts on page 331 of *The Flexible Writer* are also drawn from these sources.

a.   The consumer may use extended, limited, or routine decision-making. This depends on the degree of search, level of prior experience, frequency of purchase, amount of perceived risk, and time pressure.

b.   The fit of the continents on a map seems to be too good to be accidental. The fit is even better if, instead of the shoreline, the true edge of the continent, the continental shelf, is used. Later deformation or erosion does spoil the match at some places.

c.   There aren't any broad moral principles of justice, charity, equity, or benevolence that can be discovered in the moral systems of all cultures. There is a much deeper question that we have not touched on yet. Even if there *were* universally accepted norms, what would that fact prove? Does everybody believing something make it right? Don't we need some justification for our moral convictions that goes beyond saying, "Everybody agrees with me"?

d.   No matter how carefully a measurement is made, it is never exact. A vital part of any good experiment is an evaluation of the degree of uncertainty of the results. The evaluation of the probable range of error in an experimentally determined parameter is often almost as important as the numerical value of the parameter itself.

Questions

A question, by its very nature, invites response and gathers information to itself. That is why questions are so powerful in learning and remembering. By developing the habit of noticing and asking questions, you enhance the speed, quality, and quantity of your learning. The better your questions, the better the answers you'll find.

Writing allows you not only to relate what you already know but to learn in the process. You learn best by maintaining a curious mind, by constantly asking yourself questions. In turn, you can engage your readers by anticipating questions they will be likely to raise in response to your writing. If you wrongly assume that your readers will understand or agree with what you are writing, you might lose them in the process.

To develop the habit of asking questions, use question words to trigger them. The *wh* words in Figure 5.3 (page 118) are key words that help you to start formulating full questions. Questions can also start with words such as *do, can, are, is, were, if,* and *has,* but, as you will soon see, these questions do not generate quite the same kinds of responses as the *wh* words do.

To develop your skill in asking and responding to questions, it is important to notice differences between them. Five basic categories of questions that will help you discern these differences are (1) good questions, (2) unfair questions, (3) yes/no questions, (4) one-answer questions, and (5) rhetorical questions.

Good Questions.   "Why do some birds fly south, while others don't?" "If a tree falls in the forest and no one hears it, has it made a sound?" "Is there a God?" "Why do some people become alcoholics?" "How can we save the ozone layer?" "What happened to Uncle Frank that made everyone in the family avoid talking about him?" These and other questions are good questions. Students notice that good questions meet some, if not all, of the following standards:

- They respond to some important human need.
- They are focused and specific.
- They make you think.
- They may question popular beliefs.
- They invite more than one answer. Some of these answers may conflict with others.
- They lead to other questions.
- They suggest how you would go about answering them.
- They lead to good answers.
- They aren't unfair.
- They give you an "aha" feeling.
- They can cause strong reactions.
- They may meet with resistance from others.
- They make you say, "That's a good question."
- They can lead you to work with others.

For example, the question "How can we save the ozone layer?" is a good question because it responds to an important human need—to save the planet. The question makes you think, has more than one answer, leads to other questions about the environment, and suggests that you need to consider practical measures. The question has lead to good answers by people who are working together on the problem. It isn't a trick or unfair question. It leads people to say, "That's a good question."

Unfair Questions.   "Are you still beating your dog?" "What's the difference between a duck?" "How come someone says they saw you do it?" "You don't want another piece of my pie, do you?" "What is it like to be blown up by a bomb?" These and other questions can be seen as unfair. Unfair questions have some, if not all, of the following characteristics:

- They assume something that the responder may want to question.
- They are meant to trick responders into saying things they wouldn't want to say.
- They often lead to only one answer.
- They may have no answer.
- They may lead you to say, "That's not a real question."
- They may leave you confused as to how you would answer them.
- They antagonize the audience.
- They may undermine your purpose.

For example, the question "Are you still beating your dog?" is unfair because it assumes that the person beat the dog in the first place. The responder couldn't win. A responder who says "Yes" is admitting to beating the dog in the first place. A responder who says "No" is still admitting to beating the dog! The question may antagonize and confuse the responder. The question could undermine the questioner's purpose of trying to save the dog from abuse. A fair approach would be to first ask, "Have you ever beaten your dog?"

Some questions may be unfair because of the context in which they are asked. For example, it could be unfair and embarrassing to ask a person "What is your real hair color?" at a formal dinner. But it can be entirely appropriate for a hairdresser to ask this question of a client while in a salon. How you phrase the question is crucial. The question "What happened to my Uncle Frank?" may be a good question to ask of a relative, whereas "What did you do to him?" assumes that the relative injured Uncle Frank. "What is it like to be blown up by a bomb?" is unfair because it can't be answered by one who has had the experience. The question "What's the difference between a duck?" doesn't normally make sense. But when a comedian asks it, the question isn't unfair—it's meant to be funny.

Yes/No Questions.   "Is there an afterlife?" "Have you gone to the store?" "Are there moons around Jupiter?" "Do they make navy blue blinds?" "Will there be enough ozone layer left in the twenty-first century?" "Should there be an extra microphone for the event?" "Can you loan me money?" Such yes/no questions have some, if not all, of the following characteristics:

- They often begin with some form of the words *is, can, do, have, could/would/should,* or *will.*

- They do not invite collaboration.
- They limit the range of response.
- They may be too general.
- They can be unfair.

Because of the way they are phrased, these and other questions like them usually call for a response of "yes" or "no." Because the anticipated response is so limited, for the most part yes/no questions do not invite the kind of richness, elaboration, and collaboration that other questions do. Sometimes yes/no questions can be unfair because they assume that the topic can be dispensed with by a short answer. For many religious and nonreligious people, the question "Is there an afterlife?" is too general. The topic requires more discussion, elaboration, and interpretation. A good question about the afterlife would be more focused, as this one is: "How convincing are the arguments current Roman Catholic theologians offer in support of an afterlife?"

One-Answer Questions. "How much is 2 + 2 in the decimal system?" "What was the cause of the Civil War?" "Who is the main character in Chaucer's *Canterbury Tales*?" "What is the most important trait of a responsible thinker?" "Would any sane person ever want to kill an innocent child?" Such one-answer questions have some, if not all, of the following characteristics:

- They assume that there is only one right answer.
- They occur most often in courses where the focus is learning information.
- They can create the atmosphere of a guessing game.
- They can be satisfying to answer "right."
- They may create a competitive atmosphere.
- They may lead a person to answer without questioning the question.

For example, the question "What was the cause of the Civil War?" assumes, by the use of the word *the*, that there was one and only one cause of the Civil War. If the question were posed by a teacher in class it could create the atmosphere of a "guess what the teacher's thinking" game. Some students would settle for the satisfaction of guessing what the teacher thought at the time, while others would compete to say it first. Students who aren't good at guessing could give up and feel defeated. If these kinds of questions were very frequent, students would not be able to feel the satisfaction of responsible thinking: asking and exploring good questions, entertaining different points of view and perspectives, formulating standards, reflecting, correcting their own thinking, and collaborating with others to find interesting and provocative answers.

Rhetorical Questions.   "Would you starve little children to death?" "How many people have given their lives in Bosnia-Herzegovina?" "What more could we have done to save them?" Sometimes answers to such questions as these are meant to be so obvious that the questions are not really requests for answers. For example, the question, "Would you starve little children to death?" was used in a student's speech on children's rights to make a point: *You are not paying attention to these children—if you were, you'd donate to this fund.* The obvious answer to the question was "No." The question "How many people have given their lives in Bosnia-Herzegovina?," if used in a speech or political paper, would not be a request for statistics. The obvious answer and the implied statement is "Too many people have died." Nor is the question, "What more could we have done to save them?"—when used in this way—a request for a list of things to do. The obvious answer is "We have done all we could."

If a question is used not as a request for an answer but as a strategy to persuade an audience of a predictable answer and point, it is called a *rhetorical question.* The word *rhetorical,* in this context, means "meant to persuade."

Rhetorical questions have some, if not all, of these characteristics:

- They are asked in speeches.
- They are used to make a powerful impression on the audience.
- They are used to make a point.
- There is only one acceptable answer to each question.
- Listeners or readers know there is only one acceptable answer.
- They are statements in disguise.
- They are not meant to be answered.

Notice that context—purpose and audience—determines whether a question is used rhetorically or not. A villain might ask, "Would you starve the little children to death?" as a request for strategies. A writer seeking details to support an argument against war might ask, "How many have given their lives for this cause?" And to a Red Cross volunteer, "What more could we have done to save them?" would be a good question.

> ### *Learning to Ask Questions*
>
> 1. ***Remind*** yourself, "The only dumb question is the one not asked." Even an unfair question can lead to a better question, once the first one is addressed.
>
> 2. ***Use the question star*** (Figure 5.3) to help you trigger and generate questions.
>
> 3. ***Collect*** questions for each course that you take. Mark the questions that are likely to be asked on an exam or that may lead to reports or papers.
>
> 4. ***Collect*** questions for specific problems you want to solve, whether they are personal or social, financial or spiritual, academic or professional.
>
> 5. ***Analyze*** questions. Ask yourself:
>
>   - What kind of question is this: good, unfair, yes/no, one-answer, or rhetorical?
>
>   - What kind of response, if any, does this question require?
>
>   - How could I revise this question to be a *good* question?
>
> 6. ***Practice*** answering anticipated questions for exams, business meetings, social conversations, and interviews. Write your questions down. Freewrite in response to them, one at a time. Revise them for your purpose and audience.
>
> 7. ***Allow questions to emerge*** throughout your learning process. Respond to the most relevant ones.

*E*xplorations

1. *Together.* Consider the question "What are the three traits of a responsible thinker?" Decide, from the way it is phrased, whether it is a good, unfair, yes/no, one-answer, or rhetorical question. How would you rephrase it so that it would more certainly be a good question?

2. *Together.* Analyze and discuss the following questions. Using the standards offered in the discussion above, mark the questions as being good (G), unfair (U), yes/no (Y), one-answer (O), or rhetorical (R). Do any fit into more than one category? If so, in which contexts?

   a. What is nuclear winter?

   b. How is modern-day television different from its early days?

   c. Does the president of the United States have too big a job?

   d. Was the decision in the Sacco and Vanzetti case cruel?

   e. Who led the fight against Hitler?

   f. What is family life like in Argentina as compared to family life in the United States?

   g. Well, baseball fans, what is the world's greatest sport?

   h. What are the comparative benefits of organic and synthetic fertilizers?

   i. How should cigarettes be advertised?

   j. Are the problems of single parents being adequately addressed by local and federal governments?

3. a. *Solo.* Choose a class that is important to you or one in which you are having difficulties. During a class meeting, listen for and record the questions that are asked in the class. Mark the following letters by them to note who asks them—(T) for the teacher, (S) for students, (B) for books or other written material. Then write about what you noticed.

   • What questions were repeated?

   • Which questions did *you* feel were *good questions?*

   • How were they handled?

   • What did you notice about the source of the questions?

   • What did you learn by focusing on questions?

   • Are the questions being asked in this Exploration helpful to you?

   • What other questions occur to you about, or in response to, the questions asked in your chosen class?

   b. *Together.* Compare the results of collecting questions from your classes. Analyze them, using the instructions from Exploration 2.

4. *Together and Solo.*

   a. Choose a topic that is puzzling you in a course you are taking. Using the *wh* words as triggers, ask as many questions about the topic as you can. Next, discuss which questions are good, unfair, yes/no, one-word, or rhetorical questions. Which questions will lead you to the answers you are seeking?

   b. Write an essay on the topic, using your questions to stimulate ideas and insights. Organize your paper into a series of paragraphs, each of which poses and responds to a question. Write so that one question-and-answer paragraph leads logically to the next question and answer. As you write, allow other questions to arise. Do not require yourself to give a complete answer, especially if you are posing new good or rhetorical questions.

   c. Read these essays to each other, and discuss what you learned from doing this Exploration.

5. *Together and Solo.* Listen to a debate or interview on television. Record the questions. Discuss whether the person answers the questions. If not, how does the person "dodge" offering a direct answer to the questions posed?

6. *Together and Solo.* Turn to pages 116–121 in Chapter 5 and notice how questions help you focus in the writing process. Choose a paper someone in the class is writing and ask questions to help the author write more effectively. List these questions and analyze them using the criteria developed above.

Key Statements: The Thesis

Questions invite answers, and key statements (also called *thesis statements*) invite further elaboration, evidence, and proof. They are called *key* statements because, like keys, they unlock your mind as well as your reader's. If you have not already done so, review the sections on pages 121–128, which provide you with an in-depth discussion of how to identify and use these key or thesis statements. Complement the work in that chapter with these examples of key statements from textbooks in three different academic disciplines:

U.S. history. "Four predominant schools of thought have emerged in American history since the first graduate seminars in history were given at The Johns Hopkins University in Baltimore in the 1870s."

Geology. "Many of the materials that form the crust of the earth are useful to us."

Marketing. "Strategic planning efforts must accommodate the distinct needs of marketing as well as the other functional areas in an organization."

These "thesis" statements embody the main or key ideas the authors want to relate. They are good thesis statements because they meet some of or all the following standards:

Standards for good thesis statements

- They lead to good questions.
- They lead to other statements.
- They are focused.

For example, consider the thesis statement in U.S. history: "Four predominant schools of thought have emerged in American history since the first graduate seminars in history were given at The Johns Hopkins University in Baltimore in the 1870s." This statement invites questions such as these: What are the four predominant schools of thought in U.S. history? Why does the author name The Johns Hopkins University as a starting point? What happened in the 1870s that made that decade a turning point in U.S. history? The thesis statement leads to a long discussion of the four schools of thought and what forces influenced them. The thesis statement is focused on a particular time and doesn't try to cover all possible theories.

In the writing process—whether for an exam, an oral report, or a term paper—the purpose of writing a thesis statement is to make a commitment to a key idea so that it will trigger your memory and guide you to collect and recollect whatever further evidence you need to support your claim.

Remember that thesis statements develop in the writing process. Start with a working thesis statement. Revise and refine it as you draft your paper. A thesis statement is like a roof: it appears at the top, but first you have to construct the building under it.

*E*xplorations _____

1. *Together.* Discuss this statement: "The statements of a responsible thinker are made in the spirit of preserving or bettering human relations and the environment." What are the key words in the statement? How would you define them? Is the statement weak or strong? Why? Is the statement responsible or irresponsible? Why?

2. *Solo and Together.*

   a. Collect questions and assignments from your textbooks and class notes. Using the sidebar offered on page 127 for writing thesis statements, practice turning these questions and assignments into thesis statements. Write the statements on the board one at a time and revise your statements until they meet the standards for good thesis statements. Adjust them to be appropriately strong.

   b. *Solo.* Write an essay in response to a key (thesis) statement you developed in response to an assignment.

Learning Through the Senses

From a drop of water a logician could infer the possibility of an Atlantic or Niagara without having seen or heard of one or the other. . . . By a man's fingernails, by his coat sleeve, by his boots, by his trouser-knees, by the callosities of his forefinger and thumb, by his expression,

by his shirt-cuffs—by each of these things a man's calling is plainly
revealed.

—Sir Arthur Conan Doyle, Creator of Sherlock Holmes
"A Study in Scarlet"

Part of the education process is to sharpen your senses and mind so that
you can create new ideas from available input. Chapter 6 invited you to
explore your senses in everyday experiences. This section offers some
basic insights into how to develop academic thinking skills through the
senses.

Whenever you are writing—whether it be a paper, report, proposal,
essay, poem, or story—prime your senses by collecting pictures, audio
recordings, objects, and documents and by putting yourself in a place
where you can best gather sensations. Ask yourself the following questions:

What visual or object would be relevant for me to look at? For example, if you are writing a paper about political unrest in Somalia, find
photographs or news broadcasts depicting people and events there. When
you write, start by describing a photograph or film to provide your reader
with immediacy. If you are reporting on the Berlin Wall, you might want
to find a piece of it and describe what it feels like to hold it in your hand.
If you are writing about hairstyles in eighteenth-century Paris, you can
either find a book of pictures or ask your local video store for a movie
set in that time. (Be aware, however, that movies are not always accurate
or well researched.)

What audio would be relevant for me to listen to? For example, if
you are writing a paper about a speech, ask your librarian for a recording
of the speech made by the speaker. Or, a paper on a poem would be much
enriched by your reflecting on a videotaped reading of it by the author.

Where can I get firsthand experience of what I am writing about?
For example, if you are writing about the homeless, you may want to
visit a shelter or city bus terminal where homeless people live so that
you can better understand their problems. While you are there, if it seems
appropriate, talk with some of the homeless. When you reach for such
firsthand experiences, make sure you consider your own and other's sense
of safety and dignity. If you want to know what conditions are like in a
mine, you would want an escort; if you want to know what hang gliding
is like, you would want some training (lots of it).

*E*xplorations

1. *Together and Solo.* List visual and audio material that will help you
   prime your senses for each of the following assignments in different

Learning Through the Senses

1. ***Use the sense star*** [Figure 6.1, page 134] to remind you to collect images for all the appropriate senses.

2. ***Ask yourself these questions*** when posed with an assignment:

   - What visual or object would be relevant?
   - What recordings could enliven my process?
   - What firsthand experience could support my learning?
   - How could I trigger my memory?

3. ***Research documents,*** such as newspapers, books, reports, financial papers, letters, and journals.

4. ***Prime your senses*** by taking notes as you review your visual or audio materials. Don't expect to remember all the relevant details without this support.

5. ***Consult*** with others. Observe your object, film, or subject together. What relevant images do others notice that you have overlooked?

areas of study. Design, as well, some possible firsthand experiences that would enliven and inform the experience of doing each assignment.

a. *Geography.* Environmental catastrophes such as Three Mile Island, the Exxon oil spill, and Love Canal are jeopardizing human life and the life of our planet. Investigate your community for instances of environmental pollution. Write a paper detailing the problems and how the community is either coping with or ignoring them.

b. *Sociology.* Nursing homes can be difficult places for the elderly to pass their last years. Write a paper detailing the problems and possible solutions to them.

c. *Political Science.* Compare television and newspaper coverage of an important current event. How do the two differ in terms of the time, space, and emphases they give to different aspects of the event? How does your experience of watching a television report differ from your experience of reading the newspaper?

d. *Psychology.* Write a paper stating your position on whether or not television violence encourages violent behavior in children.

e. *Fine Art.* Write a paper showing similarities between two pieces of art shown in a gallery this season.

f. *Mathematics.* How would you go about estimating the number of leaves on a tree, grains of sand on a beach, cars that pass through a toll booth, or hamburgers eaten on average at the local diner?

    g. *Literature.* What are five of the most frequent subjects of Robert Frost's poetry?

    h. *Media Studies.* What are five main points of view (angles) that the camera takes in current horror films to terrify audiences?

    i. *Management Sciences.* Write a paper either agreeing or disagreeing with the statement "Women tend to be treated differently from men in offices."

2. *Solo.* Write a paper in response to one of the assignments in Exploration 1. Conduct your research by priming your senses and collecting notes on as many sensations as you can cover.

3. **a.** *Together and Solo.* List courses you are taking this semester. List projects, papers, and other assignments that you anticipate having to complete. In small groups, develop suggestions for visual, audio, and firsthand experiences that will help you prime your senses for the assignments.

    b. *Solo.* Complete an assignment by priming your senses. Write a report on how this affected both your experience of doing the assignment and the outcome of the assignment.

Summarizing

A summary is a concise statement—in your own words—of a longer piece of writing. Whereas writing a key statement helps you to focus what you *write*, summarizing in key statements helps you to focus what you *read*. In the act of summarizing, you connect what you read with whatever you already know. Since what you read then becomes connected to what you know, you are more likely to remember and understand what you read and to notice what questions you have about it. Good summaries meet some, if not all, of the following standards:

Standards for good summaries

- They are brief.
- They identify the author, title, focus, and context of works.
- They relay the author's main points.
- They omit most supporting information.
- They capture and honor the author's purpose and intention.

The purposes and audiences for a summary vary, and it is important to note why you are summarizing a particular piece of writing and for whom. For example, if your purpose in studying an article is to prepare for an exam that tests your recall of information, you would summarize the article, trying to guess what your instructor considers important. You would take careful notes in class, listening for points that your instructor repeats, emphasizes, likes, or dislikes. If the instructor agrees with the article, you would look for what the author emphasizes. If the instructor doesn't agree with the article (and you can often tell), you would look—in addition to what the author emphasizes—for points of disagreement.

If you were summarizing a chapter in this book in order to remember skills you personally need to develop, you would focus mostly on the parts of the chapter that were important to you, just as in a course where interpretation is important, you would focus the most on those parts of a poem, painting, or musical performance that support your interpretations.

The audience for your summary also determines how you proceed. Suppose you read an article opposing smoking. If you were summarizing the article for children, you would not stress technical language. If you were summarizing the same article for medical personnel, you *would* stress technical language.

Read the following paragraph from S. I. Hayakawa's book *Language in Thought and Action*,[22] and the discussion of three attempted summaries that follows.

> People who think of themselves as tough-minded and realistic tend to take it for granted that human nature is selfish and that life is a struggle in which only the fittest may survive. According to this philosophy, the basic law by which people must live, in spite of their surface veneer of civilization, is the struggle of the jungle. The "fittest" are those who can bring to the struggle superior force, superior cunning, and superior ruthlessness.

Summary 1

> S. I. Hayakawa thinks that people who think of themselves as tough-minded and realistic take it for granted that human nature is a struggle of survival of the fittest. The fittest are those who can bring to the struggle superior force, superior cunning, and superior ruthlessness.

Summary 1 is not brief: it is almost as long as the paragraph it attempts to summarize. It includes too many supporting details and doesn't identify the title of the work it cites.

Summary 2

> He thinks that some people are selfish and live like animals in a jungle.

How to Summarize

1. Carefully **read** the material you are summarizing, several times.

2. **Identify the purpose and audience** for your summary.

3. **Identify the author, the title, focus, and context** of what you are summarizing. Notice, for example, how the following summaries are begun:

   > In his book *Amusing Ourselves to Death,* Neil Postman argues that in the modern world we are destroying our minds in the pursuit of pleasure.

   > Joseph Campbell illustrates, in his book *Transformations of Myth Through Time,* that there are common themes in the mythologies of cultures around the world.

4. **Choose words that identify the author's purpose** in the work. So, for example, to say an author "claims" something is to suggest that what the claim can be questioned. To say an author "shows" is to suggest that you believe the author is successful in proving a point.

5. **Underline** or highlight **key words and statements.**

6. **Notice what the author emphasizes** in the title, section headings, table of contents, underlining or italics, bold print, and boxes. The author may cue you as to what is important to him or her by using expressions such as "It is important to note . . ." "The main point I want to make . . ." or "In this article I will show. . . ."

7. **Exclude most supporting details** from your summary, except those that are necessary for clarifying your main points.

8. **Rephrase only what the author says.** Do not make statements stronger or weaker than the author would.

9. **Be brief.** Place a working limit on the number of statements or words you will use in a summary. This will force you to choose what's most important. The act of choosing, itself, will help you learn. For a test, attempt to fit your summary of main points on one sheet. The summary should be significantly shorter than the original writing.

10. **Quote** directly when the author writes a statement so clearly that it's best just to copy it into your summary.

This summary is brief, but it does not identify the author or title of the work to which it refers. It misrepresents Hayakawa, who does not claim that some people live like animals in a jungle. What he says is that those people who think of themselves as tough-minded and realistic think of life as survival of the fittest. He doesn't identify himself as being one of them.

Summary 3

> In <u>Language in Thought and Action,</u> S. I. Hayakawa states that,
> according to adherents of the philosophy of tough-minded
> realism, human nature is selfish. For them, life is the struggle
> of the jungle where the fittest survive.

This is the most balanced summary of the three. It cites title and author. It is brief. It excludes supporting details. It states what Hayakawa states without attributing to him claims that he did not make.

Read this excerpt from a speech given by poet and feminist Adrienne Rich at a meeting of the New Jersey College and University Coalition on Women's Education on May 9, 1978. Then reflect on the three student summaries that follow.

> In teaching women, we have two choices: to lend our weight to the forces that indoctrinate women to passivity, self-depreciation, and a sense of powerlessness, in which case the issue of "taking women students seriously" is a moot one; or to consider what we have to work against, as well as with, in ourselves, in our students, in the content of the curriculum, in the structure of the institution, in the society at large. And this means, first of all, taking ourselves seriously: Recognizing that central responsibility of a woman to herself, without which we remain always the Other, the defined, the object, the victim; believing that there is a unique quality of validation, affirmation, challenge, support, that one woman can offer another; believing in the value and significance of women's experience, traditions, perceptions; thinking of ourselves seriously, not as one of the boys, not as neuters, or androgynes, but as *women.*

Summary 1

> Adrienne Rich, in her talk "Taking Women Seriously," says we
> should do just that. It's time we stopped treating women students
> as if they should only have babies and take care of men.

Summary 2

> In this speech, Rich says either we force women to be passive
> or we take them seriously when we teach them.

Summary 3

In her May 9, 1978, address to the New Jersey College and University Coalition on Women's Education, "Taking Women Seriously," poet Adrienne Rich argues against those who teach women to be passive and powerless. She wants teachers to educate women to believe in themselves.

Reflections _____

1. Rank the summaries from 1 to 3, with 3 being the most effective.

2. Which of the ten strategies does each of the summaries clearly illustrate?

3. Which strategies are not applied in each of the three summaries?

4. Revise the least effective summary using the strategies it missed.

5. Revise the other drafts to better represent the material being summarized.

Explorations _____

1. *Together.* To help you develop a vocabulary that relates how an author approaches a topic, do Exploration 1 on page 51.

2. *Together.*
   a. Bring in newspaper articles and cut off or cover the headlines. In small groups, write headlines that serve as summaries of the articles whose headlines you didn't see.
   b. Discuss the differences between the original headlines and what you wrote. Which are more effective for what purposes and audiences?

3. a. *Solo.* Choose a passage from a textbook you are currently using or a newspaper article that interests you. Write three different drafts of a summary for a person who hasn't read the passage. Improve your summary with each draft.
   b. *Together.* Using the suggestions and questions in the preceding Reflections, review your summaries in small groups or as a class. Discuss whether your current draft meets the standards for a good summary. Revise your summaries to meet the standards.

4. *Solo.* For your next exam, create a one-page summary using your instructor's outline, the table of contents of your textbook, or a list

of key statements. Write in your journal about what you learned by writing this summary and how you did on the exam. What improvements, if any, would you make in writing a summary for your next exam? Discuss these insights with other students.

Chapter Review

1. *Together or Solo.* Summarize this chapter for a new college student. Your purpose will be to outline the basic skills this chapter offers. Limit the length of the summary to one typewritten page.

2. *Together.* Compare and contrast the summaries you wrote for Chapter Review 1, using the suggestions in the preceding Reflections on summaries. Revise your drafts to meet the standards for good summaries.

Chapter 13

Writing to Learn II

Making Connections

This chapter offers opportunities to

—***Learn by writing***
—Use a ***learning journal*** with ***double*** and ***process entries***
—***Write essays*** to support thesis statements and theories
—Write essays that ***compare and contrast***
—***Chart*** information
—Practice the skills of ***responsible thinking***

> Writing, like life itself, is a voyage
> of discovery.
> —*Henry Miller, Novelist*

> If we knew everything beforehand, all
> would be dictation, not creation.
> —*Gertrude Stein, Writer*

Reason and Evidence

Academic disciplines based on reasoning are systems of connected statements. Some of these statements are claims and others are statements of evidence in support of the claims. Statements of evidence should be clear, relevant, and sufficient so that other people can see for themselves the truth of the claims your statements of evidence are meant to support. For example, if, in biochemistry, you claim that high-cholesterol diets may lead to heart attacks, you should be able to support your claim with evidence such as blood test results of heart attack victims. Other people should be able to review your evidence (or perform the same tests) and come to the same conclusions as you did. If, in literature, you claim that Shakespeare did not write all the plays attributed to him, you should be able to support your claim with evidence such as an analysis of writing style in particular plays. You would support your claim by using the theory that every person's writing style is as unique as her or his fingerprints. Other people should then be able to analyze your evidence—the writing style in the questionable plays—and come to the same conclusions as you did.

Chapter 12 offered you strategies for identifying key words, questions, and statements. This chapter offers you opportunities to further develop your ability to reason by connecting these key elements—supporting claims, ideas, and theories with evidence—as thinkers in different academic disciplines do.*

Drafting: Writing, Itself, Helps You Learn

In Chapter 12, intelligence was defined as the ability to make useful and creative connections between experiences. The more you write about what you experience and read, the more of these connections you will develop. Repetition is one of the foundations of learning: the mere act of writing reinforces what you learn or already know because you are repeating it as you write. You are also connecting your inner world with the outer because writing transforms ideas and feelings into a form others can experience, as well. As you continue to write, you recall previous experiences, integrate them with new material, and create new connections. Because of all these reasons and more, it is important to make and find opportunities to *engage* with words on the page.

---

*For an in-depth discussion of writing to learn, see John S. Mayhen, Nancy Lester, and Gordon Pradl, *Learning to Write/Writing to Learn* (Montclair, N.J.: Boynton/Cook, 1983).

Learning Journal

In a notebook, you record what someone else says or presents to you. In a journal, you *engage* with what you record and *make it your own.* You respond, question, argue, wonder, interpret, experiment, explore, and evaluate. Your *learning journal* is one of the most helpful tools you can use to develop yourself as a responsible thinker. The journal becomes your companion, a safe audience with whom to develop your unique perspective. Your learning journal is a source of ideas for papers, discussions, presentations, creative projects, and social interactions.

Double entries

A *double entry* offers you the combined benefits of a notebook and a journal. That's why it's called a *double entry.* On the left side of your double entry, you record key words, statements, questions, quotes, and other stimuli including drawings and diagrams. On the right side, you enter your responses to what you recorded on the left. You can create a double entry in several ways: Draw a line down the middle of your notebook page; use a stenographer's pad, which already has a line down the middle; or keep notes on the left sheet in your notebook and write your commentary on the facing right sheet. Start with the divided sheet. For some purposes you may want to switch to left and right notebook pages. Leave plenty of space for your responses. One side of your double entry will usually look emptier than the other. Some students prefer to distinguish notes from responses by using different colored pens instead of separating notes on the left from responses on the right.

Here are a number of ways in which you can respond in a double entry:

Repetition. If there is a key word, idea, or statement you want to remember, either copy it out several times just as it is or restate it several times in your own words. Here is how Lev Mansky used repetition in a double-entry response to a note taken in Introduction to Philosophy:

Appearance and reality

According to Plato, there is a difference between appearance and reality. I guess what he means is that things aren't always what they seem. He thinks that there is a reality, some truth, that is under all the appearances.

Questions. If something puzzles you, ask good questions about it. Remember that the only dumb question is, literally, the one not asked.

Sometimes, just writing out a question triggers a connection in your mind, and you find you already know the answer. Start with the words *I wonder.* Here is how Lev used questions in his double entry to continue exploring Plato's claim:

> I wonder what true reality is anyhow. I mean, who's to say? George tells me women only want to get married. But that's the way he's looking at Janice, maybe so he can avoid her. But she tells me she wants a career, and George won't listen. So, what's real there? George sees Janice one way, she sees herself in another, and I'm on the outside looking in. Can it ever be different? Is Plato dreaming that we can be certain of what's true and real once and for all?

Authority Notes.   Suppose you encounter a topic that overwhelms you. Take time to record five key statements that you already know about the topic. Start with the words *I know that.* One idea will lead to another, and you will be able to proceed with more confidence. Sometimes you encounter a topic about which you know a great deal. Take time to write about the topic to recall and reinforce what you already know so that you can absorb new information more quickly. Here is how Lev continued his responses to Plato:

> So okay, there are some things I do know are real and true.
>
> 1. I know that I'm holding a pen and this is my hand.
> 2. I know that I can read what I'm writing.
> 3. I know that I'm smelling dinner cooking. (I'm presuming my father is cooking because he always does on Tuesdays because my mother is usually late.)
> 4. I know that Plato made this claim because so many books say he did. (But they could all be wrong, so maybe it only appears that he did. But the chances are slim.)
> 5. I know that I'm smarter than I thought I was when I first started writing this.

Evaluations.   You may find yourself disagreeing with the point of view of an instructor or writer. Use your double-entry journal to anticipate arguments and to justify your current position. Start with the words *I feel that* or *I believe that.* Lev wrote this:

> I feel that Prof. Jorgenson is being too hard on Plato when she says that Plato's philosophy is outdated. Sure, I can see that the idea of a world of perfect Ideals is just wishful thinking. I can see that social and

political prejudices shape how we look at things. But, I believe (or would like to believe) with Plato that underneath it all, there *is* some solid truth. Is this wishful thinking?

Connections.   One of the most satisfying experiences is to make connections between what you learn in different courses. Look for and write out ideas from other courses that occur to you in response to an idea or statement. Start with the words *This connects with* or *This reminds me of.* Lev continued to write about Plato:

> This connects with my science course. If we couldn't believe in what we see right in front of us, the way I can believe that I am using a pen right now, then there would be nothing to hold onto. So science, the way it's set up with physical proof and math, seems to me one real way to get to truth and reality. But then Prof. J. told us that which piece of evidence is accepted by the scientific community depends on who you know. I guess we're going to have to discuss this more the way Plato did with his students.

Process entries

The focus in a notebook is to record *what* someone else is offering you. A double entry focuses on *your responses* to what others offer. *Process entries* focus on your style of learning, thinking, and responding. In process entries you do some, or all, of the following:

- Describe how you currently approach a skill or problem.
- Write what occurs to you as you work through a problem.
- Notice patterns and relationships.
- Identify difficulties.
- Explain procedures in your own words.
- Develop new ways of solving problems.
- Record what happens when you "catch on."
- Pose clear questions.

When you keep a process journal you enjoy opportunities to:

- Learn how you approach information and skills.
- Write your way through problems.
- Develop insights into your own and others' processes.
- Develop new ways of doing things.
- Develop more confidence and pleasure in learning.

José A. López, a student in Arthur Powell's Developmental Mathematics I class at Rutgers University, used a process journal to help him pass the course.[23] Here are some process entries he made as he worked through his mathematics problems. You don't have to understand mathematics to notice that José became clearer about exponents as he wrote about his process and that writing helped him to learn and to succeed.

> Today in class, I observed that when working with exponents, when I move to the right the value of the exponential number increases by one. The reverse is true when moving to the left. Also, the number of multiplication steps is the same as the exponential number. When moving to the left, I take the reciprocal of the positive value I found when moving to the right. When multiplying numbers with the bases the same, but different exponential numbers, I can add these exponents. E.g., $5^3 \times 5^1 = 5^4 = 625$. When dividing numbers whose base is the same, but have different exponents, I can subtract the second exponent from the first. E.g., $5^3/5^1 = 5^{3-1} = 5^2 = 25$.

Letters

You may find, as you write in your learning journal, that you want to share your reflections with peers and instructors. Write a letter to a classmate or instructor when you need some questions answered, are excited about an idea, want to propose a project, or just need to test some reactions. Sometimes you can just photocopy a journal entry and add a note at the top saying why you are sending that entry.

*E**xplorations*

1. *Solo.* Choose a course that is important to you and create a double entry for it in your learning journal. Try a different double-entry strategy for each of the next few meetings of the course, and notice which strategies work best for you. Write a letter to your instructor about what you have learned by writing and what more you want to learn.

2. *Solo and Together.* Contact a student or group of students in a course you are currently taking. Plan to meet once a week to discuss questions and insights that arise for you, or arrange to write each other letters. You may want to introduce double-entry strategies to your study partners. After a couple of weeks, reflect on the benefits you have gained.

3. *Solo.* Keep a double-entry journal for your courses. Write your notes on the right side and on the left formulate possible questions to which

How to Keep a Learning Journal

1. *Commit yourself.* Decide on a regular schedule for keeping your journal, such as coming to class five minutes early and leaving five minutes late so you can freewrite in your journal. Be flexible. Revise your schedule so you can honor your commitment.

2. *Choose writing tools* that best support your process: a spiral-bound notebook, a binder filled with typed pages, or a computer disk. You might want to combine strategies, such as including taped-in typed pages among your handwritten notebook entries.

3. *Focus* your entries on particular key words, statements, and questions. Tape news articles, quotes, and photocopies of excerpts into your journal for starters.

4. *Collect* ideas by freewriting, listing, brainstorming, clustering, or drawing in your journal.

5. *Organize* your entries with tabs, colored pens, or computer files.

6. *Describe* your learning processes, especially when you get stuck.

7. *Prepare* for class, exams, conferences with your teacher, or study sessions by writing in your journal.

those notes could be responding. Writing these entries will help you to prepare for exams.

4. **a.** *Together.* Discuss some problems you are encountering in other courses or at work.

b. *Solo.* Choose a particular skill or group of skills you use in another course or at a job. Write a process entry, using some of the suggestions listed above.

c. *Together.* Share your process entries from 4b with your writing class or with the instructor or students in the course for which you are developing your process journal. With the help of your writing class, you may want to compose a letter to the instructor of the course for which you are writing the process journal, explaining your process notes, what you are learning from them, and what help you need. Even if you don't send the letter, you will learn from the process of writing it. Reflect on what you learned, together.

For further Explorations on process, refer to 1 and 2 on pages 34–35.

Writing Essays: Thesis and Evidence

One of the basic ways that connections are made in science and education is by writing essays. An *essay* is far more than just a set of notes. An essay is a written report or interpretation of information, ideas, and observations. An essay presents evidence and examples to support statements and a certain point of view.

When you write essays, keep your purpose and audience in mind. In academic writing, you will often want to focus on transfer of information, development of skills, interpretation, and experimentation. If the purpose of your essay is to display how much information you have retained, then you will want to offer more examples and evidence. If the purpose of your essay is to show reasoning skills, then you might want to limit the number of examples and increase the discussion of them. If the purpose of your essay is to develop an interpretation, then you must clearly describe and evaluate what you are interpreting and support your discussion with relevant quotes and details. If the purpose of your essay is to report an experiment, you might need to summarize relevant research done by others and compare your results to theirs. In each course, you will learn the purpose of your essays and what counts as evidence for the kinds of statements made in that discipline.

Some of the main strategies for fulfilling the purposes of academic essays are to:

Analyze	Inform
Argue	Interpret
Classify	Outline
Compare	Narrate
Contrast	Question
Define	Reflect
Describe	Solve
Evaluate	Summarize
Explain	Theorize
Illustrate	

For each strategy there are different ways in which to organize your thinking and writing. Chapter 7 offers you a variety of these ways to develop your academic and professional writing. If you decide to work more as a planner on a particular writing project, you might want to adopt

> ## *Writing an Academic Essay*
>
> 1. *Read* the assignment carefully.
> 2. *Decide on your strategy for a lead.* This may be a story, a statistic, an example, or a thesis statement. Revise this lead as you draft the essay.
> 3. *Develop a key or thesis statement,* adjusting its strength to your purpose. You may need to write a first draft before you can formulate this statement.
> 4. *Position your thesis statement* either at the beginning of your essay or at the end of your lead. In some cases, your thesis statement might be delayed for your ending.
> 5. *Support* or lead up to your thesis statement with appropriate evidence and examples. Ask yourself:
>
>   • Is this the most relevant information?
>   • Is this all the information I need?
>
> 6. *Organize* the essay so that the evidence and examples combine to most effectively support your thesis statement. Use the kinds of reasoning appropriate to the purpose and audience of your essay. Choose between a deductive and an inductive approach.
> 7. *End* your essay reflecting, in some way, on your thesis statement.
>
> *Remember that the final product, your essay, may be different from the process of writing it.* You may have to freewrite, collect information, organize, reorganize, and revise several times before you settle on a thesis statement and evidence you want in the final version. *Avoid the temptation to settle for your first draft of an essay.* A benefit of the writing process may be the discovery of a better thesis statement. It's worth the extra effort to redraft your essay with the better thesis statement rather than to settle for a mere first attempt.

a structure and then work to fill it in. If you decide to work more as an explorer, you will delay organizing your work until you have discovered and created ideas through focusing and collecting.

Notice the final version of an essay that biology major John Williams produced in response to a lab assignment about the diet of Washington barn owls:[24]

The barn owl's primary source of animal food in Washington is rodents. In the pellet samples we took (which contain the fur and bones of the animals eaten by the owl at a meal), we found that *Microtus* is the owl's primary food source because there were more than twice as many *Microtus* remains (twenty-two *Microtus* to nine other rodents). This might be a preferred choice of the barn owl, but is probably a result of *Microtus* being more numerous than other prey. However, this cannot be proved from the data given. It should be noted, based on the data, that the barn owl will occasionally consume other birds. In addition, this data does not reflect the owl's vegetarian diet, which may, or may not, be significant. Moreover, this data reflects a small sample size (two pellets). A larger sample size (more pellets analyzed) might strengthen our conclusion or modify it in some way.

John begins his essay by stating his thesis:

The barn owl's primary source of food in Washington is rodents.

He supports his thesis by referring to the contents of the physical evidence: the pellets that the owl expelled after eating. John used only relevant information. He shows as well that he questions the evidence. This gives the reader more confidence that the evidence John offers has been carefully considered. John ends his essay by referring to his thesis statement, remarking that a larger sample might strengthen his statement or modify it.

*E*xplorations ─────────────────────────────

Do one or more of the following Explorations, which are designed to help you work with thesis statements and evidence. For further Explorations, turn to pages 121–128 in Chapter 5 and pages 331–332 in Chapter 12.

1. *Together and Solo.* Review the material on thesis statements offered in Chapters 5 and 12. If you have not already done so, do a selection of the Explorations corresponding to those discussions.

2. *Together.* List some essay assignments you have in your courses. In small groups, write thesis statements in response to select assignments. Together, practice writing an essay in response to one of the statements. Discuss first what the purpose of the essay is. Ask whether you are using enough appropriate examples and evidence to satisfy that purpose. If you discover a better thesis statement during the writing process, revise the essay, starting with the better statement.

3. *Solo.* Choose an essay assignment you have in one of your academic courses and formulate a thesis statement. First, determine the purpose

of your essay. Then, write an essay with appropriate evidence and reasoning to support your thesis statement. Be sure to ask yourself, "Is this information relevant? Is this information enough?" If you discover a better thesis statement during the writing process, revise the essay, starting with the better statement.

4. *Solo.*

   a. To help you prepare for your next essay exam, find a key or thesis statement in a course you are taking. Using it as a beginning, write an essay in which you offer evidence to support the statement. On your first attempt, write without referring to your notes or books. Be sure to follow the strategies on page 349. Ask yourself, as well, which of the four main academic purposes—learning information, skills, interpretation, or experimentation—the essay can satisfy. This Exploration will help you discover what you need to study or practice.

   b. To help you prepare for your next essay exam, find or formulate five questions you anticipate will appear on the exam. Answer the questions by formulating and supporting thesis statements.

5. *Together and Solo.* Read the essays you wrote in Exploration 4 with special attention to whether the writers offer enough relevant evidence to support key statements. Notice which purpose or purposes the essays are meant to satisfy. Revise accordingly.

Synthesizing: Forming Theories

The first step in any study—whether in the natural or social sciences or in the arts—is collecting observations. If you are a biologist, you might notice how a certain form of amoeba reacts to chemicals under a microscope. If you are a psychologist, you might observe babies' crying habits at different times and under different conditions. If you are an art critic, you might notice the shapes and colors an artist uses at certain periods in his life. After repeated observation, you may notice a pattern and formulate a theory—an educated guess—of what accounts for the sudden contraction of the amoeba, why and when the rhythms of babies' crying change, or how it is that the artist started to use brighter colors after becoming an epileptic.

A theory often takes the form of a key statement, or thesis, and offers you the same opportunities for development. But a theory goes beyond a key or thesis statement. In formulating your theory—your best guess—you are developing new and broader insights. Once you formulate the theory, you go back to test whether your theory is true under further observations.

Here is a list of theories from different academic disciplines. Notice that the theories attempt to organize a number of observations to say something general about their respective subjects:

1. Earthquakes can be predicted by correlations with weather conditions.
2. Oat bran can reduce harmful cholesterol levels.
3. Data collected in the United States indicate that marriage and family remain important.
4. World War II was caused by the economic devastation of Germany in World War I.
5. Companies in the United States are shifting their management styles from company-based to person-based.

These five theories may sound like facts, but actually they are the best guesses that people have made at different times. Notice that each statement must be supported by evidence and tested. For example, the first theory was held by people in the last century, before we had sophisticated instruments to measure weather and earthquake activity. Since then, no reliable correlation has been found between earthquakes and weather. The theory about oat bran does not account for other factors such as overall diet and exercise. It is the combination of diet and exercise that has been shown to reduce cholesterol. Again, this theory has to be revised and tested against different kinds of evidence.

The five theories comply with some, or all, of the standards for theories that are listed in the sidebar. For example, the third theory, that family is still important in the United States, (1) applies to many families, (2) explains why there are so many marriages, (3) forms part of a system of theories about relations between the sexes in the United States, (4) can be tested against new data, and (5) can be revised if the number of marriages decreases while divorces sharply increase.

Standards for a Good Theory

1. The theory should apply to many specific examples.
2. The theory should explain why or how something occurs.
3. The theory is part of a system of other theories.
4. The theory can be tested.
5. The theory can be revised to include new evidence.

Explorations _____

The following Explorations offer you practice in formulating and testing theories.

1. *Together.* Consider theories 4 and 5 on page 352. Which "Standards for a Good Theory" do they meet? Refer to the sidebar above.

2. **a.** *Solo or Together.* Complete the following starters of theories (or create your own):

   > Young people at a mall . . .
   >
   > Football players before a game . . .
   >
   > Hungry babies . . .
   >
   > College teachers . . .
   >
   > Meals at the college cafeteria . . .
   >
   > Rock singers . . .
   >
   > Most (kind of music) . . .
   >
   > Most movies of (time period) . . .
   >
   > (A person) is/does _____ most of the time . . .

   b. *Together.* Read the completed statements aloud and discuss whether the theories hold true. Are there relevant examples that disprove the theory? Are these exceptions that don't fit the pattern? Why or why not? How can you reformulate your theory so that it will be truer to fact?

   c. *Solo.* Write an essay in which you state a theory you developed while doing this Exploration. Observe your subject(s) closely. Support it with relevant evidence and examples.

3. *Together.* List twenty-five objects and documents that you feel should be included in a time capsule that will help people a hundred years from now formulate accurate theories about college students in your time and place. Discuss which ten objects or documents would give the most effective picture, and why.

4. *Together.* Bring strange objects to class and formulate theories as to what they are and how to use them. Describe what it is about each object that leads you to your theory. (If you know the function of an object but most others don't, you might want to sit back and make notes while others guess.) Notice which statements made during your discussion sound like statements of theory. Reflect on what you learned about theories during this Exploration.

5. *Solo or Together.*

   a. Watch a mystery program or movie, making notes as to who you think "did it" as you go along. What clues led you to your theories?

If you are watching a mystery together, stop the film before the mystery is solved. Write and support your theories of what's happening. Read and discuss your theories together. If you watch programs separately, write a short summary of the movie including only the clues that actually lead to solving the mystery. Read others' summaries and try to guess. What do you notice about how people support their theories?

6. *Together and Solo.* To practice for essay exams, collect statements from your courses that you believe are statements of theories. Drawing on your course, write an essay offering evidence in support of one of these theories.

Comparing and Contrasting

Writing essays in support of thesis statements and theories helps you to interpret and remember information. An essay strategy that is especially helpful in making connections between two or more ideas, people, objects, places, or events is to compare and contrast them. When you *compare,* you notice similarities. When you *contrast,* you notice differences. You can write a whole essay in which all you do is compare two or more subjects. You can write a whole essay in which all you do is contrast two or more subjects. When you both compare *and* contrast in a paper, you explore the balance of similarities and differences between your subjects. By comparing and/or contrasting, you learn new things, create new connections, and keep what you know clearly organized.

There are countless examples, in all disciplines, of how comparing and contrasting can help you learn, create, and organize your learning. Friedrich Kekulé discovered the chemical structure of benzene when he compared it to a coiled snake. Lewis Thomas realized how interconnected all inhabitants of this planet are when he compared earth with a single cell.

The process of learning, itself, used to be compared to an assembly line: first you learn this, then this next, and so on, with no consideration for different learning and thinking styles and needs. Much progress has been made recently, since learning is now being compared to more organic processes. For example, in his article "What True Education Should Do," Sydney J. Harris compares learning to the formation of a pearl around an irritant in an oyster.[25] For Harris, learning is a process of using mistakes to create new knowledge and understanding. If you think of the writing process as an assembly line, you may not be motivated to write. Every time you moved away from the rigid assembly line model you would feel you were doing something wrong. If, however, you see the writing process as forming a pearl, then any move that may seem like a mistake on the assembly line model would be the grain of sand around which another "pearl of wisdom" can form.

Writing Comparisons and Contrasts

Charting. To help you collect information to compare or contrast two or more subjects, it is helpful to create a chart. You can divide a sheet of paper into as many columns as you have subjects. For example, if you were comparing and/or contrasting women in U.S. history, you could create a column for each woman that you want to compare. If you were comparing marketing strategies, you could create a column for each strategy you were considering. Your subjects are written at the head of the columns, and you generate lists of phrases and statements under the subjects. As you write an item on one list, you can write a corresponding note on the others. If you can't think of something to write in one of the columns, leave a space and come back to it. Your chart will change and develop throughout the writing process, and you can add or subtract from the chart whenever you need to. If it gets too messy, recopy it.

To fulfill an assignment in an ecology class, John Williams was trying to determine which kind of owl would be best suited for rodent control in the northwest United States, an area with large open farms and small

Standards for a Good Comparison or Contrast

A good comparison or contrast meets many of the standards that a good question meets. A good comparison or contrast:

- Is clear
- Makes you think
- Helps you question your ways of thinking
- Helps you see different points of view
- Helps you learn more about each point of comparison or contrast
- Is new or generates new insights
- Helps you remember better
- Helps you formulate good questions

woodlots. This assignment called for a comparison and contrast. John created a chart in which he compared and contrasted the barn owl and the great horned owl:

Barn owl	Great horned owl
Voracious for small mammals	Aggressive predator of any available prey, including birds and cats
Eats in open fields	Eats mostly in woodlands
Eats at night and in daytime	Eats more strictly at night

Starting Comparison and/or Contrast Essays. In your introductory paragraph, state your subject, the purpose of your essay, and its significance. Here is such a statement: "Having survived a cultural move from Japan to the United States, I feel I would like to contrast my life in these two countries." Or, you can start your essay using another of the strategies for leads, which you follow up with such a statement. Here is a lead that uses examples to introduce an essay:

> In Japan, most mothers are devoted to making sure that their children make excellent grades and become successful in their lives. These mothers make it their careers. In the United States, mothers have to have their own careers as well. Having survived a cultural shift from Japan to the United States, I feel I have special pressures as a mother in this country that I didn't have at home.

In this example, the writer started with three sentences that state how mothers work in each country. The writer then wrote her thesis statement, which focuses on contrasts between mothers in the two countries.

Just as there are strong and weak thesis statements, some statements of comparison and/or contrast are stronger than others. For example, to say a car *is like* a girlfriend to some teenage males is not as strong as saying a car *is* a girlfriend. To say that teaching is not like running a factory assembly line is not as strong as saying teaching should never be conducted as an assembly line. The sidebar lists some phrases that distinguish weaker from stronger statements of comparison and contrast. Replace *X* and *Y* with your subjects. These formats work for more than two subjects, as well. Use them to get started. Then revise your statement to reflect your own style and purpose.

John formulated the following drafts of thesis statements for his comparison and contrast of the owls:

1. From data collected in class and data found in literature, it is clearly seen that the barn owl controls rodents.

2. The barn owl and the great horned owl show similarities in food habits that are potentially good for controlling rodent populations.

3. The barn owl is far superior to the great horned owl for rodent control in the northwest United States.

Sentence 1 is not a statement of comparison or contrast, because only one subject is being discussed. Sentence 2 is weak because it states only that the two owls are similar. Since you would expect similarities between owls, this is not an informative point. Sentence 3 is the strongest and most appropriate statement in response to the assignment. The statement mentions both the subjects of the comparison and incorporates the purpose of the assignment.

Organizing

Looking at your chart, or reviewing a freewrite, notice whether your main purpose will be to compare your subjects' similarities or to contrast their differences. It is far easier to *either* compare *or* contrast your subjects. However, you might prefer to explore the balance of similarities and differences between your subjects. Once you have committed yourself to

Comparisons

Weaker Statements	**Stronger Statements**
X is like *Y*.	*X* is *Y*.
X can be compared to *Y*.	*X* is always like *Y*.
X is similar to *Y*.	*X* is better than *Y*.
	X is more . . . than *Y*.
	X is less . . . than *Y*.

Contrasts

Weaker Statements	**Stronger Statements**
X is not like *Y*.	*X* is not *Y*.
X can be contrasted to *Y*.	*X* is never like *Y*.
X is different from *Y*.	*X* has nothing in common with *Y*.
	X is . . . while *Y* is . . . .

Transition Words for Comparison and Contrast

Comparisons	Contrasts
Both *X* and *Y*	Although *X*, *Y*
Just as *X*, *Y*	Even though *X*, *Y*
And	But
Also	Yet
Compares with	Contrasts with
Similarly	Conversely
	On the one hand . . . on the other hand
	Whereas
	While
	However

---

your approach, choose from these three methods for developing your essay: zig-zag, block, or combination. If you choose the *zig-zag method*, you consider a point of comparison or contrast on one line under a column of your chart and compare or contrast it to a point on the same line under other columns. You then zig-zag back and forth, point by point.

John considered both the similarities and differences between the barn owl and the great horned owl and ordered the similarities and differences according to what he thought were the most important points for supporting his thesis. This is what John wrote:

Thesis

> The barn owl is far superior to the great horned owl for rodent control in the Northwest United States.

Zig-zag between barn owl and great horned owl

> Whereas the barn owl eats mostly small rodents, the great horned owl eats any prey including other birds and cats. While the barn owl eats mostly in open fields, the great horned tends to eat in the woods. The barn owl may eat during the day; however, the great horned owl is more strictly a night predator.

Notice the words John uses to help him include both points of comparison and contrast in his sentences: *whereas, while,* and *however.*

In the *block method* you discuss all the points about one subject before turning to discuss the other subject. The block version of John's essay reads like this:

Thesis   ⎡   The barn owl is far superior to the great horned owl for
                           ⎣ rodent control in the Northwest United States.

Block on barn owl   ⎡   The barn owl has a voracious appetite for small animals.
                             It inhabits mostly open grasslands where it will eat one and
                             a half times its own weight in mice and rats in an evening.
                             The barn owl is often found near human populations, so it
                             could control prey numbers at the source of most rodent
                             problems: in the farm or farm storage areas. That is probably
                             why it is called the barn owl. Its eating habits are not limited
                           ⎣ to the evening. It can hunt also during the day.

Block on horned owl   ⎡   Although the great horned owl is an excellent predator,
                             eating large numbers of problem rodents, it is far too aggres-
                             sive a bird to introduce into an area near human populations.
                             If the great horned owl is finished reducing rodents, it might
                           ⎣ attack barnyard birds, and worse even, family pets.

In the zig-zag method, it is easier to make sure that all points of comparison or contrast are made. In the block method, you are freer to discuss each subject in more depth. Be careful to cover all relevant points of comparison or contrast by reviewing your blocks point by point. You will probably want to discuss the points in your blocks in the same order so that your reader can easily find the corresponding point of comparison or contrast in the other blocks. In a longer essay, you could use the *combination method*, zig-zagging at one point in the essay and using the block method when you want to discuss a point about one subject in more depth.

Writing essays that compare and/or contrast, you will discover and create more connections. Jot these onto your chart and incorporate them into your essay. As you reread your drafts and consult with others, count sentences or draw blocks to discern the relative amount of space you devote to each of your subjects. Strive for balance and equal time. In this process, you might discover that you favor one subject or point over another. You might need to collect more information and ideas. You may also find, as you write, that your original purpose and method change. Your subjects may be far more similar or different than you had at first believed. This is one of the main benefits of comparing and/or contrasting: it leads to new discoveries.

*E*xplorations _____

1. *Solo and Together.*

   a. For twenty-four hours, carry a small notebook in which you record comparisons and contrasts that you read or hear. Popular songs

> ### *How to Write a Comparison or Contrast*
>
> 1. ***Choose*** your subjects.
> 2. ***Chart*** similarities and differences.
> 3. ***Choose*** whether you want to focus on comparison or contrast or both.
> 4. ***Write a thesis statement.*** Present your purpose and method for the paper.
> 5. ***Organize*** your paper using either the block or zig-zag method. Either start with an outline or revise a draft using an outline you develop in process.
> 6. ***Develop*** your paper by illustrating your points of comparison or contrast with examples and sense appeal.
> 7. ***Balance*** how much you say about each subject. Draw blocks to represent the relative amounts of space you devote to each.

and advertisements are easy sources. Consider, as well, textbooks for your courses (including *The Flexible Writer*). Noticing comparisons and contrasts that are made in your fields of study will help you to learn more fully. As you record these comparisons and contrasts, note also:

- Who said or wrote the comparison or contrast

- What the situation was

- What the purpose of the comparison or contrast was

- What, if any, the response or result was

   b.   Choose ten comparisons and contrasts. Using the standards above, discuss whether these comparisons and contrasts are clichéd or "good." In your discussions, consider your notes on the situations in which these comparisons and contrasts were made.

2.   *Together.* When comparing and contrasting, be sure to work with groups in the same category. So, for example, you might compare apples with pears, but not apples with riding a bicycle, because apples and pears are both fruits, whereas apples are fruits and riding a bicycle is an activity. This Exploration offers you practice in keeping things in the same category.

   a.   Decide what category each of the following groups may represent. Then add to them, making sure that the subjects are appropriate for the categories as you discerned them.

Group A	Group B	Group C
Running	Alcatraz	Lincoln
Bending	Athens	Washington
Throwing	Arcadia	Jefferson
_____	_____	_____
_____	_____	_____
_____	_____	_____
_____	_____	_____
_____	_____	_____

Group D	Group E	Group F
Tone	Hare	Decide
Note	Rat	Affirm
Pitch	Shrew	Ask
_____	_____	_____
_____	_____	_____
_____	_____	_____
_____	_____	_____
_____	_____	_____

3. *Together and Solo.*

   a. For each of the following topics, create three categories. For example, you could say there are three kinds of restaurants: take-out, fast food, and sit-down.

Dates	Students
Doctors	Teachers
Movies	Athletes
Diets	Excuses
Ways of taking an exam	Ways of sleeping

    b. Choose one of the topics for which you created categories in 3a. Create a chart with three columns and brainstorm corresponding points of comparison and contrast. Decide whether you want to compare similarities, contrast differences, or both. Using the block, zig-zag, or combination method, write and organize an essay on your topic. Be sure to illustrate your points with specific examples and sense appeal.

    c. Read and discuss what you wrote, noticing the methods writers used. Suggest and make revisions for clarity and balance.

4. *Together.*

    a. In small groups, or as a class, choose one of the following topics. Generate two columns of at least ten corresponding points of comparison and/or contrast:

        Falling in love and getting the flu

        Treatment of the aged and treatment of the homeless

        Language used about women and language used about animals and children

        Life at age fourteen and life at age eighteen

    b. In small groups, write an essay of comparison or contrast using the chart you generated together. Formulate a thesis statement. Decide whether to use the zig-zag, block, or combination method.

5.   **a.** *Together.* Referring to textbooks, collect assignments that call for comparison and/or contrast. Help each other design the necessary charts for preparing to write about a choice of these assignments.

    b. *Solo.* Formulate a thesis statement in response to a selected assignment. Draft an essay of comparison and/or contrast using the zig-zag, block, or combination method.

    c. *Together.* Read your essays to each other and make suggestions for revisions.

Special Structures Across the Curriculum

Each academic discipline has special formats for how to write reports, essays, proposals, memos, and other types of writing. For example, in laboratory science courses you will often be asked to write reports using the following format:

1. Summary of the experiment
2. Materials used
3. Methods of collecting and observing

4. Results
5. Discussion of further applications

However, if you were interpreting a piece of literature in a basic course, you would:

1. Name the work and its author
2. State your thesis
3. Analyze the work using direct quotes
4. Write a summary

Before beginning a writing assignment in any course, be sure to ask your instructor for guidelines on how you should structure your writing within that particular academic discipline.

STUDENTS WRITING TO LEARN

Discuss one or more of the following essays using the Reflections questions and suggestions.

*R*eflections

1. For what course was the essay probably written?

2. What was the main purpose for writing the essay?

3. What thesis statement or theory is the essay trying to support or question? Underline it.

4. What evidence and examples are used?

5. Is the evidence relevant, necessary, and sufficient to support the thesis statement or theory?

6. How does the writer organize the essay? Is the organization effective?

7. What questions or suggestions for revision would you offer the writer?

Lack of Self-Awareness

Christine Vidal

In Albert Camus's *The Stranger* and Chinua Achebe's *No Longer at Ease*, the main characters are both men who did not know their inner "selves" and as a result others took advantage of them. Since "knowledge is power" (according to Sir Francis Bacon) their lack of power is an important factor in both works.

In *The Stranger*, Meursault has the backbone of a jellyfish. He has no opinion, and he does whatever is asked of him. He also lacks emotion. So, when Raymond asks him to write a letter to an ex-lover, he does so without question. Meursault is the perfect pawn, and Raymond uses this fact to his advantage. Meursault's inability to make his own decisions causes his imprisonment and finally his execution.

Likewise, in *No Longer at Ease*, Obi, too, is confused about what he wants. At first, Obi is righteous and refuses to take a bribe that is offered to him. As time passes, as the bills pile up, Obi gives in. He no longer acknowledges his righteous self. He becomes the pawn to society's evils.

Therefore, in Camus's *The Stranger* and Achebe's *No Longer at Ease*, the main characters, Meursault and Obi, fall victim to the evils of society.

This is because they do not know themselves, and so they are punished. They are guilty of ignorance.

I Love I Love Lucy

Jane Riscinti

The communicative ability of Lucille Ball's character Lucy Ricardo on the popular 1950s sitcom *I Love Lucy* is outstanding. She knows how to express her ideas in words, gestures, and facial expressions as well as employing strong manipulative behavior when she wants something. When she wants to communicate a point, it does not matter to her how crazy or overemphasized her actions may be for Lucy is comfortable with herself as a person and is not afraid to try new things.

Lucy is clever, humorous, manipulative, and a schemer. She presents these traits in her dealings with her husband, Ricky Ricardo, and her close friends, Fred and Ethel Mertz. She also thinks of herself as a rich entertainer's wife and tries to present this concept to high-society acquaintances. Lucy also tries to act sophisticated because she cares what people think of her and how she dresses.

One of Lucy's favorite lines is "Ricky, I can explain." Usually when Lucy employs this strategy she is trying to get Ricky to listen to the reasons why something happened the way it did before he has a chance to lose his temper by hollering at her in Spanish.

When Lucy is lying to her husband by shading the truth a little, she pauses after each sentence and does not look her husband in the eye, as if she was trying to believe it herself. Her eyes blink rapidly, and she tries to make them wider, to appear innocent. Lucy's voice has a lot of vocal variety, and she is not afraid to shift the volume of her voice from a high pitch to a low tone in a split second to convey her ideas.

Lucy's general body tone is of one who is not in control. When she is trying to look confident in what she is saying but is nervous, she betrays herself by speaking quickly, wringing her hands, and moving her eyes from side to side as if she was looking for a way to escape.

Lucy has good facial expressions. You can tell by looking at her face when she is about to cry. Her face gets all scrunched up; she closes her eyes and opens her mouth and bawls when she can't get her way. When Lucy is proud, her eyes get a faraway look in them, and she straightens her posture.

I Love Lucy is a classic example of comedy at its best. Lucille Ball's use of language and physical props created a style that is imitated by many but accomplished by none. With the passing of Lucille Ball, we have lost someone who was able to make us laugh and understand human nature at the same time.

Electronic or Pipe Organ

Frank Dos Santos

There are different types of organs: pipe and electronic. The electronic organ is much cheaper than the pipe organ. The old churches of Europe had and still have beautiful pipe organs. The modern church in America is turning to the electronic organ, because it is much cheaper to maintain and repair.

A religious service that has a pipe organ is much more beautiful than one with an electronic organ. First of all, the pipe organ is more elaborate than the electronic. It has a beautiful wood finishing and is decorated with pipes. The sound is much more real than the electronic one because it is produced from a pipe and not a speaker. Wind is blown from blower to blower into a leather housing where it is stored and pressurized until it is called for. The organist presses down on a key and the pipe that it corresponds to will speak. The sound of the organ changes by putting down different sounds called stops; putting them down changes the volume of the organ also.

The electronic organ is totally different: it doesn't have a blower or pipes. Instead it has a computer that reproduces the sound. Some electronic organs come very close to reproducing the sound of a pipe organ. This holds true for the Allen Organ. This electronic organ uses a sampler. That is, it records the sound of a pipe organ electronically, and reproduces the sound whenever the key is pressed down. Although the sound comes close to the pipes, it still isn't the same. But the churches of America, because of a lack of money, are dealing more and more with the electronic than the pipe organ.

The Development of the Rocket

Edem Ikurekong

The history of the rocket has been traced to the Chinese as far back as three thousand years ago. Even though it was discovered three thousand years ago, it wasn't put to use until nearly a thousand years later. The early rocket was very crude in design and construction. It was known at that time as *xio pon*, which means "traveler." Since then the rocket has undergone a series of changes and modifications. The result is that we can boast of it as the sole agent for delivering satellites and other space cargo.

At one time the rocket was used in sending messages such as war declarations and to communicate with remote regions difficult to reach by ordinary means of transportation. One of those areas included Sholla and Belolla in the Chinese enclaves. The latter is now known as Taiwan. Later rockets were made to travel across Arabia to North American territories for trade purposes but were still in their crude stage. Early rockets had a rectangular shape, which greatly hindered their efficiency since scientists of that time knew little or nothing about aerodynamics and their importance.

Rockets changed drastically both in performance and shape after an Egyptian scientist conducted an impromptu experiment. Mohammed Ibn Tatar, who was 6 foot 7 inches tall and who was described in an Egyptian chronicle as a serious thinker, is not a household name in the scientific world and particularly aviation industries. Omitting his name is the same as drinking coffee without sugar. Mohammed, a mathematician and physicist in Alexandria, was repairing his father's house when he realized that using polymer plastic would be the best bet since it is unaffected by atmospheric chemicals and other environmental hazards. He, therefore, cut a piece of polymer plastic 8' × 11". Holding it in his mouth, he climbed the ladder to the roof. Getting to the top, he dropped the piece from his mouth. Mohammed had no choice but to watch it drop. He also had no choice other than to go down for it. This time he thought it would be better to roll the piece into a cylindrical shape. Mohammed decided not to handle it in his mouth so he placed it under his arm. Due to perspiration, when he took it to the top, the piece became slippery and dropped again. Here Mohammed watched it drop and compared the time difference. The second drop seemed to get to the ground in less time than the first. He then tried a deliberate experiment to find out what was happening.

Mohammed discovered that the wider surface of the first piece of plastic and the four corners increased pressure on the upper surface as well as on the lower surface of the piece. As a result, there was no free and even distribution of air pressure at the vertex, hence the first piece couldn't pierce through the air layers with ease. On the rolled drop, Mohammed noticed that the cylindrical body allowed no pressure to build up at any point on the surface; there was also no vertex, hence there was even and easy penetration through the air layers. He wrote books on the issue which were well received. This is why modern aircrafts, rockets, and even space vehicles assume cylindrical shapes externally. The new shape increases fuel efficiency by 80% and speed by 75%.

The Chinese developed what is known today as a stabilizer, which makes a rocket stable in flight. Its initial design was a long, seven-foot stick. In 1845, a British aerospace scientist, Michael Stanton, invented and designed triangular wings which are used today by all in every aerospace industry as stabilizers in rockets, airplanes, and spacecrafts.

Ellen Goodman's "Checks on Parental Power"

Eleticia Colon

"Checks on Parental Power" is an essay written by Ellen Goodman. It talks about stories of parents who decide to send their children to mental institutions. In the essay, Goodman attacks the position taken by the Supreme Court and argues the point of view of the children being placed in mental institutions. There are many ways that parents could try to understand their children. The parents should be there when their children really need them and not send them away. This is why I agree with Goodman's point that placing children in mental institutions, without recognizing their right to be heard, is wrong.

When I read this essay, it shocked me knowing that the Supreme Court agreed with parents who placed their children in mental hospitals and denied the children their right to a hearing before institutionalization. In the beginning of the essay, Goodman wrote three stories which gave me an idea of what the rest of the essay was going to be about. In a part of the essay, Goodman stated that the right of the parents to make decisions about bringing up their children is in conflict with the rights of children to their freedom. Children should not be placed in a mental institution because they have terrible behavior. Children should be treated as adults: a simple hearing before incarceration was recommended in the essay. This made me think a lot about the issue. The word *incarceration* attracted my attention so that I even looked it up in the dictionary. I agree with the part that children must be treated as adults would be when placed in a mental hospital. Adults have rights—why can't children have rights too?

Ellen Goodman asked whether it's more important to protect a child's freedom or to protect a parent's right to dispose of the child's fate. There was also a part of the essay that really helped me to understand some things. It was when she compared signing a child into a mental hospital with signing the child into a general hospital to have tonsils taken out. Taking out a child's tonsils only lasts a couple of hours, and it's not harmful. Placing a child in a mental hospital is forever.

I conclude that Ellen Goodman made her point so clearly that she even persuaded me to agree with her opinion against parental power. The essay was well written; she supported her statements. I also like the way she used words such as *devastating, infringement,* and *promiscuous.* They were exciting and new words for me.

Chapter Review

Solo or *Together* respond to the following:

1. If you were an instructor of writing, what five points from this chapter would *you* stress in teaching student writers? Why?

2. Which strategies offered in this chapter were either new to you or made clearer?

3. Which strategies do you need to further develop? How do you plan to incorporate them into your writing process?

Chapter 14

Writing for Power

This chapter offers opportunities to

—Explore **the dynamics of power**

—Analyze **the power of language**

—Distinguish appeals to **emotion, status,** and **reason**

—Develop strategies for **writing for power**

—Identify and revise **faulty reasoning**

> The pen is mightier than the sword.
> —*Edward Bulwer-Lytton, Novelist*

The Power of Language

Every day you are confronted with billboards, television and radio commercials, newspaper and magazine advertisements, junk mail, packaging, fast talking, arguments, and other kinds of pressure by people trying to convince you to buy, act, think, do, and be what they want you to buy, act, think, do, and be. The first sentence of this paragraph, itself, is a kind of pressure: Agree with me; here are all these many examples that you can't ignore. The difference between a billboard and this book is that here you have more of a choice about whether you will agree. This book offers you reasons to do and believe what it suggests. A billboard does not offer you reasons, because advertising is meant to limit, not to expand, your range of choices.

Power can be defined as the ability to choose what you want to do, and to be what you want to be. When what you want is compatible with what others want, there is no need to struggle for power. However, if there is a conflict, if there are limited resources (time, space, people, things, or energy), if there is confusion, fear, anger, or any other form of resistance, power has to be taken, relinquished, or negotiated.

Language is the most valuable tool we have for managing power. "Talk it out," "you have my word for it," "as good as her word"—these, and other expressions, remind us of the power of words without which we could be reduced to physical conflict. In fact, that's what happens between nations when diplomatic talks fail.

This chapter offers you opportunities to develop your awareness of how to use language to protect and assert your own power. You will be offered strategies and opportunities to persuade, to negotiate, to assert, to argue,* to propose—in short, to write for power.

The following Explorations will help you identify issues or problems on which you want to write for power. The rest of the chapter will guide you through different phases of the writing process as you develop one or more essays on the issues or problems that you identify here.

Explorations

1. **a.** *Together.* List and then discuss experiences you have had in which someone convinced you to do something or act in a certain way you didn't want to—drinking alcohol at a party, talking with someone you would rather avoid, accepting a job, putting out a cigarette, or buying an object or service. Use these questions to stimulate your discussion:

     *   Who was the person who convinced you?
     *   What attracted you to or repelled you from doing or acting as the person wanted?
     *   How did you comply?
     *   How did the person convince you to do or act as you did?

---

*In this chapter, different forms of the word *argument* are used to refer to reasoning aimed at proving the truth or falsehood of claims. These arguments are not necessarily fueled by disagreement, though they might be. Unless otherwise indicated, these words are not used to refer to angry interchanges.

- What kinds of nonverbal pressure did the person use?
- How did the person use language?
- Looking back, how do you feel about what happened?
- Do you wish you had responded differently? If so, how?
- What, if anything, could you do now to reverse the results of that experience?

b. *Solo.* Freewrite on one incident you identified in 1a. How does writing about the situation affect you now?

c. *Solo.* Freewrite on a current situation in which someone is trying to convince you to do something or act in a way you don't want to. How does writing about this situation affect you?

2. **a.** *Together.* Name and discuss experiences in which you tried to convince someone else to do, think, feel, or act in a certain way, such as lend you a car or money, have a date with you, hire you for a job, or take sides with you against someone else. Use these questions to stimulate your discussion:

- What was the situation?
- Were you successful? If so, how did you accomplish it?
- What strategies and pressures, verbal and nonverbal, did you use?
- If you were not successful, why do you think you failed? How do you wish you had approached the situation?
- Successful or not, what have you learned from the experience?
- Have your interactions changed since then? If so, how? If not, why not?

b. *Solo.* Freewrite on an incident you identified in 2a. How does writing about this incident affect you?

3. *Together and Solo.*

a. Bring current newspapers and magazines to class. Using them for ideas, create a list of issues and problems in which power is being asserted, taken, surrendered, or negotiated. Include local issues such as homeless people sleeping in the corner park, national issues such as the Equal Rights Amendment, and global political issues such as free immigration. Add to this list as you work through this chapter. Avoid broad, often-discussed issues such as abortion, drugs, capital punishment, or mercy killing unless (1) one of these issues specifically affects you or someone close to you, or (2) you have a fresh approach to it.

b. List issues and problems of power that arise for you or others at home (such as quiet hours), at school (such as grades), at work (such as fair salaries), and elsewhere.

c. Choose an issue that is important to you, and think of people— such as particular relatives, friends, and people in the news—with whom you would like to discuss the issue. Consider who would be the most appropriate person for you to approach.

d. Write a letter to someone about an issue identified in 3a, b, or c. Try to convince this person of your point of view on the issue.

e. Write a dialogue between two parts of yourself or between yourself and someone else concerning a specific issue. What do you learn?

Appealing to Your Audience

In his *Rhetoric,* the ancient Greek philosopher Aristotle identified three kinds of appeals:

- Appeals to *emotion* (fear, anger, greed, sexuality)
- Appeals to *status* (character, expertise, believability)
- Appeals to *reason* (logic, evidence, proof)

Appeals to *emotion* focus on the emotional reactions of the *audience.* Appeals to *status* focus on the believability of the *writer.* Appeals to *reason* focus on the *words and statements* the writer uses. Appeals to emotion respond to the first four levels of need that psychologist Abraham Maslow identified: survival, security, power, and love. (See page 383 for further discussion of Maslow's theory.) Appeals to status respond to needs for security, power, and self-esteem. Appeals to reason respond to the highest-level needs: love, communication, self-esteem, and self-fulfillment.

Knowing Your Audience

Ask yourself the following questions whenever you are writing for power:

- Whom do I want to reach?
- What does my audience know?
- What does my audience need?
- What is important to my audience?
- What is my audience's point of view?
- What language will trigger a response?

Appeals to Emotion

When a commercial shows you a crumpled and shattered car and red ambulance lights flashing in the background, you are supposed to feel so much fear, anger, and helplessness that you won't drink and drive. When two healthy-looking people are pictured smoking cigarettes together and broadly smiling, you are meant to associate cigarettes with happiness, health, and social success. These advertisements appeal to your emotions.

In writing, the television commercial against drunk driving or the billboard favoring smoking would be translated into vivid descriptions using strong language to appeal to your emotions. In an advertisement against drunk driving, you would expect expressions such as *kills, destroys,* and *every 15 seconds someone is involved in an accident with a drunk driver.* In an advertisement for cigarettes, you would expect expressions such as *Alive with pleasure; You've come a long way, Baby;* and *I'd walk a mile* (which is meant to remind some people of a line in a romantic song that is followed by the line "for one of your smiles").

When emotional appeals take advantage of people's fears, misrepresent the truth, or try to manipulate people into doing what they would otherwise not choose, they are irresponsible. But if the commercial against drunk driving could effectively save lives, and if an appeal to the emotions of authorities could result in better care for the needy or the oppressed, an appeal to emotions may be legitimate.

Appeals to Status

If Arnold Schwarzenegger tells you to drink Lookgood, you are meant to believe that, since he is so well-built and since he tells you to drink Lookgood, he must drink it too. Advertisers want you to believe that Lookgood is what makes Schwarzenegger strong and that if you drink Lookgood

---

Appeals to Emotion

In deciding whether to use an emotional appeal, ask yourself the following questions:

- What is important to my audience?
- What emotional appeal would be appropriate and responsible?
- What are some strong words that I can use to appeal to emotions?
- Could I use stronger words or examples to appeal to my audience's emotions?

you will be like Arnold Schwarzenegger, too. Similarly, you are more likely to believe Sharon Berman, *M.D.*, on issues of nutrition than Sharon Berman, *M.A.*, because an M.D. is supposed to be better educated on issues of health. (Of course, a person with an M.A. degree may know more about the issue than a person with an M.D. But you would discern this by examining the evidence a person offers for claims, not the status of the person.) Other, more subtle ways to appeal to the status of a person include tactics that are used to convince you to do something because *everybody else does it* or because something's been done in a certain way for a long time.

In writing, appeals to status include expressions that indicate that the person who is writing or the persons being cited are believable. The Lookgood commercial would include terms such as *protein-rich, 30% more energy, vitality,* and *results in ten days.* A report on nutrition would include not only the same terms as the Lookgood commercial but also technical terms that indicate Dr. Berman's familiarity with medical science. Some of these terms and expressions could be *amino acids, enzyme activity, double-blind study,* and *standard deviation.*

Appeals to status that take advantage of people's respect and admiration for the powerful and successful, that try to manipulate and use people to act in ways that they wouldn't otherwise choose, are irresponsible. But you are wise to consider the advice of Sharon Berman, M.D., on nutrition because what she says is likely to be backed up by a knowledge of medicine. And if you can successfully find a believable authority to quote in an argument, then you are wise to do so. When you are writing or speaking, your audience will be considering whether you are believable. Showing

Appeals to Status

In deciding whether to use an appeal to status, ask yourself the following questions:

- Who does my audience know?
- Who would my audience believe?
- How can I convince my readers that I know the best and most relevant information on this subject?
- Can I use stronger sources to support my arguments?
- Which words will show that I know what I am writing about?
- Could I use stronger or more technical language to gain the confidence of my readers?

that you know how to draw on the expertise of others increases your status in the minds of your readers.

Appeals to Reason

When you make an emotional appeal, you are trying to manipulate your readers to believe or to do something because it would *feel* right to them. When you make an appeal to status, you are trying to pressure your readers to believe or to do something because you or *someone else believes or does it.* When you appeal to reason, you are asking your readers to believe or to do something as a result of the *evidence and arguments* you offer. Because an appeal to reason allows your readers more freedom to make up their own minds, it is the most powerful appeal. If your readers adopt your point of view, they will do so because they freely choose to.

The writing process is ideally suited for reasoning. Focusing enables you to clarify your claims and evidence. Collecting enables you to find support for your claims. Organizing enables you to develop connections both within your sentences and between them. Consulting enables you to develop your purpose and sense of audience. Revising gives you opportunities to deepen your understanding and your ability to communicate.

Appeals to reason include statements reporting personal observations or experiences, relevant examples, comparisons, contrasts, scientific reports, statistics, and other forms of evidence. In addition, appeals to reason are organized in a logical order to show how the evidence and examples prove claims.

For example, a tree surgeon may claim that the best way to manage

---

Appeals to Reason

In deciding whether to use an appeal to reason, ask yourself the following questions:

- What does my audience know?
- What would my audience believe?
- What examples or evidence can I use to support my position?
- Which reasons are most relevant?
- What reasons contradict my position? How can I respond to them?
- How can I best organize my reasons?
- What expressions can I use to show the relationships between my claims and my evidence and examples?

Forms of Reasoning

Reasoning often takes the following forms in which *X* and *Y* can be replaced by statements:

If *X*, then *Y*.	Whenever *X*, then *Y*.
X only if *Y*.	If *Y*, then necessarily *X*.
X causes *Y*.	Because *X*, therefore *Y*.
Since *X*, *Y*.	*Y* is the result of *X*.

contagious Dutch elm disease is to remove a tree at the first sign of infection. Suppose you have two beautiful elms in front of your house and one of them is showing signs of the disease. In order to convince you, the tree surgeon could appeal to reason by telling you about incidents in which alternative treatments were tested and failed. In addition, the tree surgeon could explain how the disease is spread and show you how your uninfected tree may be in danger.

Suppose you wanted to start a new child care program that employs the elderly in your community. You could appeal to the pity or guilt of the local authorities. You could have a celebrity adopt the cause and speak for you. Or, you could provide the authorities with arguments, reports, and statistics to show that communities with such programs have significantly reduced child care and nursing home costs.

Appeals to reason are often expressed in forms that link causes with effects, problems with solutions, evidence with conclusions, and prior events with results.

Here are two examples of appeals to reason using two of the options listed in the sidebar on Forms of Reasoning:

> Since the carburetor was clogged, the engine could not turn over.
>
> If the government doesn't cut back on spending, then we are sure to suffer from inflation.

Presented with statements such as these, readers are in a position to consider the reason offered (*X*) and decide whether it is adequate to support the claim (*Y*).

Combinations of Appeals

The most powerful writing integrates appeals to emotion, status, and reason in a balanced way, and the same statement can be an appeal to all three. Read and reflect on Ellen Goodman's article "Checks on Parental Power."[26] Focus on the combination of appeals she uses to make her points. Use the questions and suggestions that follow to guide you.

Checks on Parental Power

Ellen Goodman

First, consider the stories.

Appeal to emotion

An eleven-year-old retarded boy was brought to a mental hospital with a teddy bear under his arm. His parents were, they said, going on a two-week vacation. They never came back.

A twelve-year-old "tomboy" and truant was committed to a mental hospital by her mother after school authorities threatened the woman with prosecution.

Appeal to emotion

A seven-year-old boy's mother died one year, and he was committed the next year by his father—two days before the man's remarriage. The diagnosis: a reaction of childhood.

Consider, too, the story of one child committed because he had "school phobia," another because she was "promiscuous," a third and fourth because they were "difficult" or even "incorrigible."

Questioning status

Then, when you've heard the stories, listen to Justice Warren Burger insist that the "natural bonds of affection lead parents to act in the best interests of their children."

Last Wednesday the Supreme Court assured all parents—the confused and the pathologically indifferent as well as the caring and concerned—an equal right to put their kids in mental hospitals. Last Wednesday they denied all children—the odd and the unwanted as well as the ill—an equal right to a hearing before being institutionalized.

Questioning status

And they did it on a wish and a myth: that parents—and those bureaucratic "parents," state agencies—know best. It took seven years and four separate Supreme Court hearings to achieve this disappointing decision.

Appeal to status

Lawyers from Pennsylvania and Georgia, and children's advocates, argued that minors deserve the same treatment adults have: a simple hearing before incarceration. They argued that children facing a mental institution deserved the same treatment as children facing a penal institution: a hearing.

But the Justices, especially Burger and Potter Stewart, were convinced that these children didn't need any advocate other than their parents, or any check on parental power other than the institution's own medical team. In roughly thirty-eight states, they left the fate of children up to parents and hospitals.

"That some parents may at times be acting against the interest of their child creates a basis for caution, but is hardly a reason to discard wholesale those pages of human experience that teach that parents generally do act in the child's best interest," wrote Burger.

The conflict was between the right of the parent to make decisions about bringing up their children, and the rights of children to their liberty, and to due process. Burger and Stewart, both ardent advocates of extreme parental supremacy, interpreted the constitution to read, Families First.

Appeal to reason

I agree that most parents do want to act in the "child's best interest." But the law is not necessary to protect children from wise and sensitive parents. Nor is it made to "interfere" with families functioning smoothly on their own.

Appeal to status

As David Ferleger, the Pennsylvania lawyer who argued this case, put it: "We all want to protect the integrity of a family where it exists. But when the family wants to incarcerate a member, it has already created a break. There is no longer a united family to protect."

Appeal to reason

At that point, the question is whether it's more important to protect a possible, and devastating, infringement of the child's liberty, or to protect the right of a parent or state guardian to dispose of that child's fate.

Appeal to reason

A family in stress may not have the information and emotional stability to make a good judgment. A state agency may not care. Nor can we trust the hospital for an impartial judgment. If surgeons have a bias toward surgery, institutional psychiatrists often have a bias toward institutional psychiatry. Psychiatry is hardly an infallible science, as Burger knows, and there are many children in hospitals now who are simply not mentally ill.

Appeal to reason

The justices compared signing a child into a mental hospital with signing him into a general hospital to have his tonsils out. But a tonsillectomy takes hours, not years. And it does less harm.

Appeal to emotion

Parents obviously have and must have a wide range of decisions over their children's lives. But they don't have absolute power and never have. They cannot refuse immunization for their kids or keep them uneducated. They cannot (at least yet) forcibly sterilize them, order them to become a transplant donor, commit incest or abuse them.

Appeal to reason

Nor should they have the right, without another impartial source, to deprive children of something equally as fundamental as their liberty, by putting them away in an institution. In this case (which bodes badly for other children's rights cases coming before the court), the majority of the justices have sided with a parental power that is virtually unchecked.

Appeal to emotion

Chalk one up for the folks who dropped off the boy with the teddy bear.

---

*R*eflections

1. Which parts of Goodman's article do you find most effective? Why?

2. What basic human needs are at issue in this article?

3. Who is Goodman's anticipated audience? Describe the typical person you believe Goodman is trying to reach—age, gender, education, class, parental status, and so on.

4. Do you agree with the way the marginal notes identify the different appeals? If so, say why a given portion is making the indicated appeal. If you disagree, name the appeal you believe Goodman is making.

5. Identify appeals made in unlabeled portions of the article.

6. Which appeals work most effectively for you? Why?

7. What purposes does Goodman have for the article? Are they mainly to connect with, separate from, or negotiate with her audience? What is she hoping to accomplish?

8. What are the different points of view being taken and considered in Goodman's article? What is the common ground between them?

9. Do you believe the article will fulfill the purposes you identified for it? If so, why? If not, why not?

10. Write a letter to Ellen Goodman, focusing on how she presents her case. State whether you agree or disagree with her and why. Illustrate your letter with your own examples.

*E*xplorations

1. *Together and Solo.* Read the following examples. Mark appeals to emotion *E*, appeals to status *S*, and appeals to reason *R*. Discuss the examples, using these questions as guides:

   - Does it make an appeal? If so, go on to the following questions.

   - Which words and expressions make a strong appeal?

   - What kinds of appeals do these words and expressions make?

   - Which need or needs are being addressed?

   - Which kind of appeal is predominant?

   a. "Thanks, New Hampshire Institute of Photography. Since enrolling, I've opened my own studio and already grossed over $7000. I love it!" (A version of this was written in a magazine next to a photograph of a young woman holding a long telephoto lens.)

   b. "If you don't teach your children the facts of life, one day, AIDS may be a fact of life for you." (This statement was written especially for this Exploration.)

   c. "Stefan Edberg and third-seeded Ivan Lendl advanced to the third round of the Australian Open." (This statement was made on the sports page of a newspaper.)

   d. "In a study recognized by the American Medical Association, researchers found that a program of exercise, diet, and relaxation significantly lowered the cholesterol levels of heart patients. If you want to avoid heart attack, stroke, and other life-threatening consequences of a high-fat diet, start today to readjust your life-style." (This appeared in a community newsletter.)

   e. "The only way to end all wars is to strike hard and fast at all would-be Hitlers now!" (This statement was made by a citizen making an editorial statement on a news show.)

2. *Solo and Together.* Using newspapers and magazines, identify three examples each of appeals to emotion, status, and reason. (You may

find that most of the material combines appeals.) Then apply the directions in Exploration 1 to one of these examples.

3. *Together and Solo.* Revise examples collected in Exploration 2 so that they appeal to reason.

4. *Together and Solo.*

   a. List television programs and movies that focus on court trials. Choose one episode, movie, or trial. Take notes in which you record the different kinds of appeals that attorneys and witnesses are using to support their positions. To help you in your note taking, use a different sheet of paper for each position. Mark appeals to emotion *E*, appeals to status *S*, and appeals to reason *R*. Of course, you may want to mark a given piece of evidence with more than one letter.

   b. Either in writing or in discussion, report what you observed and learned about the case and the appeals favored by the participants.

5. a. *Solo.* Choose a power issue you identified either in your own life or in the news. Decide whether you want to address an audience that agrees with you, disagrees with you, or is neutral on the issue. Ask yourself the following questions:

   • Which need or needs am I addressing?

   • How do I hope to affect my audience?

   • What purpose or purposes do I have in mind?

   • What changes in thinking, attitude, or action do I want to effect?

   • Which appeal or combination of appeals will most effectively create the changes I want to make with my particular audience?

   b. Freewrite a draft of a paper on your chosen issue, addressing the purpose and audience you have chosen.

   c. *Together.* Discuss your drafts with special attention to purpose, audience, points of view, and appeals.

Power and the Writing Process

The writing process is ideal for developing and asserting power. Clearly stating your purpose, understanding your audience, focusing your mind and energy, organizing your strategies, collecting your resources, consulting with others, and revising and refining your reasoning all empower you and strengthen your position.

Establishing Needs

Psychologist Abraham Maslow ranked human needs in the following order, starting with the most basic:[27]

- Survival
- Security
- Power
- Love
- Communication
- Self-esteem
- Self-fulfillment

The most basic needs for survival must be met first: these include the need for food, shelter, and clothing. Human beings also need the security that a social structure can provide. A social structure includes provisions not only for those who are strong, independent, and healthy but also for children, the elderly, the ill, and the poor.

Humans need a sense of power to be able to realize what they need. The drive for money and possessions, above and beyond basic necessities, reflects the need for power. The need for community and love is the next level of need. Animals also need survival, security, power, and social contact. But what makes humans unique is their ability to meet their needs through words, to create new ideas and systems, and to implement them. Human beings also have the unique ability to reflect on and value themselves and the world through language—to realize that people are both unique individuals and fundamentally like all other human beings. Whenever you write for power, reflect on the kinds of needs you are addressing and which ones are your priorities for a particular writing project.

Naming Your Purpose

Writing provides you with opportunities to do some, or all, of the following:

- Connect (flatter, yield, agree, accept)
- Separate (blame, insult, undermine, stalemate)
- Negotiate (propose, discuss, bargain, adjust)

If your purpose is to connect with and to be accepted by your audience, emphasize needs and purposes you have in common. This process is usually referred to as "establishing common ground." For example, if you were writing a letter of application for a job, you would decide which of your abilities corresponded to the job description. You would emphasize what you could bring to the job, because the job is the common ground between you and the employer.

If your purpose is to separate from your audience, you should project the consequences of how you try to separate. For example, if you wanted to resign from a job because of sexual harassment, you could write a scathing letter to your employer. This letter would serve the purpose of expressing your frustrations; however, the letter could also be used against you if you ever brought legal charges against your employer. You could write a letter in which you resign without explanation. This would serve your purpose and still provide you access to other employees and records should you want to press charges. But you would not be expressing your frustration. A third alternative would be to resign with a short statement citing sexual harrassment as your reason.

If your purpose is to negotiate with your audience, assess, as fully as you can, what you have in common, what conflicts of interest you may have, and how you can both benefit from the negotiations. In both connecting and negotiating, it is crucial to establish a common ground of human needs that all parties can understand. You establish common ground first by becoming aware of how different people can view the same events. Read Table 14.1, in which some typical parent/child interactions are recorded. Notice the internal messages behind the spoken words (written in parentheses). Notice the common ground of needs the parent and child share.

In each of the sets of positions in the table, the parent and the child are disagreeing over some kind of power. The parent wants to control the child's time, for example, whereas the child wants the freedom to decide about time. However, in many disagreements you can find some common ground of needs with which all parties can identify. Establishing common ground helps you avoid nonproductive disputes and power struggles. In the case of time, both parent and child could recognize the need for safety and self-esteem and negotiate a way to ensure a pleasant evening for all.

*E*xplorations _____

1. *Together.* Two people can volunteer to enact a dialogue between a parent and child, using one of the interactions from Table 14.1 as a starter. The rest of the class can serve as directors. Follow these two stages:

T A B L E   1 4 . 1   *Finding Common Ground*

Parent	Child
"It's correct for you to have an 11:00 curfew."	"You don't trust me."
(I'm really scared you're going to be hurt. I won't be free to relax if I have to worry about you.)	(I want to be free to decide when to come back. I won't be able to relax if I'm afraid of missing curfew.)

Common ground: Need for security and self-esteem.

"When I was your age I wasn't even thinking about a car."	"Everybody in my class has a car except me."
(I feel insecure about the budget.)	(I feel embarrassed to ask for rides.)

Common ground: Need for power.

"Get your feet off the coffee table."	"It's my house too."
(I need respect for my things.)	(I don't want to feel unwanted.)

Common ground: Need for security.

"We have always gone to the shore as a family."	"I want to be with people my own age. Your friends are boring."
(I feel you are growing away from us and don't want to see you go.)	(I feel stifled.)

Common ground: Need for communication.

"Sex is a beautiful thing, after your wedding day."	"But that's not what your generation did."
(I'm terrified of sexually transmitted diseases.)	(Why do we have all these terrible sexually transmitted diseases today?)

Common ground: Need for security and love.

First, allow the parent and child to maintain their own positions without considering the other person's point of view. The directors can interrupt when either parent or child starts to "give up" her or his position.

As a class, discuss what is wrong between the parent and child.

Second, the parent and child start as they did before, but this time they try to discover their needs and establish common ground. The directors can interrupt when either the parent or child starts to retreat to a one-sided point of view.

> ### *Naming Your Purpose*
>
> In formulating your purpose, ask yourself the following questions:
>
> - Why am I writing this?
> - Do I want to connect with, separate from, or negotiate with my audience?
> - What is the point of view of my audience?
> - What common ground do I share with my audience?
> - How much can I hope to accomplish with this audience?

As a class, compare this interaction with the first one. What do you learn? Can you apply any of the insights developed in this Exploration to your own life? If so, how? If not, why not?

2. **a.** *Solo.* Refer to the power issues you identified in doing the Explorations on pages 371–373. Choose an issue or think of others that are important to you.

　　b. *Together.* Do the following for each issue:

　　　　Establish at least two points of view.

　　　　Create a chart, similar to Table 14.1, in which you compare the different points of view. Write statements that people would make from those perspectives and the inner messages behind the statements.

　　c. *Solo.* Using your chart as a starter, write a dialogue between two people with differing points of view on your issue. Ideally, this dialogue should involve specific people.

　　d. *Solo.* Referring to basic needs—survival, security, power, love, communication, self-esteem, self-fulfillment—establish some common ground between the two points of view.

　　e. *Together.* Read these dialogues to each other and suggest ways to revise the dialogues so that the perspectives are clear and strong. *Notice opportunities for establishing common ground.* How did you benefit and what did you learn from writing the dialogues?

Focusing

There are many ways to focus yourself and your audience when you write for power:

- Quoting
- Illustrating
- Stating
- Questioning
- Using sense appeal

Which combination of strategies you use will depend on your style, purpose, and audience. However, when you write for power, it is essential that you state what you want to prove or accomplish, at least to yourself.

The process of stating your problem will help you to decide how much to try to accomplish. Suppose you felt, as student Helen Kwok did, that Chinese students at your college were isolated. You could state the problem in these ways:

- Students are segregated in this college.
- Chinese students don't feel comfortable at this college.
- Chinese students are not able to eat food in the college cafeteria that is in keeping with their traditional diets.

The first statement is much too general. It includes all the students in the college and all possible kinds of segregation. The word *segregation,* itself, is strong. In an appeal for some action, the word could incite unnecessarily strong emotions and perhaps confusion. The second statement is more specific because it focuses on Chinese students. It is easier to address the problems of one group of students at a time. However, *don't feel comfortable* can mean so many things that it is impossible to know how the Chinese students feel or what would make them more comfortable. The third statement is far more focused. It specifies Chinese students and points out one problem they have in one setting. It is easy to think of ways to provide cafeteria food that would bridge the gap between home and school. By focusing in this way, you can actually start to assume power over the situation.

When you are attempting to formulate a statement of your problem and your purpose, you may find that you have to experiment and rephrase until you find a focus. Before you can settle on a working focus, you may have to collect information and ideas. You may find yourself interviewing and consulting others.

To benefit the most from the writing process, proceed both as a planner (formulating statements to get you started) and as an explorer (discovering statements and ideas as you draft your letter or essay). In your final draft, you may place your focusing statements in a variety of positions (see the sidebar on page 190).

Explorations _____

1. *Together and Solo.* If you have not already done so, turn to pages 122–125 and read about the differences between strong and weak statements. Do one or more of the Explorations in that section.

2. *Together and Solo.* For each of the following sets of statements, decide which is most specific and which is most general:

    a. Pornography diminishes both men and women.

        Thomas Johnson should not have his contract renewed as gymnastics coach at Millstream College because he has accepted a contract to be a centerfold model in a pornographic magazine.

        The number of pornographic magazines published in the last ten years has increased 250 percent.

    b. The beef-growing industry is directly related to the destruction of the rain forest in South America.

        There is a delicate balance between the insects, plants, and animals in the rain forests.

        We are all responsible for the well-being of our planet.

Focusing for Power

To help you focus, ask yourself the following questions:

*   What exactly is the issue or problem?
*   How can I most directly present the issue or problem?
*   How much can I accomplish effectively with my current resources?
*   Is my statement of the problem clear?
*   Is my statement sufficiently strong for my purposes?
*   Is my statement fair and true?
*   Is all my supporting evidence relevant?

    c. People should be able to learn and write in the language in which they were raised.

    For a Mexican American, Spanish is the language of warmth and intimacy.

    In order for students to learn computer programming, there has to be a language that all international communities can share.

3. a. *Solo.* Return to the power issue you have chosen to address. Phrase a statement of the issue or problem in at least three different ways, ranging from the most general to the most specific.

   b. *Together.* Read your statements to each other. Choose the ones that are the most specific. Revise the statements so that they are as strong or as weak as you want them to be for your purpose and audience.

Collecting for Power

To formulate and develop your position on an issue or problem, you need to collect information and ideas. Otherwise, you may be repeating old prejudices and beliefs and not taking the opportunity to discover and invent better ideas. Collecting, like other phases of the writing process, will be determined by the particular purpose and audience for which you write. The better you focus, the easier it will be to find the kinds of evidence, examples, and appeals you need to support your position. The better you conduct your collecting activities, the more empowered and successful you will be to fulfill your purpose.

    Helen Kwok wrote a proposal on the problems Chinese students have with feeling isolated at her college.[28] She used a variety of collecting strategies. She *surveyed* the members of the Chinese Culture Club at her college, asking them about their concerns. After *listing* these concerns, she *focused* on the problems with the cafeteria. She then *observed* the kinds of foods that were served in the cafeteria and their methods of preparation. Since she is Chinese and eats a traditional diet, she was able to *recall her own experiences.* She *collected data* on the cost of a microwave oven and how it would be cost-effective to buy one for the Chinese Culture Club.

    As part of her collecting activities, Helen *anticipated objections and resistances* that her proposal might raise, including problems with maintenance and funding. This is a crucial strategy for anyone writing for power. As you present your case and your arguments, your readers—especially if they are predisposed against your position—will be thinking of objections

> ### Collecting for Power
>
> For help in collecting what you need, ask yourself the following questions:
>
> - What evidence or examples would best help me to make the kinds of appeals I want to make to my audience?
> - Who can I ask for information?
> - What method of collecting could I use?
> - What is the most efficient way to collect what I need?
> - What objections or resistances do I anticipate from my readers?
> - How can I directly address and defuse these objections and resistances?

to your points. If you show that you know these objections and can maintain your position nonetheless, your argument will be much more effective:

- You show yourself to be thoughtful and reasonable.
- You show that you can identify with those who disagree with you.
- You create an atmosphere of cooperation.
- You use others' disagreements to strengthen your case.
- You reduce the number of objections others can make.

Here are some transitional phrases you can use in anticipating objections:

"You might object that . . . ."

"Some people have argued that . . . ."

"I know what it means to have been on the other side of this issue."

When you present your counterargument, you can use expressions such as these:

but	nevertheless
even so	nonetheless
however	on the other hand

Explorations _____

1. *Together and Solo.* Consider the issues you are exploring in writing for power. Using the questions listed in the sidebar on Collecting for Power, decide what information you need to fulfill your purpose and

to make the kinds of appeals you want to make to your audience. Choose from the following list of collecting strategies:

Listing	Brainstorming
Clustering	Charting
Observing	Experimenting
Interviewing	Firsthand experiences
Dialoguing	Researching written materials

2. *Together and Solo.*

   a. In small groups or as class, present objections to the points that might be raised in response to the essays you are writing for power. Offer examples to disprove objections. Anticipate how others might resist. Do this to be helpful: it's better to test yourself with your working partners than to encounter resistance from a true adversary.

   b. Choose the most difficult objections to each paper. Brainstorm examples and ways in which these objections can be quieted or disproved.

   c. *Solo.* Revise your paper, directly addressing anticipated objections.

Organizing for Power

Organizing, like other phases of the writing process, will be determined by the particular purpose and audience for which you write. The better you organize, the easier it will be for your audience to absorb and respond as you want.

Structures. You can write for power using many different structures and forms. These include:

- Letters of application and complaint
- Letters to editors and companies
- Résumés
- Legal documents
- Proposals
- Term papers
- Business memos and reports
- Newspaper, magazine, and journal articles
- Book-length discussions
- Speeches

- Scripts
- Lectures
- Debates

How you organize what you write depends on what form best suits your purpose. You wouldn't write a job application as you would a television script (unless you were applying for a creative position at a television station).

Shapes.   There are two directions from which you can present your case when you are writing for power. You can state your position and purpose and then provide your examples and evidence. This is *deduction.* Or, you can shape your presentation by offering a series of examples and evidence and then conclude by summarizing them into a key statement of your position and purpose. This is *induction.* The sidebar on page 190 charts some options you have in using deductive and inductive reasoning.

In combining strategies, you can move back and forth from stating a position and supporting it with examples and evidence to offering examples and evidence and stating your position on them afterward.

Whether you use deduction or induction depends on the effect you want to make and your personal style. Experiment with both. You may find that in revising a paper you will want to switch completely from one strategy to another. In either case, focus on the lead and the ending. These are the strategic points where you either engage your readers or lose them. The more cleanly you organize what you write, the more confidence your audience will have in what you say. In short, the way you organize is an indirect appeal to status: "See how well I write—I must know what I'm talking about." Notice how Helen organized her proposal (see pages 393–394) to install a microwave oven in the office of the Chinese Culture Club.

Helen arranged her proposal using headings, underlining, and white space so that it looks official enough for her to be taken seriously by her audience. Helen begins her proposal by establishing common ground: She is a member of the Chinese Culture Club writing to its president, who is Chinese himself. Helen states her purpose and outlines the problems that led to her proposal. She continues by stating the advantages and practical considerations of her proposal. Notice how Helen considers the points of view of all the people concerned and anticipates any practical objections to her proposal. She ends her proposal clearly stating the support for her plan. The proposal finishes with a personal note that reestablishes common ground and invites negotiations.

```
     To : Mark Ho, President
   From : Helen Kwok, Treasurer
   Date : November 1, 1994
Subject : A proposal to install a microwave oven in the office of
          the Chinese Culture Club
```

The Purpose

Based on a food service survey conducted among our members, I am
writing to propose the installation of a microwave oven in the
office of our club. Since there is no microwave oven in the college
that is available to the general students, all the members feel
that it will be beneficial to have one in our club. Moreover, we
can improve our public relations by allowing other students to
use it.

Problems with the Hot Catering in College Cafeterias

Most Chinese like to eat hot food. The usual diet of our members
at home is hot steamed rice served with hot meat and vegetables.
However, according to the survey, all of our members feel that
the hot meal served at the cafeteria is unsatisfactory. First of
all, it costs around $4 to $5 for a meal in both Downs Hall and the
College Center cafeteria. Moreover, the two cafeterias serve
only Western food. Sometimes, the food is cooked with some
special flavors that taste strange to us. Therefore, many Chinese
students prefer to bring their own lunch. The only problem is that
the food is prepared in the morning or even the night before. By
the time they have lunch, the food is cold. Rice gets hard when
it is cold. It not only tastes bad but will also hurt the stomach.

Advantages of a Microwave Oven

With a microwave oven, students can prepare their food at home
and still enjoy a hot meal during lunchtime. Moreover, according
to the survey, homemade lunch generally costs $1 to $2 less than
buying a hot meal in the cafeterias. Members can also prepare hot
drinks by heating up water in the microwave oven. As a club that
truly cares about its members, I think we should help members by
installing a microwave oven. Moreover, we could allow other Kean
College students to use it so that they can warm their homemade
hot dogs, cakes, or lasagnas. This will help us to improve our
public relations.

Cost

Microwave oven (GE, model 27KWH)	$171
Electrical Power	5 per month

Maintenance

The microwave oven can be managed by executive members during their office hours. Moreover, we can save the maintenance costs by having our members clean the oven. According to the survey, all the members are willing to take part in the maintenance. We have 65 members. On average, each member is responsible for just 1.4 days per semester.

Funding

The initial cost of the oven can come from member donations. Since we have 65 members, each of them would have to contribute only $2.15. Based on the survey, all of the members feel that that is a fair price. The cost of power can be covered through use of our club's funds granted by the Student Organization.

Conclusion

Based on the survey, all the members are willing to support the plan because they can have a better diet at a lower cost. In order not to disappoint them, I feel that we should install a microwave oven before winter. I will be glad to discuss the plan during our executive board meeting.

*E*xplorations

1. *Solo.* Consider the issues you are exploring in writing for power. If you have *not* already drafted a paper on the issue, use the questions and suggestions listed in the sidebar to organize your strategies. Then draft an essay to fill in your structure. If you have already drafted your paper, create an outline of it to determine your organization. Reorganize your paper for clarity. Use headings, where appropriate. Refer to the guidelines for deduction and induction on pages 189 and 190.

2. *Together.* Read and respond to each other's drafts, with special emphasis on organization.

Consulting for Power

When you are writing for power, it is very valuable to present your papers in process to those who can offer you a clear sense of what you are doing and whether you are likely to reach a particular audience. If you are working in small groups, ask one person to completely support you in your position, one person to disagree as much as possible, and one person to help you to find common ground. The more you rehearse different

Organizing for Power

For help in organizing what you write, ask yourself the following questions:

- What kinds of appeals should I use in my lead?
- How can I design a lead that clearly focuses my reader's attention on my concerns?
- What formatting would help emphasize the points I want to make?
- What is the most effective order for my supporting examples and evidence?
- How much do I want to emphasize any given point?
- Is every point and example relevant?
- What possible objections can I anticipate, and how can I manage them?
- Do I provide smooth and reasoned transitions between ideas and examples? Between major points? Between paragraphs?
- What point do I want to emphasize in my ending?
- What tone is appropriate for my ending?

points of view in this way, the more likely you will be able to anticipate and manage objections or resistance. In addition, you will benefit from insights into human nature that others can offer you that would take you much longer to formulate by yourself.

As you write, as you consult with others, and as you learn more through writing, you will find ideas and create strategies to accomplish what you want. Even if you have already given what you write to your prospective audience and have gotten a response, you may want to write further, retract some of what you wrote, add to it, or reinterpret it in some way. You can revise by directly incorporating your audience's response; then send it back to your audience.

Revising Faulty Reasoning

As you move back and forth between the phases of the writing process, identify and revise any faulty or irresponsible appeals that may undermine your purpose. The following are some of the most frequently used faulty appeals to reason. Often *faulty reasoning* is a misused appeal to emotion or status, masquerading as an appeal to reason.

Ad Hominem.   *Ad hominem* means "to the man" in Latin. In an ad hominem argument, the truth of a statement is judged not by whether the statement is valid but by who states it. It is an example of a misuse of appeal to status. Whether a well-known politician or your next-door neighbor tells you that Rocketcar is your best value, you have to judge the car by its own merits. Conversely, you can't judge the merits of your doctor's diagnoses by whether he or she agrees with your politics. The following are two examples of ad hominem reasoning:

> I wouldn't believe a thing she tells me about honesty and relationships. She hasn't had her own hair color for years.
>
> If Professor Singer says it, I'll do it.

Sometimes an ad hominem attack is buried in a rhetorical question, such as "How can an undergraduate understand a professor's point of view?" or "Who, if not a mother, can feel deeply for children?" The first question assumes that being an undergraduate makes a person unsympathetic to professors. The second question assumes that being a mother guarantees a love for children. Neither of the assumptions is true.

Be careful of abusing your own status. Don't expect others to believe you just because of who you are or what you have done. Saying things such as "I know because I'm older" or "Do it because I said so" not only shows your inability to reason but invites others to rebel.

Counteract ad hominem arguments by separating statements from the person making them. Ask yourself, "Is it true just because X says so?" "Do the person's other activities or traits make a difference to this point? If so, how?"

Mudslinging.   *Mudslinging* is an extreme form of ad hominem reasoning. Mudslinging is an aggressive attempt to discredit or attack a person's statement by attacking the person instead of judging the statement on its own merits. For example, suppose a male politician believed in supporting AIDS research. A mudslinger would state that the only reason the politician supports AIDS research is because he must have AIDS and if he has AIDS then he must be homosexual. Furthermore, the mudslinger might aggressively attack homosexuals and suggest that the politician be impeached.

Counteract mudslinging with these questions:

- What is your evidence for that claim?
- What is the source of your evidence?

- What difference do the person's other activities or traits make to this point?

Point out that overemotional appeals to status are confusing and destructive. Avoid mudslinging, yourself—it usually backfires.

Hasty Generalizations. Be wary of claims that ask you to believe something is true for every person, place, time, thing, or event. If these generalizations are made in response to only a few examples, they may be *hasty generalizations*. Just because you have had a bad experience with one make of car doesn't mean that all cars of that make are faulty. Just because one person dies while playing a violin doesn't mean that all violins are lethal. Another expression for *hasty generalizations* is *jumping to conclusions*. Jumping to conclusions can damage friendships, strain marriages, cause political friction, and discredit you in your profession.

Know, however, that many generalizations—such as "The sun rises every morning" or "Unprotected sex enhances the likelihood of contracting AIDS"—are useful, if not necessarily true for all time. A time may come when the sun goes cold, but for now we must trust its cycles if we are to feel secure. A cure for AIDS may someday be found, but for now it's best to protect ourselves against the devastating disease. A counterexample to a generalization does not mean that there isn't some truth in the generalization, only that it is not true in all cases.

Counteract hasty generalizations by offering examples that discredit them: *counterexamples*. If someone says all Model Q cars are jalopies, you might point out the counterexamples of Model Q cars that are not jalopies. If someone says gardening is too much trouble (meaning that *all* gardening is too much trouble), you might point out the counterexamples of avid gardeners who thrive on planting and tending their crops.

Stereotyping. *Stereotyping* is making a judgment about a whole group of people based solely on a few traits the members have in common, such as gender, race, religion, or age. Stereotyping—whether stated in positive or negative terms—can be harmful. A stereotyping statement such as "Men are good at controlling their emotions" may seem complimentary, but it is problematic in many ways: the statement puts undue pressure on men to tamp down emotions; it depreciates men who are expressive; and, by implication, it depreciates women. Stereotyping others negatively may serve to make you feel more powerful in comparison with them, but it severely reduces your opportunities for meeting, learning, and connecting with people who may be different from you. Stereotyping limits your personal growth and can backfire. If you degrade others, part of you will also be fearful of the judgment of others. This fear will reduce your power.

Counteract stereotyping both in yourself and in others, by treating persons as individuals, not as categories. Be aware of stereotyping statements. Look for examples of people who don't fit the stereotypes. Offer counterexamples to people who stereotype. You will find that counterexamples of stereotypes are abundantly available. (For further discussion and work on counteracting stereotyping, turn to pages 298–302 in Chapter 11, "Writing to Bridge Cultures.")

Either-Or Fallacy.   There are rarely only two sides to an issue—good or bad, right or wrong, yes or no—because there are many ways to present an issue. In fact, give someone only two options and you may invite resistance. "What do you mean we have only two options: war or economic devastation?" Also, an extreme either-or position is much harder to live up to, as in "Either you buy this product or you will go bald." Be wary of any claim that seems to suggest only two sides or ways of viewing a situation.

Counteract the either-or fallacy by devising further alternatives. Introduce your objection with expressions such as these:

"There are more than two sides to this question."
"We can synthesize a position somewhere in between."
"Let's create a compromise."

Evading the Question.   Do you ever notice when people change the subject or don't answer questions? For example, after ordering an attack on a foreign government's building, a politician was asked if her country was trying to assassinate the minister in charge of the building. She replied, "We are not targeting any individual." She was not answering the question. Her statement could imply that her government was targeting a group of individuals that included the minister. And if you read her statement emphasizing *any,* the statement could imply, "We're not targeting just *any* individual. We are targeting an *important* one." She was *evading the question,* a tactic that avoids reasoning about the issue at hand.

Counteract the problem of evading the question by frequently asking these questions:

- Is this person answering the question?
- Is this person addressing the issue?
- Is this response relevant and to the point?

Be sure to ask these questions of yourself, as well.

False Comparisons. *False comparisons* are often used when a person is trying to overpower an audience in some way. Consider these two examples using comparisons:

> We must use force to make people accept our religion as the only true breath of life. We would force breath into a suffocating child to save her, wouldn't we?

> If there is a rotten apple in a barrel, remove it completely or it will ruin all the apples. A radical mastectomy is perhaps the only reliable procedure for breast cancer.

It is true that we would all want to resuscitate a suffocating child. It is not clear that accepting a particular religion is the only way to "breathe life" into a person. The comparison is questionable. Similarly, a tumor can be as ruinous to the body as a rotten apple is to other apples. But a breast is not significantly like an apple. Apples in a barrel are far more similar than different parts of a body are. Also, it is not clear that cancer works in the same way that chemicals in a barrel of apples do.

Counteract false comparisons by first noticing that a comparison is being made. Notice how the things being compared are alike. Are these similarities relevant to the issue being presented? If the things being compared are not significantly alike, show how they are significantly different.

Explorations

1. *Together and Solo.*
   a. Identify faulty reasoning in the following statements. Which appeal or combination of appeals is each making: to emotion, to status, to reason?

      - In response to the question of how many casualties we have sustained so far, let me say that we are in the process of reevaluating our reports from the field.
      - How can John Updike write about women when he's a man?
      - If you're not willing to write this memo regarding the promotions, then you aren't qualified to remain on this job.
      - His mother was a drug addict, his father an alcoholic, and his uncle a thief. How can he possibly run a hospital?
      - Women were born to bear children, not heavy responsibilities.
      - Skiing is like jumping off a bridge: sooner or later you stop.
      - Either you're with us or you're not.

    b. Revise and add to the statements in 1a so that they will form true appeals to reason. For example, the first statement would be more honest if the person said either "I don't know" or "We have found four bodies so far."

2. *Together or Solo.*

    a. Collect examples of faulty reasoning from newspapers and magazines, especially on editorial pages and in letters to the columnists and editors. Listen for faulty reasoning in debates and speeches on television, radio, and in person.

    b. Choose some examples of faulty reasoning. Revise the speech or piece of writing so that it is a true appeal to reason. What changes in the message? What would change for the persons who used the faulty reasoning if they had used your versions?

3. *Together and Solo.* Read the papers you are writing for power, and identify any statements or arguments that use faulty reasoning. Revise them into true appeals to reason.

Results

In order to effect changes through writing, it is important that you reach the right people. Write to individuals you know personally, to the editor of your local newspaper, to the manager of a television or radio station, to people in government (both local and national), to associations such as the American Medical Association, and to places of business and commerce. Distribute what you write to people in your community, workplace, school, and wherever else is appropriate for your purposes. Be bold. Someone in power may respond as you wish. Write to become that person in power, yourself.

Exploration

Solo and Together. List appropriate audiences to whom you could send the papers or letters you are writing for power. Be specific. Choose your audience and send your work. Share the results with each other. If appropriate, write and send more in response.

STUDENTS WRITING FOR POWER

Read the following student essays. Discuss one or more of them, using the questions and suggestions offered here. Be sure to point to specific parts of the essays to support your discussion.

*R*eflections

1. What need is motivating the person to write the essay?

2. What is the purpose of the essay—to connect, to separate, or to negotiate?

3. How does the writer engage the audience?

4. What appeal or combinations of appeals (to emotion, to status, or to reason) is the writer using?

5. Does the writer attempt to establish common ground? If so, where and how? If not, should the writer have done so? Where and how?

6. Does the writer use a thesis statement? If so, what is it?

7. Does the writer focus the essay with clear, specific, and relevant examples, images, or quotes?

8. Does the writer anticipate and address possible objections and resistances? If so, how?

9. How does the writer organize the essay? Discuss the title, the lead, the body, and the ending. Does the writer use induction or deduction?

10. Does the writer fall into any faulty reasoning? If so, name it.

11. Write a letter in response to the writer of the essay that most affects you. What questions and suggestions would you offer the writer? Why?

12. Write an essay on some issue that occurred to you as you were reading these essays.

The Dark Side Of Abortion

Dave Witthuhn

Abortion is a confusing issue that fires the emotions of everyone. I should warn both the conservatives and liberals in advance that I'm about to throw "another log on the fire." To understand my views, you first need to know the current issues in debate. The popular titles for the

401

debating groups are *The Right to Life,* who take the conservative position, and *Pro Choice,* who take the liberal side.

The conservatives believe that every human being has a right to life, the fetus is a human being, and killing a human being is morally wrong. Thus, abortion is morally wrong. They will go to great extremes, armed with a mountain of facts, to convince you that the fetus is a human being. Their stance hinges on this premise.

The liberal view proposes that abortion should be a woman's right to choose but restricted in some way. The phrase "restricted in some way" presents a lot of controversy within the liberal camp. It seems that they cannot agree on when the fetus becomes a human being. The problem here revolves around their inability to define the point at which the embryo or fetus becomes a human being. There are as many ideas of when this happens as there are people in their ranks. When the embryo or fetus becomes human is anyone's unscientific guess. For the sake of argument, I will accept that this happens at conception.

With all this confusion, we are asking the same original question: When is abortion permissible? The answer lies in the conservative statement "Killing a human being is morally wrong." We, as a people, have condoned and even glorified the killing of our fellow human beings in numerous wars. I'll prove this statement is faulty, because there are situations when killing is justified and accepted.

While in the military, I worked frequently on aircraft carrier flight decks. This environment is considered one of the most dangerous places in the world to work. One day an accident occurred. A man was crushed between a piece of heavy support equipment and an airplane. He was still alive and in no pain. After he was examined by the ship's surgeon, it was determined that the separation of the equipment from the aircraft would result in the man's immediate death. Meanwhile, the next cycle of flight operations was preparing to start. Because of the accident's location, the next launch of combat missions would be held up. The commanding officer ordered the separation and the man died immediately at the moment the order was carried out.

The dark side, in any issue, is a point of view that excludes morality. Now, set aside morality and examine the event on the flight deck, as it is, in the light of simple reality. An accident happened; it was neither intended nor wanted. The man had a right to life, but his life was terminated early. The commanding officer's decision boiled down to one fact: this man's continued life was inconvenient considering the circumstances. Therefore, it was necessary to terminate his life so the mission could continue. All this may sound cold and heartless, but you cannot deny that it was a rational choice devoid of morality.

Now, let us take another look at abortion from the dark side's point of view. A woman becomes pregnant. The pregnancy was an accident. It was neither intended nor wanted. The resulting embryo or fetus has a right to life, but continuing this life is inconvenient considering the circumstances. The woman decides to have an abortion, which results in the immediate termination of the life within her. Why is this situation wrong to so many people, when the previous situation on the ship is considered right? I contend that morality is conveniently imposed on women who choose abortion and not on the commanding officer who chose to terminate a human life. This is nothing more than a double standard and unfair.

In summary, many people use morality as a standard on which to base their decisions. This is a faulty guideline, because morals can differ greatly between cultures and even individuals. This makes morality an inconsistent idea providing no real standard to rely on.

Using morality also allows an individual to fall into the trap of judging another person unfairly while hiding behind inconsistent morals. History is full of notorious events brought on by a group of people imposing their morals on another group. Our United States Constitution was written to safeguard our freedoms and rights from the abuse of this situation, by establishing a separation of church and state.

In conclusion, it is my duty to support the right of any woman to choose an abortion, free of any moral considerations on my part or on the part of any group. As I have said, invoking morals in this issue leads to judgment and condemnation. Even if I believe abortion is wrong, I have no right to interfere or judge when a woman chooses abortion as an option. For the religious conservatives reading this, I'll close with two quotes: "Judge not that ye be not judged" and "He that is without sin, let him first cast a stone at her."

Ignorance Breeds Hate

Bryan Worthy[29]

In today's society, the educational system is based on a Eurocentric point of view. This means that everything we (citizens of the United States) learn is based on a European viewpoint. The omission of the true importance of the African race and its diaspora creates misunderstanding between the African American and the white American. The black child and the white child are being taught that blacks were slaves, while white people of that time were God-fearing, Christian people (a hypocritical lie). The African-American child who hears this will feel inferior, and the white child, in turn, will feel superior. This thought of "being better" than others causes racism.

To correct this problem, we need to teach the correct history, not the false one educators have been teaching. An example of this is how society teaches that Moses was white. Moses was raised in the Egyptian pharaoh's home for a number of years. The pharaoh believed Moses to be his natural son. If Egypt is in Africa and the King of Egypt thought Moses was his son by birth, wouldn't that make Moses dark-skinned? The inclusion of the history of African Americans and its importance will balance out the importance of white Americans. Therefore, the two races will have a better understanding of each other and eliminate most of the ignorance.

In conclusion, hate is a direct result of distorted facts, similar to the ones I just presented. So, for any hope of a peaceful future between the races, teach the correct past, or there will be no future.

The Unkindest Cut

Tamara Tolbert

> Wife tells court sex assault drove her to "unkindest cut" on husband.
> —*The Star Ledger,*
> Associated Press, Tuesday, November 9, 1993

Ex-Marine John Wayne Bobbitt was accused of forcing his wife Lorena Bobbitt to have sex with him against her will. She claimed he always came home heavily intoxicated and repeatedly raped her. So one night, after she was raped, she left and went to the kitchen to get a glass of water. That's when she saw the knife. Flashbacks of him brutally having sex with her, pleasing only himself, went through her mind. The next thing she knew, she was in the room, removing the covers and cutting off his penis.

Moreover, to make matters even worse, she drove off with his penis in her hand. Once she realized it, she threw it out the window. Fortunately, the police found his penis and it was quickly sewn back on him. The thing that really gets me is that he didn't respond right away after being cut. Now the only reason to me that he didn't react was because he was drunk.

Consequently, they were both being tried in court: Mr. John Bobbitt for sexual assault, and Mrs. Lorena Bobbitt for malicious wounding. She admitted to cutting off his penis but he denied all charges of sexual assault. I think he was lying because I see no reason for her to go to such drastic measures unless she was going through a lot of stress and physical and emotional pain.

When you compare the two types of pain they were going through, you come up with two very disturbed people. Mr. Bobbitt had been through some very intense physical pain. His operation lasted ten hours. Afterward, the result was that there is a possibility that he wouldn't ever be able to sexually perform again. Still and all, I feel as though he deserved it. I say that because too many men nowadays drink too much alcohol. If he wasn't getting drunk all the time and then coming home to disrespect his wife, none of this would have happened. So he should have learned a very valuable lesson: never abuse what you have because a person can only take so much. Too bad he had to find out the hard way.

Mrs. Bobbitt, on the other hand, was going through some mental and emotional pain. She had to deal with the fact that she was a victim of sexual assault. Most likely, she'll need some therapy. Nevertheless, she'll have to pay the price for her malicious act on her husband's genitals. Hopefully, she has learned a lesson from this also. That is when you're being abused, leave immediately! Don't let matters get worse before you act.

They'll both have plenty of time to think over what put them where they are. That should help them realize their mistakes and hopefully they won't repeat them again in the future.

Hunting

Vincent Moore

To me, hunting is a misunderstood sport in many parts of the United States. Where I am from, Oregon, hunting is understood and is passed down from generation to generation. It is a common sport and it is among the majority.

Hunting is much more than the actual killing itself. It's not the killing that makes a hunter keep hunting; it is the feelings that are experienced while out there all alone—maybe a little cold and most definitely quiet. At least there aren't any people noises, except for the occasional plane passing overhead. I say quiet, but actually there is plenty to hear; it's just that the noises that are heard are pleasant and enjoyable to hear. The wind blowing through the pines and rustling up the leaves, the morning songs of the birds, and the sound of cold water running over the rocks of a nearby stream are just some of the sounds heard while hunting.

I'm not trying to make anyone a hunter. I'm just trying to explain what hunting is about from a hunter's point of view. To better explain what hunting is like for me, I am going to take you through a day of hunting.

The day begins as I walk into the dark quiet woods to my "stand" (a designated area). I try not to disrupt the woods, though I feel anything around could hear the beating of my heart. This walk takes only fifteen minutes, but it feels like it has taken an hour before I have reached the stand. Once there, I quickly, but quietly, settle in and get comfortable. Still in the early morning darkness I sit in the cold, with a slight wind blowing in my face. For a while it is very quiet until the sun slowly begins to rise. With the darkness slowly fading to light the birds begin to chirp, and the squirrels begin to play, jumping from tree to tree.

It is cold, lightly snowing, and the sun is directly overhead. I haven't heard or seen a thing all morning and I am beginning to become uncomfortably cold. I keep thinking about how nice it would be to be in my car, warming up and heading home. As I am about to give in to the cold, I begin to hear something. It sounds like cold dead tree limbs banging together in the wind. As I look for the tree that is making the noise, I catch movement. It is coming from directly in front of me. At first, all I can see is flashes of white. Through heavy brush, I begin to see the outline of not one, but two deer. They are bucks, and the noise I hear did not come from the wind and a dead tree but from the antlers of these two bucks while fighting. They are too far off to shoot, but nonetheless, my heart begins to pound. The two bucks have my full undivided attention for their hour-long standoff. I am no longer cold and wanting to go home.

This experience will long last in my memories of hunting. Seeing something like that made that day's hunt one of the best. Some might say, if hunting is just enjoying nature, then why is it necessary to kill? This is where tradition and growing up with hunting comes in. Everyone I know that hunts does not hunt for the trophy, but they eat what they kill. The sport is hunting, not killing. The majority of the hunting day consists of relaxing and enjoying nature. The actual killing of an animal does not make the hunt more enjoyable or memorable. To be quite honest, one of my most memorable days of hunting didn't end with a kill. This may be hard for some to understand, but where I come from this is a common sport and it is understood.

Kindness Doesn't Pass in Class

Marcus Raines

This is a story of a young man who is in the twelfth grade and about to graduate. His name is Ralph. He has done moderately well in the majority of his classes except one. This is his geometry class. His geometry class is taught by his very kind and nice Aunt Jean. Ralph's Aunt Jean has been helping Ralph out, but not in a good way. She has passed him for quizzes that he took but didn't pass. At the time Ralph was feeling pretty sure of himself. He was getting good grades and hardly doing any work.

Now it's time for the final exam. Students who have studied, passed, and absorbed all of the work throughout the year are ready for the test. One day before the exam Ralph sees some of his friends studying in the lunchroom. They are reciting formulas, doing problems, and drawing shapes. They are doing this as if they were born with the information inside of them. Ralph just sits on the side, watches, and says, "I'll study tonight before I go to bed, and even if I don't pass, my Aunt will help me out." Later that night Ralph tries to cram for the exam. He doesn't know anything; everything is just in scrambles. So Ralph lies down and feels terrible. He also feels guilty. He feels he has been cheated this time. He thinks, "How will this help me in college? I might pass, but I don't know the work. I won't know anything." Ralph knows this because he had his Aunt for Algebra 1, too. So Ralph says, "I'm going to cram for the test." This doesn't work. Everything is still in scrambles. Ralph turns over and starts to cry. He feels very bad and scared—scared because he has to get at least an *A* on the exam to pass for the year.

The next day Ralph confronts his Aunt and tells her not to coddle him anymore and that he feels bad. But his Aunt tells him not to worry and that she will help him through this last exam because otherwise he will never pass. Ralph screams, "No, no, I don't want your easy passes anymore." The exam proceeds but Ralph isn't there. So, he fails for the year and repeats his senior year because of the kindest but cruelest aunt, Aunt Jean.

So the next time you take a course because you think it's going to be easy or because you think you can cheat your way through, remember this story of Ralph. Sooner or later, it'll all catch up with you.

Chapter Review

Solo or *Together* respond to one or more of the following:

1. This chapter provides a variety of strategies for writing for power. Which five strategies do you believe are most important, and why?

2. What are you and your writing partners hoping to accomplish in writing for power?

3. Do you believe you will be successful in accomplishing what you set out to do in writing for power? Why or why not?

4. What more could you do in writing for power on your current project?

5. Which parts of this chapter do you anticipate reviewing in the future? Why?

Chapter **15**

Grammar

This chapter offers opportunities to

—Develop *perspective* on grammar

—Experiment with *phrases* and *clauses*

—Connect sentences for *meaning* and *style*

—*Revise* fragments, run-ons, comma splices, and misplaced modifiers

—Adjust your writing for *pronoun and verb agreement*

—*Revise* your writing to comply with nonsexist academic and professional standards

---

Grammar is a piano I play by ear. All I know about grammar is its power.
—*Joan Didion, Fiction writer*

Learning to write is not a matter of learning the rules that govern the use of the semicolon or the names of sentence structures . . . it is a matter of making meanings.
—*Ann E. Berthoff,*
Philosopher of Composition

How to Use This Chapter

Here are some possible ways you can use this chapter:

1. Work through the whole chapter, doing selected Explorations as you proceed.

2. Focus on a particular point of grammar until you are satisfied that you understand it. Collect examples of it in your readings. Look for it in your writing. Focus on it when you consult with others during the writing process.

3. Go straight to the Explorations; if you get stuck, read what precedes them.

4. In a small group or solo, create a lesson on a particular point of grammar. Illustrate your lesson with examples you have collected, especially in your own writing and in the writing of other students.

5. Review Chapter 9, "Revising." Remember that you don't have to name every part of speech or every kind of grammatical usage in every piece of writing to write appropriately. However, if you have had difficulty with particular kinds of usage, it can be helpful to learn how to identify them by name in your own writing. Ultimately, as long as you learn to revise your own writing, whether or not you are a grammarian won't matter.

6. If you work with a computer grammar checker, identify patterns you need to change in your writing. Work with the portions in this chapter that address your concerns.

If you have used grammatical terms before, you may notice that, in some cases, this chapter uses different terms. For example, the word *and* is called a *connector* instead of a *conjunction. Connector* is a more common word that better describes what the word does. Words such as *however* and *therefore* are called *afterthoughts* instead of the more technical *conjunctive adverbs*, which can be confused with *connecting adverbs*.

Grammar, Purpose, and Audience

Grammar is a description of how the different parts of a language are organized. In some languages, the order in which you put words is not as important as it is in English. In English, there are vast differences in meaning between "She saw me through" and "She saw through me" or between "The dog bit John" and "John bit the dog." The differences are determined by the order and the relationships of the words—the grammar of the sentences.

What is considered "correct" grammar is determined by who is in power, who is teaching, and how people are currently using language in different situations. How the powerful speak and write is what will be taught to those who also want to be powerful in the same way. For example, it was much more fashionable at the turn of the century to write long, complex sentences in advertisements because people were used to reading and had the time and patience to do so. Read the following advertisement. Notice how long the sentences are:

> **Genuine Castille Emollient Soap for Ladies and Gentlemen.**   Within the boundaries of polite society, there are many ladies and gentlemen who prefer a soap that offers more amenities than those offered by the local general store. For this distinguished clientele that understands the advantages of a true emollient, we offer Genuine Castille Emollient Soap, imported directly to our Emporium, or to your local apothecary.

Radio, television, and other electronic mass media did not exist at the turn of the century. Today, written advertisements have to flash their messages much more quickly because people are used to instant visual messages. Therefore, advertisements are more likely to communicate today by short sentence fragments. The same advertisement, above, could be written this way:

> Castille soap. Natural and gentle. Back to basics. In finer stores, everywhere.

More than likely, this ad would be accompanied by a picture or photograph that would imply a complete message. Or, if the words *Castille soap* appeared in places normally used for advertising—such as a billboard or on television—you would know that the implied message is "buy Castille soap."

Sentence fragments are not usually acceptable in academic and professional writing (other than ads), partly because the messages in school and work are far more complex than just "buy this today." Also, academic and professional writing is not normally accompanied by sufficient visual or audio aids to communicate complete messages.

Other forces, as well, determine what is considered correct grammar. If you come from a community that has historically had less political power, then your rules of how to use and organize language may not be favored by those who have more political power. As poet Robert Frost once said, "You can be a little ungrammatical if you come from the right part of the country." In other words, what is considered acceptable depends on who you are with and where you came from. In fact, the word *glam-*

our—which means exciting, ideal, or glorified—originally came from a mispronunciation of the word *grammar*. Teachers were the only people with advanced education in many communities. Grammar, and knowing rules of reading and writing, became associated with being the best, or the ideal. At some point someone heard the word *grammar* as *glamour*, and a new word was coined. The word *glamour* is now used to mean *ideal*.*

The grammars of spoken language are different from the grammars of written language, partly because gestures and tones of voice complete spoken but not written communication. Spoken language is often more economical than written language. For example, *ain't*, a word usually used in speaking, can mean "is not," "are not," "has not," and "have not." *Ain't* is a four-in-one word. However, *ain't* hasn't yet become acceptable in written language. Many other words and expressions are acceptable and very useful in spoken language but haven't yet been incorporated into most academic and professional writing.

Yet another factor in determining the grammar of a language is individual style. Within the framework of a language community, there is a full range of individual styles or patterns of speaking and writing. Style is like a fingerprint. In fact, some experts can identify who you are by the patterns they notice in your writing. You may be someone who prefers to write long sentences with many phrases. Someone else may have a more spare style of short sentences with few modifying phrases. But unlike your fingerprints, your style can be developed and changed. So, as you write and experiment with writing, you may find your style changing for different purposes and audiences. There is no one right style, only different styles for different meanings.

As you work with grammar, resist the temptation to settle for merely correct sentences. It is far easier to write short sentences with simple structures than it is to strive for more complex sentences that connect and interweave ideas in more meaningful and interesting ways. Remember the quote from Laura Silwones on page 27, "You have to try something harder to do better."

This chapter outlines the elements of grammar as they are used in academic and professional communities today. How you speak and write in your home community (with friends and family) and the kinds of writing you see in advertisements, school, and the professions may be different—not better or worse in themselves.

---

*William Safire discussed this word origin in his December 13, 1987 column, "On Language," in *The New York Times Magazine*. He, in turn, was citing W. V. Quine's book *Quiddities: An Intermittently Philosophical Dictionary* (Cambridge, Mass.: Harvard University Press).

Understanding and developing skills that help you to use language for different purposes, audiences, and communities will empower you. You will gain the trust and confidence of more people and learn from them, in turn. Such flexibility in using language could even enable you to change others' ideas of what is grammatically acceptable. Remember, as you learn more about grammar, that *all* the elements of writing are meant to help you create meaning, express yourself, communicate with others, and get things done.

*E*xplorations

1. **a.** *Together.* Discuss your experiences with grammar using the following suggestions and questions:

    - List words you would use to describe your previous experiences with grammar. Why would you use these words?

    - Are there cultural differences between how you speak English with friends and family and how you are expected to write for academic and professional purposes? What are some of the specific differences?

    - Do your experiences with grammar affect your perception of yourself as a writer? If so, how? If not, why not?

    - What reactions do you have to focusing on grammar now?

    - What do you hope to learn, specifically, by working with this chapter?

    b. *Solo.* Using insights developed in your discussion in 1a, write a letter to your instructor about your experience of grammar.

2. *Together and Solo.* Read the following examples and decide which ones are standard academic, casual contemporary, or neither. With whom, when, where, how, and why would these expressions be appropriate? Revise those that are not standard and contemporary English into sentences that are. How do the meanings of the examples change as you revise them? In what situations would the nonstandard phrases be appropriate?

    a. Yes. I can understand why you feel that way. I really can.

    b. Having checked the card catalog and the *Index to Periodical Literature*, she approached a reference librarian for assistance.

    c. Hungry am I.

    d. I mean like what 'm I s'posed to do, Miss?

    e. Whilst the spring doth come and the wind doth blow, thou wilt weep.

f. Because she refused her position to concede, the council her rights removed.

3. *Together and Solo.* Discuss how the two sentences in each set differ in meaning:

   a. John cooked because Mary cleaned.
   Mary cleaned because John cooked.

   b. She saw me through.
   She saw through me.

   c. "John, won't you help me?"
   "John, you won't help me?"

   d. All dogs are animals.
   All animals are dogs.

   e. Should the bridge be mended, I will cross it.
   The bridge will be mended; I should cross it.
   The bridge should be mended. Will I cross it?

4. *Together and Solo.* Discuss the meanings of the following sentences, which can be read in different ways. Under some interpretations the sentences have unintended or humorous meanings because of word orders and omissions. Revise the sentences to make better sense.

   a. Droughts turn deer to crops.

   b. He was raised by his grandparents because his mother died in early infancy.

   c. Youths drink and rob baker.

   d. The town meeting talked garbage.

   e. Detective denies his suicide.

   f. Jury gets drunk driving case.

5. *Together.* List words and expressions that you or others use that are not acceptable in the academic or professional writing you have done. Define the expressions. Revise them into something that sounds more academic or professional to you.

PARTS OF SPEECH

To understand how language is organized, grammarians analyzed it and categorized words into different parts of speech. The sidebar presents a quick review of the most basic parts of speech, followed by Explorations that help you identify them in your own writing.

Explorations _____

1. *Together or Solo.*

   a. Turn a piece of lined paper sideways and write the parts of speech across the page on the red line. Under these headings, list the following words according to the parts of speech you believe they are. Test words in sentences if you are uncertain. Some words may belong under more than one heading.

one	inn	kind
lightning	because	gentle
light	without	purse
belonging	reflection	geography
lug	sold	near
magically	were	oh
outcry	make	pick
vault	only	

Parts of Speech

Nouns (n): Names for persons, places, activities, things, e.g., *child, town, pen*

Pronouns (pro): Noun substitutes, e.g., *she, whoever, themselves, this*

Adjectives (adj): Words that modify nouns and pronouns, e.g., *dazzling, red, legal*

Articles (art): Words that point to nouns, e.g., *a, an, the*

Verbs (v): Words for actions and states of being, e.g., *run, wonder, exist*

Adverbs (adv): Words that modify verbs, adjectives, and other adverbs, e.g., *slowly, next, there, only*

Prepositions (prep): Words that introduce phrases, e.g., *in, of, at*

Connectors (con): Words that join, e.g., *and, but, yet, while, which*

Interjections (interj): Words that exclaim, e.g., *yes, well, wow*

      b. Using a dictionary, add to these lists so there are at least ten words in each. The dictionary will offer abbreviations, such as the ones in parentheses in the sidebar, to indicate which parts of speech a word can serve.

2. *Solo.* To become aware of the elements of your own writing style, analyze something you have written. Use the following questions and suggestions to guide your analysis:

   - Which words do you repeat?

   - Do you tend to begin your sentences with certain words?

   - Are your sentences generally long or short?

   - Count up the words on a handwritten page (or half of a typewritten page). Mark what part of speech each word is, using the abbreviations in the list of the basic parts of speech in the sidebar. Count how many of each part of speech you have.

   - Do you use connectors?

   - Do you use more adjectives than different kinds of verbs?

   - Do you often use forms of the verb *to be,* such as *am, is, was,* or *were?*

   - What parts of speech do you tend to use more than others?

   - What did you learn about your writing style?

   - What do you like about it?

   - What do you not like about it?

   - How could you develop your style for greater variety in parts of speech?

3. *Together or Solo.* Using the instructions in Exploration 2, notice stylistic patterns in each other's writing. Revise your papers for more variety.

SENTENCES

Suppose you read the word *tree* in the middle of an otherwise blank page. A word written in such isolation has little meaning. You don't know why the word was written or what to make of it. To write, you need to know how to connect ideas into meaningful sentences. A sentence presents a *subject* for the reader to consider and a *verb* that tells the reader what to make of it, as in these two simple sentences:

> The tree stands alone
>
> The tree is being removed.

Although you might not know which tree is being referred to, you start to understand why the word *tree* is written on the page. Meaning starts to develop. A sentence may also include phrases and other clauses that further modify (add to or change) its meaning.

Phrases

A *phrase* is a group of words that has a subject (a noun) but not a verb, or a verb (with or without an object) but not a subject. A phrase with a subject but no verb is started by a *preposition. During the Revolution* has a preposition and a subject but no verb. Prepositional phrases usually function as adjectives or adverbs, modifying the meaning of subjects, verbs, or objects in sentences. A phrase with a verb but no subject is started by the *participle* of the verb. *Fighting injustice* has a verb, *fighting,* and an object, *injustice,* but no subject. Verb phrases, when used as modifiers, usually function as adjectives.

Prepositional Phrases

Prepositional phrases are phrases introduced by prepositions, such as *at, below,* and *in.* Here are some well-known prepositional phrases:

After the fall	Between the acts
Into the woods	Of mice and men

Some of the most common prepositions are listed in the sidebar. Other phrases may be added to the simple sentences above to make them more meaningful:

Prepositions

about	except	over
above	for	since
after	from	than
at	in	through
because of	inside	to
before	into	toward
below	near	under
between	next to	until
by	of	up
despite	on	with
during	out	without

The tree stands in front of Town Hall.

The tree is being removed from the lawn.

Verb Phrases

A phrase may start with a verbal. A verbal is a form of a verb that is not used as the main verb in a clause. (Clauses are discussed on pages 422–431.) A verbal may be a present participle, a past participle, or an infinitive. If a phrase starts with a verbal, it is called a *verb phrase.*

The *present participle* is formed by adding *-ing* to the present tense of a verb. For example, *walking* is the present participle of *walk* and can introduce verb phrases such as *walking down the street* in the sentence "Walking down the street, the dog wagged its tail." Note that not all verbs ending in *-ing* introduce modifying phrases. Some verb forms ending in *-ing* function as nouns, as in the sentence "*Walking* is good for your health."

The *past participle* of *regular verbs* is formed by adding *-d* or *-ed* to the present tense. For example, *walked* is the past participle of *walk* and can introduce verb phrases such as *walked twice around the block* in the sentence "Walked twice around the block, the dog was satisfied." Notice that in the sentence "Walking down the street, the dog wagged its tail," the word *walking* refers to what the dog is doing. In the sentence "Walked twice around the block, the dog was satisfied," the dog is having something done to it: the dog is being walked.

The past participle of *irregular* verbs is not formed by adding *-d* or *-ed* to the present tense. The present participle of the irregular verb *stand* is *standing,* but the past participle is *stood.* Notice that in the sentence "Standing alone, the potted tree grew well in the sun," the word *standing* refers to what the tree itself is doing. In the sentence "Stood alone, the potted tree grew well in the sun," *stood* refers to what was done *to* the tree. To help you form verb phrases using past participles of irregular verbs, the sidebar presents a list of commonly used irregular verbs that includes the present tense, the past tense, and the past participle of each. If you are not sure of how to form the past participle of a verb, consult the dictionary. Unless it offers an irregular past tense or past participle, form the past participle by adding *-d* or *-ed.*

If *to* is followed by a verb in the present tense, *to* is not used as a preposition. *To* and a present tense verb together form an infinitive, as in this example: "Harry loves *to cook.*" An infinitive may also be used as a noun, as in this sentence: "To cook is Harry's greatest joy."

*E*xplorations _____

1. *Solo and Together.* Collect twenty-five examples of prepositional phrases from *The Flexible Writer.* See if you can find at least one example for each of the prepositions listed in the sidebar on page 418.

2. *Together or Solo.* Form prepositional phrases with each of the words listed in the sidebar on page 418. To explore the meaning of the prepositions, use the word *tree* as the object. Notice how certain prepositions will not work with *tree.* For example, *between the tree* does not make sense because you need two objects with *between.* A more appropriate prepositional phrase would be *between the trees.* Add adjectives to make interesting phrases.

3. *Solo and Together.* Collect examples of verb phrases from a book you are currently reading for another class or purpose. Endeavor to find both present and past verb phrases.

4. *Together or Solo.* Form the present and past participles of each of the following verbs. If you are uncertain whether a verb is regular or irregular, consult the sidebar on regular and irregular verbs or the dictionary.

walk	break	be	type
draw	got	drive	burn

Regular and Irregular Verbs

Present Tense	Past Tense	Past Participle
am,* are, be,** is	was, were***	been
beat	beat	beaten, beat
become	became	become
begin	began	begun
bite	bit	bitten, bit
blow	blew	blown
break	broke	broken
bring	brought	brought
burn	burned, burnt	burned, burnt
burst	burst	burst
buy	bought	bought
catch	caught	caught
choose	chose	chosen
come	came	come
do	did	done
draw	drew	drawn
dream	dreamed, dreamt	dreamed, dreamt
drink	drank	drunk
drive	drove	driven
eat	ate	eaten
fall	fell	fallen
find	found	found
fly	flew	flown
forget	forgot	forgotten, forgot
get	got	gotten, got
give	gave	given
go	went	gone
hang (suspend)	hung	hung
hang (execute)	hanged	hanged
has, have	had	had
hear	heard	heard
hide	hid	hidden
hurt	hurt	hurt

Present Tense	Past Tense	Past Participle
keep	kept	kept
know	knew	known
lay (put)	laid	laid
leave	left	left
let (allow)	let	let
lie (recline)	lay	lain
ride	rode	ridden
ring	rang	rung
rise (get up)	rose	risen
run	ran	run
say	said	said
see	saw	seen
set (place)	set	set
shake	shook	shaken
sing	sang	sung
sit (be seated)	sat	sat
sleep	slept	slept
speak	spoke	spoken
stand	stood	stood
steal	stole	stolen
strike	struck	struck, stricken
swear	swore	sworn
take	took	taken
teach	taught	taught
throw	threw	thrown
wake	woke, waked	woken, waked, woke
wear	wore	worn
write	wrote	written

*Normally, *am* is used only with *I* as in *I am* in academic and professional writing.

**Normally, *be* is not used as a singular or plural verb in academic and professional writing. However, *being* is often used as a present participle.

***When verbs are formed with helping verbs such as *is, are, was, were, been, had, has, have, do, does, get,* and *got,* they are followed by either the present or the past participle as in *is forming, is formed,* or *have been forming* and *have been formed.* Note that other than the simple past tense, past tenses are formed with the past participle.

5. *Together or Solo.* Discuss each of the following groups of words. Which
    are prepositional phrases? Which are present tense verb phrases?
    Which are past tense verb phrases? Which are infinitives? Which are
    none of these?

    a. To the park

    b. To go swimming

    c. Swimming in the pond

    d. Walked across the field

    e. Because of walking

Clauses

A clause is constructed of a subject and a verb. Every sentence is a clause,
but not every clause is a sentence. Only an *independent clause,* containing
a subject and a verb, is a sentence. A *dependent clause* also has a subject
and a verb, but a dependent clause functions as an adverb, an adjective,
or a noun. An adverb, an adjective, or a noun cannot function independently of a sentence. The meaning of a dependent clause *depends* on the
main or independent clause in which it is incorporated.

Independent Clauses

An independent clause has two elements: a subject (what the sentence
is about) and a verb (what the subject does, is, or has done to it). The verb
may stand alone; or the verb may have an object, as, for example, the
word *ball* in the sentence "Sam threw the ball." All sentences are or
contain independent clauses. What makes a sentence a sentence is that it
carries a *complete* message. Only a sentence that contains an *independent
clause* is a sentence, because as its name implies, it stands alone.

A sentence can be as short as one word, as in the sentence "Write."
You is the implied subject, and *write* is the verb. An independent clause
with no attached dependent clauses is referred to as a *simple sentence.*
The end of a sentence is marked by a period, question mark, or exclamation
point—appropriately called *end marks.* Sometimes a word or a couple of
words will be followed by an end mark without being a sentence. For
further discussion of such "sentences," refer to page 435.

Here are two *simple* sentences:

1. The diseased elm trees were removed from Linwood.

2. Trees in the neighboring towns were stricken with Dutch elm
    disease.

> **Connectors**
>
> | and | nor | so |
> | --- | --- | --- |
> | but | or | yet |
> | for | | |

Trees are the subjects in these sentences. *Were removed* and *were stricken* are the verbs.

A *compound sentence* is composed of two or more sentences connected by a comma *and* a sentence connector such as one of those in the sidebar. The two sentences above can be joined into a compound sentence by using a comma and a sentence connector.

> The diseased elm trees were removed from Linwood, but trees in the neighboring towns were stricken with Dutch elm disease.

It is important that you choose the sentence connector that best expresses your meaning. If the word *so* were used in the compound sentence above, it would mean that the trees in neighboring towns became diseased *because* the trees were removed from Linwood. But the trees were removed *to save* neighboring trees. The sentence joined by *but* means that they became diseased *even though* the sick trees in Linwood were removed. Choose your sentence connectors carefully to create sentences that say what you mean.

Although in the past grammarians did not deem it acceptable to start a sentence with a sentence connector, such as *and* or *but,* it is no longer considered "wrong" to do so. But it's up to you. And it will depend on the effect you want to make on your readers.

Afterthoughts. Sometimes an independent clause will follow another independent clause to which it is closely connected (see Figure 15.1). But instead of using a sentence connector, you can use words that signal *afterthoughts.* Such words are listed in the sidebar on page 424. Here are some examples of pairs of independent clauses; the second clause in each pair is an afterthought. Notice that the two sentences contain semicolons and that a comma follows the afterthought word:

> The diseased elms were removed from Linwood; nevertheless, trees in the neighboring towns were stricken with Dutch elm disease.
>
> The trees in the neighboring towns were stricken with Dutch elm disease; indeed, it did no good to remove the elms from Linwood.

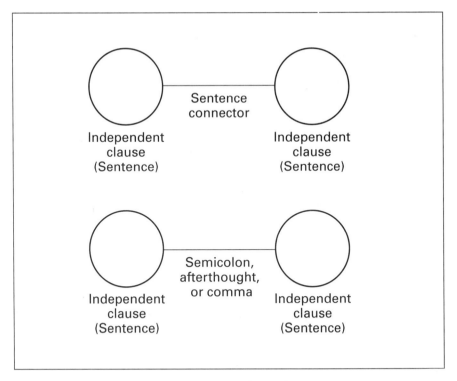

F I G U R E   15.1   Connecting Independent Clauses

Dependent Clauses

A *dependent clause* contains a subject and verb and is introduced by a word that connects it to an independent clause. Dependent clauses contain ideas that are dependent on, or not as central as, the independent clauses to which they are attached. There are three kinds of dependent clauses:

Afterthoughts

accordingly	hence	nevertheless
also	however	otherwise
besides	indeed	so
consequently	in fact	then
finally	likewise	therefore
furthermore	moreover	thus

adverbial, adjectival, and *noun.* A sentence that contains a dependent clause is called a *complex sentence.*

Adverbial Clauses.   Adverbial clauses contain ideas that are dependent, or not as central, as the independent clauses to which they are connected. Adverbial clauses help to change or modify the meaning of the main, independent clause. *Adverbial clauses work like adverbs because they answer the questions when, where, how, and why.* They tell you something is happening, has happened, or will happen. They begin with connecting adverbs such as those listed in the sidebar.

These are some examples of adverbial clauses:

Even though the diseased elm trees were removed from Linwood

If you want a reliable compact convertible

Wherever there are children at risk

Notice that these clauses do not carry a complete message. When you read one of them, you look for the rest of the sentence. The rest of the sentence would be the independent clause.

Adverbial clauses can be written at the beginning, the middle, or the end of a sentence. For example, you could incorporate the first adverbial clause above as follows:

1. *Even though the diseased elm trees were removed from Linwood,* trees in the neighboring towns were stricken with Dutch elm disease.

Connecting Adverbs

after	even though	unless
although	if	until
as	in order that	when
as if	rather than	whenever
as long as	since*	where
as soon as	so that	wherever
because	than	whether
before	though	while

*The expression *being that* is sometimes used to mean *since.* Normally, *being that* is not used in academic and professional writing.

2. The trees in the neighboring town were stricken with Dutch elm disease, *even though the diseased elm trees were removed from Linwood* and the neighboring trees were far away.

3. The elm trees in the neighboring towns were stricken by Dutch elm disease, *even though the diseased elm trees were removed from Linwood.*

Where you place the adverbial clause is determined by what you want to emphasize. You will usually start your sentence with the point you want to emphasize. Because sentence 1 starts with the fact that trees were removed, that is the emphasis of the whole sentence; sentence 2 emphasizes the trees in the neighboring town because those trees are mentioned at the beginning and the end of the sentence; and sentence 3 emphasizes that the trees were stricken with Dutch elm disease.

How you modify or change the meaning of your main, independent, clause will be determined by the connecting adverb that you use. If, for example, you used the word *because* instead of *even though* in sentence 1, the whole meaning of the sentence would change.

> *Because* the diseased elm trees were removed from Linwood, trees in the neighboring towns were stricken with Dutch elm disease.

This version of the sentence states that the trees in the neighboring town were stricken with disease *because* the trees were removed from Linwood. Unless the removal process itself transferred the disease, this sentence doesn't make sense in this situation.

Adjectival Clauses.   Adjectival clauses contain ideas that are dependent on the independent clauses to which they are attached. *Adjectival clauses function as adjectives because they modify the nouns in sentences.* Adjectival clauses begin with connecting adjectives such as those listed in the sidebar. These are some examples of adjectival clauses:

Who inspected the trees

Which was meant to stop the spread of Dutch elm disease

Notice that these adjectival clauses are incomplete. When you read them, you look for the rest of the thought. The rest of the thought would be the independent clause. For clarity, place the adjectival clause as close as possible to what it explains. For example, notice how the adjectival clauses above are embedded in the following sentence:

> Mary, who inspected the trees, ordered the removal of the stricken trees that would spread Dutch elm disease.

> ### *Connecting Adjectives*
>
> that   whom
>
> which   whose
>
> who

If the adjectival phrase were placed much later, it would confuse readers:

> Mary ordered the removal of the stricken trees that would spread Dutch elm disease, who inspected the trees.

This sentence implies that Dutch elm disease, itself, had inspected the trees. That's absurd.

Remember that *who* is used to refer to persons, *that* is used to refer to persons or things, and *which* is used to refer only to things or events.

Noun Clauses. Noun clauses contain one of the connecting pronouns listed in the sidebar on page 429 and a verb. Noun clauses are dependent clauses because they cannot stand alone. A noun clause functions as a noun—a subject or an object that must be incorporated into an independent clause.

Here are some examples of noun clauses. Remember, the connecting pronoun transforms the whole clause into one noun:

> Whoever owns an elm tree
>
> That they couldn't save the trees

Read alone, these noun clauses are not meaningful. They must become either a subject or an object in an independent clause (a sentence):

Noun Clause as Subject:

Whoever owns an elm tree knows it may be stricken.

That they couldn't save the trees was a tragedy.

Noun Clause as Object:

They notified whoever owns an elm tree.

They knew that they couldn't save the trees.

Figure 15.2 shows how clauses can be combined into complete sentences.

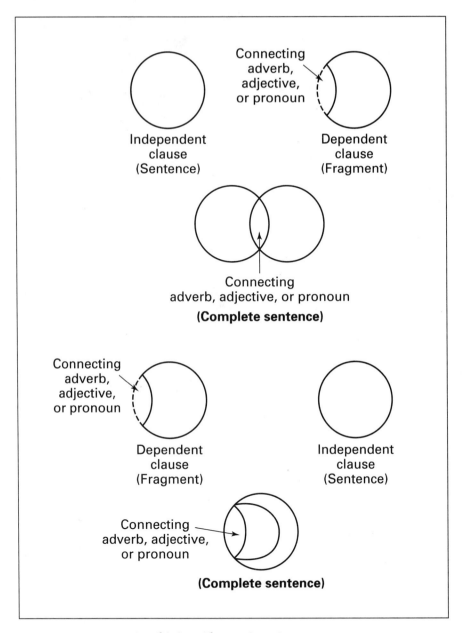

FIGURE 15.2 Combining Clauses into Sentences

Sentence Variety

If every sentence you wrote were short and started with the word *the,* your style would become choppy and boring for your readers:

Connecting Pronouns

how	whichever	whomever
that	who	whose
where	whoever	why
which	whom	

> The storm started at 3:00. The rains were heavy. The forecasters were warning drivers. The drivers were swamped. The flash flooding swamped the drivers. The rescue squads were swamped too.

Compare this choppy report to its revised version:

> The storm, starting at 3:00, produced such heavy rains that despite the forecasters' warnings, not only drivers but rescue squads who were on the scene were swamped by flash flooding.

This sentence connects ideas and shows how they are related to each other. Notice some of the connecting devices:

Verb Phrase: starting at 3:00

Prepositional Phrases: at 3:00, despite the forecasters' warnings, by flash flooding

Adjectival Clause: who were on the scene

The revised sentence is far more meaningful because it communicates how the author connects events. In your own writing, endeavor to use a variety of phrases and dependent clauses to connect and weave ideas into interesting sentences.

Sentence connectors; connecting adverbs, adjectives, and pronouns; and participles and prepositions allow you to combine sentences to introduce meaning and variety into your style. Compound sentences are formed by using sentence connectors. Complex sentences are formed by using adverb, adjective, and pronoun connnecters. *Compound-complex sentences* include both a compound and a complex sentence:

> Mary, who inspected Linwood, ordered the stricken trees to be removed, but the trees in the neighboring towns were stricken with Dutch elm disease.

The sentence is complex because it contains a dependent clause, in this case starting with *who*. The sentence is also compound because it combines two independent clauses. In this case, the independent clauses start with *Mary* and *the trees* and the sentence connector is *but.*

Explorations _____

1. *Together and Solo.* Identify which of the following groups of words is a prepositional phrase, a verb phrase, an adverbial clause, an adjectival clause, a noun clause, a sentence, or some combination of these. Start by circling prepositions, verbals, and connectors. Add punctuation to complete sentences.

   a. During the nineteenth century

   b. Enduring the tedious conversation long enough, George finally fell asleep

   c. After the peace talks concluded

   d. After the hurricane

   e. Whoever finds it in his or her best interest

   f. Who you are often depends on who you know

   g. Because of him

   h. Because she refused to concede her position

   i. Approved for release, the prisoner spent the last night in prison distributing presents

2. *Together and Solo.* This Exploration provides you with an opportunity to practice writing dependent clauses. Choose words from the lists of nouns and verbs below. Feel free to add your own. Write serious clauses or humorous ones.

Nouns	**Verbs**
dust	wind (wound)
man	dive (dove)
courage	take (taken)
child	watch
bus	swirl
coin	go (gone)
coffee	reach
freedom	forgive (forgiven)
watch	clear
wind	excuse

   a. Referring to the list of connecting adverbs on page 425, write five dependent clauses.

    b. Referring to the list of connecting adjectives on page 427, write five dependent clauses.

    c. Referring to the list of connecting pronouns on page 429, write five independent clauses.

3. *Together and Solo.* Identify the following sentences as simple, compound, complex, or compound-complex, and offer reasons for your choices. Start by circling connectors.

    a. I went to the store, I bought what I wanted, and I'm glad I did.

    b. The kimono was worn in festivals to show the quiet elegance of pattern and fabric.

    c. Everyone knows that there is more to magic than meets the eye, but sometimes even professional magicians have a hard time seeing beneath the surface.

    d. Comparing Mount Olympus and Valhalla, the anthropologist showed how much different cultures have in common.

    e. When we created the Stallion, we weren't content to make a different car.

4. *Together and Solo.* Combining the clauses you wrote in Exploration 2, write five compound and five complex sentences.

5. *Solo and Together.* To identify your style, review one or more of your own papers using the following strategies:

    a. Identify which groups of words are prepositional phrases, verb phrases, adverbial clauses, adjectival clauses, and noun clauses. Circle the word or words that lead you to identify the groups of words as you do.

    b. Mark your sentences as simple *(S)*, compound *(C)*, complex *(X)*, or compound-complex *(CX)*. Count the sentences. Notice which kinds of sentences you tend to favor.

    c. Discuss which patterns you tend to use. Are there any patterns that you don't use? Do your sentences tend to be too long or too short? How could you introduce more variety and meaning into your writing?

    d. Revise your paper so that you have a greater range of phrases, clauses, and kinds and lengths of sentences.

    e. Discuss how your meaning changes with these revisions.

Parallel Construction (‖)

In order to show your reader that you consider certain ideas to be equally important, organize them into similar or *parallel* grammatical structures. If, for example, one of your ideas is expressed in a prepositional phrase, and all the other ideas you have to express are equally important, express all the ideas in prepositional phrases. Notice what happens in the following two sentences:

> George went to the dry cleaner, the drugstore, and the bakery.
>
> George went to the dry cleaner and to the drugstore, and then he went to the bakery.

In the first sentence, because all George's stops are expressed using an article-noun structure ("the _____"), the bakery is no more or less important than any other stop George made. In the second sentence, the bakery is clearly a reward for having done his errands. All the other stops take a preposition-article-noun structure, but the bakery deserves a whole independent clause.

Using parallel structures also provides you and your reader with a sense of order and *balance*. Notice how parallel structures are used in the following well-known expressions:

Parallel constructions	Nonparallel constructions
To be or not to be: that is the question.	To be or having lost your existence: to have that question.
I came; I saw; I conquered.	I came; there were things to see; victory was soon mine.
All's well that ends well.	If something ends well, all went well.
A penny saved is a penny earned.	A penny saved is someone earning money.
A time to love, a time to hate; a time of war, and a time of peace.	A time to love, having been hated; to have time for war; you should want peace sometimes.

*E*xplorations

1. *Together and Solo.* Compare each nonparallel expression above to its original. To help you identify structures, circle words, punctuation, parts of speech, and phrase and clause structures that repeat. How are the meanings of the nonparallel expressions different? Which of each of the two expressions is more memorable? Why?

2. *Together and Solo.* Read the following expressions. What parallel structures are being used? To help you identify structures, circle

words, punctuation, parts of speech, and phrase and clause structures that repeat.

    a. What did you do? Why did you do it? What will you do next?

    b. Having exhausted the medical supplies, having lost all the equipment, having tried all possible procedures, the doctor finally quit.

    c. Fireworks, barbecue, clear sky, ice cream, and friends—what more could we ask for on the Fourth of July?

    d. When chickens read and pigs fly, I'll organize my files.

3. *Together and Solo.* Listening to song lyrics, and noticing what you read, collect examples of parallel structures.

4. *Together and Solo.* Review your own papers for parallel structures. Mark problems with parallel structure with the symbol ||. Revise them for greater balance.

PROBLEM SENTENCES

In academic and professional writing, most sentences must be complete and unified. Groups of words that are supposed to be sentences but don't meet these standards are called *fragments, run-ons,* or *comma splices.*

Fragments (frag)

Fragments are incomplete sentences. They usually come in the form of words, phrases, or dependent clauses punctuated with end marks—periods, question marks, or exclamation points—as if they were sentences. The following fragments are examples of phrases punctuated as sentences:

Prepositional phrases

In the garden.

During the operation?

Verb phrases

Spinning the wheel!

Dragged through the swamp.

Including these.

In some cases, transitional phrases signal fragments, as in these examples:

In some cases, dependent clauses.

For example, the money he stole.

Not to mention her lung capacity.

To be sure, ten dollars.

The following dependent clauses are examples of fragments. Their connecting words do not connect them to independent clauses.

Adverbial clauses

Because the experiment had not been properly designed?
Even though there were many arguments in favor of the defendant.

Adjectival clauses

Who had been inoculated against rubella.
Which was the first time the region had been explored!

Noun clauses

How you present yourself.
That the storm had passed over!

In some instances, single words can be correctly punctuated with end marks, as in the case of one-word answers to questions or a series of short questions. Strictly speaking, however, these words are not sentences:

Did they attempt to help the endangered seals? *No.*
Who was helping Carmen? *Mary? Kyomi? Jacob?*

A group of unpunctuated words can be long and still be a fragment. Even a long group of words can be missing an independent clause:

> *Whoever* explored the region for the first time and was confronted with the spectacle of the snow-capped mountains after the arduous climb in dangerous terrain.

How would you complete the sentence?

Fragments may make your readers work too hard to understand you. Readers may give up because they are confused, or they may actually misread your intent. Fragments can also give your work a choppy, unconnected quality that may undermine your purpose. Revising fragments will help you to clarify what you want to say and to establish a better relationship with your readers.

Identifying Fragments

The first step in revising fragments is to identify them. Use the following strategies to help you. Mark fragments with the word *frag.* If in the beginning you can't identify fragments in your own work, consult with others to help you to develop your skills.

Strategy 1. *Check short sentences.* Do they start with prepositions, participles, or connectors? Do they start with transitional phrases such as *for example* or *not to mention?* If so, go to strategy 3 or 4.

Strategy 2. *Read the paper aloud. Stop at every end mark*—period, question mark, or exclamation point. Exaggerate the stop. Notice if that breaks the connection between ideas. If so, go to strategy 3 or 4.

Strategy 3. *Circle prepositions, participles, and transitional phrases* that start "sentences." Are these groups of words fragments? Consult with others to establish whether you tend to start fragments with certain prepositions, participles, or transitional phrases. If you do, regularly monitor the "sentences" that start with such words. Circle the words. Go to strategy 5.

Strategy 4. *Circle dependent clause connectors.* Often, writers who write fragments tend to fall into a pattern of beginning fragments with dependent clause connectors such as *although* or *because* (connecting adverbs), *which* or *that* (connecting adjectives), or *whoever* or *that* (connecting pronouns). Notice whether you tend to write fragments that consist of dependent clauses starting with these words. If you do, read through your papers for fragments that start with these words. Circle the first word of these "sentences." Go to strategy 5.

Strategy 5. *Review "sentences" by marking subjects and verbs.* If a series of words does not have both a subject and a verb, it cannot be an independent clause.

Fragments

A fragment is a nonsentence word group punctuated as if it were a sentence. Fragments can take these forms:

Noun	Transitional phrase
Verb	Adverbial clause
Prepositional phrase	Adjectival clause
Verb phrase	Noun clause

Identifying Fragments

If you tend to write fragments, notice if there are particular words with which you tend to start them. These ideas can help you identify fragments:

1. Check short sentences.
2. Read the paper aloud. Stop at end marks.
3. Circle prepositions, participles, and transitional phrases.
4. Circle dependent clause connectors.
5. Review sentences by marking subjects and verbs.

Reflection

Together or Solo. Read through the following student paragraph. Using the strategies offered above, identify fragments.

> If only I could sleep. In the bedroom alone. I want to hide from the world. In and out of the kitchen. In and out of the bathroom. I'm wandering. Help! Agoraphobia. For example, when I have to go to the store. I can't do it. I live on deliveries and catalogs. Shop from the shopping channel. Safe. Since I have a computer and a phone. My job is making sales calls. But now I'm getting scared of making calls. Help!

Revising Fragments

Once you have identified a fragment, you can revise it using one of the following strategies.

Strategy 1. *Delete the fragment.* Sometimes a fragment is a remnant of an undeveloped thought or a typo. Delete any fragments that don't add to the quality or readability of your writing.

Strategy 2. *Give nouns verbs.* If your fragment is just a noun or noun clause without a verb, give it a verb. This subject has no verb:

Fragment: The best dog in the show

Here a verb combines with the subject to form a sentence:

Sentence: The best dog in the show was trained by a ten-year-old girl.

This noun clause has no verb:

Fragment: Whoever goes to the Fashion Institute of Technology

This can be revised into a sentence by adding a verb:

Sentence: Whoever goes to the Fashion Institute of Technology *must cope* with Manhattan's transportation system.

Or the noun clause can be added to a subject and a verb that needs an object:

Sentence: The transportation system serves whoever goes to the Fashion Institute of Technology.

Strategy 3.   *Give verbs and verbals subjects.* If your fragment is a verb or verbal without a subject, revise it by giving it a subject:

Fragment: Walked in the park
Sentence: Jeremy walked in the park.
Sentence: Walked in the park, the dog was happy.

Fragment: Including the garage fees
Sentence: Including the garage fees, the bill came to $300.

Strategy 4   *Connect phrases to sentences.* If your fragment is either a prepositional or verb phrase and the fragment is next to an independent clause, turn the end mark either preceding or following the phrase into a comma. Depending on which sentence it should be linked to, finish the sentence. In the following example, the strings of words starting with the participle *Accumulating* and the preposition *To* are fragments because they are only phrases. *The ice choked the region* is a sentence.

Fragments and Sentence: Accumulating for thousands of years. The ice choked the region. The dinosaurs flourished. To the south.

Full sentences can be formed from this example by attaching the phrases as follows:

Sentences: Accumulating for thousands of years, the ice choked the region. The dinosaurs flourished to the south.

Strategy 5.   *Delete connectors or participles.* Sometimes you can create an independent clause (a sentence) just by deleting a connector or participle. In the following example, the strings of words starting with the participle *Accumulating* and the connecting adverb *While* are fragments:

> *Fragments and Sentence:*   Accumulating for thousands of years. The ice choked the region. While the dinosaurs flourished to the south.

Full sentences can be formed by deleting the participle and connecting adverb. Note that the resulting prepositional phrase *For thousands of years* is added to the sentence *Ice choked the region.*

> *Sentence:*   For thousands of years, ice choked the region. Dinosaurs flourished to the south.

Strategy 6.   *Connect fragments to sentences.* If your fragment is a dependent clause, and if it is either preceded or followed by a complete sentence, you can connect the fragment to one of the sentences. Depending on the sense you want to make, turn the period *preceding* or *following* the dependent clause into a comma. Here are three sentences. The clause starting with *because* is a fragment; it contains only an adverbial clause.

> The colleges sponsored a tennis tournament. Because there were so many injuries. They hired a sports doctor to coach the players.

If you attach the fragment to the preceding sentence, it will read as follows:

> The colleges sponsored a tennis tournament because there were so many injuries. They hired a sports doctor to coach the players.

The first sentence now states that the colleges sponsored a tennis tournament because there were so many injuries. That's silly. Tournaments are not sponsored because of injuries. This is what happens if you attach the fragment to the sentence that follows it:

> The colleges sponsored a tennis tournament. Because there were so many injuries, they hired a sports doctor to coach the players.

The second sentence now states that a sports doctor was hired because there were so many injuries. This makes sense. Whenever you attach a fragment to a complete sentence, make sure it appropriately expresses your meaning and purpose.

*E*xplorations _____

1.   *Together and Solo.*

   a.   Read the following advertisements and texts from product labels that use words, phrases, and dependent clauses as if they were

> ### Options for Revising Fragments
>
> 1. Delete the fragment.
> 2. Give nouns verbs.
> 3. Give verbs and verbals subjects.
> 4. Connect phrases to sentences.
> 5. Delete connectors or participles.
> 6. Connect fragments to sentences.

sentences. Identify the fragments in each example. Circle prepositions, verbals, and connectors to focus your work. Turn the examples into complete sentences by deleting words, adding your own, or reorganizing. Use connecting adverbs, adjectives, or pronouns to add variety and meaning to your revisions. How do the meanings change? Would your revised versions satisfy the purpose of the advertisements? If so, with which audiences? If not, why not?

1) How gender plays a role in the roles we play. The season premiere of *Our World* shows how gender affects how we see ourselves. How others see us. How it shapes our human identity. How do gender roles evolve? Are they a privilege? Or a prison?

2) Alaska. Where the bald eagles soar above your head. Where whales dive and otters splash right before your eyes. Alaska. If not now, when?

3) Sun-dried grapes. Because anything less is a compromise.

4) A Viking masterpiece. Wrought of tempered steel. 24K gold. Sterling silver. Hand-set crystal handles.

5) Well tolerated by most highly allergic individuals. No tablet binders, coatings, or colorings. Daily dose: one tablet with each meal.

6) Financial aid available. If you are eligible.

7) Wherever. Whoever. Whenever. Lion's Limousines.

    b. Bring magazines to class and find advertisements that use words, phrases, or dependent clauses as if they were sentences. Revise the advertisements so that they are written in complete sentences.

2. *Together.*

    a. Sometimes the best way to break a habit is to overdo it: eating too much chocolate or smoking too much at once can make you sick of chocolate or smoking. If you tend to write fragments by using dependent clauses as if they were sentences, this Exploration will help you to become aware of this tendency and to break the habit. In small groups, write a very long sentence fragment using a series of dependent clauses started by adverbial connectors.

The goal is to write the longest sentence fragment without finishing it with an independent clause. An example of such a long fragment may sound like this:

> After the first frost encrusts the ground, when the ground starts to thaw, before the April rains fall, if you plan to grow leafy vegetables, as soon as you can, whenever it's a warm day . . .

Be sure to write dependent clauses and not just phrases. Recall that some words function as prepositions or connecting adverbs, depending on whether or not they are followed by a subject and verb.

    b.   Write these group fragments on the board and discuss whether they contain any independent clauses that finish the sentences. Write independent clauses that would turn the long fragments into sentences.

3. *Together or Solo.* Revise the paragraph filled with fragments on page 437. Strive to use as many of the strategies as you can. Use your imagination to add variety and interest to the resulting sentences.

4. *Solo and Together.* Identify fragments in your own papers and mark them *frag*. Revise them into complete sentences. Discuss how the meaning of your paper changes and clarifies with these revisions.

Run-ons

Technically, run-on sentences are two or more independent clauses that have been punctuated as if they were all one sentence. No connectors or punctuation marks are used to distinguish clause from clause. Some sentences, although they seem to run on and on—using a string of connectors—are *psychological* run-ons. The following sentence is a psychological and not a technical run-on:

> Because Harry was so determined to stuff and bake the turkey himself, Tania, who has always wanted him to follow his passion for cooking, promised to do all the shopping and cleanup to give Harry the support he needed during a busy season at his job, when otherwise he would have been too pressed to do all the usual shopping himself.

Because run-ons make it difficult to know where one sentence ends and another begins, they can confuse the reader. Read the following run-on sentence:

> John loves to run some other runners don't.

On first reading the sentence, you might read that John is running runners, the way a boss can run workers. By the time you read through the line, you realize that there are two separate thoughts. So you have to reread from the beginning of the line. Readers soon tire of having to reread and organize your words for themselves. Furthermore, run-on sentences make your writing seem cluttered and rushed. Readers will not want to spend any more time on your work than you do. But *just because a sentence is long doesn't mean that it is technically or even psychologically a run-on.* This long sentence is not a run-on:

> The research lab at the top of the hill is so hard to see from the bottom because it is behind the hill, which is thick with trees and shrubbery.

However, *even a short sentence can be a run-on,* as in this example:

> Run don't walk.

Punctuate the sentence so that it won't read as a run-on.

Comma Splices (CS)

A special form of run-on is the comma splice. Comma splices are two or more independent clauses that have been punctuated as one sentence with only commas between them. The word *splice* is used as in the splicing together of tape or film. Here is an example of a comma splice:

> Maya Angelou has written several volumes of poetry, *Just Give Me a Cold Drink of Water 'Fore I Diiie* was the first and appeared in 1971.

In this example, the comma should be a period, because "Maya Angelou has written several volumes of poetry" is an independent clause and so is the clause that follows it.

One of the most common patterns of comma splices occurs in sentences that begin with pronouns, as in the following examples:

> Teenage pregnancy is a growing epidemic, it concerns me a lot. My parents worked hard to raise us, they never even complained.

These comma splices are to be distinguished from pronouns that follow a dependent clause, as in these correctly punctuated sentences:

> Because teenage pregnancy is a growing epidemic, it concerns me a lot. Although my parents worked hard to raise us, they never even complained.

Identifying Run-ons and Comma Splices

Consulting with others will help you to develop and sharpen your ability to identify run-ons and comma splices. Use the following strategies to help you.

Strategy 1. *Read the paper aloud. Do not stop for a breath unless there is an end mark*—period, question mark, or exclamation point. If you tend to write run-ons, have someone read your papers to you. Sometimes this will be enough to help you identify run-ons. Then go to strategy 3 below for identifying run-ons.

Strategy 2. *Circle pronouns.* A common way to create a run-on comma splice is to use a series of pronouns, as in the following example:

> *He* was not an unhappy child, *he* was content to care for his younger brothers, *he* cooked and mended their clothing, *he* created bedtime stories.

If you tend to link clauses that start with pronouns without using a sentence connector—*and, but, for, nor, or, so, yet*—between at least the last two of the clauses, circle the pronouns that are subjects in your paper. Write the symbol *CS* above commas that splice independent clauses together.

Strategy 3. *Mark subjects and verbs.* Mark the subjects, verbs, and connectors. Determine which parts of sentences are dependent and independent clauses. Then, mark any sentences that run independent clauses together as if they were only one sentence. Mark them with the symbol *RO.*

Strategy 4. *Circle commas.* Read each segment that is marked off between commas or a comma and an end mark. If the segment is an independent clause, if it is not connected to other sentences by a sentence connector, and if there are no dependent phrases or clauses attached to it, you have a comma splice. Analyze the example in strategy 2, using this system.

Strategy 5. *Distinguish technical from psychological run-ons.* Striving for variety and complexity in your sentence structure can help you to develop your mind and earn your readers' respect. Don't artificially

---

Identifying Run-ons and Comma Splices

1. Read the paper aloud. Do not stop for a breath unless there is an end mark.
2. Circle pronouns.
3. Mark subjects and verbs.
4. Circle commas.
5. Distinguish technical from psychological run-ons.

---

shorten or break up psychological run-ons unless they are also technical run-ons, or confusing or boring to readers.

Reflection

Together or Solo.   Using the strategies offered above, identify run-ons and comma splices in the following student paper. Distinguish psychological from technical run-ons.

> I am writing about my fiancée, she is the youngest in her family, she always had people there for her, doing things for her, like making decisions for her, solving all her problems, and that was because they would always think she wasn't able to make her own decisions or solve her own problems. Her parents were very loving and caring, she was always protected by them, in reality she was never alone.
>
> When my fiancée turned 15 years old, her mother passed away, she died of cancer, it was very painful for my fiancée. After that happened she moved in with her sister, and continued attending school. As the years passed by, she would talk to her family about getting her own apartment, a new car, finishing college, and getting her life going on her own, but she was surrounded by criticism, family members would always tell her, you can't manage on your own, its too hard and you'll never make it, because you were never alone, there was always someone there for you, helping you out. Then they would tell her, it would be a waste of time for her to even try, because she would just end up back home. So that in turn made her stop and think about everything, it made her afraid of going out and getting what she really wanted in life, which was being an independent person, and having things of her own.

Revising Run-ons and Comma Splices

How you revise a run-on will depend, as it does for revising fragments, on your meaning and emphasis. Choose from the following four revising strategies.

Strategy 1. *Add end marks.* Place a period, question mark, or exclamation point (depending on the purpose of the sentence) at the ends of your independent clauses. The following sentence is a run-on. Place a period where you believe one of the sentences ends.

> The Pilgrims and Puritans fled to New England to escape religious persecution some of them persecuted those who didn't share their beliefs.

Strategy 2. *Add sentence connectors.* Place a sentence connector—*and, but, for, nor, or, so, yet*—between independent clauses. The run-on above can be revised as follows:

> The Pilgrims and Puritans of New England sought to escape religious persecution, *but* some of them persecuted those who didn't share their beliefs.

The comma has been added to separate the two long sentences, helping the reader distinguish the two ideas. The sentence connector *but* not only removes the run-on, but it also creates a much stronger statement. The word *but* provides a transition and meaningful link between the two sentences, showing an ironic contradiction in the behavior of some of the Pilgrims and Puritans. The word *but* shows that the writer objects to the behavior of the Pilgrims and Puritans who persecuted others.

Sentence connectors can be used with a series of parallel sentences, as well. One way to revise the comma splice from above is as follows:

> He was not an unhappy child, he was content to care for his younger brothers, he cooked and mended their clothing, *and* he created bedtime stories.

The sentence connector *and* is placed between the last two sentences. The preceding commas function like the word *and* when the connector is thus added.

Strategy 3. *Place a semicolon between two independent clauses.* The word following the semicolon is not capitalized unless it is a proper noun. The run-on above can be adjusted as follows:

The Pilgrims and Puritans of New England sought to escape religious persecution; some of them persecuted those who didn't share their beliefs.

The semicolon separates the two independent clauses while showing that the two ideas are closely related. This version does not imply the judgment made when the word *but* linked the two clauses.

Strategy 4. *Create afterthoughts.* Create a transition between independent clauses by placing a semicolon after an independent clause, followed by an afterthought word and comma. (Refer to the sidebar of afterthought words on page 424.) The run-on above can be revised as follows:

The Pilgrims and Puritans of New England sought to escape religious persecution; however, some of them persecuted those who didn't share their beliefs.

The semicolon divides the two sentences while showing that the ideas are linked. The word *however* emphasizes and clarifies the nature of the connection being made between the ideas. The comma following *however* causes the reader to pause briefly and thus notice the emphasis even more. Notice that this version also implies a judgment about the Pilgrims and Puritans.

Strategy 5. *Introduce a connecting adverb, adjective, or pronoun* to make one clause depend on the other. If necessary, change the order of clauses. Reword portions of the sentences. In some cases, use commas to mark off clauses. Notice how the meaning changes when a connector is introduced and clauses are reordered:

Connecting adverb

Although the Pilgrims and Puritans fled to New England to escape religious persecution, some of them persecuted those who didn't share their beliefs.

Connecting adjective

Some of the Pilgrims and Puritans *who* fled to New England to escape religious persecution in turn persecuted those who didn't share their beliefs.

Connecting pronoun

Some of the Pilgrims and Puritans fled to New England to escape religious persecution only to persecute *whoever* didn't share their beliefs.

Options for Revising Run-ons and Comma Splices

1. Add end marks.

   _____ ? _____ .

2. Add sentence connectors.

   _____ , (connector) _____ .

3. Place a semicolon between two independent clauses.

   _____ ; _____ .

4. Create afterthoughts preceded by a semicolon and followed by a comma.

   _____ ; (afterthought), _____ .

5. Introduce a connecting adverb, adjective, or pronoun.

   (Connector) _____ , _____ .

   _____ (connector) _____ .

   _____ (connector) _____ _____ .

*E*xplorations

1. *Together and Solo.* Using the five strategies offered above, revise the following run-on comma splice in five different ways. Discuss how the meanings of these five versions change and vary.

   > He was not an unhappy child he was content to care for his younger brothers he cooked and mended their clothing, he created bedtime stories.

2. *Together and Solo.* Read and identify which of the following sentences are run-ons or comma splices. Mark them *RO* or *CS*. Revise run-ons and comma splices in at least three ways. How do the meanings change?

   a. While Mark didn't agree with the verdict, he respected the legal procedures that led to it.

   b. Julius Caesar crossed the Rubicon, he said there was no turning back.

   c. O'Keefe painted skulls and other bones suspended in the sky most people find her work to be haunting.

    d. Music relaxes the mind, soul, and body tempo is the most important factor in its effect.

    e. I'm not going to let my coach down since she has been there to help, I'm going to try my best, because I want to show her that her help matters, and that's what I'm most concerned about now.

3. *Together or Solo.* Revise the paragraph filled with run-ons and comma splices on page 444. Strive to use as many of the revising strategies as you can. Use your imagination to add variety and interest to your resulting sentences.

4. *Together and Solo.* Identify run-ons and comma splices in your own and others' papers. Mark them with the appropriate symbols, *RO* or *CS.* In small groups or solo, revise these papers so that the sentences are effectively separated. Use a variety of strategies to break up run-ons. Discuss why you chose to revise as you did and how the revisions changed and clarified meaning.

Misplaced Modifiers (mod)

Modifiers are words and groups of words that modify or change the meaning of what you write. The simplest modifiers are adjectives, adverbs, and prepositional phrases. More complex modifiers are verb phrases and dependent clauses. When using a modifier, you should place the modifier as close as possible to what it is modifying, so that you will avoid confusing your reader. Also, if you misplace a modifier, you may find yourself unintentionally saying something humorous. For example, read the following sentence, which has a misplaced adjectival clause:

> The child was put to bed by his father who was crying and fretting with fatigue.

Of course, a father can be reduced to tears from fatigue. But the sentence above sounds humorous. The author most likely meant to say the child was crying and fretting from fatigue. Because the word *who* is closer to *father, who* sounds as if it were modifying *father* and not *the child.*

    Be especially careful with verb phrases. The first subject that follows the verb phrase is what the verb phrase is modifying, as it does in the following sentence:

> Wrapping the broken vase in cloth, *Leslie* found the missing piece inside.

If the sentence had been written as follows, it would be illogical:

Wrapping the broken vase in cloth, the missing piece appeared inside.

What this sentence implies, since *missing piece* is the first thing that follows the phrase *wrapping the broken vase,* is that the missing piece, itself, was wrapping the broken vase. That, of course, is absurd.

Similarly, the sentence would be confusing if the verb phrase followed the independent clause, "Leslie found the missing piece inside."

Leslie found the missing piece inside, wrapping the broken vase.

This implies that the missing piece, again, is wrapping the broken vase. Putting the verb phrase right next to Leslie would be more appropriate:

Leslie, wrapping the broken vase, found the missing piece inside.

This sentence clearly states that Leslie, and not the missing piece, is wrapping the broken vase, because *wrapping* is right next to *Leslie.*

Explorations

1. *Together and Solo.* Read the following sentences and identify modifying clauses and phrases. Discuss what the sentences imply. If a sentence is confusing or unintentionally humorous, revise it. In some cases, you can do this by moving the modifiers so that they are closer (or as close as possible) to what they modify.

   a. The swimming pool is very near our house, which is pleasant in hot weather.

   b. Running the risk of losing their jobs, the toys were being made on the factory premises by the workers for homeless children.

   c. Many people enjoy skiing having lived in Colorado.

   d. Proven to be effective, the town adopted the new water filtration system.

   e. The deer was injured by a car which jumped over the pasture fence.

   f. The coach lost the sixty pounds which improved his health tremendously.

   g. Same Day Laundry will not tear your clothes in machines, which we do carefully by hand.

2. *Together and Solo.* Review your own papers for problems with misplaced modifiers. Mark these problems *mod* and revise for clarity.

AGREEMENT

Subjects and verbs must agree in number (both are singular, or both are plural). Pronouns must agree in number and person (first, second, or third) with the people, places, or things to which they refer. As you will see, problems with agreement can confuse and turn away your readers. In this section, you will have an opportunity to review and refine your skills with subject-verb and pronoun agreement so that you can fulfill your purpose and engage your audience.

Subject-Verb Agreement (S-V)

Singular subjects take verbs with singular endings, and plural subjects take verbs with plural endings. Create subject-verb agreement with verbs in the present tense and subjects that don't end with -s in the singular, by adding an -s or -es to *either* the subject or the verb *but not both*. For example, notice where the -s's are in the following sentences:

The dog walks.   (singular subject and verb)

The dogs walk.   (plural subject and verb)

Notice that irregular verbs follow this pattern as well:

The book is lost.   (singular subject and verb)

The books are lost. (plural subject and verb)

The horse has won.   (singular subject and verb)

The horses have won. (plural subject and verb)

The tower does not stand anymore.   (singular subject and verb)

The towers do not stand anymore.   (plural subject and verb)

The singular subject *dog* does *not* end with an added -s; therefore, the verb ends with an added -s. The plural subject *dogs* ends in an added -s; therefore, the verb does *not* end with an added -s. The same holds true for subjects and verbs that normally end with -s in their basic form, as for example the nouns *class* and *harness* or the verbs *pass* and *press*. The only difference is that -es is added to one or the other. Notice where the -s's or -es's are added in the following sentences to maintain subject-verb agreement:

The class pass**es**. (singular subject and verb)

The class**es** pass. (plural subject and verb)

The class walk**s**. (singular subject and verb)

The dog pass**es**. (singular subject and verb)

Some plural words are not formed by adding *-s* or *-es*. They include these:

Singular	Plural
child	children
curriculum	curricula
datum	data
deer	deer
foot	feet
goose	geese
she, he, it	they
louse	lice
moose	moose
mouse	mice
person	people
woman	women

Treat them as you would other plural words. Do not add the *-s* or *-es* to their verbs:

The children walk to school.

The five deer pass along the highway.

The people do not accept the new government.

Most plural subjects are created either by adding *-s* or *-es* to the singular form. Another way to form plural subjects is to join subjects with *and*. *An apple and a pear* is a plural subject and would take a plural verb (without an *-s* or *-es*) such as *make* in the sentence *An apple and a pear make a healthy lunch.*

Some subjects *seem* to be plural but are treated as singular, especially in academic and professional writing. These are *collective* nouns; pronouns formed with *any, every, no,* and *some;* and constructions using *each, either,* and *neither.* The rest of this section details how to identify and create subject-verb agreement with these singular subjects.

Collective Nouns.   Some nouns apply to more than one thing but take a singular verb (with an *-s* or *-es*). These are called *collective nouns.* Collective nouns refer to groups of things and are considered to be singular units. The following nouns are examples of subjects that would take a singular verb:

class	family	school
college	flock	society
committee	government	team
community	group	tribe
company	herd	world
faculty	jury	

Here are examples of how to match such collective nouns with singular verbs in the present tense. *Don't be distracted by phrases with plural objects that precede the verb:*

The committee of doctors meets every week.

The team of players *is* going to win every game it plays.

The society makes its own rules.

Any, Every, No, and Some.   Some pronouns sound as if they should be treated as plural constructions but are treated as singular constructions in academic and professional writing. These pronouns are created by combining a word from the left column below with a word from the middle column.

				anybody
				anyone
any				everybody
every	+	body	=	everyone
no		one		nobody
some				no one
				somebody
				someone

All these words, from *anybody* to *someone,* take a singular verb (with an added *-s* or *-es*). An easy way to remember that words such as *everybody* take a singular verb is to notice that *body* and *one* are singular. Here are examples of how to match singular verbs in the present tense with these constructions. *Don't be distracted by phrases or clauses with plural objects that precede the verb:*

> Every**one** in the groups *is* working well with others.
>
> Any**body** who knows those dances go*es* to that club.

Each, Either, and Neither.   *Each, either,* and *neither* are used with singular verbs (with an added *-s* or *-es*). Here are examples of how to match singular verbs in the present tense with these words. *Don't be distracted by phrases with plural objects that precede the verb:*

> **Either** of the newspapers give*s* a forecast.
>
> **Each** person writing the television scripts *is* a professional.

To Be, To Have, and To Do.   Be especially aware of subject-verb agreement when you use forms of the verbs *to be, to have,* and *to do.* These verbs are the most basic verbs in the English language and are used in all forms of writing by all communities. As Chapter 11 shows, language variations mark out different communities. Because forms of *to be, to have,* and *to do* are so widely used, you have to be especially flexible in adjusting your use of them as you move from one cultural setting to another. Notice that the verbs for third person singular all end in *-s: is, has, does.* Refer to the following sidebars when you are revising your work for subject-verb agreement.

Present Tense of *To Be* (Present Participle: *Being***)

	Singular		**Plural**	
	Subject	*Verb*	*Subject*	*Verb*
1st person:	I	am**	We	are
2d person:	You	are	You	are
3d person:	He, she, it, or singular noun	is	They or plural noun	are

*Normally, *be* is not used as a singular or plural verb in academic and professional writing. However, *being* is often used as a present participle.

**Normally, *am* is only used with *I* as in *I am* in academic and professional writing.

Present Tense of *To Have* (Present Participle: *Having*)

	Singular		Plural	
	Subject	*Verb*	*Subject*	*Verb*
1st person:	I	have	We	have
2d person:	You	have	You	have
3d person:	He, she, it, or singular noun	has	They or plural noun	have

Present Tense of *To Do* (Present Participle: *Doing*)

	Singular		Plural	
	Subject	*Verb*	*Subject*	*Verb*
1st person:	I	do	We	do
2d person:	You	do	You	do
3d person:	He, she, it, or singular noun	does	They or plural noun	do

*E*xplorations

1. *Together and Solo.* Circle the subjects and verbs in the following sentences, and discuss whether the subjects and verbs agree in number, according to academic and professional standards:

   a. The committee need funds in order to study the fiscal crisis.

   b. Every person has to account for his or her own output.

   c. An apple and a pear keeps the doctor away.

   d. He want to apply to dental school within the next three years.

   e. The very idea that electricity can cause cancers seem ridiculous to some people.

   f. Neither of the teams want to lose.

2. *Together and Solo.*

    a. Using the list of collective nouns, write a variety of sentences in which the subjects are collective nouns and the verbs are in the present tense.

    b. Using the list of words formed with *any, every, no,* and *some,* write a variety of sentences in which the subjects come from the list and the verbs are in the present tense.

    c. Using the words *each, either,* or *neither* as subjects, write a variety of sentences in which the verbs agree in number with the subjects.

    d. Write a variety of sentences in which you use the present tense singular forms of *to be, to have,* or *to do.* For a challenge, use subjects recommended in Explorations 2a through 2c.

3. *Together and Solo.* Identify the subjects and verbs of sentences in one of your papers. Discuss whether the subjects and verbs agree. If they don't, mark them *S-V.* Revise any sentences in which the subjects and verbs don't agree.

Verb Tense Consistency (V-C)

Study the timelines offered in the sidebar, which show you how different verb tenses are formed to indicate when something occurred. The first timeline shows the basic tenses. The second timeline shows how to form verb tenses that indicate activities or conditions in progress. A regular verb, *cook,* and an irregular verb, *ring,* are used as illustrations. Notice that all but the present and past tenses are formed by use of participles. The timeline for basic tenses uses the *past participle.* The timeline for actions in progress uses the *present participle.* (Refer to pages 418–419 for a discussion of how to form participles. The sidebar on pages 420–421 shows some irregular verbs.)

Provide your reader with a clear sense of when things happen. Unless you are very clear in your transitions, do not shift from one verb tense to another within or between sentences and paragraphs. Notice how confusing the following sentence is:

> I walk through the door and talked to the coach who will be standing by the equipment.

The sentence starts in the present tense with the verb *walk,* quickly shifts to the past tense with the verb *talked,* and then shifts to the future with *will be standing.* It would be much clearer if the verbs agreed in tense

Verb Forms

Present Tense	Past Tense	Present Participle	Past Participle
cook	cooked	cooking	cooked
ring	rang	ringing	rung

Basic Tenses

Past Perfect	Perfect	Past	Present	Future	Future Perfect
(Earliest event; before other past events)	(Done up until now)	(Done)	(Now)	(To come)	(To be completed)
had cooked	has (have) cooked	cooked	cook	will cook	will have cooked
had rung	has (have) rung	rang	ring	will ring	will have rung

Progressive Tenses (continuous actions or conditions)

Past Perfect	Perfect	Past	Present	Future	Future Perfect
had been cooking	has (have) been cooking	was (were) cooking	is (are) cooking	will be cooking	will have been cooking
had been ringing	has (have) been ringing	was (were) ringing	is (are) ringing	will be ringing	will have been ringing

so that all were in the present tense or all were either in the past or future. Read the following examples, which are consistent in tense:

Present tense

I *walk* through the door and *talk* to the coach who *is standing* by the equipment.

Past tense

I *walked* through the door and *talked* to the coach who *was standing* by the equipment.

Future

I *will walk* through the door and *will talk* to the coach who *will be standing* by the equipment.

Explorations

1. *Together or Solo.* Turn back to Ben Burton's essay on pages 135–137. Notice that it is written in the present tense. Revise all the verbs into the past tense. How does this change the tone and meaning of the essay? Which version do you prefer and why?

2. *Solo.* Write a paragraph, entirely in the present tense, describing how you arrived at a given destination today. This paragraph will give your readers the feeling that they are moving through the day with you.

3. *Solo.* Write a paragraph, entirely in the past tense, describing the most memorable occasion you experienced last year.

4. *Together.* Discuss the paragraphs you wrote in Explorations 2 and 3. Focus on whether you were consistent in your use of verb tenses.

5. *Together and Solo.* Review your papers in process for consistency in verb tense. Circle all your verbs, and look for any shifts that could confuse your audience. Mark distracting shifts *V-C*. Revise your work for verb tense consistency.

Pronoun Agreement (pro)

A pronoun holds the place of a noun and refers to it. Sometimes it is not clear to whom or what a pronoun refers, especially in written English. The added challenge is to make sure that number, gender, and case agree as well. In this section, you have opportunities to explore and practice pronoun agreement for reference, number, gender, and case.

Pronouns and Reference

The *reference* of a pronoun is the noun that comes before the pronoun to which the pronoun refers. In the following sentence, *environmentalists* is the reference of the pronoun *they*.

> Environmentalists may ask us to do more work than we are used to, but they are our guides for preserving the planet.

Sometimes it is not clear what the reference of a pronoun is. For example, in the following sentence, *her* can apply to more than one person:

> Marilyn told Janet that her promotion was approved.

The pronoun *her* can refer to Marilyn, or Janet, or even another person. Sometimes the context will resolve the confusion. Often it will not. The example above could be clarified by revision. In this case, Janet was promoted:

> Hearing that Janet's promotion was approved, Marilyn called to tell her the good news.

In this case, Marilyn was promoted:

> Relieved that the committee had approved her for promotion, Marilyn felt free to tell her friend, Janet.

Pronouns, Number, and Case

Pronouns must agree in number with the person, place, or thing to which they refer. Pronouns must also be in the proper case—subjective, objective, possessive, or reflexive—depending on the role they play in the sentence. Refer to the sidebar on pronoun case as you consider these issues.

If a construction is singular—a singular noun; a collective noun; forms of *any, every, no, some, either, neither,* and *each*—any pronoun that refers to that construction must be singular too. (Refer to pages 450–453 for a review of singular constructions.) Notice that the pronouns in the following sentences are all singular because they are referring to singular constructions. Notice, as well, that they are subjective, objective, possessive, or reflexive, depending on what role they play in the sentence.

Unless *John* excels on the entrance exam, *he* will not be able to enter the college of *his* choice.

The *faculty, itself,* decided to waive *its* salary increase so that no one would be fired.

Nobody wants to make up *his* or *her* mind on the issue.

Each woman chose *her* own speciality in the engineering class.

Neither of the doctors told us how *she* or *he* wanted to proceed with the treatment.

Someone on the men's swimming team had neglected to practice *his* backstroke.

Pronouns that refer to plural nouns must be plural, as well:

The *members* of the faculty decided to waive *their* salary increases so that no one would be fired.

The *women* chose *their* own specialties in the engineering class.

The *doctors* told us how *they* wanted to proceed with the treatment.

Pronouns and Consistency (P-C)

Provide your reader with a clear sense of who or what you are talking about by being consistent with your use of pronouns. Do not shift back

The Four Cases of Pronouns

	Subjective		Objective		Possessive		Reflexive	
	Singular	*Plural*	*Singular*	*Plural*	*Singular*	*Plural*	*Singular*	*Plural*
1st	I	We	Me	Us	My/Mine	Our/Ours	Myself	Ourselves
2d	You	You	You	You	Your(s)	Your(s)	Yourself	Yourselves
3d	He	They	Him	Them	His	Their(s)	Himself*	Themselves*
	She	They	Her	Them	Her/Hers	Their(s)	Herself	Themselves
	It	They	It	Them	Its	Their(s)	Itself	Themselves
	One	Ones	One	Ones	One's**	—	Oneself	—
	This	These	This	These***	—	—	—	—
	That	Those	That	Those***	—	—	—	—

*Normally, *hisself* and *theirselves* are not used in academic and professional writing.

**Notice that *one's* is the only possessive pronoun formed by an apostrophe and *-s*.

***Note that *this* and *that* are singular pronouns and *these* and *those* are plural. When used as adjectives, they must agree in number with nouns and verbs.

and forth from first person (*I*) to second person (*you*) or third person (*he, she, one,* or *it*). Notice how confusing the following sentence is:

> If *one* considers the amount of time it takes to grow a tree, *you* feel a sense of responsibility toward the use of paper.

The sentence starts with the general pronoun *one* and then shifts to *you.* Your reader would expect *one* again, and so *you* is jarring (especially since *you* could be addressing the reader).

A more subtly confusing shift in pronouns occurs when you use the second person *(you)* when you are really talking about yourself. This is a habit that some people have when talking in person. The character Radar in the television program "M*A*S*H" had a tendency to use the word *you* in this way:

> You feel bad when your mother is having trouble on the farm and you're thousands of miles away and you can't do anything about it.

Radar, himself, was the one whose mother was having trouble. He, himself, was feeling frustrated.

In writing, be direct. Use *I* if you are speaking for yourself. For example, I could say, "You would hope that this example is clear" when actually it is more accurate to say, "I hope that this example is clear." Also, if you use *you* in your writing, be sure that you are addressing your reader directly. Do not use the second person *you* form when it would be more accurate to use the third person.

Pronouns and Sexism (P-Sx)

Language embodies gender differences. English retains remnants of old sexist beliefs. Starting with the end of the nineteenth century, we have made strides in establishing equal rights for both sexes. But there is more to do. In writing, you can avoid sexism by paying close attention not only to what you write but also to how you use pronouns that refer to gender. Here are several strategies.

Strategy 1. *Refer to both sexes.* You may have noticed that in some examples in this book *he or she, his or her,* and *him or her* are used. In the past, only the masculine form of the pronoun was used to refer to both men and women when words such as *somebody* or *each* were being used. You may also have noticed that this book does not comply with the customary order of always referring to the male gender first. Always putting the male gender first in such expressions is sexist. Create a balance by sometimes reversing the order. Use *she and he, her and his, her or him* as well. Of course, if everyone being referred to is female, use the feminine pronouns. Likewise, if everyone being referred to is male, use the masculine pronouns. If you find that your writing is overburdened with constructions such as *he or she,* use one of the following strategies.

Strategy 2. *Use plural forms, instead.* If you are referring to people in general, use the plural form. Instead of writing "A teacher is frequently asked for his or her ideas," write "Teachers are frequently asked for their ideas."

Strategy 3. *Switch from focus on persons to focus on ideas, activities, states of being, or things.* Instead of writing "A teacher is frequently asked for her or his ideas," write "A teacher's ideas are frequently sought." In the second version, the subject of the sentence is not *teacher* but *ideas.*

Explorations

1. *Together and Solo.* Circle the pronouns in the sentences below and draw an arrow to their references. Discuss the following for each sentence:

    *   Do the pronouns agree in number with their references?
    *   Are the pronouns consistent?
    *   Do the pronouns agree in number?
    *   Are the pronouns in the correct case?
    *   Are the pronouns free of sexism?

    a. When Brenda was in New York visiting her sister, she took her to the theater quite often.

    b. When you take first-year English, they have to be prepared to learn how to write term papers.

    c. Everybody got their coats and left.

    d. Each of the men brought his proposal to the meeting.

    e. Because the Hungarians were so charming and hospitable, my friend and I enjoyed visiting it.

2. *Solo and Together.*

    a. Listen for examples of people using *you* when they mean to speak about people in general, or when they are indirectly speaking for themselves. Record as much as you can of what they say. Share these in class.

    b. Identify instances in your writing in which you use *you* not to address the reader but to speak in general or for yourself. Revise the papers to comply with standards of academic and professional writing.

3. *Together and Solo.* Revise the following sentences to remove any sexism. However, be careful not to remove appropriate gender distinctions. Make sure your pronouns agree in number and person and that the references are clear.

    a. When a doctor treats a patient, he must respect his right to refuse certain treatments.

    b. If a parent has to stay home with a sick child, she must have the opportunity to make up the time at work.

    c. A person who breastfeeds knows the satisfaction of giving his or her baby the best start in life.

    d. The average person knows more about what celebrities think than his locally elected officials.

    e. The president of the United States must be aware of his or her responsibilities as commander in chief.

4. *Together and Solo.* Following the instructions in Explorations 1 to 3, discuss your own work. Circle your pronouns. Mark problems with *pro*, *P-C*, or *P-Sx*. Revise your papers for pronoun agreement, reference, consistency, and nonsexist language.

GRAMMAR REVIEW

Read the following "Blooper Rules of Grammar" that ask you to do what they don't do themselves. Revise the rules so that—although they will be less funny—they won't contradict themselves.

1. Each verb agree with its subject.
2. A pronoun agrees with their antecedent.
3. Don't never use no double negatives.
4. Everyone should use standard grammatical structures in their papers.
5. Using parallel structure, or not to use it, is your decision.
6. A fragment.
7. Comma splices are run-ons, run-ons are not always comma splices.
8. Having an important effect on meaning, you should always place the subject right after the verb phrase.
9. One must not shift your point of view.
10. When you write about a professional, do not be sexist in your treatment of him.
11. Run-on sentences ask your reader to absorb too much at once you should avoid using them besides they are hard to end.
12. The order of your words should your language community reflect.
13. Be consistent in how you used verb tenses within a sentence.

*C*hapter Review _____

Solo or *Together* respond to one or more of the following:

1. Which parts of this chapter did you most appreciate, and why?

2. If you were an instructor of writing, which points would *you* stress from this chapter? Why?

3. Record questions that arose for you as you were working with this chapter, and discuss these in small groups or as a class.

4. How do you plan to change as a writer as a result of working with the grammar section of the Handbook?

5. Which parts of this chapter do you anticipate rereading?

Chapter 16

Punctuation

This chapter offers opportunities to

—Develop perspective on how **punctuation** works

—Recognize **myths about punctuation**

—Learn the **purposes** of different punctuation marks

—Experiment with punctuation to alter **meaning**

—**Revise** your writing for your **purpose** and **audience**

No iron can pierce the heart with such force
as a period put at just the right place.

—*Isaak Babel, Short story writer*

Punctuation gives us the human voice, and
all the meanings that lie between the words.

—*Pico Iyer, Essayist*

How to Use This Chapter

You will find yourself focusing on different points of punctuation, depending on your needs and interests and on the guidance of your instructor. Don't expect yourself to learn punctuation *once and for all,* because you will learn and develop new insights into punctuation as long as you continue to read and write. Here are some possible ways to use this chapter:

1. Work through the chapter in the order in which it is written, choosing and doing Explorations as you go.
2. Refer to different parts of this chapter according to which punctuation element or mark you need to focus on.
3. Go straight to the Explorations; if you get stuck, read what precedes them.
4. Display a copy of the punctuation chart in the sidebar printed on page 466, for easy reference during the writing process.
5. Adopt a particular punctuation and focus on it until you are satisfied that you understand its basic uses. Collect examples of it in your readings, use it consciously in your writing, and focus on it when you consult with others during the writing process. When you are revising, notice whether that punctuation could be added or deleted to enhance your meaning.
6. Create a lesson on a particular punctuation mark. (Refer to Exploration 3 on page 496.)

Punctuation, Purpose, and Audience

When you talk with someone in person, you communicate with more than just your words. You communicate with the tone, the loudness or softness, the pace, and the rhythm of your voice, and you communicate with your pronunciation, facial expressions, and body gestures. All these nonverbal cues give your listener a greater sense of what you're saying than your words alone could. In writing, punctuation serves the same purpose as your voice, expressions, and gestures. For example, in his article "In Praise of the Humble Comma," Pico Iyer[30] remarks on the difference between these two expressions:

Jane (whom I adore)
Jane—whom I adore—

The parentheses in the first expression make the writer's adoration an afterthought, something that can be hidden. The dashes in the second expression highlight and emphasize the writer's feelings toward Jane. The meaning of an expression can change depending on the context, or situation in which it appears. If the expression "Jane (whom I adore)" appeared after the author had stated he adored Jane many times in what he was writing, putting "whom I adore" in parentheses (as an afterthought) might make sense. If the writer had already emphasized "Jane—whom I adore" before and kept on emphasizing it, the reader would start wonder-

Punctuation Chart

Name	Mark	Origin	Meaning	Gesture	Use	Example
apostrophe	'	"step up"	contract / possess	flick away / beckon	contraction / possession	it's / John's
comma	,	"to cut"	introduce / add	mark off	introduction / modifier / transition / comments / series	In the beginning, / John, the tallest one, / However, / Socialism, at least in theory, / a, b, c, and d
colon	:	—	point	to point	list / emphasis / summary	He saw the following: / He knew: this was it.
dash	—	"to rush"	emphasize	rush	interruption / list	Jane — whom I adore — / The numbers — 1, 2, 3 —
ellipsis	. . .	"fall short"	omit	cut		The first . . . the last.
exclamation point	!	"call out"	emphasize	jab	emphasis	Help!
hyphen	-	"under one"	treat as one	connect	link / line ending	high-priced / end-ings
parentheses	( )	"to put beside"	set aside	hide	insertions	Jane (whom I adore)
period	.	"cycle"	end	finish	sentence	Walk.
question mark	?	"to ask"	inquire	invite	questions	Why?
quotation marks	" "	"exactly what"	highlight	highlight	direct quotes / irony / titles	"Why?" she asked. / It's "cool." / "Silent Night"
semicolon	;	—	half-stop	balance	sentences	Run; stop.
underlining (italics)		—	emphasize	draw attention	emphasis / mention / some titles	She knew / I is the first word in I, Claudius / Gone with the Wind

ing if the writer really meant it. So, although each punctuation element has its own personality, what it means also depends on where it appears. Raised eyebrows can mean many things, depending on the situation, from surprise to terror. When you are punctuating, be sensitive not only to the phrase, clause, or sentence you are punctuating but also to how the phrase, clause, or sentence fits into the larger piece.

Myths About Punctuation

Myths about punctuation may distract you from its main purpose: the making of meaning. Here are some of those myths.

> *Myth 1:* There is only one right way to punctuate a sentence.
> *Myth 2:* Punctuation always follows speech patterns.
> *Myth 3:* The best way to learn punctuation is by filling in blanks in a workbook.
> *Myth 4:* A sentence is a complete thought by itself.

As you work through this section, you will realize that these and other beliefs are only myths. You will be offered guidelines for using punctuation meaningfully, that is, to fulfill your purposes with your choice of audiences. You will be offered much more than the rules, for it is a myth that there is one best way to punctuate a sentence in any and every context. For each punctuation element, you will be offered a discussion of its strength, meaning, and the gesture it can make in a given situation. In addition, you will be offered some of the standard uses of that punctuation.

Strength. When language was chiseled into stone slabs in ancient Greece and Rome, the chiselers had to save space; therefore, they left no spaces between words and ran the words in two directions (see Figure 16.1). Otherwise, if the slabs were long enough, it would have been hard

FIGURE 16.1 Words Chiseled into Stone

to find the way back to the beginning of the next line. The Greeks called this kind of writing *boustrophedon*. The word means "the way oxen move" and refers to how oxen would pull the plow in a field going *up* one row and turning at the end to go *down* the next. But, as you can see, it's hard to tell on the slab where words begin or end. The first punctuation element was the dot placed between words to separate them. Later, space itself was used to separate words, to emphasize their identity, or, in short, to punctuate words. For the purposes of our discussion, we will expand the definition of punctuation to include white space and other typographical elements that communicate any kind of separation, emphasis, or gesture.

Some punctuation elements do more than others. If you were to rank punctuation marks according to whether they were stronger or weaker, the comma would be "weaker" than the period, because the period marks off whole sentences, whereas the comma usually marks off only parts of sentences or lists.

Meaning.   In the discussion of punctuation elements below, you will be offered guidelines for how to use punctuation to communicate your tone and attitude toward your subject, purpose, and audience. Punctuation often determines your meaning and how it will be read by others.

Gesture.   Punctuation is a translation into written form of the body and voice gestures that accompany spoken language and lend it meaning. Therefore, the discussion of punctuation below will include comments on what gesture each punctuation element can make.

Explorations

These Explorations are designed to help you recognize how much you know about punctuation and meaning and to interest you in learning more.

1. *Together.* List words you would use to describe your previous experiences with punctuation. Why would you use these words? Do your experiences with punctuation affect your perception of yourself as a writer? If so, how? If not, why not? What reactions do you have to focusing on punctuation now? What do you hope to learn, specifically, by working with this chapter?

2. *Together. A physics of punctuation.* The object of this Exploration is to rank punctuation marks according to their relative strengths. List all the punctuation elements you can think of, including capitalization and different sizes of white space. You may want to start the list with the "weakest" punctuation element, either word spacing or capitalization, and end the list with the space suggested by the covers

of a book. All other punctuations go in between. Rank the punctuations according to how much each element can do in terms of the following: emphasis, size of expressions the punctuation marks off, flexibility, and so on. For example, the semicolon can be ranked between the comma and the period. But where would you put the colon, and why? There is no absolute ranking. The important thing in this Exploration is to become aware of your current ideas about punctuation. As you discuss the rankings, you will notice what you know, which aspects of punctuation you focus on, and what questions you have about punctuating.

3. *Together.* Read the following groups of words. For each group, discuss how meaning changes with different punctuations.

   a. Woman, without her man, is a savage.[31]
      Woman! Without her, man is a savage.
      Woman! Without her, man is a savage?
      Woman without! Her man is a savage.

   b. He told her he was into shuffleboard, soap operas, and Lawrence Welk, before she managed to slip out the back door.

      He told her he was into shuffleboard, soap operas, and Lawrence Welk. Before, she managed to slip out the back door.

   c. Johnny's probably out there in the waiting room sitting in Dad's lap. Mary looks tired.

      Johnny's probably out there. In the waiting room, sitting in Dad's lap, Mary looks tired.

The Elements of Punctuation

Capitalization

The word *capitalize* comes from the Latin word *caput,* which means "head." To capitalize a word means one or two things:

1. The word heads or starts a new segment of your writing.
2. The word is capitalized as a gesture of respect.

To start a new segment of writing, capitalize as follows:

1. *Capitalize the first word of a sentence.*
2. *Capitalize the first word of a quoted sentence.* Capitalize the first word after an interruption only if it begins a new sentence.

   "*If* you want a healthy garden," she said, gesturing to her compost heap, "you have to be willing to put up with some discomfort."

3. *Do not capitalize the first word after a colon unless it begins a sentence.* If a sentence follows the colon, capitalization is optional.

The following are guidelines for capitalizing as a gesture of respect:

1. *Capitalize proper nouns,* including names of specific persons, places, religions, nationalities, languages, institutions, courses, historical periods, organizations, days of the week, months, holidays, movies, documents, and brand names.
2. *Capitalize titles* when used as part of a specific name, as in "*Dr.* Martha Cottrell" or "Sammy Davis, *Jr.*"
3. *Capitalize all the major words in titles and subtitles* in books, articles, and creative works, unless the author specifically avoids doing so: Beethoven's Sixth Symphony is usually referred to as "*The Pastoral Symphony.*"

The Comma (,)

The word *comma* comes from the Greek word *koptein,* which means "to cut." The comma marks off some word or words that *cut into* a phrase or clause in the same sense as you would *cut into* a waiting line. The comma marks off words that are used to introduce or modify other expressions. A comma means you are (1) introducing a sentence or idea or (2) adding an idea.

Without the comma, words, phrases, or clauses that have been introduced into a sentence could confuse a reader. For example, notice what happens without the comma in the following example:

If you fly Maryann will join you.

When you start reading this sentence—*If you fly Maryann*—it sounds like an airline advertisement, implying that *Maryann* is either the name of an airplane or a human being who can be flown like an airplane. You have to reread the sentence and regroup the words for yourself to realize that the clause *If you fly* is separate from the main point, which is *Maryann will join you.* If the comma is added in the logical place, before *Maryann,* the meaning of the sentence becomes clear on first reading.

A misplaced comma can be very expensive, as well. For example, it happened once that a congressional clerk was supposed to write, "All foreign fruit plants are free from duty." This meant that only fruit plants were to be admitted into the country without extra import cost. But in the process of writing, the clerk introduced a comma so that the sentence read: "All foreign fruit, plants are free from duty." The comma implied a list that included fruit and plants because a comma sometimes functions as an abbreviation for *and.* The comma cut the important adjective, *fruit,* away from the word it modified, *plants.* This change cost the U.S. government over $2 million, because *all* fruit and *all* plants, not just fruit plants, were admitted without import cost.

> *Note:* If a clause or a phrase cannot be cut out of a sentence without seriously altering the meaning, do not mark it off with commas. Read your sentence without the clause or phrase marked off with a comma or commas, and decide whether the essential thought has been altered.

When the comma indicates an introduction, it is traditionally used as follows:

1. *Use the comma to mark off introductory word groups, such as adverbial clauses or phrases (starting with connecting adverbs or prepositions):*

> During the march on Washington, the protesters encountered supportive bystanders.

> Because all new cars will have antilock brakes, driving in foul weather will be safer.

2. *Use the comma to mark off certain adjectival clauses or phrases that modify nouns or pronouns.* If the clauses or phrases are essential to the meaning of the sentence, do *not* mark them off from the rest of the sentence:

> Genetic engineering, which is a much disputed enterprise, is being researched in certain major universities.

In this sentence, the adjectival clause (starting with *which* and marked off by commas) is not essential to the meaning of the sentence. If you cut out the clause "which is a much disputed enterprise," you would still have the essential message, which is "Genetic engineering is being researched in certain major universities." There are, however, adjectival clauses that *are essential* to the sentence. The following sentence does not make sense because commas mark off the essential adjectival clause starting with *who:*

> People, who live in glass houses, shouldn't throw stones.

The commas mean that the clause could be cut out. But the sentence "People shouldn't throw stones" does not include the essential information that people *who live in glass houses* are jeopardizing themselves if they throw stones. The more reasonably punctuated sentence is this:

People who live in glass houses shouldn't throw stones.

There are phrases called *noun phrases* that reidentify a nearby noun. *If the noun phrase is not essential to identifying a specific person, place, or thing, mark it off with commas:*

> Neil Postman, author of *Amusing Ourselves to Death*, argues that television is reducing our ability to reason.

If the noun phrase is essential to identifying a specific person, place, or thing, don't use commas:

> The movie *Casablanca* has recently been colorized.
>
> The poet Robert Frost wrote "The Road Not Taken."

If commas marked off the word *Casablanca*, then that word could be cut out of the sentence. The sentence would not retain its essential meaning, for it would read, "The movie has been recently colorized." You would not know which movie was being referred to. Similarly, to write *poet Robert Frost* is the same as writing *General Patton*. You would not separate the word *General* from *Patton* or *poet* from *Robert Frost* by commas because the words *General* and *poet* provide essential information concerning the persons' roles.

3. *Use the comma to mark off transitional expressions.* Afterthought words, such as *however, moreover,* and *nevertheless* (see page 424 for a complete list), and transitional phrases, such as *in fact* and *for example* are sometimes marked off by commas.

> Moreover, the year-end report does not reflect contracts awarded in the fourth quarter.

4. *Use commas to mark off side comments or afterthoughts that preface or interrupt the sentence.*

> Yet, looking at the Ancient Egyptian wall paintings for the first time, one may find them bewildering.
>
> Socialism, at least in theory, is an attempt to improve conditions for all humans.

5. *Use the comma to mark off expressions that introduce or modify direct quotations.*

> "Henry," he said, "I just remembered the answer to your question."

6. *Use the comma to mark off direct addresses, questions, introductions, and expressions that serve as throat clearers.*

Mr. President, I want to object to the new tax policy.

Yes, they won the battle but lost the war.

Well, it's about time.

When the comma indicates something is being added, it is traditionally used as follows:

1. *Use the comma with dates, addresses, and titles.*

On July 17, 1984, the defendant entered the premises of my client, Cynthia Horton, M.D., at 1400 Washington Street, Bellville, Maine.

2. *Use the comma between items in a series.* This includes series of independent clauses, as in the first example:

Caesar came, he saw, and he conquered.
The butler purchased apples, caviar, and ham and cheese.

There are no commas between *ham* and *cheese* because they are often thought of as going together. A comma inserted between them would imply that one could be cut off from the other within the context of the sentence.

Confusing Commas.   There are several uses of the comma that cut off parts of sentences in confusing ways. Whenever you are deciding whether to use a comma, notice which part or parts of a sentence the comma marks off. Sometimes, a comma may seem to mark off a part of a sentence for one reason when it is actually marking it off for another. In the examples below, you will be shown confusing uses of commas and commas that are used correctly although they appear to be incorrect:

1. *Do not cut off verbs from their subjects or objects.*
Confusing:
Caring for an infant, can be both the most frustrating and rewarding task a person can do.
Jonathan crammed, all the cashews he could fit into the box.
Clear:
George, the cake decorator, created a huge basketball out of chocolate cake and orange icing.

The comma after *decorator* is marking off the phrase *the cake decorator.* It is not cutting the subject, *George,* from the verb, *created.*

2. *Do not use a comma to begin or end a series,* unless the comma ends a phrase or clause (in which case the comma is used not to mark off the series but to mark off the phrase or clause).

Confusing:
You should read a full range of materials including, newspapers, journals, magazines, and books, to make sure you have collected ideas from many different sources.

Clear:
For the new chicks, ducklings, and goslings, the incubator was the first parent they knew.

The comma after *goslings* is not ending the series *chicks, ducklings, and goslings;* it is ending the whole phrase starting with *For.*

3.   *Do not use a comma before parentheses.*

Confusing:
Whatever the effectiveness of vigorous exercise, (whether in individual or team sports), there is no substitute for a healthy diet in weight control.

4.   *Do not use a comma when the* and *joins two subjects, verbs, or phrases.*

Confusing:
The temple provided a place for worship, and served as a meeting place.
Some people don't realize the effect that fathers' use of drugs can have on the body, and future of their unborn children.

Clear:
The temple provided a place for worship and a shelter for passersby.

5.   *Do not use a comma to separate noun clauses from their verbs.*

Confusing:
Whoever wants to succeed, must work.

Clear:
Whoever wants to succeed must work.

*E*xplorations _____

1.   *Together and Solo.* Explain the differences in meaning in the sentences in Exploration 3 on page 469. In your explanation, refer to parts of the discussion of commas.

2.   *Together or Solo.* Circle all the commas on half of a page of one of the books you are reading. (You may choose a page from this book, if you like.) Why is each comma used? (In answering this question, refer to the explanations and examples of uses of the comma, above.) How does each comma help you better organize and understand what you are reading? Would you add or delete any commas? Why or why not?

3. *Together.* Punctuate the following sentences in two (or more) ways. Discuss how capitalization and commas change the meanings of the sentences. *To test whether a comma or commas should be included, experiment with cutting out parts of sentences they mark off.* If the sentence loses its essential meaning, then do not use the comma or commas. You may find that some punctuations create humorous sentences. In what situations would the different versions probably be used?

a. come and watch the elephant eat debbie
come and watch the elephant eat debbie

b. during the mexican american war 1846 1848 general santa anna lost every battle he fought

during the mexican american war 1846 1848 general santa anna lost every battle he fought

c. the author of mind your own beeswax a self published novel made some serious points

the author of mind your own beeswax a self published novel made some serious points

d. i suspect you were right there
i suspect you were right there

e. camps that do not make safety the first priority should be shut down

camps that do not make safety the first priority should be shut down

f. when he swallows his eyes blink
when he swallows his eyes blink

g. therefore if we consider the effects of citrus on scurvy as in the example of early british sailors we will realize how some diseases have simple dietary solutions

therefore if we consider the effects of citrus on scurvy as in the example of early british sailors we will realize how some diseases have simple dietary solutions

h. the battleship formerly berthed in newport news virginia is now on active duty

the battleship formerly berthed in newport news virginia is now on active duty

i. she powdered her nose her appearance and her claims met the requirements for the modeling job

she powdered her nose her appearance and her claims met the requirements for the modeling job

j. god rest ye merry gentlemen
god rest ye merry gentlemen

4. *Together.* Write a long sentence in which you try to include every use of the comma cited in this section.

5. *Together and Solo.* Review your own papers, focusing on the comma. Where can commas be added or deleted to support your meaning and guide your reader? Revise your papers accordingly.

The Hyphen (-)

The word *hyphen* comes from the Greek word *huphen,* which means "together" or literally "under one." The gesture the hyphen makes is to connect. To use a hyphen means one of two things:

1. Two words or parts of words are to be treated as one.

2. Two expressions, though treated as one, need to be distinguished.

The hyphen can give a powerful message, as the following example shows. According to Steven Greenhouse, in his March 28, 1990, article for *The New York Times,* during the 1990 revolutions in Eastern Europe, the Czechs and the Slovaks found themselves in an ethnic battle over a hyphen. The Slovaks wanted to rename Czechoslovakia "Federation of Czecho-Slovakia." The Czechs argued that including the hyphen is divisive because it implies that the Czechs and the Slovaks are separate and need to be put together.

When the hyphen indicates that two words or parts of words are to be treated as one, it is traditionally used as follows:

1. *Use the hyphen to connect two or more words that function as an adjective before a noun.* Otherwise, the two words are separate.

She wrote a well-turned phrase.	Her phrase was well turned.
They sell a high-priced camera.	Their cameras were high priced.
Use a double-entry journal.	Write a double entry.

2. *Use the hyphen when the dictionary indicates that a word is currently being treated as a hyphenated word.* Many words in English were originally two or more words, but, since they were so often used together, after a while they became treated as one, such as the word *waterworks.* These words are called *compound words.* Here are some examples of related words. (Remember that connected adjectives are hyphenated only *before* the nouns they modify.)

Hyphenated	Compound	Separate
water-cooled (adj)	waterworks	water tower
high-riser (n)	highlight	high school
news-ready (adj)	newspaper	news release

In addition, you will discover other words that are hyphenated in current usage. These include some you may already know:

sister-in-law (n)   no-show (n)   good-for-nothing (n)

3. *Use the hyphen to connect fractions and compound numbers.*

one-fourth   thirty-nine

4. *Use the hyphen to connect words broken across lines.* If a word must be divided at the end of the line, there are several guidelines to follow.

- *Divide words between syllables.* If you have a question as to where a syllable ends, consult your dictionary, which places dots between syllables. The same word root may be hyphenated in different ways for different forms of the word. For example, *indication* is hyphenated as in-di-ca-tion. But *indicative* is hyphenated as in-dic-a-tive. Sometimes, you may even want to check different dictionaries if you have a question. Here is an example of a hyphenated sentence:

  We stored the lawn furniture, brought the garden hose in-doors, and dragged the garden tools into the garage for safe-keeping.

- *Never divide a one-syllable word at the end of a line.*
- *Always make sure that more than one letter is at the end of a line when you hyphenate and that three or more letters begin the next line.*
- *Divide a hyphenated word at the hyphen only.*

5. *Use the hyphen with prefixes such as* all-, ex-, *and* self-.

all-encompassing   ex-boss   self-fulfilling

6. *Use the hyphen in some words to separate confusing double or triple letters.* When the hyphen indicates that two expressions, though treated as one, need to be distinguished, it is traditionally used as follows:

re-create   cross-stitch   pre-engineered

*E*xplorations _____

1. *Together and Solo.* In small groups or solo, search through the dictionary and find thirty words that are hyphenated. Find thirty compound words—two or more words that function as one unhyphenated word.

2. *Together or Solo.* In small groups or solo, list thirty hyphenated adjectives. These may include ones you find in the dictionary and ones you create yourself. The ones you create may be serious or humorous.

3. *Together and Solo.* Choose a page from this chapter and mark words to indicate which ones could be hyphenated at the end of a line and where the hyphens could be placed. For example, the previous sentence could be marked as follows:

    > Choose a page from this chap-ter and mark words to in-di-cate which ones could be hy-phen-at-ed at the end of a line and where the hy-phens could be placed.

    Use the dictionary to confirm your hyphenations.

4. *Solo.* Keep an ongoing list of hyphenated and compound words from your readings.

The Apostrophe (')

The word *apostrophe* comes from the Greek words *apo* and *strophe,* which together mean "step up." The name "apostrophe" describes how the punctuation looks. An apostrophe means one of two things:

1. A letter has been removed. The apostrophe contracts what's left. (Think of the apostrophe as a hand flicking a letter away in order to pull the other letters together, as in the word *don't.*)

2. You want to indicate possession. The apostrophe points to the owner. (Think of the apostrophe in this case as a hand cupped toward the owner.)

When the apostrophe indicates a letter has been removed, it is traditionally used as follows:

1. *Place the apostrophe where the letter has been removed, and contract what's left into one word.*

they are	=	they're
do not	=	don't
she is	=	she's
something is	=	something's
something has	=	something's
let us	=	let's
1992	=	'92
it is	=	'tis, it's
because	=	'cause

A special case is the contraction of *will* and *not:*

will not	=	won't

Note that the word *ain't* is a contraction of *am not, is not, are not,* or *have not. Ain't* is not normally used in academic or professional writing, but this word is an example of the economy and elegance of spoken language: one word can have many uses.

2.   It's *is always a verb contraction of* it *and* is *and never a possessive pronoun.*

When the apostrophe is used to indicate possession, apply the following guidelines:

1.   *If the noun in the singular does not end with an* -s, *add an apostrophe and an* -s.

Singular: consumer   Possessive: consumer's

2.   *If the noun in the singular ends with an* -s, *add an apostrophe and an* -s.

Singular: hippopotamus   Possessive: hippopotamus's

3.   *If the noun is plural and ends in an* -s, *add only an apostrophe.*

Plural: parents   Possessive: parents'

4.   *If you have conjoined nouns, add an apostrophe and an* -s (*or an* -s *and an apostrophe, depending on the noun) to the last noun only.*

Conjoined noun: Mary and William

Possessive: Mary and William's

Conjoined noun: Teachers and parents

Possessive: Teachers and parents'

5. *Pronouns such as* everyone *and* somebody *take an apostrophe and an* -s.

everyone/everyone's   somebody/somebody's

6. *Except for* one's, *possessive pronouns never take an apostrophe and an* -s *because they already indicate possession by themselves.*

hers, his, its, ours, theirs, yours

Remember that the possessive pronoun *its* does not have an apostrophe so that you can distinguish it from the contracted verb *it's.*

The only possessive pronoun that uses an apostrophe is *one: one's.* Otherwise, it could not be distinguished from the self-contradicting word *ones,* which implies more than one of something that is only one. If you want to say that the number *1* is used more than once, write *1s.* Both the contraction of *one is* and the possessive of *one* are written as *one's.* It is the only pronoun that functions this way.

7. *Use an apostrophe and an* -s *to pluralize lowercase letters used as letters, capital letters that would otherwise be confusing, and abbreviations.*

Sydney wrote her *y*'s with elaborate curls.

They embroidered the cloth with *S*'s, *A*'s, and *I*'s.

The audience was filled with M.D.'s and Ph.D.'s.

Do not use an apostrophe to pluralize numbers or words as words.

They dressed to the 9s.

We don't want to hear any *ifs, ands,* or *buts* about it.

*E*xplorations

1. *Together and Solo.* Discuss how the meanings change in the following phrases and sentences. Imagine the situations in which the statements would be used. Which are confusing or illogical? How and why? Revise confusing or illogical phrases and sentences to make sense.

   a. I won't do it 'cause I don't want to.
      I will not do it because I do not want to.

   b. Everybodys' opinion is to be considered in the decision.
      Everybody's opinion is to be considered in the decision.

   c. Her parents' house is in disrepair.
      Her parent's house is in disrepair.

   d. Do'nt think twice, its' all right.
      Don't think twice, it's all right.
      Don't think twice, its alright.

   e. I've had it.
      I have had it.

2. *Together and Solo.* Choose papers you are currently writing and review them, focusing on the need for apostrophes. Add or delete apostrophes to clarify your meaning.

Quotation Marks (" ")(' ')

The word *quotation* comes from the Latin *quo,* which means "what." Literally, quotation marks mean "exactly what." The gesture or function of quotation marks is much like that of two spotlights highlighting *exactly what* is between them. To use quotation marks means one of two things:

1. You are indicating the exact words between the quotation marks.

2. You are drawing attention to an expression.

When quotation marks indicate exact words, they are traditionally used as follows:

   1. *Use quotation marks to indicate another person's* exact *words, whether they were spoken or written.* These are called *direct quotes.*

> Malcolm X once said, "Power in defense of freedom is greater than power in defense of tyranny and oppression."

Indirect quotes, which refer to what someone says, are not placed within quotation marks. Indirect quotes are often, though not always, signaled by *that.*

Direct quote:
The engineer said, "The bridge is on the verge of collapse."

Indirect quote:
The engineer said that the bridge was on the verge of collapse.

Words mentioned as words, traditionally placed between quotation marks, are now italicized. Refer to page 492 for a full discussion of how to punctuate words as words.

2. *Use single quotation marks to indicate a quote within a quote.*

"Stop saying 'you know' all the time," she said in exasperation.

3. *Use quotation marks around titles of news and magazines articles, poems, stories, songs, chapters or sections of books, and television and radio programs.*

> The article entitled "The Taste of Fresh-Brewed" offered an analysis of thirty-three name-brand coffees.
> "Married with Children" is a satire on late-twentieth-century family relations.

4. *Use quotation marks to indicate meaning.* There are times when you want to refer to meaning. Notice this sentence:

Apostrophe means "step up."

The expression is a shortened way of writing the following:

Apostrophe means *exactly what* the expression "step up" means.

5. *Traditionally, the way to set off long quotes of more than four or five typed lines is to indent and single-space them.* When you are making long quotes, check what style your academic discipline uses.

> The important matter is to find your own style, your own subjects, your own rhythm, so that every element in your nature can contribute to the work of making a writer of you. Study your own pages; among them you are to find some idea—preferably, this time, a fairly simple one—which offers you a good, obvious nucleus for a short story, an expanded anecdote . . . or a brief essay. You will have something to say on the subject which is more than a superficial comment. (Dorothea Brande, *Becoming a Writer* [Boston: Harcourt, 1934], p. 139.)

6. *When writing dialogue, indent for the beginning of each change of speaker.*

> James Smith, deeply troubled, went to a psychiatrist.
> "My brother," he said, "thinks he's a chicken. He goes around pecking at things on the floor, squawks constantly, and flaps his arms."
> "Oh," the psychiatrist said. "How long has he been acting this way?"

"About six months," James said.
"Why didn't you come in sooner?" asked the psychiatrist.
"To tell you the truth," James replied, "we needed the eggs."

7.   *Use quotation marks for repetitions in lists.* The quotation marks
indicate that exactly what is written above should be repeated:

For extended physical therapy	12/7/94	$ 50
"	"	12/14/94	$100
"	"	12/21/94	50

When you are drawing attention to an expression, use quotation marks
in the following ways:

1.   *Use quotation marks to indicate that a familiar word is used in
an unusual way:*

The hyphen is one of the "weaker" punctuation marks.

2.   *Use quotation marks to introduce slang or technical terms.*

Some of our sophomore classmates have a serious case of "beautyism."
The contract was mostly "boilerplate."

3.   *Use quotation marks for an ironic tone:*

Bart Simpson is not exactly an "overachiever."

(Note that members of some academic and professional communities do
not favor using quotation marks to draw attention to slang or puns or to
create an ironic tone.)

Traditionally, quotation marks combine with other punctuation elements as follows:

1.   *Within quotation marks.* Commas and periods are placed within
quotation marks at the end of quoted material.

"To begin," she said, "is half the work."

2.   *Outside quotation marks.* Colons and semicolons are placed outside quotation marks at the end of quoted material.

Judge Wilson said, "The verdict stands"; nonetheless, the lawyers were already preparing another appeal.

Question marks and exclamation points are placed within quotation marks only when they are part of the quoted material. Compare the following two sentences:

Why did George say, "Go away"?
Why did George say, "Go away?"

The first sentence asks why George asserted "Go away." The question mark ends the whole sentence. The second sentence implies that George was asking whether or not to go away because the question mark ends only the quote itself. If George were asking a question, the sentence would be more appropriately written and punctuated as follows:

Why did George *ask*, "Go away"?

The Ellipsis (. . .)

The word *ellipsis* comes from the Greek word *elleipsis*, which means "to fall short." Use ellipsis points to indicate that you have deleted material from a quotation. Ellipsis points cut. Normally, ellipses are not used at the beginnings or ends of quotations. Put single spaces before, after, and in between. Note that the plural form of *ellipsis* is *ellipses*.

Neil Postman writes, "Thinking does not play well on television, a fact that television directors discovered long ago. . . . It is, in a phrase, not a performing art."

*E*xplorations _____

1. *Solo.* Look through one of your textbooks from another course and find examples of quotations within the text. Notice how the author introduces quotes and which are indented and which single-spaced.

2. **a.** *Solo.* Choose a statement you recently read or heard that is meaningful to you in some way. Quote the statement *directly*, and write an essay about what it means to you. In your essay, refer to words and expressions in the statement.

   b. *Solo.* Write about your chosen statement, quoting the author *indirectly*. In this essay, do not refer to exact words and expressions used by the author.

    c. *Together.* Read, discuss, and compare the differences between the essays in which you quote directly and the essays in which you quote indirectly. How do the meanings change? Which essays do you prefer, and why?

3. *Solo.* Choose a page of a book that interests you. Highlight several key phrases or sentences. (Refer to pages 123–129, 322–324, and 331–335 for discussions of key words and statements.) Write a short essay relating what the author says. Report what the author says in one long direct quote. Use ellipses to indicate portions that you have left out of what the author wrote.

Parentheses [( )]

The word *parenthesis* (singular form of parenthes*es*) comes from the Greek words *para, en,* and *tithenai. Para* means "beside," *en* means "in," and *tithenai* means "to put." *Parenthesis* literally means "to put beside." A parenthetical remark adds extra material, afterthoughts, and tangents to the discussion. To put something between two parenthes*es* (note that this is the plural form of *parenthesis*) means that, if necessary, the added remark could be removed. Parentheses hide what is between them. That is why the example of "Jane (whom I adore)" could be so disappointing to a lonely Jane. Depending on the situation, parentheses can also serve the purpose of befriending or distancing a reader. Compare the attitudes that the following two examples can portray:

> We have to buy the more expensive gift for the boss (if you know what I mean).

> You look really terrific (for your age).

There are two situations in which parentheses are traditionally used:

1. *Use parentheses to mark off comments.*

> When you harvest herbs for drying, cut only the tops of the plants, about a third or quarter of its growth. (Parsley and chives can be cut further down.)

> Art lies to us to tell us the (sometimes disquieting) truth.

2. *Use parentheses to mark off or enclose letters or numbers.*

> The Graduate Management Admissions Test (GMAT) is required by most graduate schools of business.

The Fujiwara period of Japanese art (897–1185) was centered on the capital and dominated by the Fujiwara family.

If a whole sentence is included within parentheses, the end mark goes within the parentheses. If parentheses are included within a sentence, other punctuation marks that belong to the main sentence are put outside of the parentheses.

*E*xplorations

1. *Solo.* Collect at least five examples of the use of parentheses in books, newspapers, and magazines you are currently reading.

2. *Together.* Discuss the examples of uses of parentheses you collected. Revise several sentences to experiment with removing parentheses. Create additional sentences if necessary. What happens to the meanings of the sentences when formerly parenthetical expressions are incorporated into the regular text?

The Colon (:)

The word *colon* comes from the Greek word *kolon,* which refers to a unit of rhythm in poetry. The origin of the word does not clearly capture the meaning of the colon. Think of the colon as the tips of two fingers pointing either to indicate a list or to emphasize what follows. To use a colon means one or both of two things:

1. You are directing attention.
2. You are further explaining or summarizing.

When the colon directs attention, it is traditionally used as follows:

1. *Use the colon after an independent clause to direct attention to a list or a quotation, or after the salutation in a business letter.*

There are three things you should never do at a cocktail party: put a lampshade on your head, drink from a bottle, or arrive early.

Robert Foster states: "Venus is named for the goddess of love because it is visible only near sunrise and sunset."

Dear Ms. Winokur:

Note that when the colon is used to introduce a list, it must be preceded by a complete independent clause. Although this convention of punctuation is in transition, the following uses of the colon are *not* currently standard for academic and professional writing:

> The four major experts commenting on the economy were: Hale, Leisenring, Ratajczak, and Foster.
>
> The panel of judges consisted of: skaters, gymnasts, and ballet dancers.

2. *Use the colon to explain or to summarize.*

> As I was falling asleep in Professor Dorman's class, I knew: This was going to be the end of me.
>
> Hunting stories have a long history: they appear in different forms on the New England frontier of the eighteenth century.
>
> Elizabeth Bishop wrote about fishermen, sandpipers, and seals: images of the sea.

Do *not* capitalize the first word after a colon unless it is a new sentence. If a new sentence follows the colon, capitalization is optional.

> When you go to Rome, visit the popular sites: the Tivoli Gardens, the Roman Colosseum, the Bernini Fountains, and the Sistine Chapel.

The Semicolon (;)

Think of the semicolon visually. It is half period and half comma. The semicolon is used for balancing parts of sentences in one of two situations:

1. When a period is too strong a break
2. When a comma is insufficient to mark off a part of a sentence

1. *Use a semicolon when a period is too strong a break between independent clauses, and there are no connectors* (and, but, for, nor, or, so, yet).

> The physician recommended that the terminal patient take that special vacation; there was nothing else the doctor could do.
>
> The carousel is still a favorite in amusement parks; people ride it more than the Ferris wheel.

2. *Use a semicolon when you use a word to make a transition into an afterthought, such as* nevertheless, furthermore, hence.

> The job market was frozen; nevertheless, Mary was resourceful enough to get hired.

3. *Use a semicolon when a comma is insufficient to mark off a part of a sentence.* This occurs usually when the items in the series contain internal punctuation.

> The mechanic had a whole shopping list of repairs to make: adjust the fan, air conditioner, alternator, and power steering belts; change the transmission, brake, and cooling system fluids; and tune-up, align, rotate, balance, and repaint anything that he could find.

The Dash (—, --)

The word *dash*, used as a verb, means "to rush" or "move quickly." As an adjective, *dash* means "spirited" or "stylish." The dash, used as punctuation, gives writing these same qualities. Think of a dash as an arrow with two heads. Whereas parentheses hide what is written between them, the dash emphasizes or points arrows to what it marks off. Sometimes the dash is used when a list interrupts a sentence and a comma is too weak and a colon too strong. In sum, using a dash means one of two things:

1. An expression is to be emphasized.
2. A list or comment is being framed.

1. *Use the dash to emphasize.*

> Jane—whom I adore—is not only a successful business executive but a sensitive artist as well.
>
> Any increase or decrease in the proportion of people between the ages of sixteen and twenty-five in the total population affects the crime rate—which is what has happened over the past couple of decades.

2. *Use the dash to frame lists or restatements.*

> The most famous baseball players—people such as Babe Ruth, Joe DiMaggio, and Lou Gehrig—are immortalized in the Baseball Hall of Fame in Cooperstown, New York.
>
> As the large "baby boom" generation—people born between 1946 and 1964—passed through its youthful years, crime rates rose sharply.

Because the dash is very strong, avoid overusing it. When you type a dash, use two hyphens. Do not leave spaces before or after the dash.

*E*xplorations

1. *Solo.* Collect examples of sentences that use the colon, the semicolon, or the dash, or some combination of them. Revise the punctuation

in three of the sentences using commas or parentheses where possible.
How do the meanings change?

2. *Together and Solo.* Write sentences using the following sequences of punctuation. You can write as much or as little as you want in the spaces between the punctuation marks. For sequences a, b, and c, experiment with using the same sentences and discuss how the meaning changes with the different punctuation marks.

a. _____ ; _____ .

b. _____ : _____ .

c. _____ — _____ .

d. _____ : _____ , _____ ; _____ ; _____ .

e. _____ — _____ , _____ , _____ — _____ .

3. *Together and Solo.* Review your own papers, focusing on colons, semicolons, and dashes. Where can these punctuation marks be added or deleted to support your meaning and guide your reader? Revise your papers accordingly.

End Marks

The Period (.)

The word *period* comes from the Greek word *periodos*, which means "cycle" and implies an end. To use a period means that you have completed something. It means "stop, reflect." The traditional uses of the period are as follows:

1. *Use a period to end sentences that are not questions or exclamations.*

Robert Frost's career as a poet did not really begin in earnest until he was nearly forty years old.

2. *Use a period to end short answers to questions.*

Did the company reimburse me after I had called them six times?
No.

3. *Use periods in abbreviations according to current customs.*

etc.   450 A.D.

e.g.   6:00 P.M.

The Question Mark (?)

The word *question* comes from the Latin word *quaestio,* which means "to ask." This mark is normally an invitation for a response. The traditional uses of the question mark include the following:

1. *Use a question mark after a direct question.*

Did the governor report the exact amount of fiscal deficit for the year?

Note that some questions, called rhetorical questions, are not genuine invitations for answers. Usually the situation will determine whether a question is rhetorical. A rhetorical question—implying that there is only one "right" answer—is meant to create a bond between the writer and the audience. (For a full discussion of rhetorical questions consult page 328).

Is there any reason for this murder of innocent people?
Are you ready to pay less taxes?

2. *Use question marks in a series of short questions, even if the questions are not complete sentences.*

Will they research all the possible contributing factors to the development of cancer? Diet? Genetics? Environment? Life-style?

Notice that all the questions in the series begin with a capital letter.

The Exclamation Point (!)

The word *exclamation* comes from the Latin word *exclamare,* which means "to call out." *Use exclamation points after words, phrases, or sentences that deserve sudden emphasis.* Do not overuse the exclamation point. Because the exclamation point *demands* attention, much like a jab in the arm, it can overwhelm and distance the reader. Notice the difference in your reactions to the following two versions of the same sentence:

Help! These are the worst problems we've had in decades! There's a recession! Environmental destruction! Political tensions! What next?! No one seems to be catching on! We're committing suicide on this planet!

Help! These are the worst problems we've had in decades: a recession, environmental destruction, political tensions. What next? No one seems to be catching on. We're committing suicide on this planet.

If you had to choose, who would you vote into a responsible government position, the one who wrote the first version or the one who wrote the second? Why?

Explorations ⎯⎯⎯⎯⎯⎯⎯⎯⎯⎯⎯⎯⎯⎯⎯⎯⎯⎯⎯⎯

1. *Solo.* Review the sections on fragments and run-ons in Chapter 15. Do some of the corresponding Explorations that address concerns you have with punctuating sentences in your own writing.

2. *Solo.* Collect examples of sentences for all the uses of end marks reviewed above. Use newspapers, magazines, or books as your resources. Change the end marks on three of these sentences. Do the meanings change? If so, how? If not, why not?

3. *Together and Solo.* Review your own papers, focusing on end marks, colons, and semicolons. Where can these punctuation marks be added or deleted to support your meaning and guide your reader? Revise your papers accordingly.

Underlining (Italics)

Written language has progressed from its earliest forms of marks on sand and stone to ink on paper. Today, typewriters and computers offer further ways of creating meaning and guiding the reader's attention with the written word. These typographical punctuations include italics (underlining), boldfacing, and shading. This discussion will focus on underlining (italics) because it is the most commonly used and available typographical punctuation. The more sophisticated typographical punctuations function, in part, as underlining (italics) does.

Italics are a slanted typeface on a printed page that some computer programs allow you to use in conjunction with a regular typeface in the same paper. The working manuscript of this book was not printed with italics. Instead of italics, words were underlined. However, in its printed form, words that were underlined are now in italics.

Underlining is meant to emphasize or draw attention.

1. *Use underlining to emphasize.*

The company will *not* abandon this project.
Scientists are insisting that *yodoxin* is the cure.

2. *Underline titles of books, plays, magazines, newspapers, pamphlets, musical and artistic works, and long poems.*

In one semester, Lindsey studied *War and Peace, The Merchant of Venice, Forbes Magazine,* Beethoven's *Pastoral Symphony,* Chicago's *Dinner Party,* and Browning's *Sonnets from the Portuguese.*

3. *Underline foreign words introduced into part of a sentence.* Do not underline words that have been incorporated into English, such as *rendezvous* or *laissez-faire.*

In ancient Hawaii, members of a family would hold a *ho'oponopono* until everyone in the gathering agreed to a peaceful solution to a problem.

4. *Underline words, letters, and numbers mentioned as themselves.* To *use* a word as part of your discussion is different from *mentioning* it as itself. To understand the difference between using and mentioning a word, read the following sentence:

Boston has six letters.

This sentence is absurd because the city of Boston is likely to have more than six letters (in or out of envelopes) at any one time. The word *Boston* is being *used* in that sentence as if it were any other word. But the following sentence *does* make sense:

Boston has six letters.

What this sentence says is that the word *Boston* has six letters, because the word *Boston* is in italics. The italics emphasize the word to signal the reader that *Boston* is being mentioned as a word. In your own writing, underline words, letters, and numbers that you mention as themselves.

*E*xplorations

1. *Together and Solo.* The purpose of this Exploration is to give you practice in distinguishing whether a word, letter, or number is being *used* or being *mentioned* as itself. Read the following sentences. Which make sense and which don't? Which words should or should not be underlined? Revise them by underlining words, letters, and numbers that are mentioned as themselves.
   a. Chicago is a large city.
   b. Chicago is north of *Cleveland.*
   c. Othello had 3 daughters.
   d. 3 is a sacred number in many religions.

    e. How do you spell Cleveland?

    f. The G was barely visible on the slab.

    g. 1 is the loneliest number.

    h. Los Angeles means "the angels."

    i. Los Angeles means a lot to my Uncle Frank.

2. *Together.* The purpose of this Exploration is to give you practice using quotation marks, writing dialogues, and underlining to mention words. Review the use of quotation marks in direct quotations. Then brainstorm a list of overused words and expressions, such as *like, you know, yup, uh-huh, really,* and *good.* In pairs, or small groups, write dialogues that would last at least two minutes between a person who overuses a certain expression and another person, irritated by the repetition, who is trying to stop him or her from overusing the expression. Underline words when you are mentioning them:

> "I wish you would stop saying *you know* all the time."

> "Well, you know, it's a habit just like saying *like*—if you know what I mean."

Read the dialogues aloud. Although the dialogues may be serious, they are likely to be humorous.

Paragraphing (¶)

Usually, paragraphing marks off larger units of writing than end marks normally do. The word *paragraph* comes from the Greek words *para* and *graphos,* which together mean "writing to the side." Back during the days when language was carved into stone, one of the ways that new units of thought were marked off was by making marks by the sides of lines. Today, the white space that follows the last sentence of the previous paragraph, and the space indentation at the beginning of the line, mark off the beginning of a major shift in thought in a piece of writing. These white spaces do one or both of two things for your readers:

1. The white spaces frame out, and therefore emphasize, a major unit of thought.

2. The white spaces give your readers a breather so that they can reflect or readjust for a transition.

Because of these two functions of the paragraph, the end of a paragraph is a place to write those things that you want to have a lasting effect.

    A paragraph can be as short as one word. For example, suppose there was a long paragraph describing a terrifying experience. It could be followed by a one-word paragraph:

Help!

The word *help*, framed by all that white space, cannot be missed. However, a sentence can be pages long, as often happens in legal documents. Forget any rigid rules you may have heard about how many sentences or how many paragraphs you should write in a given essay or other piece of writing. Forget, as well, any rigid rules about how long a sentence ought to be. Instead, challenge yourself to write shorter or longer sentences and paragraphs to develop your style and shape your words to fulfill your purpose and capture your audience.

*E*xplorations

1. *Together or Solo.* Review the section on "The Body" on pages 182–200 in Chapter 7. Do the Explorations that follow it.

2. *Together and Solo.* Review your own papers in progress for paragraphing. Notice if your paragraph breaks mark off sentences that belong together. Do your paragraph breaks give your readers time to reflect on what you've written, or do you rush readers from one idea to another without pauses? Revise your papers accordingly.

PUNCTUATION REVIEW

Read the following "Blooper Rules of Punctuation" that ask you to do what they don't do themselves. Revise the rules so that—although they will be less funny—they won't contradict themselves.

1. Don't, use a comma, where it isn't, necessary.
2. Its important to use apostrophe's with care.
3. The period. Is a mark of punctuation. Which is used only at the ends of sentences.
4. Do not separate a term of respect from the name of a person just because poet, W. S. Merwin didn't use punctuation.
5. Do not—under any circumstances—whether in business, academic, or personal writing—overuse the dash—it puts a strain on the reader.
6. Do not create overly-long-and-complex words with hyphenation.
7. NEVER capitalize a word all the way through unless it is a HEADING BECAUSE it is not acceptable in academic or professional writing.
8. Do not use "quotation marks" to draw "attention" to familiar expressions in "academic" writing.
9. Do not be someone, who overuses commas, and marks off phrases, that must be included, in the sentence, without commas.
10. Don't overuse exclamation points!!!!!

*E*xplorations _____

1. *Together and Solo.* Punctuate the following, using as great a variety of marks and elements as would make sense.

   because john was worried that people would not like him if his party was not successful as it was last time when he had it catered and he was able to afford it since he came into the inheritance which he blew on a weekend in las vegas he bought a pineapple ham cheesecake champagne salami horseradish and ritz crackers thinking he would make finger foods they all loved all of it went well although they thought he looked a bit bedraggled

2. *Together.* Divide your class into small groups. Each group is to find a long sentence or a group of sentences in some newspaper, magazine, or book, preferably with a variety of punctuation. Type the sentence (or

sentences) without any punctuation or capitalization and distribute copies to another group or groups. Each group is to punctuate these sentences. Then compare your versions with the originals. How are your punctuations similar or different from the originals? How do your sentences differ in meaning from the originals? Which versions would work best with which purposes and audiences? How would you change your own or the original versions?

3. *Together.* Divide the class into small groups. Each group is to adopt a particular punctuation that members want to learn more completely. Prepare a lesson for someone who will be entering college or for a grammar school child. Find or create examples to illustrate your lesson. Prepare explorations to engage your audience. Use the ideas in this chapter, but vary them and make them your own. Refer to other books to enrich your presentation. If you decide to use an idea directly from this chapter or any other work, be sure to follow the conventions of quoting.

Chapter Review

Solo or *Together* respond to one or more of the following:

1. Which parts of this chapter did you most appreciate, and why?

2. Record five statements from this chapter that you want to remember.

3. Which Explorations did you like best, and what did you learn from doing them?

4. What did you learn about yourself as a writer?

5. If you were an instructor of writing, which points from this chapter would *you* stress in teaching student writers? Why?

6. Record questions that arose for you as you were working with this chapter, and discuss these in small groups or as a class.

7. How do you plan to change as a writer as a result of working with this chapter?

8. Which parts of this chapter do you anticipate reviewing?

Endnotes

1. From John Steinbeck, in *Writers at Work, Paris Interviews*, ed. George Plimpton, 4th series (New York: Penguin, 1976), p. 183.
2. From Virginia Woolf, "A Sketch of the Past," in *The Virginia Woolf Reader*, ed. Mitchell A. Leaska (New York: Harcourt, 1984), p. 4.
3. William James, "Habit: Its Importance for Psychology," in *The Writings of William James*, ed. John J. McDermott (Chicago: University of Chicago Press, 1977), pp. 11–19.
4. These distinctions are an adaptation of James Britton, "Notes on a Working Hypothesis about Writing," in *Prospect and Retrospect: Selected Essays of James Britton*, ed. Gordon M. Pradl (Montclair, NJ: Boynton/Cook, 1982).
5. From J. L. Austin, *How to Do Things with Words* (New York: Oxford, 1962).
6. From Donald Carroll, ed., *Dear Sir, Drop Dead: Hate Mail Through the Ages* (New York: Collier of Macmillan, 1982), p. 103.
7. From Ferd Nauheim, *Letter Perfect: How to Write Business Letters That Work* (New York: Van Nostrand, 1982), p. 141.
8. From School Boys of Barbiana, *Letter to a Teacher* (New York: Random House, 1970), p. 93.
9. From *Anne Frank: The Diary of a Young Girl* (New York: Doubleday, 1989), p. 12.
10. Old woman/Young woman drawing is from Myers & Myers, *The Dynamics of Human Communication*. Copyright © 1973, McGraw-Hill Inc. Reprinted by permission. Original drawing by E. G. Boring.
11. Reprinted by permission of Marvin H. Scilken. The writer is the editor and publisher of *THE U*N*A*B*A*S*H*E*D™ LIBRARIAN*, GPO Box 2631, New York, NY 10116.
12. Debbie Bober's essay was written with the guidance of Gregory Ryan at Kean College.
13. From Sir Arthur Conan Doyle, "The Six Napoleons," in *The Complete Sherlock Holmes Treasury* (New York: Avenel Books, 1976).
14. From Peter Elbow, *Writing with Power* (New York: Oxford, 1981), p. 54.
15. From Neil Brown, *Asking the Right Questions* (Englewood Cliffs, NJ: Prentice Hall, 1986), p. 40.
16. From Judith Viorst, "What Me? Showing Off?" *Redbook*, November 1982, p. 17.

17. From Emily Hancock, *The Girl Within* (New York: Fawcett Columbine, 1989), p. 32.
18. From "Meditations on a Photograph," copyright © 1983 by Susan Mitchell. Reprinted from *The Water Inside the Water.* Published by Wesleyan University Press and reprinted by permission of University Press of New England.
19. "Memory: It Seems a Whiff of Chocolate Helps," *The New York Times*, July 10, 1990, p. C2.
20. From Rena Cobrinik, "Let's Hear It for Pickled Herring," copyright © 1984 by The New York Times Company. Reprinted by permission.
21. Avantika Patel, Fred Ampofo, and Silvia Trillo were writing with the guidance of John Gruesser at Kean College. Debbie Chung's essay was written with the guidance of Jessie Reppy, director of the ESL Program at Kean College. "Body Language" first appeared in *Accents: Writings by Students in The ESL Program at Kean College of New Jersey, 1989–1990* and is reprinted by permission.
22. From S. I. Hayakawa, *Language in Thought and Action*, 5th ed. (New York: Harcourt, 1990), p. 4.
23. From Arthur B. Powell and José A. López, "Writing as a Vehicle to Learn Mathematics: A Case Study," in *Writing to Learn Mathematics and Science* (New York: Teachers College Press, 1989), p. 168.
24. John Williams was writing with the guidance of Jay Mahoney at Kean College.
25. From Sydney Harris, "What True Education Should Never Do," *Chicago Daily News*, 1964.
26. From Ellen Goodman, "Checks on Parental Power," copyright © 1979, The Boston Globe Newspaper Company/Washington Post Writers Group. Reprinted by permission.
27. From Abraham Harold Maslow, *Motivation and Personality*, 2nd ed. (New York: Harper & Row, 1970).
28. Helen Kwok was writing with the guidance of Mary Scotto at Kean College.
29. Bryan Worthy was writing with the guidance of Sue Woulfin at Kean College.
30. From Pico Iyer, "In Praise of the Humble Comma," *Time*, June 13, 1983, p. 80.
31. I am indebted to The Cooper Union for the Advancement of Science and Art for their exhibit "Period Styles: A Punctuated History," New York, March 22 to April 22, 1988.

Index

Abbreviations, 489
Academic writing, 295,
    317–69. *See also*
    Disciplines, academic
Ad hominem, 396
Adjectival clauses, 426–27,
    435, 448, 471
Adjectives, 415, 417
    connecting, 426, 427, 428,
        429, 436, 446, 476
    hyphenated words as, 476
Adverbial clauses, 425–26,
    435, 448
Adverbs, 415, 417
    connecting, 410, 425, 426,
        428, 429, 436, 446
    See also Afterthoughts
Advertisements
    appeals, 370–71
    grammar in, 411
Aesthetic writing, 43, 45, 257
Afterthoughts, 410, 423, 424,
    487
Age, 306–308, 310–12
    and point of view, 306–307
Agreement, 450–62
    pronoun, 450, 457–61
    subject-verb, 450–55

verb tense consistency,
    455–57
Apostrophe, 459, 478–81,
    482, 495
Appeals, 373–77
    combinations of, 377–79
    to emotion, 373, 374, 377,
        379
    faulty, 395–96
    to reason, 373, 376–79
    to status, 373, 374–75, 378,
        387
Arguments
    counterargument, 390
    supporting, 184–85
Articles, 415, 432
Attitude
    and audience appeal, 60
    biased, 145–46
    objective, 145–46
    self-defeating, 4, 9, 38
    subjective, 144–45
    and tone, 62–63
Audience
    adjusting to your, 66–68
    in bridging cultures,
        293–97
    choice of, 66

grammar and, 410–13
    identifying, 29, 30, 38, 45,
        56–57, 60, 67, 210, 373
    kinds of, 55–56
    punctuation and, 465,
        467–68
    purpose and, 50
    in summarizing, 335–36
    tone and, 62–63
    in writing to learn, 320–21
    in writing for power,
        373–77
    in writing process, 31,
        65–67
Authority notes, 344

Biased writing, 145–46
Block method, in comparison
    and contrast, 187,
    193–94, 358–59
Body, 182–200
    language, 312–13
    leads and, 188
    shaping, 189–95
    strategies of development,
        182–88
    writing process and,
        196–200

Brainstorming, 80–81, 216

Capitalization, 469–70, 487, 495
Case, 458–59
Cause and effect, 186, 376
Change, fear of, 10
Charting, 355–56
Choosing, 92, 96–100
Chronological order, 182–83
Classification, 186
Clauses, 422–31
    adjectival, 426–27, 435, 448
    adverbial, 425–26, 435, 448
    dependent, 422, 424–27, 428, 429, 434–35, 436
    independent, 422–24, 428, 430
    noun, 427, 429, 435
Clichés, 160–61
Clustering, 71, 82–84
Coherence, 32, 167
Collecting, 69–86
    clustering, 82–84
    for comparison and contrast, 355–57
    dynamics of, 69–71
    focusing and, 66, 72, 92–93
    interviewing, 84–86
    in journals, 73–81
    listing and brainstorming, 80–82
    memories, 265–71
    organizing and, 72, 168
    for outline, 197
    senses and, 133–40
    sources for, 70
    using memorabilia, 70, 265
    using photographs, 268
    in writing for power, 381, 389–91
    and writing process, 31, 67, 71–73
Colon, 466, 486–87
Comma, 423, 438, 445, 470–74, 495
    confusing, 473–74
    misplaced, 470–71
Comma splices, 442–48
    identifying, 443–45
    revising, 445–48
Commitment, 4, 11–12, 31, 247, 332

Common ground, establishing, 383–85, 394
Comparison
    clichés, 160–61
    to communicate experience, 158–60
    false, 399–400
    See also Comparison and contrast
Comparison and contrast, 186–87
    block method, 187, 193–94, 358–59
    collecting for, 355–57
    in essays, 356–62
    good, standards for, 355
    organizing methods, 357–59
    thesis statements, 356–57
    words expressing, 188, 358
    writing process for, 360
    zig-zag method, 187–88, 194–95, 359
    See also Comparison
Complex sentence, 425, 429
Compound-complex sentence, 429
Compound sentence, 423, 429–30
Compound words, 476–77
Computer, 18
    spelling/grammar check and, 241
    typographical punctuation and, 491
Conjunctions. *See* Connectors
Conjunctive adverbs. *See* Afterthoughts
Connecting adjectives, 426, 427, 428, 429, 436, 446, 476
Connecting adverbs, 410, 425–26, 428, 429, 436, 446
Connecting pronouns, 427, 428, 429, 436, 446
Connections, making, 342–69
    comparing and contrasting, 354–62
    drafting to learn, 342–49
    reason and evidence, 342

special structures in various disciplines, 362–63
    student writings, 364–69
    theory formation, 351–54
    thesis and evidence, 348–51
Connectors, 410, 415, 423, 424, 429, 436, 443
    in revising fragments, 439
    in revising run-ons/comma splices, 445–46
Connotation, 63, 64, 67
Consulting, 33, 38, 202–29
    collecting and, 72–73
    focusing and, 93–94
    organizing and, 168
    with other writers, 202–203
    in writing for power, 381–82, 394–95
    writing process and, 67
    See also Writing workshop
Contractions, 479
Contradictory/controversial lead, 172–73
Contrast. *See* Comparison and contrast
Coordinating conjunctions. *See* Connectors
Copy-editing, 212
    checklist, 241, 242
    strategies for, 237–46
    symbols, 238
Cultures, bridging, 290–315
    defining cultures, 290
    language and culture, 293–95
    points of view, 297–308
    reasons for bridging, 292–93
    student writings on, 309–15
    and writing process, 302–15

Dash, 466, 488, 495
Deduction, 190, 289, 392
Defining, in leads, 171
Denotation, 63
Dependent clauses, 422, 424–27, 428, 429, 434–35, 436
Development. *See* Body

Diagramming, 189, 191–95, 197–98
Dialects, 295
Dialogue, 482
Diary, 73. *See also* Journals
Disciplines, academic, 320
  based on reasoning, 342
  formats for reports in various, 362–63
  key statements in, 331–32
  key words in, 322
  making connections between, 345
  points of view, 320–21
  purpose and emphasis in, 348
Documents, 70, 265
Double entries, in learning journal, 343–45
Drafting
  focusing in, 92, 97–98
  to learn, 342–47
  in memory writing, 261–62
  process of, 33

Editing. *See* Copy-editing
Education
  academic disciplines, 320–21
  attitude toward, 10
  purpose in, 53–54, 320–22
  through senses, 332–35
  teacher role in, 7, 29, 38
  See also Disciplines, academic; Responsible thinking
Either-or fallacy, 398
Ellipsis, 484
Emotion, appeals to, 373, 374, 382, 384
Emphasis, expressions for, 193
Endings
  effective, 179
  examples for, 193
  strategies for, 179–81
  writing, 181–82
End marks, 422, 435, 438, 445, 485, 489–90
Essays, 36, 45
  comparing and contrasting in, 356–59
  example, 349–50
  process of writing, 349
  purpose of, 348

thesis and evidence in, 348–51
Ethnicity, 290, 302–304
Evading the question, 398
Evaluations, 344–45
Evidence
  in appeals to reason, 375–76
  collecting, 389
  in essays, 348–51, 352
  statements of, 342
  in writing for power, 392
Examples
  collecting, 389
  counterexamples, 397, 398
  illustrating, 111–18, 184
  shaping, 193
  supporting statements, 348
Exclamation point, 422, 483, 490, 495
Experimentation, as purpose in education, 54
Explorer's approach, to writing process, 37, 150, 151, 156, 168

Failure, fear of, 9
Family history, 279–81
Fears, about writing, 8–11, 38
Flashback, 182, 183, 275
Flexibility, 38–39
Focusing, 87–165
  choosing and, 96–100
  collecting and, 66, 72, 92–93
  dynamics of, 88
  explorer's approach to, 150
  identifying focus, 210–11
  illustrating and, 111–16
  in journals, 56, 71, 75–76
  on key statements, 121–28, 331–32
  on key words, 322–24
  organizing and, 93, 167
  planner's approach to, 151
  purpose and, 65–66, 89–92
  on questions, 116–21, 324–31
  quoting and, 105–13
  revising/consulting and, 93–96
  with sense appeal, 131–65
  on senses, 152
  specifying and, 100–105

strategies, 87–130
  on topic, 73
  in writing for power, 387–89
  writing process and, 31–32, 89–130
  in writing to remember, 261–64, 271–74
Foreign words, 492
Formal writing tasks, 35–36
Fragments, sentence, 434–41
  identifying, 435–37
  revising, 437–41
Freewriting, 4, 13–15, 71
Future perfect tense, 456
Future tense, 456, 457

Gender
  pronouns and, 458, 460–62
  roles, 304–306, 314–15
Generalizations, hasty, 397
Glossary of misused words, 506–509
Goals, time management and, 16
Grading, 223–29
  holistic scoring, 224–29
  scoring grid, 228
Grammar, 409–63
  agreement in, 450–62
  correct, 411–12
  individual style in, 412
  parts of speech, 415–16
  purpose and audience, 410–13
  review, 463
  sentences, 417–49
  spoken and written, 412

Habits, writing, 16, 20
Hasty generalizations, 397
Historical background, in lead, 172
History
  family, 279–81
  personal, 275–79
Holistic scoring, 224–29
Homonyms, 503–505
Hourglass shape, 191, 192
Humor, in leads, 173
Hypen, 476–78, 483, 488
Hyphenated words, 476–77

I, use of, 460
Ideas, collecting, 31

Illustrating
  in body, 183–84
  focusing and, 111–18
  leads, 169
Imaging
  in endings, 180
  in leads, 169
  See also Senses
Independent clauses, 422–24,
  428, 430, 486, 487
Induction, 189, 190, 392
Inductive reasoning, 189, 191
Infinitive, 418, 419
Informal writing tasks, 35–36
Information, as purpose in
  education, 53
Intelligence, 318, 342
Interjections, 415
Interpersonal writing, 43,
  44–45, 46, 257
Interpretation
  purpose in education, 53,
    54
  thesis and evidence, 348
Interviewing, 71
  for family histories, 279,
    280, 281
  purposes and audience for,
    84
  strategies for conducting,
    84–85
Introductions
  comparison and contrast
    in, 356
  punctuating, 471, 472–73
  thesis in, 349
  See also Leads
Inverted V-shape, 191, 192
Irony, 483
Italics, 491–93

Journals, 73–79
  double entries, 343–45
  focused, 56, 71, 75–76
  kinds of, 73–76
  learning, 74–75, 343–47
  personal, 73–74
  process entries, 74, 345–46
  strategies for keeping,
    78–79, 347
  training, 75
  writer's, 74, 234–37
Jumping to conclusions, 397

Key statements. *See* Thesis
    statements
Key words, noting, 322–24

Language
  academic, 348–50
  body, 312–13
  changing your, 10
  communities, 295, 453
  and culture, 293–95
  dialects, 295
  power of, 370–71
Leads, 168–77
  effective, 168
  ending and, 179–80
  examples of, 193
  false, 174–75
  matching with body
    development, 188
  outline for, 196
  process of writing, 173–77
  strategies for, 169–73
Learn, writing to. *See*
    Connections, making;
    Education; Responsible
    thinking
Learning journals, 74–75,
    343–47
Letters
  audience for, 65–66
  punctuating, 485
  purpose in, 57–58, 65–66
Lists
  punctuating, 473, 482–83,
    486–87, 488
  of topics, 80

Mastery needs, 29
Meaning
  connectors for, 426
  in ending, 180
  punctuation for, 468–69,
    482
  and purpose, 147–54,
    256–61
  and spelling, 499
  and word order, 410
  writing for, 28
Memorabilia, 70, 265
Memories, 255–88
  accessing, 256
  aids for, 265–71
  family history, 279–81

finding meaning in
    difficult experiences,
    258–60
  focusing with sense appeal,
    271–74
  focusing with statements,
    261–64
  importance of, 255–56
  meaning and purpose in
    writing, 256–61
  personal history, 275–79
  student writings on,
    281–88
Mnemonic devices, 500
Modifiers, misplaced, 448–49
Mudslinging, 396–97
Myths, about writing, 3–7

Need
  basic needs, 373, 382
  to bridge cultures, 392–93
  to focus, 89–90
  to learn, 317–18
  and meaning, 28
  to remember, 255–56
  and writing for power,
    382–83
  in writing process, 29–30
Networking, 222
News event, in lead, 172
Note taking, 319, 322–24
Noun clause, 427, 428, 429,
    435
  connecting pronouns in,
    427, 428
  as subject and object, 427
Nouns, 415, 417, 459
  collective, 452
  joined, 479
  proper, 470
Number/case pronoun,
    458–59
Numbers, 480, 485, 492

Object
  noun clause as, 427
  of verb, 422
Objective writing, 145–46
Observations
  focusing on, 154–55
  forming theories from,
    351, 352
  objective and subjective,
    144–46

Organizing, 166–200, 212
  body, 182–200
  collecting and, 72, 168
  for comparison and
      contrast, 357–59
  dynamics of, 166–67
  endings, 179–82
  explorer's approach to, 156
  focusing and, 93, 167
  leads, 168–77
  personal memories,
      274–81
  planner's approach to, 156
  sensations, 154–58
  structures, 167
  titles, 177–79
  in writing for power, 381,
      391–94
  writing process and, 32–33,
      67, 167–68
Outline, working, 195
Outlining, 195–97
Outsider, being an, 298–99,
      309–10

Pacing, 198
Paragraphing, 493–94
Parallel construction, 431–32
Parentheses, 466, 485–86
Participles, 417, 418–19,
      420–21, 439, 453–54,
      455, 456. *See also* Verb
      phrases
Parts of speech, 415–16
Past participle, 418, 419,
      420–21, 455, 456
Past perfect tense, 456
Past tense, 419, 420–21, 456,
      457
Perfect tense, 456
Performance needs, 29
Period, 422, 439, 466, 489–90
Personal history, 275–79
Personal journals, 73–74
Photographs, as memory
      aids, 265–68
Phrases, 417–22
  prepositional, 417–18, 429,
      431–32, 448
  verb, 417, 418–19, 429,
      448–49
Planner's approach, to
      writing process, 36–37,
      151, 156, 168

Plural subject, -verb
      agreement, 450–51
Poetry, 45, 46
Point of view
  age and, 306–308, 310–12
  audience and, 60
  cultural, 297–98
  denotation and
      connotation, 62–63
  ethnicity and, 302–304
  gender and, 304–306,
      314–15
  outsider, 298–99, 309–10
  senses and, 133, 145
  showing and telling,
      140–42
  subjective and objective,
      144–46
  in various disciplines,
      320–21
  in writing workshop,
      216–17
Possession, 479
Possessive pronouns, 459
Power, 370–408
  audience appeal and,
      373–77
  defined, 371
  of language, 370–71
  student writings on,
      401–407
  and writing process,
      382–400
Prepositional phrases,
      417–18, 429, 431–32,
      434, 448
Prepositions, 415, 417, 418
Present participle, 418, 419,
      453–54, 456
Present tense, 418, 419,
      420–21, 455, 456, 457
  to be, to have, to do,
      453–54
Problem and solutions,
      focusing on, 185
Process analysis, 185–86
Process journals, 74, 345–46
Procrastination, 17–18
Progressive tenses, 456
Pronouns, 415, 443
  agreement, 457–61
  connecting, 427, 428, 429,
      436, 446
  and gender, 458

number/case, 458–59
  possessive, 459, 479–80
  reference of, 458
  and sexism, 460–62
  singular/plural, 452–53
Proper nouns, 470
Publication, writing for,
      33–34
Punctuation, 464–96
  capitalization, 469–70
  chart, 466
  defined, 468
  elements of, 470–93
  end marks, 422, 435, 438,
      445, 485, 489–90
  myths about, 467–68
  paragraphing, 493–94
  purpose and audience and,
      465, 467–68
  review, 495
Purpose, 42–54
  aesthetic, 45, 257
  in bridging cultures,
      292–93
  in collecting, 66
  in education, 53–54,
      320–22
  in essays, 348
  in focusing, 89–92
  grammar and, 410–13
  identifying, 29, 30, 50,
      209–10
  interpersonal, 257
  kinds of, 43–48
  in leads, 170–71
  in letters, 57–58, 65–66
  meaning and, 147–54,
      256–61
  punctuation and, 465,
      467–68
  for revising, 232
  self-expressive, 257
  in writing for power,
      383–85
  in writing process, 31,
      65–67
  in writing to remember,
      256–61

Question mark, 422, 466, 490
Questions, 324–31
  and answer strategy, 185
  to develop senses, 143
  for ending, 180

Questions, *continued*
  for focusing, 116–23, 211
  good, standards for, 325
  on information, 324
  in interviewing, 84
  for leads, 172
  learning to ask, 329
  for making connections,
    343–44
  for meaning, 258
  one-answer, 327–28
  phrasing, 325–26, 327
  rhetorical, 328
  unfair, 325–26
  yes/no, 326–27
Question star, 117–18
Question words, 117, 118,
  324
Quotation marks, 481–84,
  495
Quotations
  direct/indirect, 481
  for endings, 180
  for focusing, 105–11
  how to quote, 109
  for leads, 170
  long, 482
  punctuation with, 472,
    481–84, 486

Reading aloud
  to consult, 208
  to revise, 241
Reading for meaning, 160
Readjusting, 247
Reason, appeals to, 373,
  375–77, 378–79, 381
Reasoning
  ad hominem, 396
  disciplines based on, 342
  faulty, 395–96
  forms of, 377
Recopying, 246
Redundancies, 91–92, 212
Relevance, focusing and,
  90–91
Remember, writing to. *See*
  Memories
Repetition
  for emphasis, 193
  in learning journal, 343
  in learning to spell,
    499–500
  in lists, 482–83

and redundancy, 91–92,
  212
Reports, format of, 362–63
Responsible thinking,
  317–40
  focusing, 322–32
  need to learn, 317–18
  note taking, 319, 322–24
  points of view, 320–21
  purposes in education,
    320–22
  qualities of, 318
  questions, 324–31
  senses and, 332–35
  summarizing, 335–40
  thesis statements, 331–32
  writing for, 318–20
Revising, 231–53
  collecting and, 72–73
  consulting and, 217, 219
  copy-editing, 237–46
  faulty reasoning, 395–99
  focusing and, 93–96
  levels of, 246–47
  organizing and, 168
  progress review, 250
  purposes for, 232
  reflecting on process,
    249–53
  run-ons/comma splices,
    445–48
  sentence fragments,
    437–41
  strategies for, 232–33
  to-do list, 233–34
  in writer's journal, 234–37
  in writing for power,
    395–99
  in writing process, 33, 38,
    67–68, 247–49
Rewriting. *See* Revising
Rhetorical questions, 328
Run-on sentence, 441–48
  identifying, 443–45
  psychological *vs.*
    technical, 441–42, 444
  revising, 445–48

Scales/balance, 193, 194
Self-expressive writing,
  43–44, 46, 257
Semicolon, 423, 424, 446,
  466, 487–88
Senses, 32, 131–65
  assessing, 211

collecting and, 133–40
comparisons/clichés and,
  158–61
focusing and, 152
illustration and, 184
learning through, 332–35
meaning/purpose and,
  147–54
as memory aids, 271–74
organizing and, 154–58
point of view and, 133, 145
showing/telling and,
  140–44
student model for
  discussion, 162–64
subjective/objective
  modes and, 144–47
Sense star, 134
Sentence, 412, 417–49
  clauses, 422–31
  comma splice, 442–48
  complex, 425, 429
  compound, 423, 429–30
  compound-complex, 429
  fragments, 434–41
  parallel construction,
    431–32
  phrases, 417–22
  problem, 434–49
  run-on, 441–48
  simple, 422–23
  variety in, 428–30
Sentence connectors. *See*
  Connectors
Sex differences, 460
Sexism, pronouns and,
  460–62
Shaping
  combined strategies,
    392–94
  deduction/induction in,
    189, 190, 392
  diagrams in, 189, 191–93
Showing, sense appeal and,
  140–44
Simple sentence, 422–23
Singular subject, -verb
  agreement, 450–51
Skills, as purpose in
  education, 54
Spatial order, 183
Specifying, 100–105
Statements
  argument and, 184–85
  of evidence, 342

illustration and, 183–84
weak and strong, 357
See also Thesis statements
Statistics, in lead, 173
Status, appeals to, 373,
374–75, 376, 382, 383
Stereotypes, 298, 300–301,
397–98
Storytelling, 171
String of pearls shape, 191,
193
Structures and forms,
362–63, 391–92
Styles
of composing, 36–37
in grammar, 412
Subject
of clause, 422, 424
noun clause as, 427
of phrase, 417
in revising fragments, 438
showing relationship to,
171
singular/plural, 450–51
-verb agreement, 450–55
Subjective writing, 144–45
Subordinate clauses. *See*
Dependent clauses
Subordinating conjunctions.
See Connectors
Success, fear of, 8–9
Summarizing, 319, 335–40
in endings, 181
good, standards for, 335
purpose and audience for,
335–36
strategies for, 337
Supplies, writing, 18–19
Surveying, 70
Syllables, hyphen and, 477
Synthesizing, 351–54

Tape recorder, 18
Teacher, role of, 7, 29, 38
Telling, sense appeal and,
140–44
That. See Who, which, that
Theories, forming, 351–54
Thesis statements
of comparison and
contrast, 356–57
evidence supporting,
348–50
focusing and, 121–28,
331–32

formulating, 125–28
good, standards for, 331–32
in lead, 170
strong and weak, 122–25
theories in form of, 351–52
Thinking, responsible. *See*
Responsible thinking
Time management, 16–18
Titles
italicized, 491–92
process of writing, 177–79
punctuation in, 470,
481–82
strategies for, 177
working, 178
Tone, 62–63
Topics
authority notes, 344
brainstorming, 80–81
choosing, 96–99
listing, 80
outlining, 195–97
Training journals, 75
Transitional words, 487
for anticipating objections,
390
for cause and effect, 186
for chronological order,
183
for classifying, 186
for comparison and
contrast, 188, 358
linking statement and
arguments, 185
linking statement and
example, 184
for problem and solution
strategy, 185
in process analysis, 186
punctuation with, 472
for question and answer
strategy, 185
for spatial order, 183
Typewriter, 18, 491

Underlining, 491–93
Unity, 167

Verb phrases, 417, 418–19,
429, 434
misplaced modifiers,
448–49
See also Participles
Verbs, 415, 417, 422, 424

consistency, 455–57
irregular, 420–21
participles, 418, 419,
420–21
regular, 420–21
-subject agreement, 450–55
tenses, 418, 419, 420–21,
455–56
to be, to have, to do,
453–54
V-shape, 189, 191, 192

Who, which, that, 427, 435
Word order, 410
Working plan, 195
Workshops. *See* Writing
workshops
Writer(s)
becoming, 1–25
consulting with other,
202–203
new, 38
practicing, 38–39
See also Writing workshop
Writer's journal, 74, 234–37
Writing
barriers to, 3–7
committed *vs.*
uncommitted writer,
11–12
fears about, 8–11
freewriting, 4, 13–15
myths about, 3–7
reasons for, 1–2
time management in,
16–18
See also Writing workshop
Writing process
collecting and, 71–75
composing styles in, 36–37
focusing and, 31–32,
89–130
formal/informal tasks in,
35–36
meaning and, 28
of new *vs.* practicing
writers, 38–39
organizing and, 32–33, 66,
167–68
phases of, 28–34
revising and, 33, 38, 68,
247–49
Writing space, 19
Writing tools, 18–19
Writing workshop, 204–29

Writing workshop,
   continued
acknowledgments, 223
checklist for, 218
grading, 223–29
personalities, 216–17,
   219–20
practical considerations for
   conducting, 204–206

problems and
   opportunities in, 217,
   219
purposes of, 206
responding to writing,
   206–15
variations in conducting,
   220–23

Zig-zag method, in
   comparison and
   contrast, 187–88,
   194–95, 359